THINKING
UP A
HURRICANE

Martinique Stilwell

PENGUIN BOOKS

PENGUIN BOOKS

Published by the Penguin Group
Penguin Books (South Africa) (Pty) Ltd, Rosebank Office Park, Block D,
181 Jan Smuts Avenue, Parktown North, Johannesburg, 2196, South Africa
Penguin Group (USA) Inc, 375 Hudson Street, New York, New York 10014, USA
Penguin Group (Canada), 90 Eglinton Avenue East, Suite 700, Toronto, Ontario, Canada
M4P 2Y3 (a division of Pearson Penguin Canada Inc)
Penguin Books Ltd, 80 Strand, London WC2R 0RL, England
Penguin Ireland, 25 St Stephen's Green, Dublin 2, Ireland (a division of Penguin Books Ltd)
Penguin Group (Australia), 250 Camberwell Road, Camberwell, Victoria 3124, Australia
(a division of Pearson Australia Group Pty Ltd)
Penguin Books India Pvt Ltd, 11 Community Centre,
Panchsheel Park, New Delhi – 110 017, India
Penguin Group (NZ), 67 Apollo Drive, Rosedale, Auckland 0632, New Zealand (a division of
Pearson New Zealand Ltd)

Penguin Books (South Africa) (Pty) Ltd, Registered Offices:
Rosebank Office Park, Block D, 181 Jan Smuts Avenue, Parktown North,
Johannesburg, 2196, South Africa

www.penguinbooks.co.za

First published by Penguin Books (South Africa) (Pty) Ltd 2012

Copyright © Martinique Stilwell, 2012

ISBN 978-0-14-353034-3

All Caribbean photographs taken by Robert Ravensburg
Cover by Michiel Botha
Printed and bound by CTP Printers, Cape Town

For Alice and Ruby

And in memory of those lost along the way

Name	Comment
Allison	
Colleen	Accessible storytelling. Fast
Cathy	paced, poignant & honest.
Carla	
Debbie	
~~Jackie~~ Elsa	So interesting : Past Rand reference resonates
Kapsie	Compelling: I neglected duties to read on !!!
Margie	Chilling portrait of an abusive father. Adventure to the MAX.
Paula	
Sue	Different + very interesting
Sandy	
Ursula	
Wendy	
Karen	V. interesting. Loved it.
Tina	Inspiring. very good.

Ships are the nearest things to dreams that hands have ever made.
Robert N Rose

A sailor's joys are as simple as a child's.
Bernard Moitessier

I once knew a writer who, after saying beautiful things about the sea,
passed through a Pacific hurricane, and he became a changed man.
Joshua Slocum

CONTENTS

Vingila's Voyage

St Helena
Jamestown

Ascension
Georgetown

The Caribbean
Puerto Rico
British Virgin Islands
Anguilla
St Martin
Barbuda
Antigua
St Croix St Kitts
Monserratt
Gaudeloupe · Marie Galante
Dominica
Martinique
St Lucia
St Vincent & the Grenadines Barbados
Grenada · Mapion Is.

Fernando de Noronha
Bay of Dolphins

ASIA

Chagos Arch.
Christmas Island
Cocos Keeling
Ashmore Reef
Darwin
Thursday Is.
Solomon Islands
Vanuatu
Marquesas
Samoa
Society Islands
Cook Islands

INDIAN OCEAN
AUSTRALIA
Cairns
Brisbane
New Caledonia

PACIFIC OCEAN

NEW ZEALAND

The Pass
Omoka
Penrhyn

Suwarrow
Piyades Pass

Western Samoa
Tonga

New Caledonia
Loyalty Islands
Noumea

Solomon Is.
Bougainville
Honiara
New Georgia
Gaudalcanal
Bellona

Panama
Colon — San Blas
Panama City
Las Perlas
Panama Canal

Galapagos
Santa Cruz
Isabella
Floreana — San Cristobal

Marquesas
Nuku Hiva — Ua Huka
Motane
Fatu Hiva

Society and Tuamotos Is.
Tahiti

ICELAND

ASIA

NORTH AMERICA

NORTH ATLANTIC OCEAN

AFRICA

Caribbean Islands

Panama

Galapagos

Baia Peñas

Fortaleza

Fernando de Noronha
Recife

SOUTH AMERICA

Salvador

Ascension

St Helena

MADAGASCAR
Rodrigues
Réunion
Mauritius

SOUTH ATLANTIC OCEAN

Richards Bay
Durban
Port Elizabeth
Cape Town
Mossel Bay

INDIAN OCEAN

Vanuatu
Banks Islands
Espiritu Santu
Port-Vila

Chagos Arch.

Rodrigues
Port Mathurin

Mauritius
Port Louis

St Denis
Réunion

Cartography by James Berrangé

Part 1

SOUTH AFRICA

1

BENONI

I didn't want my father to buy *Vingila*. When we first saw her, she smelled bad, like mushrooms left in a cardboard box. Her hatches and portholes were covered by a tarpaulin that blocked the light below decks and turned us all to ghosts as we explored her cabins. Her hull was painted old swimming pool blue and her decks had been sprinkled with coarse river sand and coated with epoxy to form a crude non-slip surface. Her scuppers wept rust. Later I learned that she had terrible lines: her prow was stubby and far too high, her stern too broad. Her cabin-top, with its three milky windows of scratched plexiglass, sat clumsily on her decks.

A photographer named Vincent, who dreamed of circumnavigating the world, built *Vingila* in his backyard and named her after his three children: Vinca, Gita and Lars. Perhaps the attention he lavished on the boat led to the breakdown of his marriage, but after the lawyers had settled, Vincent's ex-wife had a yacht to sell.

The evening after we went to inspect *Vingila*, my mother asked my twin brother Robert and me if we should buy the boat. We were seven years old and in grade two at the time. Although we lived far from the sea, my father, who said life was too short to spend it all living in a house and working, was going to sail around the world and take my mom and Robert and me with him. My mother's poodle Pepe was coming too, but not Laura, our pointer, because she was too big. Mom looked at Robert first, who usually didn't speak much because he was shy. He just shrugged and smiled. Even at seven he didn't like to commit, and not to something as momentous as a sailing yacht. Then my mother turned to me and asked if we should buy *Vingila*.

'No, I don't want it,' I said.

'Why not?'

'I don't like the washbasin.'

'You don't like the washbasin? Why not?'

The basin filled me with horror. It was turquoise, and lumpy with dried globs of dusty glue that ran and oozed like worms working their way up from the outflow. Just looking at it induced a surge of nausea and the texture of rough bumps on smooth porcelain took me back to bilious dreams of fevers and tonsillitis. I tried to explain this to my mother.

'The washbasin's so dirty,' I said, 'it makes me feel funny.'

'I tell you what,' she said, for she knew that my father had already bought the yacht, 'when we get the boat you can clean the basin, all right?'

My father's friend Charlie Kingma had found *Vingila* while browsing the classified adds, but she was never Dad's first choice. He wanted a Hinckley, a yacht he had seen in the magazines that cluttered our house. Hinckleys were sleek vessels, thoroughbreds with racing lines, gleaming white topsides and decks of caulked teak. But they came from America and their price was beyond the reach of a Benoni electrician. Other yachts, however, were to be found closer to home. Some people, fearing the end of apartheid and South Africa's imminent collapse, were building ferro-cement boats in their backyards. But Dad said he didn't want a hull of concrete draped over a skeleton of steel. Although such

4

yachts were inexpensive and easy to make, he said they were ugly and weak. One crack and the seawater was in, rusting the metal bones, and then there was nothing you could do about that. My father wanted style and strength in a boat and if he couldn't afford both, he'd choose strength. So for him it was a Hinckley, or a vessel with a hull of steel, or nothing. Steel boats were scarce, but Dad was good with his hands; he knew how to weld and could fix almost anything with the contents of his toolbox. He was seriously considering building a yacht of his own when Charlie Kingma phoned one weekend to say he'd found the right boat.

Charlie and Trish, my parents' friends, would be sailing with us. They had pageboy hairstyles like Purdy from *The Avengers* and they dressed in matching outfits which Trish laid out every morning. Charlie, with a wide smile and a gap between his front teeth, was big, and the outline of his underpants showed through the seat of his pale slacks. Trish blow-dried his hair for him. They had no children or pets and their house was decorated with fluffy white carpets and vases of pampas grass. Charlie was very artistic, my mother said. He chose the colours for the walls of their rooms and the vase for the pampas grass. He was handy too and had made their coffee table from a glass door which he painted green. He liked to work with wood. After returning from an army camp one year, he carved my brother an exact replica of an R1 service rifle from pine and stained it black. Whenever Robert went on the street with his new toy, Mom received calls from the neighbours warning her that her son was in possession of a firearm.

Trish owned an orange fondue pot and a lava lamp. We had nothing like that in our house. We had dogs. The linoleum in our kitchen was cracked and the carpet tiles covering the remainder of our floors were a shade of brown that Mom said didn't show dirt. My mother had bought the tiles on special and had laid them herself. They were so scratchy that every fall resulted in oozing carpet burns. I felt so unsuited to my surroundings that I often imagined I was adopted. I pictured my real parents as slick and stylish with a house full of lava lamps and fluffy carpets.

My father first met Charlie in the reception office of the local foundry. Ignoring the calendars of girls in bikinis advertising ball bearings and heavy machinery, the two men focused instead on the marine equivalent: a photograph of a white yacht flying a spinnaker and racing across an impossibly blue sea. After a period of silence, as the two men stood side by side looking at the yacht, my father cleared his throat. He had been born in the Transvaal, far from the sea, into a family that feared the ocean. After dropping out of high school and finishing an apprenticeship as an electrician, he had gone to London. England had not worked out quite the way he hoped and, completely broke, he had found passage back to South Africa on a Scottish fishing boat. The cook was a drunk, the captain verging on psychotic and a storm in the Bay of Biscay had driven them to seek shelter in Monaco where, for the first time, Dad had seen private sailing yachts. He was hooked. From that time on, he wanted a yacht of his own. When I was born – an unexpected twin to my much anticipated brother – he named me Martinique, after an island he planned to visit when he sailed around the world.

'See that?' he said to Charlie in the foundry, pointing a grime-ingrained finger at the picture on the calendar. 'I'm going to have one of those someday.'

Charlie, a sales rep in white shoes, looked my dad over, taking in the oil-stained workman's clothes and a pair of intense eyes partially shielded by practical glasses.

'Actually,' he said, 'me too. I'm also going to have one.'

On his next visit to the foundry Charlie brought atlases and maps, and my father, after washing his hands as best he could, sat beside him, poring over sailing routes and destinations. Before long they were friends. Candles flickered late into the night, casting shadows in the pampas grass while my parents gathered at the green glass coffee table chewing morsels of fried beef from Trish's fondue pot and talking about sailing. The plan was that my mom and dad would buy or build a boat first and then Charlie and Trish would help them sail it for a while before getting one of their own.

After Dad bought *Vingila* she was delivered to my aunt and uncle's place on the outskirts of Benoni. She would stay there for two years. Uncle George, Aunty Enid and their five children lived with my Oupa and Ouma on a plot, which in different hands might have been a small farm but instead was a stretch of grassy land with a swimming pool, a tennis court and a single oily sheep tethered to a tree stump. The sheep, named Braaivleis, had been bought to be eaten, but when nobody had the heart to kill her, she'd become a low-grade, rather neglected pet.

On the first weekend that we visited *Vingila* on the plot, Dad told Robert and me that things would be different from now. There was serious work to be done on the yacht and that he hadn't brought us to the plot to play with our cousins and slack off. We were expected to pitch in and pull our weight and if we didn't there would be trouble. Thus Robert and I were introduced to boat work. Every weekend and even some afternoons we worked on *Vingila*. We learned to sand and varnish wood, to scrape and paint and to clean our hands afterwards with turpentine. We discovered that epoxy tar and anti-fouling stung and left red marks on our skin. I learned to clean marine glue from washbasins. Our fingernails split and our hands roughened as *Vingila* gradually, over the months, grew sea ready.

She was sandblasted to bare steel and covered with seven coats of paint. Dad stripped the old river sand and laid cork decking. He assembled rigging and one thrilling day we raised her beautiful gold masts. He bought winches, sheets, halyards, blocks and anchors.

At night after finishing at the foundry he read books with titles like *Essentials of Seamanship* and *Teach Yourself Sailing the Easy Way*.

He ordered sails from Hong Kong and enough canvas arrived to fill the vast sail locker in *Vingila*'s roomy stern. We would never learn to properly use the mizzen trysail, or the staysail. The genoa, spread out on the lawn, was immense, a frothy wedding dress for a giantess. The cloth of the storm jib was so heavy we couldn't fold it. The idea that wind could tear a sail so thick was inconceivable.

At the end of her second year at the plot, Dad booked a crane which arrived and lifted *Vingila* onto a truck. Workmen strapped our boat into the truck's cradle with her gold masts trussed together like a pair of chopsticks. The men tied 'abnormal load' signs to her stern. When the truck pulled out of the yard, heading for Durban and the ocean, Dad left with it. It was 1977 and I was nine years old.

There is a reef in Benoni, but no sea. Instead of beaches there are mine dumps: piles of yellow sand brought up as ore from shafts drilled into the earth and ground fine to extract the gold. While my father had worked in the foundries, my mother took us to play on the dumps which to us were as good as any beach. On the weekends before Dad bought *Vingila* and we were put to work, Robert and I visited our Nana and Chummy, Mom's parents, who lived in Alberton. Chummy had a runabout and was a member of the Germiston Aquatic Club where he taught us to waterski on Germiston Lake: a pool of water clotted with weed and surrounded by picnic sites, a mini-golf course and the highest concentration of gold refineries in South Africa.

Dad had a skiboat which we took to the coast for fishing holidays but apart from ten days my parents spent on a yacht in Mozambique, we had no sailing experience. Unless you counted the time that Mom and Dad took us to the drive-in, with the dogs in the back seat, to watch

Dove, a film about a blond teenager with rumpled hair who sailed around the world by himself. He had lots of cats, and when one fell overboard and was eaten by a shark, I cried. I hoped that when we went sailing Pepe, our poodle, would be okay, but Mom told me not to worry, we would look after Pepe.

While Dad was on the truck carrying *Vingila* to the sea, Mom moved to her parents' house in Alberton. *Vingila*'s road trip was expected to take a week by the back roads, avoiding the highways and their bridges, and during that time Mom had a lot to do before meeting up in Durban for the boat launching. She arranged storage for the furniture we hadn't sold or given away. My parents' bed, for example, was hoisted into the roof of my uncle's garage and my mother's twin-tub washing machine was wedged beside his car. We owned a pair of small houses in Benoni, originally built for mine workers, and Mom finalised rental arrangements with the new tenants. At 5 Master Street where Robert and I had lived since we were born, a new family had moved in, and the mother asked Mom to keep us kids outside because she didn't want my brother and me disturbing the baby. While Mom and the woman talked, I stayed on the porch, trying to see through the curtains and find out what they had done to my bedroom, until the woman came out and shooed me away, which made me want to cry.

To finance our trip Dad had cashed in his modest savings which we hoped could be stretched out for the two years my parents thought it would take us to sail around the world. The rent from the houses, it was decided, would go towards paying off the bonds and a little would be set aside for emergencies. What kind of emergencies, I wondered.

The morning that we left Nana and Chummy's house to meet my father in Durban, Mom sent me to say goodbye to my dolls who were sitting propped in a row against the pillow of my bed in the spare room.

I picked up Patsy, my favourite, and cradled her in my arms. She was moulded from hard pink plastic and her bald head was as big as a real baby's. She was a birthday present from Nana who had sewn her dress and bonnet from an opalescent, slightly gritty blue fabric and trimmed it with lace. When I tilted Patsy backwards her glassy eyes closed and her eyelids, with their soft nylon lashes, made a clicking sound. I was kissing her goodbye when my mother, wearing a pair of cut-off jeans and a jersey over her tank top, came into the room. She had tears in her eyes and I saw that the time was right to make a play for what I wanted.

'Please, Mom,' I said.

'Your father won't like it, you know.'

'Please. Just one, just Patsy. I love her.'

My mother sighed. 'All right, just her. We can make room.'

Mom's powder-blue Peugeot 404 was in the carport loaded up and ready to go. Robert and Pepe were waiting in the back seat. Nana, her hair freshly set in a permanent wave, stood in the passage wearing a polyester pantsuit and an unhappy smile on her face while Chummy sat in the kitchen brushing off his sports jacket for work and folding tissues to stow in his breast pocket. Neither of them wanted us to go. They had never liked my father and didn't approve of his plan to sail around the world with their grandchildren, and they did not like the fact that my parents knew nothing about sailing, even though my mother had assured them we would learn as we went.

Nana kissed me goodbye. 'Be a good girl, now,' she said and my eyes filled with tears. Robert and I were Nana's first grandchildren and we had spent at least one weekend a month with her since our infancy. She looked after us when we were sick and taught us songs. She made clothes and knitted jackets for my dolls. Each year she and Chummy took us on holiday, to places like Bourke's Luck where we looked at the potholes or to Margate where we swam in the sea and bought greasy packets of samoosas on the beach. I did not want to leave her, or my

Chummy. I liked spending the weekends in Alberton where we had our own toys and got to eat bacon and eggs for breakfast. I liked going waterskiing on Germiston Lake. And I liked my school in Benoni where I had friends and played on the netball team. My grandmother kissed me again and hugged me hard enough for it to hurt. 'I'll be waiting for you to come back,' she said.

Chummy joined her as she followed us outside. They stood on the ramp beneath the carport holding their two miniature pinschers as we drove away, waving until my mother's car was out of sight.

On the drive to the coast my mother was chatty. We played I-Spy and stopped often to let Pepe have a drink and lift his leg. Laura, our wild red-eyed pointer, had gone to live on a farm where she would soon be caught in a leopard trap and die, although we did not know that yet. Driving made me feel happier. The silvery winter sky and blond mealie fields of the highveld gave way to pine plantations and green sugar cane. It warmed up and the winter air which made my nose bleed grew humid as we descended from the escarpment. My mother pulled off her jersey and drove in her tank top, saying how exciting it was that we were going to live on a yacht. I whispered in Patsy's ear, telling her stories about the boat and the cabin in the stern we would share.

It became steadily hotter in the car and Robert, bored and jealous of the attention I was paying my doll, dug a bony elbow into my rib, starting a squabble and forcing Mom to draw a line across the back seat with her finger to separate us. From opposite windows we glared at each other while Pepe lay in the front foot well, panting. My mother – sensing mutiny – looked into the rear view mirror and said, 'At least you'll have someone to play with in Durban.'

'Who?' said Robert.

'Those kids on the junk,' Mom said.

'Oh them.'

'They seemed very nice,' my mother said.

Maria Jose, the junk, came from Bangkok but flew a Swiss flag. On a previous holiday while visiting the Durban yacht club, we'd seen her tied to the dock. She was painted black, with wide, mysterious-smelling hatches, and sails the colour of dried blood. The white eyes on her bow – to see where she was going my mother said – had an eastern slant. As we stood staring at her, a bearded man with a great square forehead and a lump of a nose, climbed out of a hatch. He was followed by two boys of about twelve or thirteen. They ignored us completely, talking amongst themselves in a strange language.

'Excuse me,' said Dad.

The man looked up, but did not return my father's smile.

'Do your children go to school?' Dad asked.

The man pointed at the older of the two boys who continued to ignore us. 'See this boy? Over there? I'll tell you now that he is thirteen years old and he can sail and navigate. So you tell me, why does he need to go to school?'

In spite of some imperfections in the man's logic, this was exactly the answer my father wanted to hear. Many years later when Hans Klaar, the boy who could navigate, was in his twenties, he would apply to study marine biology at the University of Hawaii. His application would not be considered – navigational qualifications weren't a prerequisite for the course, or any other university course for that matter. Instead of becoming a marine biologist, he would be relegated to a life of yacht deliveries, vanilla trading, orchid smuggling and intermittent stints working as a postman in his native Switzerland. That was far into the future, however, and in Durban in the 1970s, Ernest Klaar, Hans' father, was not concerned about his children's future.

'I don't know if I want to play with those kids on the junk,' said Robert, 'they didn't seem very friendly to me.'

'They're just different,' Mom answered. 'Once you get to know them you'll see.'

When we drove into Durban, Mom stopped at the first petrol station with a public phone and called the *Natal Witness*, a city newspaper. She told the news desk we'd be launching a yacht in a few hours and asked if they wanted to send a reporter. Over the preceding months my mother had developed quite a taste for appearing in the newspapers and we had made the third page of the *Rapport* several times, but only in black and white. At the height of our fame, a few months before leaving Benoni, we hit the jackpot, scooping the front page of the *Citizen*, a popular English daily. The photograph, in full colour, showed us assembled on the stern of our landlocked boat, happily waving goodbye to the photographer. In the picture, Robert, his hair nearly as white as mine, wears army camouflage and we both have guns slung in holsters around our waists. (The photographer had asked us to put down the pine R1 service rifle and Dad's old shotgun.) My father is unsmiling; he hated reporters and newspapers, but my mother, who holds Pepe in her arms, makes up for it by laughing. The caption explained that Frank and Maureen Stilwell, together with their twins Robert and Martinique, and a seafaring poodle named Pepe, were planning to sail around the world. The voyage, including a side trip to the Mediterranean Sea, was expected to take two years.

'Are you sure this'll hold the boat?' My brother spoke above the zap and flash of welding machines. A crash of metal came from the dry dock where a throng of dockworkers was overhauling a cargo ship. We had reached Durban harbour and were squatting on *Vingila*'s trailer in the shade of her hull, watching the crane men slide canvas slings beneath her keel. The air smelled salty, of anti-fouling, diesel and dead barnacles.

'It'll hold much heavier boats than this,' a workman replied, tightening a strap.

Vingila, with a full keel, was made of 11-millimetre steel plates welded together. She weighed 17 tons in total. As the men worked to secure her, I tried to keep all that weight between me and my father because I didn't want him to see me. We had been apart for a week and upon our arrival at the shipyard I had run in search of him. I saw him from a distance talking to the crane driver and looking important – in the centre of things – and I wanted to stand beside him, holding his hand and for people to know that I was his daughter. I ran with Patsy on my hip, her glossy dress glinting in the sun, her eyelids clicking each time my foot hit concrete. After the long car ride I felt excited and I planned to throw myself into his arms, but when I got near him, I slowed and stopped. His eyes, fixed on Patsy, were hard blue stones and his top lip, thinned to nothing, had curled into an tight, upside down smile.

'What the bladdy hell is this?' he said, pointing at Patsy.

'Oh Frank, it's just a doll,' my mother said from behind me. 'I said we could make room for it. Please.'

'No. We're not having a bladdy doll on the yacht. Okay?' And he turned his back on us to continue talking to the crane driver, while Mom led me back to the car.

Patsy sat in the Peugeot while the men secured *Vingila* for launching. I hoped to smuggle her aboard later; it would be difficult – she was rather big – but I would manage, somehow. If that didn't work, Patsy and I would run away together and live on the Durban docks, or make our way back to Nana in Alberton. I pictured Dad's face when he found out that I'd gone. I thought of him searching the harbour and asking people if they'd seen me. He'd be sorry then.

A crowd of dockworkers on a tea break gathered to watch the launching. They laughed among themselves, smoked and offered mocking advice to the crane men, who responded by treating *Vingila* casually; kicking out the props and flicking her ropes as the crane took up slack and she rose from her cradle. Through the gap beneath her airborne keel, I saw my mother trying to introduce a *Natal Witness* reporter to my scowling father.

For a moment our boat hung in mid-air, immobile, dark and solid. Then the crane swung her over the wharf and lowered her into the water. As she touched the sea, the dockworkers fell solemn and silent. A cheer broke out. She was floating – more than floating really – she was alive. She gave a shiver and, tugging at her warps, nosed the dock with her bow. Patsy briefly forgotten, I climbed aboard with Robert and helped my parents put out fenders, stumbling at the unfamiliar movement of the deck under my feet. Pepe watched from the wharf until a helpful bystander scooped him up and handed him to us. He came over cringing, like a furry black comma.

Then Dad, with his smile the right way up again, handed Mom a bottle of Cold Duck sparkling wine and a heavy duty welding glove. We assembled on the bow. The reporter with his camera stood on the dock as my mother, flanked by her twins and confident in her welding glove, smashed the bottle hard against *Vingila*'s blunt prow, showering us all in sticky wine and shattered glass. The next day our photograph appeared in black and white on page three of the *Natal Witness*. The reporter got both my and *Vingila*'s names wrong, and wrote that the Stilwell family hoped to set sail for Mauritius within five weeks, which was the first I had heard of it.

2

DURBAN

Dad hunched in the dim passage beneath *Vingila*'s centre cockpit, the upper part of his body lodged in the cubby hole we called a radio room. In his right hand, he held the microphone of our new VHF radio. Behind his shoulder, a porthole opened into the cockpit, through which I saw my mother's foot as she stood at the helm. By shifting my position from where I squatted on the main saloon floor I could look along her bare leg and torso, right up to her anxious face.

Dad twiddled the radio knobs, swallowed and exhaled audibly. Then, squeezing the button on the microphone, he cleared his throat and said: 'Port control. Port control. Port control. Over.'

Static hissed in the void and was replaced for an instant by a curt voice.

'This is port control. Come in. Over.'

Dad swallowed again and took another breath.

'This is yacht *Vingila*, *Vingila*, *Vingila*. Do you copy us? Over.'

'Yes, *Vingila*. We copy you.' The voice sounded bored.

'We request permission to leave the harbour. Over.'

'Granted. Over and out.'

Outside my mother was still anxious.

'What did they say, Frank?' she asked.

'They said we could leave the harbour.'

'Really, are you sure? We can leave the harbour and go out to sea?'

'Of course. That's what boats do, you know, they go to sea.'

Dad took the helm and we motored out. It was September and our boat had been afloat for three months. Never mind Mauritius in five weeks, we had yet to make it out of Durban harbour, although twice a week, in light winds and with the engine running, we had raised our sails and tacked back and forth in the sheltered waters of the port between the container terminal and the granite wharf, learning to sail. The first time the wind had caught the great white wing of *Vingila*'s mainsail and pushed her over, my mother screamed, but with passing weeks we had come to accept heeling over as a normal and even as a necessary component of sailing. We weren't always sure which direction the wind was blowing, but we came about or gybed anyway, with varying degrees of success. We learned the basics. Beating: wind just off the nose. Tacking: zig-zagging into a headwind by coming about. Reaching: wind on the side. Running: wind on the stern. Broad reaching: something between reaching and running. On calm water among the tugs and pilot boats, we relaxed and began to enjoy ourselves. Pepe crept out from beneath Mom's feet in the cockpit and strutted the decks, barking at seagulls, while a gentle wind blew up tiny wavelets amid the oil slicks.

After some weeks of this my father decided that we were ready for the open sea. With Mom at the helm we motored down the narrow straight bordered by a line of jumbled dolosse. At the mouth we met a few swells and the wind picked up. Further out, the sea didn't look quite as tranquil as water we were accustomed to, but Dad and Robert went ahead and raised not only the mainsail but the jib too. Once past the shelter of the bluff, conditions changed quickly: the sea turned milky-looking, stirred up, the wind strong and gusty. Then a series of breakers advanced, steep and topped with froth.

'Frank,' said my mother from the wheel, 'Look there ...'

A hefty swell approached our bow. Directly ahead the water tilted from the familiar horizontal to an incline so steep that the summit began collapsing on itself. Looking up at the wave brought back memories of a roller coaster ride I had taken once; and how, when the coach began its slow, horrible ascent against gravity, I knew with absolute certainty that begging my mother for a ticket had been a terrible mistake – I wanted to get off. And I couldn't.

Vingila met the wave and, rearing as if she had been whipped, displayed a surprising new capacity for vertical motion. Climbing the slope, she reached the top and balanced briefly on the sharp edge of the crest. Then she fell.

My mother's mouth opened and a thin high sound emerged from it. I grabbed at a hand rail, too afraid to cry, but missed and slid across the non-skid deck, losing skin on the way. At the bottom of the trough our boat collided with unexpectedly solid water. Stunned, she lay on her side; scuppers submerged and her cockpit flooded. Dislodged objects clattered in the cabins below. Then the jib sheet – ineptly cleated – pulled free, sending the sail thrashing and the sheets streaming into the water – horribly close to our rudder and spinning propeller.

'Cut the engine before we foul the prop!' Dad pushed his way to the bow and began wrestling the sail. 'Release the halyard,' he yelled at my brother who was standing dumbstruck on the cabin top, mesmerised by the chaos.

Abandoning the helm, Mom joined Dad to tackle the sail at the bow while Robert, jolted from his trance, loosened the halyard. Pepe, wet and wild-eyed, clawed his way from the flooded cockpit and tried to jump overboard. Mom snatched a passing leg to pull him back.

'Get inside Nicky,' she said, 'and take the dog with you!'

The main saloon looked as if it had been ransacked. Cushions were strewn about, cups and plates lay scattered on the floor and the latch of the shoe cupboard had loosened and the door was swinging open, discharging an intermittent volley of footwear. The curtains hung at an unnatural angle, lifting up occasionally to touch the ceiling. Wedging myself into a corner between the table and Dad's fishing tackle box, I sat and cried while Pepe vomited repeatedly into a cushion.

After bringing the sails down without fouling the prop or wrecking *Vingila* on the breakwater, Dad turned our boat around and we motored back to the calm of the yacht club and our moorings.

'I don't want to go out to sea again,' I told Mom.

'Don't worry,' she said, 'when we learn how to do it properly, it'll get better.' She didn't look convinced.

The administrators of the Point Yacht Club allocated boat moorings according to a strict social hierarchy. Sleek racers and expensive cruisers lay in the basin nearest the clubhouse; foreign yachts were meshed together like flies in a spider's web at the international jetty; and stretching out into the harbour, shabbier boats and newcomers like ourselves bobbed on moorings. Squeezed between a pair of lumpen ferro-cement vessels, we held the second last position. We didn't see much of the man on *Elusive* to our left, but Glen and Margie on *Chummy* were friendly. They had built the boat themselves in their backyard in Brakpan and were planning to sail to Australia with their two children.

'There's no future here in South Africa,' Glen said.

'We're thinking of the kids,' Margie added. 'And at least this way we can get our money out.'

They never did get their money out. Two years later we would hear that *Chummy* had sunk on a reef off Costa Rica.

Back on *Vingila* after our first meeting with the *Chummy* family, my father said to my mother as they undressed for bed: 'I'm not running away from South Africa, Maureen. You know that, don't you?'

'I know, Frank,' she replied. 'I know.'

'Anyway,' he said, standing in his underpants and socks, 'the blacks are never going to get this country. If I need to come back and fight for it, I will.'

Thrust together in the isolation of our remote moorings, we saw a lot of the *Chummy* family. Getting ashore was difficult because we didn't have an outboard engine for the dinghy and we weren't good enough oarsmen to row far. The club employed a Zulu ferryman called James, whom we summoned by horn, but he was old and hard of hearing and the Seagull engine he tended was temperamental. People on the boats around us called him using aerosol cans topped with red plastic funnels which produced, with minimal effort, yelping sounds of a startling intensity, but Dad said they were wasteful and expensive and instead he made us blow a brass horn which gave a strangled yodel that was never quite loud enough. It was generally easier just to play with the kids on the boat next door than get to land.

In October of 1977 after four months on the boat Robert and I turned ten and with my birthday money from Nana, I bought a small microscope. It came with a kit which included a prepared slide labelled 'silver berry scaly hairs'. They may have been pollen, plankton or parasites, I never found out for sure, but they were stained in dreamy shades of purple and pink and I could spend hours looking at them. When I got tired of that I caught the fleas on Pepe's tummy to squash onto slides. Magnified, they were horrible creatures with segmented abdomens, spiky legs and huge fanged mouths.

Hans and Alex, the Swiss boys from the junk *Maria Jose*, came to visit, but they weren't interested in my microscope and the silver berry scaly hairs. They stomped through the boat, from bow to stern, staring at our curtains and bedspreads.

'Why are you doing that?' they asked Robert, who was washing lunch dishes. 'That's woman's work. Your sister should be doing it.'

The boys were sinewy and had their father's large hands; they would both grow very tall. Alex was better looking than Hans, and both were excellent sailors. I was invited aboard *Maria Jose* just once. Below decks it was quite empty, except for two barrels; one filled with dried beans, the other with rice. It was all the family could afford to eat. Ernest, their father, had been a member of the French Foreign Legion and had fought in Vietnam. He showed my dad the guns he carried on *Maria Jose* and told him stories of sailing in Thailand and escaping pirates in the Philippines. He said it was essential to be armed and Dad said he knew that already; we had shotguns and a high-powered hunting rifle on *Vingila*. Back on the boat Dad asked Mom to start cooking more beans and rice. Shortly after that *Maria Jose* sailed for Madagascar. Although Ernest did not say so at the time, they were in search of sunken treasure.

In November foreign yachts arrived from across the Indian Ocean. Following the trade winds, they came via Christmas Island, Mauritius and Madagascar, bringing friends for Robert and me. Boys with skateboards.

David was an only child, an American, who sailed with his family on *Resolve*, a Hinckley. He was as pale and blond as his beautiful long-haired mother. His dad's name was Simon, but both David and his mother called him 'Sigh'. David wore a Rolex and rumour had it in the yacht club that the family owned an international tyre company. David invited me to his yacht to make key-ring ornaments. We poured perspex into moulds in which we arranged small toys, stones and shells, and I tried not to spill any on the gleaming wooden floors.

Urbine and his family had sailed from Sweden across three oceans on *Saga*, a sturdy Nordic ketch with a shiny red hull that reminded me so much of a boiled sweet I sometimes felt an urge to lick it. Urbine was thirteen and spoke perfect English. His Bermuda shorts hung perilously from his hips when he tick-tacked and did 360s on his skateboard. But in spite of his long sun-bleached hair and good looks, he was shy, with a smile that was always friendly and sweet. From the moment I first said hello to him, I wanted a skateboard of my own and began nagging Mom. She was still feeling bad about Patsy, my doll, who had been posted back to Nana in Alberton, and she surrendered without too much resistance.

When a letter arrived from Nana with the news that Patsy was safe and waiting for me on the spare bed, I barely had time to answer it my days were so full. Mornings we had school work, from books sent by Mom's sister Annette, a teacher at Alberton Primary School. My mother taught us only maths and English, having decided we could learn other subjects like geography, biology, and history informally as we went along. After we finished school, we did boat work and in the afternoon, once we had eaten lunch, we were allowed ashore to skate, which was the part of the day I waited for.

'What's wrong with your food?' my father asked me.

It was a hot day in December and we sat around the lunch table with the sun streaming through *Vingila*'s curtains. Summer in Durban was humid – sweat ran down the back of my knees and my bare legs stuck to the vinyl cushions. My mother had chosen vinyl because it was easy to keep clean. In addition to re-upholstering the cushions of the main saloon, she'd covered the plywood floors of my cabin with brown carpet tiles left over from our house in Benoni.

I looked at my sandwich – dyed orange cheese and a slice of tomato on government brown bread. The same thing we ate every day. I usually liked it; now I couldn't take a bite. I had other symptoms too: I was dreamy, moody and more irritable than usual with my brother.

'Nothing's wrong with the food,' I said. 'I'm just not hungry.'

From across the table I felt Dad's gaze focus on me through the lenses of his glasses, like sunlight through a magnifying glass. I felt like an ant.

'I know what your problem is,' he said, 'you're in love.'

Robert nudged me and sniggered. I gave the matter some thought and decided my father was probably right. My feelings took the form of daydreams, which were all of boys on skateboards, and one boy in particular: Urbine. I rescued him from dangerous but poorly defined situations involving trains, trucks, deep water, fire and skateboards. After I'd saved him, I would cradle his head in my lap until he regained consciousness. When his brown eyes finally opened and gazed into mine they would brim with respect, gratitude and love.

Robert nudged me again, harder this time.

'Get a move on,' he said. 'We don't have all day, you know,'

In the cockpit our skateboards lay on their backs, like a pair of dead bugs. The previous day Urbine had said he would teach me to do 360s and I yearned to get ashore, to feel my board scuttle to life under my feet, but I wasn't going anywhere until I'd eaten. I took a bite of my sandwich, which turned to crumbs and sawdust in my mouth. I forced it down with a sip of water.

'Can't we go and play now?' I asked.

'Not before you've washed the dishes,' said Mom.

Robert smirked at me. I couldn't hit him because my mother was watching, so I kicked him hard under the table instead. As he jerked his legs away the vinyl seat covers made a sucking sound, like a gasp of surprise.

'It's your turn to dry,' I said.

My parents announced that *Vingila* would leave Durban for Cape Town in early January, six months after launching. The original plan to sail to Mauritius five weeks after putting our boat in the water had never been mentioned again. However, since our initial unsuccessful attempt at open-water sailing, we'd joined forces with Glen and Margie from *Chummy* and, alternating between the two boats, had sailed outside the harbour several times a week.

We would motor past the breakwater and, depending on the wind direction, tack to the ships lying at anchor several miles from the coast, wave at the staring crewmen on the rails who were yearning for land, and then come about and run back. If the wind blew from the north-west we ran to the ships and tacked back. Very rarely, in a true westerly, we reached in both directions. Our confidence improved.

Mooring, however, remained a problem: *Vingila*, 17 tons of steel without brakes, was difficult to stop, particularly in a crosswind. We seldom got it right first time and that made us nervous. The advantage to our mooring site lay in its distance from the yacht club, away from the eyes of sailors who spent more time drinking beer in the bar and providing commentary on others than they did sailing. Given a chance, they would no doubt have had much to say about us. Dad hated them.

'Those wankers at the club with their fancy boats think we'll never do it,' he often told Mom. 'They think we'll get to Brazil at most and run home with our tail between our legs, leaving *Vingila* behind with a For Sale sign tied to her shrouds. They're wrong. And one day I'm going to come back and rub their noses in it.'

As the year drew to a close we made ready to leave for Cape Town. From conversations with our fellow sailors, it became apparent that they thought the Cape of Storms to be the most dangerous leg of the standard circumnavigation route. Seasoned sailors expressed their worry and concern. Some were going so far as to engage professional crew and send their children and wives ahead by plane. We heard talk of frequent gales, the strongest of which could push northwards against the south-flowing Agulhas current to create rough, unsettled seas and the occasional rogue wave up to a hundred feet high.

When Mom brought me a South African history book from the library, my own feelings of unease deepened. I read that the first Europeans to discover South Africa were the Portuguese who came by sea and found the rocks of our coast to be as sharp as needles. Agulhas means needle in Portuguese. They wrote that the vicious reefs and shoals had an insatiable appetite for ships and spat out their broken hulls like fish bones, littering the shore with wrecks. The early explorers were constantly blown back by tremendous fronts and, because they didn't have charts, were terrified that they'd reached the end of the world and were about to fall off the edge. Bartholomew Diaz was the first European to get past the southern tip of Africa and, having been fortunate enough to survive once, went back later for more and died. A particularly rough patch of coast – which sailors came to call The Ship's Graveyard – was thought to have claimed both his vessel and his life. I searched through the sailing books on the shelf above Mom and Dad's bed, looking for more recent accounts of navigating the Cape of Storms and hoping to find encouraging news but each story was the same: storms, high seas, strong currents and reefs. And – unlike us – Robin from the *Dove*, Bernard Moitessier and Joshua Slocum were all experienced sailors. It was just our bad luck to begin our circumnavigation by tackling a coast that had given sailors far better than us a good thrashing and taken more than a few lives.

In preparation for the voyage Mom sealed macaroni and rice in plastic canisters with squares of ether-soaked gauze to kill weevils. Following recommendations in a sailing manual, she removed the labels from our tins of corned beef and dehydrated vegetables and varnished them according to a colour coded system. The book said we should do this, so that when the cans got wet and their labels fell off, the tins wouldn't rust and we would still know what was in them. I tried to imagine how the cans under my bed could get wet enough for their labels to fall off.

Charlie and Trish took leave from work in Benoni and arrived just after Christmas with three big suitcases packed with stylish new foul weather gear, several pastel outfits and their hairdryer.

'I've given you Nicky's cabin,' Mom told them. She only called me Martinique when she was angry. 'She doesn't mind. Really. Do you, Nicky?'

Trish turned to me with a smile that didn't quite reach her eyes and spoke in a false gush, admiring my mother's curtains and thanking me for being so kind.

My cabin, with its two narrow bunks separated by a work bench and a vice, lay just fore of the open sail locker in *Vingila*'s stern. That night, from the spare bunk in my parents' cabin – my new sleeping place – I watched Charlie shift and turn, trying without success to fit his large frame into my short bed.

The following day we woke to find ourselves surrounded by jungle. There'd been flooding inland and the harbour, brown with mud, was choked with floating islands of vegetation. *Vingila* crawled with life; insects, spiders, dragonflies and giant beetles – survivors of the deluge. A snake lay on the bow, coiled around the anchor winch, perhaps believing it had climbed the mooring lines to safety. Dad identified the reptile at once as poisonous – a black mamba – and, while we watched from the cockpit, beat it to death with the truncheon we used on fish.

I found a young chameleon carefully pacing the toe rail as if he were measuring it out, and I decided to keep him as a pet; I thought he could live on the curtains in the main saloon and come sailing with us. Charlie agreed that it was a great idea and nobody gave a thought to what he would eat.

On New Year's Eve, the night before our planned departure, we went ashore to the yacht club. While the adults drank on *Betty-J*, an American sloop skippered by Leonard Pratt, an airline pilot, and his wife Betty, I skateboarded in the dark with Urbine and the other kids. As the evening wore on, we broke into successively smaller groups. Later in the night Urbine and I found ourselves alone in the brown shadows of the boatyard's sodium lights. Beneath the covered yachts on trailers, we sat rocking our skateboards, chatting and laughing while the humid night air swirled around our shoulders in warm eddies.

'It's nearly midnight,' Urbine said. 'Want to watch the fireworks with me from *Saga*?'

'What about the others?'

'They went to David's boat, but that's okay. Just us is fine.'

The sound of laughter and clinking glass came across the water from *Betty-J* as Urbine made a nest of sails at the bow. His parents and sister were out and we had the boat to ourselves. Wrapped in folds of white cloth and close enough for me to feel his breath on my cheek, we watched squibs and rockets explode. And, as the last emergency flares drifted gently down from the sky, trailing pink smoke and the smell of cordite, his hand crept slowly over the sails until it was holding mine.

The first day of 1978 saw *Vingila* sailing into a headwind over a choppy sea the colour of bile. Foam streaked the waves like white spittle. With their faces turned to the wind Charlie and Trish sat on the weather rail, the bright hues of their new jackets accentuating the ashen tone of their skin. A steady rain of salt spray, rising from the waves smacking the hull broadside, had settled on Charlie's hair, removing its bounce and clumping the strands together to expose receding temples and a thinning pate.

Pepe sat at my mother's feet in the cockpit wearing a new harness, his leash clipped into the life-lines. As a further measure to stop him jumping over board, Dad had tied netting to the guard rails.

In spite of the headwind, low grey clouds and our late return home from the previous night's festivities, we had left our mooring early.

After they'd finished drinking on *Betty-J*, Dad and Charlie woke James, the ferryman, by shouting and banging on the walls of his Wendy house in the car park. He took a long time to emerge and didn't return their wishes for a happy new year. When we got to his boat the Seagull engine refused to start. He had to rub it down with handfuls of petrol from a jerry can before it finally coughed to life and puttered us home. The following morning brought pallor and regret, but because Charlie and Trish were on leave and time was limited, we slipped our moorings and sailed out of Durban.

After several hours of pounding into steep waves, the entrance of the harbour still remained clearly visible off the starboard side. The sails were full and pulling, but we weren't making forward progress because each time *Vingila* surged forward, she met with a wave that stopped her in her tracks. I went below to check my chameleon and found him holding on to a flapping curtain, looking happy enough. After spending some time alone at the stern looking deeply into the water, Charles came inside and asked my mom for headache tablets. Later, when the main saloon table worked free of its latch on the bulkhead and fell to the floor – ripped out by the hinges, Durban was still in sight. Dad decided we couldn't sail to Cape Town without a table, so we turned around and ran back to port where, after coffee for the adults and Ovaltine with powdered milk for Robert and me, we got into our bunks and fell asleep to the sound of wind whining in the rigging. Our circumnavigation would have to wait for another day.

3

CAPE OF STORMS

Three days after finally leaving Durban in fair winds, we passed the town of East London. My chameleon, resisting the temptations of tinned meatballs and spaghetti, baked beans or similar delicacies, hadn't eaten since I'd found him. With no cockroaches or flies to catch, he refused to open his mouth to alternatives. He clung to the curtains of the main saloon, growing smaller and darker daily. His skin became dry, wrinkled and ill-fitting. I was feeding him water from an eyedropper when we sailed past East London. Because the skies ahead were so clear and the breeze was so mild, we failed to notice our falling barometer and the growing haze on the horizon behind us.

About 800 sea miles lie between Durban and Cape Town. The journey, in good conditions, should take around a week. Because storms are so common, we expected at least one front, which we hoped to avoid by sheltering in one of the ports scattered along the coast. We didn't want to meet a gale at sea. We'd experienced a few storms in Durban, and on our moorings they were nasty enough. In strong winds the harbour turned white with foam and waves crashed against our hull and broke under our stern while James lashed the ferry to the dock, retiring to his hut and leaving us stranded for days. We learned to read the weather. Southerly gales were presaged by a falling barometer, oppressive heat and a hazy horizon. Almost exactly the atmospheric conditions we failed to notice until after East London had disappeared from view.

In the event of a storm off the coast of South Africa, opinion on sailing strategy was divided. Some yachtsmen believed it best to get close to land, away from the strong current and high waves, but nearer the shoals and rocks. In later years, with GPS providing accurate and frequent information on a boat's position, this advice would make sense. We, however, were sailing a decade before the simplest satellite navigation systems became available. Sextants and manual calculations yielded no more than two sets of co-ordinates per day, depending entirely on the skill of the operator, a clear horizon and a view of the sun unobscured by cloud. In that case it was safest to keep away from the coast, seaward of the swathe of strong current, the continental shelf and the 200-metre line. But for some reason Dad didn't want to sail into deeper water and kept the coastline within sight. We were sailing where everybody had said we shouldn't, exactly where the waves would be most dangerous in a storm. And since leaving Durban my father had not brought out his sextant once.

'Take Pepe and go below!' Mom said.

Her glasses were frosted with spicules of salt. Water, dripping from the points of her fringe, dissolved the concretions in curvy trails. Through such a varied gradient of refraction I wondered how she could see at all. She had taken the helm, a position for which good vision didn't seem optional.

The haze that we had failed to notice on the horizon as we sailed past East London had grown until it engulfed the sky, bringing gusts of wind that abraded the surface of the water in dark patches, whipping up white caps. Ragged clouds approached, their edges trailing sloped veils of rain. The first drops fell, stinging our cheeks.

'I can't worry about you as well, Nicky,' my mother said. 'Take the dog and get inside!'

In bad weather everybody had a job. Mine, it was becoming apparent, was to look after Pepe. That suited me just fine, I was ten, weedy and bookish, incapable of pulling hard on a sheet and skinny enough to feel I could be blown away in a strong wind. I wanted to go below. Actually I wanted my crochet blanket. My mother, a prolific seamstress, first started crochet work in the early 1970s, producing dozens of string bikinis, several tasselled ponchos for us children and the dogs, and a blanket each for Robert and me. Our blankets – multicoloured, with mustard and brown dominant – were made from easy to wash acrylic wool and, in spite of all the decorative holes, were surprisingly warm. Going below, I scooped a shivering dog into my arms, wrapped my blanket around my shoulders and sat on the floor, making up stories in my mind – daydreaming myself far away from the pitching and shouting, the clattering of sails and the endless high-pitched lament of the rigging.

After a while Trish stumbled down the stairs and pushed past into her cabin. She didn't return my greeting. Soon my brother came inside too.

'Why are you sitting down here with a blanket on your head?' he asked, lifting the edge and peering at me. 'Are you crying again?'

I wiped my eyes.

'No,' I said, 'I'm singing to Pepe.'

Robert was drenched but he looked as calm as ever. He never spoke much; anything I wanted to know could usually only be extracted by careful questioning.

'How's things outside?' I asked.

'Okay,' he said. 'Fine.'

Vingila jolted as if she had collided with a wall. The curtain flew up to the ceiling, my chameleon pinned to it like a brooch. Robert, knocked off his feet, snatched at a grab rail.

'Seems a bit wild to me,' I said. 'How's the sea look?'

'Rough.'

'Really? That doesn't sound good.'

'It's okay. They put the storm jib up.'

'The storm jib! We've never used that before.'

'Well, we're doing six knots with it now.'

'*Vingila* hasn't done that before.'

He looked thoughtful. 'Mmm, you're right, she hasn't.'

Then he yawned and said, 'I'm going to sleep.'

Unlike me, my brother could sleep anywhere. As *Vingila* bashed through waves, he pulled his crochet blanket from the forepeak, wrapped himself in it, lay down on the floor and shut his eyes. After a while Mom stuck her head down the hatch.

'How's Pepe?' she said.

'Sleeping,' I replied.

At the sound of his name, Pepe lifted his head and tried to make his way towards her, claws skating over the wet plywood floorboards. I pulled him back by a leg and wrapped him in my blanket. He was shivering and rolled his eyes.

'Go to sleep,' I said.

With East London now behind us and to windward, 80 miles lay between *Vingila* and the next port of safety, Port Elizabeth. Fortunately the gale blew in the same direction as the current; we encountered no rogue waves and could reach with it, which was faster and safer than either beating or running. The following day, still under our storm jib, we turned and beat into Port Elizabeth harbour, tacking towards a high wooden pier. The young woman who took our lines introduced herself as Lynnath Beckley. She told us that she'd seen us tossing on the waves from the balcony of her flat with her telescope that morning. She referred to our storm as a blow and she wanted to know how we had coped and if there was anything she could do for us.

A hot shower and a good night's sleep was what we wanted. For that matter, it's all anyone wants after being at sea. Charlie had additional cravings. Suffering more than the rest of us from my mother's experimental cooking with canned dehydrated vegetables, he wanted a steak, from a steak house, followed by strawberries and cream for dessert. Lynnath said she could help and began by driving us to the yacht club where she signed us in as guest members. I took my chameleon along. Stick-like and withered, he could barely hold his head up and I left him in the yacht club garden on a dusty shrub, hoping he would catch a fly and live.

Lynnath told us she was a marine biologist. She was sturdy and boyish with cropped hair, unshaven legs and functional rather than beautiful frames on her glasses. When I learned that she had personally discovered and named two new species of plankton, I immediately wanted to become a marine biologist myself. The next time she visited she brought me a starter kit: two well-slides wrapped in tissue paper, a box of cover slips and – reeking of formalin – a jar of zooplankton she'd collected in Antarctica. With her help I learned how to use an oil immersion lens and to tell the difference between isopods and amphipods. The microscopic crustaceans looked much like Pepe's fleas, but without the awful mouth parts. A day or two after meeting us Lynnath expressed a desire to join our circumnavigation. She told my parents, who didn't quite believe her, that she would see us again in the Caribbean.

We weren't keen to leave Port Elizabeth. The people were friendly and generous and the showers at the yacht club were warm. Also, the weather wasn't right. My father hoped, unrealistically perhaps, to wait for a steady northerly wind, but Charles and Trish were in a rush to reach Cape Town and so we left Port Elizabeth the morning after Charles had had his steak. My father wasn't a gracious dinner guest. After moving to the yacht he had said that on our budget of five rand a day we would not be eating in restaurants any more. Charles, however, had a job and money to spend and wanted to make the best of his holiday, which thus far had been fairly dismal. He was determined to celebrate, so at his request Lynnath lent us her car for the outing to a steak house. Charles and Trish wore matching baby-blue pantsuits, and their hair – like their mood – was buoyant, for they'd been delighted to discover a socket for their hairdryer at the yacht club. The restaurant, with frilled polyester tablecloths and matching napkins, was deserted except for a single waiter, and we took a seat and ordered our steak well done, without a hint of pink.

After the steak Charles asked the waiter for strawberries and cream.

'They're not on the menu,' the waiter said, 'but I'll check with the manager.'

My father flinched. We never bought strawberries; he thought they were frivolous and far too expensive. And we never asked for anything that wasn't on the menu.

'I checked with the manager,' the waiter said when he came back, 'we'll find some.'

'Fantastic!'

Tossing a silky fringe from his eyes, Charles turned a gap-toothed grin on Robert and me.

'I'm sure you two won't say no to some strawberries and cream,' he said.

Robert and I exchanged glances. Of course we wanted strawberries; they were an unimaginable treat but, afraid of my father, we couldn't say yes. Silence stretched between us and Charles's fading grin.

'What will it be?' the waiter asked.

Charlie recharged his grin.

'Strawberries and cream for everyone!' he said.

'Not for me,' Dad said, looking at my mother.

'Or me, thanks,' said my mother, who loved strawberries.

'Well, I want some,' said Trish, 'and I think Nicky and Robert do too.'

Feeling like traitors, we ate our strawberries under the baleful eye of my father. Charlie paid the bill but Dad remained sullen all the way back to *Vingila*.

When we left the next day the wind was blowing on the nose and we had to beat against it. Dad claimed *Vingila* could steer herself to windward if the helm was 'balanced', but in reality our sails were usually stalled. The log may have read three to four knots, but any forward motion we made was probably due to the current. Our jib lacked telltales and we hadn't heard of the close hauled groove, much less how to get into it, so *Vingila* jackknifed into the waves and made very slow progress.

Over the ensuing days, tension grew between my parents and Charles and Trish. My father felt that Charles had pushed him to leave, and held him responsible for the bad weather. The constant uncertainty about our position, and the heavy seas, grey skies, rain and strong winds were not what Trish had in mind when she had agreed to go on a sailing holiday. In fact, as we spent day after day in our foul weather gear, the memory of every picture we had ever seen of a yacht sailing over calm blue water seemed to return to taunt us. And nothing had prepared us for how much foul weather gear stank.

My parents spent hours on deck dodging spray and peering at the distant coast through the salty lenses of their glasses, struggling to compare it with the line drawings in the pilot book. As far as they could tell, one series of hills looked much like another. At night, from the top of waves, they struggled to identify individual lighthouses by the frequency of their flashes. For some reason my father was not using his sextant to navigate.

I didn't know it at the time but two weeks before leaving Durban, Dad had given our nautical almanac away. The book, with its tables of the rising and setting times of the sun, moon and navigational stars for different latitudes, was essential for celestial navigation. Only a limited run of copies were printed each year, and in 1978 they sold out. My father, a man who forbade us ever to borrow or lend anything, gave our almanac to the skipper of an American yacht, who promised to post it back to us from Cape Town but never did.

Dad had attended several celestial navigation courses; first in Johannesburg, and then in Durban. He had a full set of charts, two beautiful sextants and a gleaming brass chronometer nestled in a velvet-lined mahogany box. He had all the necessary books and tables but he also had a secret. He didn't know how to navigate. Years later he confessed to me, 'I just couldn't get it into my head. I tried and tried but I couldn't.' His family were artisans who worked in foundries and mines; his father was a fitter and turner. Studying was considered a waste of time and reading a pretension, so my father never completed high school. A talented mechanic, he could solve complicated electrical wiring problems in his head, but when it came to maths and formal learning he was lost. And he was too proud and insecure to admit it. Mom, with matric and three years of teacher training college, was probably better equipped to assume navigational responsibilities, but in our family it had been decided that navigation was a man's job, and my father's in particular. So when our nautical almanac was not returned, we set off without it, with only my father aware that it wouldn't have made a difference anyway.

We seldom knew exactly where we were, or how far from the reefs, except on the rare occasions when we met a ship and asked them, on our VHF radio, for their position. Without short wave, we couldn't receive weather reports and it seemed we sailed aimlessly in a gale that blew constantly from the wrong direction.

When Charles and Trish weren't outside on watch they lay in my cabin, leaving the main saloon to us. Mealtimes were strained. At night I heard them whispering, squashed together in a single bunk, and once I thought I heard Trish crying.

Twice a day, my mother took Pepe outside in his harness for a walk to the stern, where he squatted with difficulty, before returning to the blankets, to lie coiled as tightly as a ball of rags. Robert and I, like most children, were resilient; we simply accepted our new reality and endured. If this was the sailing Mom and Dad wanted to do, then we had to do it. It wasn't as if we had a choice. As the sea grew rougher we moved from our cabins at the extremities of the boat to the main saloon floor, where we lay in our crochet blankets with Pepe and our books. I didn't often feel scared because although I accepted dying as a vague theoretical possibility, at the age of ten I did not yet believe I could actually die. I also did not quite realise the extent of the danger and neither, I suspect, did my mother and brother. I read a lot. I finished the few children's stories aboard and began working my way through our collection of adult thrillers. My parents didn't censor our reading and, rocking in my blankets to the motion of the boat, I sought out the sex scenes and read them with a mixture of fascination and disgust, while *Vingila* shuddered and heaved; thrusting and plunging through the waves, blasted intermittently by sudden gouts of white spray.

Between books, I daydreamed of Urbine, wrestled my brother and tormented the dog. As the days passed, it began to feel as if we had all been ill and were trapped in that interminable phase of convalescence characterised by monotony, broken sleep, weak legs, sweaty bodies, knotted bedclothes, and irritability. It became difficult to remember another way of living and there seemed no reason to believe our state would ever change.

My memory of Mossel Bay is hazy. I remember going to town and finding cans of peach flavoured fruit nectar in the supermarket. They were the most exotic drinks I'd ever seen and, although we were still in South Africa, I felt as if we had arrived in a foreign land. After some discussion, my parents agreed to break their budget and buy two cans. We returned to find a deserted boat. A letter lay on the table. Charles and Trishia apologised for leaving so unexpectedly, but they had found a last minute flight back to Johannesburg. They wished my parents all the best for the trip to Cape Town and onwards around the world.

We left Mossel Bay alone, just the four of us. Up until then we'd always had other adults aboard; spare hands to tug on lines or take the helm. *Vingila* was not an easy boat to sail – the halyards and sheets for the main and mizzen sails were scattered over the deck, and two people were needed to operate our winches. As we didn't have either a wind vane or an autopilot, my parents would now be forced to share the watches between themselves. However, with Trish and Charles gone, the time pressure was off and we could wait for the right weather conditions before leaving. Which we did, sailing away from Mossel Bay with the wind at our beam and not a cloud in sight. For two days we slept in our own cabins and drank fruit nectar on the deck in the afternoon, before the conditions turned and we found ourselves once again beating into a gale over dark green waves and living in foul-weather gear.

Mom and Dad had red waterproofs of good quality; dungarees with black elastic shoulder straps and jackets with elaborate zippers. Robert and I wore fluorescent apricot anoraks with a rubber lining that looked and smelled of mustard – adult jackets without zips that my mother had found in the bargain bin at the yacht chandlers. Their hems came to our knees and we wore them like dresses, with the sleeves rolled up. Holding our breath, we pulled them over our heads, trying to avoid the rank, ammoniacal smell that nevertheless puffed up from their necks in warm little blasts whenever we moved.

As the days passed, Mom and Dad didn't get much sleep because of their nights on the helm. Dad suggested Robert and I should take watch during the day, so that he and Mom could rest. One morning, after a night of particularly high winds, Dad handed the wheel to Robert. *Vingila*, wind abaft, was reaching under her storm jib and a reefed main. As he went through the companionway Dad turned to see Robert standing barefoot in his foul weather jacket with a wave as high as the mizzen spreaders behind him. In a rare show of concern – he never did it again – Dad took the wheel and sent Robert below. The swell, at least as big as a house and about as steep, with a toppling crest, bore down on us, but *Vingila* simply rode it and the ones that followed. We were getting to know our boat; she was slow, heavy and unresponsive, but she was strong and dry, and most of all, she was extremely forgiving, for which we probably owe her our lives.

Cape Agulhas, which lay ahead, was reputed to have the worst weather of the entire coast. Shallow sandbanks stretch out to sea, marking the confluence of two oceans: the warm Indian and the icy South Atlantic. The collision of currents confuses the waves, stirring up the shallow water. Cold plankton-rich upwellings attract fish, birds and, in spite of the danger, fishing boats. I remembered reading that Diaz lost his life somewhere here, on his third voyage around the Cape. In angry seas, pounding waves worked the caulk from between the planks of old ships and the crew members not occupied above deck tending sails kept below, bailing for their lives. Sometimes, a ship simply fell apart and sank. I found myself wishing I hadn't done quite so much reading. *Dove*, the teenage single-hander's little sloop in the movie, also nearly came to pieces in these waters. Once round the Cape, Robin, the youthful captain, was able to see daylight where his cabin-top joined the deck and he had to stop at Gordon's Bay for extensive repairs. Even Joshua Slocum, the first person to complete a solo circumnavigation and an excellent seaman, had difficulty passing the point. He wrote in his book *Sailing Alone Around the World* that his beloved boat *Spray* spent all day off the Cape trying to stand on her head and, what's more, gave him every indication that she would succeed at it before nightfall.

The trouble with not knowing where we were, was that we didn't know if we'd reached Agulhas or not. In heavy wind and angry swells, we pounded through a group of penguins, wondering when things would get worse. A passing fishing boat, running home for shelter, gave us our position over the VHF radio. We were sailing over the banks of Agulhas. Mom suggested a celebration, but the sea was too rough and, besides, several days of beating still lay ahead before we reached the shelter of Simon's Town.

'Baarp!'

Surrounded by fog, *Vingila* rolled on water as glossy as syrup.

'Baaarp!'

'It's getting louder,' Mom said.

We'd left Simon's Town that morning in light north-westerly winds, a clear blue sky and good spirits. After Agulhas we'd taken a rest while the storm blew itself out. Dad said there was only a day between us and Cape Town and we might as well wait for the right one. We had nothing to worry about, he said, Cape Point would be great, in calm weather.

'We're going to have a lovely time,' my mother said as we weighed anchor. 'It'll make up for the storms. We'll see Cape Point – it's beautiful – and the Twelve Apostles, and Table Mountain.'

Docking at Cape Town would mark the end of the first leg of our round the world voyage and was a reason to celebrate. Neither Robert nor I had been to Cape Town before. It's gorgeous, my mother said, just wait till you see it. The most beautiful city in the world. We waved goodbye to Simon's Town.

'This is what it's about,' my father said, walking to the foredeck and stretching out his arms to take in the placid water of False Bay and its surrounding mountains. 'What a way to end the trip. On a high note.'

Half an hour later a thick fog rolled in and we couldn't see a thing. The wind died and the horizon shrank to a white circle a few metres from our hull. We might have been immersed in a glass of milk. Except that there were rocks, and kelp beds and ships in the milk. Many ships. They began blowing their foghorns.

'Baarp!'

'That's close,' Mom looked panicked. 'What now, Frank?'

'Blow our horn back, of course.'

My father brought out the brass trumpet that had consistently failed to summon James the ferryman in Durban. He lifted it to his lips to produce a familiar harsh yodel. We waited for a response. There was silence, a thick foggy hush.

Then: 'BAAARRP!'

'Are they answering us, or just hooting?' Mom asked.

The ship's horn, much louder now, was joined by the heavy drone of a marine engine and the cutting pulse of a propeller, both of which grew so loud we could barely hear our own frantic bleating in return.

'I wish we had bought one of those aerosol horns,' Mom said. 'And I don't want to say it, but how long does it take for a ship to turn? Or stop?'

'Don't be stupid,' Dad said, 'even if they don't hear us, they'll pick up *Vingila* on their radar.'

I glanced at the small silver radar reflector hanging from our mizzen mast. It looked more like a talisman than a safety device, and somewhat extraneous too, considering our entire vessel was made of steel. Crossing my fingers, I imagined men in peaked white caps on the bridge of the ship, calm and in control, their eyes drifting professionally over banks of screens, searching for blips. Almost immediately, this picture was replaced by a much less reassuring vision of the same men standing in the passage *outside* the control room, taking a smoke break and chatting, or thumbing the pages of a magazine. I forced my mind back to the first image.

The deep intestinal rumblings of the ship grew louder; by all indications it was bearing down on us. My father took the helm – a sure sign of the seriousness of the situation – and sent us to the bow as lookouts. Surrounded by white, I felt helpless and oddly exposed; blind and vulnerable, like a sinner about to be struck by the hand of God. I considered my recent reading material and wondered if this was my punishment for being so interested in sex: to be run down and sunk by a ship in the fog. Maybe praying would help. Perhaps, if he knew I was sorry, God would change his mind. Dear God, I thought, I know I've been reading a lot of bad things lately ... I was considering an appropriate conclusion to my prayer when we met three sharp, unexpected waves and entered a band of freshly churned water. A multitude of bubbles rose to the surface, releasing the smell of diesel as they popped. The ship had crossed our bow, leaving us in its wake. It was impossible to know if they had ever even been aware of our presence.

We motored on inside a white cocoon, guided by dead reckoning and our compass and almost completely unsure about our position. After several hours my father noticed a change in the motion of the sea. The change was subtle, more of a feeling or a suspicion really, than anything specific.

He turned off the engine and listened.

'What's that?' he whispered. 'Can you hear it?'

Listening carefully, we could just make out the faint suck and wash of waves breaking on rocks, although in the fog it was impossible to locate the source of the sound. Dad sent us to the bow again. Slowly *Vingila* felt her way forward, like a blind person groping without a cane. I caught the mineral odour of seashore and decayed marine vegetation, and saw dark shapes floating in the sea. From the bow, we spotted the rocks at roughly the same time as we reached the kelp bed. I should have finished that prayer, I thought, because God didn't seem to be through with me yet. For the second time in a day it looked as if we were about to wreck our boat. But Dad stayed calm, thrusting *Vingila* into reverse, and hauled her head round and – in coils of seaweed 30 feet long with stems as thick as saplings – made a sharp about-turn back into the gloom. We had escaped.

Several hours later when the wind picked up, it blew the fog away to reveal the back of Table Mountain, its attendant Apostles and the white beaches and the palm trees of Camps Bay. I knew from the library book that Francis Drake passed here in 1580 on his way home after three years spent pillaging Spanish settlements, collecting spices and establishing trade ties with Indonesia. In spite of losing four of the five boats he had started out with, he was feeling chipper. He even had time to make a snotty entry in his journal. He wrote that he 'found the report of the Portuguese, who affirm that this is the most dangerous cape in the world, never without intolerable storms and present dangers to travellers which come near, to be most false. This cape is a most stately thing, and the fairest cape we saw in the whole circumference of the earth.' So much for those lily-livered Portuguese, but he was right, without the fog the Cape was pretty.

After the shroud of fog lifted, the sun came out and the sea shed its grey skin and shone a deep jewel-blue. With her white sails and a lacy bow wave, *Vingila* sailed across Table Bay, looking almost smart enough to be on a calendar. It was the third of February and a full month since we'd embarked on a maiden voyage which we'd hoped would take no more than eight days. In the Royal Cape yacht basin we were ushered to the berths for visiting yachts where we tied up among the blue-water cruisers, some of which we recognised from Durban. Our status in the sailing community had risen a notch, although I wasn't completely sure we deserved it.

Part 2

ATLANTIC OCEAN

4

CAPE TOWN

Wind quality and direction, the nature of the sea, and the motion of the boat combine and interact with a human element – expectations, health, moods and relationships between the people aboard – to form the background of an ocean voyage. Fish caught, whales sighted, bread baked and books read, create the focal points. Once port is reached and the boat safely docked, sailors can stand back and assess the whole. In Cape Town we could confidently say that *Vingila*'s maiden voyage had not been good. Slow progress, bad weather, incompetence, conflict among the crew, inedible food and tawdry books formed an experience so unpleasant I couldn't bear to look back at it. But at least we didn't die, and we still had our boat.

With the outcome of sea journeys so random, unpredictable and potentially fatal, it's hardly surprising sailors are a superstitious lot. In the face of unrelenting bad weather and ill luck the seamen of old would start casting their eyes about, searching for a jinx – something or somebody to blame. Over centuries the superstitions piled up. Never leave on a Friday, the first Monday in April, or the second Monday in August. Starting a cruise on 31 December is bad, to which we could add, from experience, that 1 January isn't much better. The French forbid mentioning the word *'lapin'* aboard. The English won't say 'drowned' while afloat and refuse to paint a hull green. On *Vingila* we were safe from the misfortunate effects of priests, redheads and green hulls, but Mom presented a problem. Women on a boat are very bad luck, acceptable only if carved from wood and in naked form. So right from the start, fortune – it seemed – wasn't on our side. But it got worse. Boat names ending in 'a' are bad luck, as are dogs near fishing tackle boxes. A dog vomiting on a tackle box, while not specifically mentioned, could only be worse. Certain seabirds bring good fortune, but penguins aren't among them, as we had learned for ourselves off Cape Agulhas. Some superstitions are more specific: a shark following a ship's wake is a sure sign of death among the crew and looking back as a vessel leaves port ensures it will never return. Once I heard that, I found it impossible to resist backward glances. Fortunately we were circumnavigating.

Superstition aside, certain ocean routes are kinder than others. The tropical South Atlantic, in which hurricanes are unknown, seldom sees a gale and has trade winds that blow steadily and – while nothing is guaranteed – good weather and a pleasant voyage can be expected. After Cape Town my father assured us the sailing could only get better.

Eva Fox stood in the cockpit of *Foxtrot*, the sleek ketch she shared with her husband Al, and invited me aboard. I very much wanted to accept her invitation but my last visit to their boat in Durban hadn't gone well and so I was hesitant. Not that Eva had been unfriendly or anything, far from it, she was an accomplished and graceful hostess. The problem, according to my father, had been with me.

Eva gave me an encouraging smile. I was surprised she even remembered me. In Durban they'd been moored at the foreign jetty, while we had been relegated to the riff-raff on the moorings. In Cape

Town we'd been given a place with the other visiting yachts and I walked past *Foxtrot* several times a day and often stopped to admire the boat, peering through her portholes when I thought no one was watching. She looked fast and seaworthy, with a mahogany panelled interior and Persian rugs in muted tones complementing the tasteful scatter cushions and drapery. Thinking of the orange curtains and brown carpet in my own cabin intensified my suspicion that I had somehow been placed in the wrong family. One day, I decided, my real parents would claim me and introduce me to grandparents like Al and Eva.

The Foxes were aristocrats of the cruising world, and in Benoni I'd seen their pictures in the cruising magazines stacked around our house. They were an athletic American couple in their sixties with silver hair and white teeth that contrasted nicely with their golden, unlined skins. More than fifteen years of sailing, several circumnavigations, and thousands of sea miles under the keel had left them surprisingly unweathered. They looked airbrushed. Their yacht was unweathered too, like a poster boat for blue-water cruising.

From the moment *Foxtrot* first sailed into Durban, my parents were determined to visit. They'd read so much about the Foxes, they almost felt they knew them. Dad suggested we go in small groups to improve our chances of an invitation and chose me to accompany him on the first foray. Our strategy worked. We were invited into the cockpit and offered drinks. We talked about sailing for a while and then Eva asked if we knew anything about seashells. We shook our heads. She took us inside to a polished walnut cabinet and pulled out drawers of beautiful, glossy, spiky, patterned shells. The result of years of dedicated collecting, she said. I had never seen anything so wonderful.

'What's that one?' I asked, pointing out a cone shell which looked as if someone with a shaky hand had tried to draw the continent of Africa on its back.

'*Conus geographus*, the geographic cone. It's deadly poisonous. One sting will kill you.'

Not sure how to respond, I giggled. A simpering, little-girl giggle. Although I wasn't usually giggly, I adopted a girly persona for the remainder of the visit, hoping to charm Eva and make her like me. I tossed my hair and asked questions I thought would make me sound intelligent. I looked at all her shells. I batted my eyelashes and flirted. I desperately wanted to make an impression. Dad watched with narrowed eyes.

Afterwards he told Mom, in my presence, that the visit might have gone well if I hadn't 'acted so stupid'. In our family 'acting stupid' was a crime second only to 'thinking you were clever', something else I was often accused of. Growing up, I constantly stumbled between these two forms of unacceptable behaviour. Robert, quiet, non-committal and as brave as a hero in a Western, didn't have the same trouble. After Dad's comment, my impression of the visit to *Foxtrot* changed. Waves of self-loathing swamped me. It became clear that I'd behaved like a vacuous clown and I was sure Eva hated me. Now here she was in Cape Town several months later, inviting me aboard again. And she'd even remembered my name. I was afraid to accept because I so wanted to be liked by her that I didn't know how to behave.

'Do you eat cookies, Nicky?' Eva asked.

I nodded. I knew cookies were only biscuits but the unfamiliar name gave them an exotic appeal.

'Come aboard then. I've got something for you.'

I couldn't say no. Eva poured me a glass of cold milk from their fridge and while I ate my cookie we chatted. She told me their sail from Durban had been peaceful. Watching the weather patterns, they had taken shelter before the storms brewed and so had travelled only in good winds. They had met interesting and friendly people en route and in East London had found a pair of rare cowries to add to their collection.

'How was your sail?' she asked.

My natural inclination was to tell a story, only slightly embellished, of how awful it had been: the howling winds, crashing seas, terrible food and wind shrieking constantly in the rigging. I wanted to tell her that our crew had run away and that I was worried my father couldn't navigate, but I tried instead to be more like my brother.

'Fine,' I said.

She unlatched a cabinet and removed a rectangular object.

'For you, honey,' she said, handing me a book.

No one had called me honey before, but I didn't mind it too much. The book was small and white. Under the title – *Seashells of the World* – were a few amateur looking paintings of shells.

'And here's something else.'

She passed me a flat cardboard box. Straw protruded through the perforations on its base and *Cape Grapes* was stamped in green ink across the lid. I wondered why Eva was giving me grapes. Opening the box I found, partially submerged in straw – as if they were living in a strange grassy habitat on the bottom of the sea – a collection of textile cones, money and serpent-head cowries, augers and a single spiky murax. All good specimens.

'You can identify them using your new book,' Eva said. 'It's the start of your shell collection.'

I didn't know quite how to thank her without acting stupid.

During our two months at the Royal Cape Yacht Club each member of the family found a private form of happiness. For Pepe, joy lay in getting ashore whenever he wanted. With *Vingila* tethered to a walk-on mooring, he was free to come and go as he pleased, obstructed only by the occasional sunbathing seal which he could bark at. For him the pontoon from our boat led directly to paradise; a car park filled with tyres where he didn't have to crouch and stagger as he had done at sea, but could lift his leg again like a proper dog. My mother found happiness in a small shop downtown selling dried fruit and bargain cheese. There, in addition to buying wedges of yellow cheddar, she could indulge her lifelong – but seldom satisfied – addiction to hanepoot raisins. My father found his bliss drinking wine in the afternoons on a yacht called *Betty-J*, swapping sailing stories with Leonard Pratt, the retired airline pilot he'd befriended in Durban. Now he had stories of his own to tell and, with a sea voyage behind him, a slightly higher status in the yachtie community.

One afternoon, warm sun falling in the cockpit and wine glasses filled to the brim from a five-litre cask – for in addition to grapes the Cape had cheap wine – he settled down for another chat with Leonard. He began telling the story of how we rounded Cape Agulhas.

'So I said to the ship, "What's your position?" and they said, "Do you want to know our position or yours?" And I said, "Well, actually I really want to know my position." And when they gave it to me, I asked, "Are you sure this is correct?" They said, yes, we were off Cape Agulhas and we should carry on sailing as we were for a few hours and then turn right.'

Instead of laughing, Leonard just looked at him and said, 'You're having trouble navigating, aren't you?'

I flinched, waiting for the explosion, the expletives, the horrible upside-down smile, but Dad simply looked back at Leonard and said, 'Yes.'

The next day Leonard took my father to Green Point Lighthouse and showed him how to shoot sights. This is where the real skill of celestial navigation lies; using a sextant to measure the angle of the sun to the horizon, a task far easier to perform on solid land than from a pitching deck. After explaining the use of the almanac and sight reduction tables, Leonard helped Dad through the calculations, concentrating on method rather than theory. When Dad, using his parallel rulers and dividers for the first time, drew lines on a chart which intersected roughly over Cape Town, Leonard congratulated him and told him he could navigate.

Ignoring Cape Town's mountains, ancient vineyards and beaches, Robert and I found our happiness roaming the boatyards and car parks of the docks and yacht club with our skateboards. Using canvas and abandoned railway sleepers, we built a fort in a dusty corner of an empty lot and hung out there with David, the rich American from the Hinckley *Resolve*, with whom I had made plexiglass ornaments in Durban, and Gary and Hudson, a pair of brothers living on a boat called *Scud*.

'Did you know,' Gary told my mother the first time he met her, 'that when Joshua Slocum came to South Africa he met your president Paul Kruger who told him it was impossible to sail around the world because the earth was flat. How backward is that?'

'Really?' answered Mom without looking up from the bikini she was crocheting. 'Very interesting.'

Gary knew a lot about Joshua Slocum because *Scud*, their sloop, was a replica of Slocum's *Spray* and had been built in the same town and even from the same type of wood as *Spray*. Gary's dad wore his beard in the style of Captain Slocum and, on special occasions, a bowler hat too. *Scud*, just like *Spray*, had no electricity or engine and the family used kerosene lamps for light, and long oars to row in and out of port.

Gary, who was fourteen, had opinions on everything. Like David's new skateboard. After his old one was stolen, David's parents bought him the best board in Cape Town. It had a body of transparent plastic with a kick tail, and polyurethane wheels with slick bearings that would ride over anything, but Gary didn't like it.

'It's not authentic,' he said. 'Skateboards should be flat and made of wood. With small wheels. My dad says our boards are truer to the spirit of skateboarding.'

I'd skated on Hudson's board before and had been thrown off the pier onto the rocks below when it came to a dead stop after hitting a small stone. I knew David had the better board, but like the others, I said nothing because Gary was older than us and the leader. Even David agreed with him and so found his wonderful new board unsatisfactory and coveted Hudson's old skateboard with its awful wheels.

We were in the fort one day when Gary showed us his new digital watch, an ugly thing, with a cheap plastic strap. We all admired it. David looked at his own watch, a Rolex, and didn't like what he saw.

'I'll sell this,' he said.

'How much?'

'Thirty dollars.' It was worth considerably more.

'Nah,' said Gary, shining the face of his digital timepiece. 'Who wants a watch like that?'

But I did, and I told my mother about it.

'If he wants to sell a real Rolex for thirty dollars you should buy it,' she said, showing the first signs of a scavenging habit we would all develop. But when I went back to David with the money, he told me his parents had forbidden him to sell the watch.

There were girls at the yacht club too, although they didn't skate or come to the fort because they said it was too dirty. Belinda and her younger sister Kim on *Antoinette* were South African. Their divorced mother Grace, with wild grey hair and a smoker's laugh, was trailing her ex-husband and his new girlfriend as they sailed their yacht *Odette* to America. Grace always needed crew. Young men applying for the post seldom stayed long and needed continual replenishing from a stream of new recruits. The two girls didn't skate but on Friday evenings, while our parents drank at the bar, Gary and Hudson turned down the kerosene lamps in *Scud*'s saloon and ignited joss sticks in the Balinese incense burner. Once darkness fell Hudson, in his best white shirt, clamped me to his stocky chest and we danced through the clouds of incense smoke while Gary kissed Belinda, and Robert, David and little Kim watched.

Shortly before we left Cape Town *Maria Jose*, the Swiss junk from

Durban, arrived. The last we had seen them they were setting sail for Madagascar some months earlier. Ernest immediately invited Dad aboard. Stacked inside the cavernous holds were numerous objects of different sizes all wrapped in hessian sacks. Ernest unwrapped one to reveal a large beautiful Chinese jar.

'Ming dynasty, I've been told,' he said.

He went on to explain that the family had found sunken treasure on the Bassa da India reef in the Mozambique Channel.

'A few years back we nearly lost *Maria Jose* in a certain place,' Ernest said. 'It was so dangerous the way the wind and the current came together and nearly forced us onto the reef that I thought other ships might have run into trouble too. So when we got back to Durban I went to the libraries and did my research, gathered scuba gear and returned to search.'

Hans, the eldest son, had found the sunken ship. After several days of unsuccessful diving with his father and brother Alex, he had gone snorkelling by himself one afternoon and discovered cannons poking from the sand. It was the wreck of the *Santiago*, a 900 tonne Portuguese nau which had struck the reef and gone down in 1585 on her way to India. Her captain and officers made off in the only lifeboat leaving the four hundred passengers behind to drown. After finding the cannons the Klaar family had spent three hard months diving every day the weather allowed and salvaging everything they could. By the time they sailed away Ernest had aboard twelve bronze cannons, six Ming jars, some jewels which he didn't show Dad, and sacks and sacks of silver coins. He admitted that one of the jars had worked its way loose in rough seas and had been broken en route to Cape Town.

'I've decided to leave the porcelain here for safe keeping,' he said. 'The rest of the stuff I'm taking to Europe to sell.'

Even with the holds of their ship crammed with treasure the Klaar boys still didn't have enough cash to buy skateboards and Alex and

I worked out a scheme where he would rent my board in return for seashells. Whenever the southeaster gale blew he'd arrive at *Vingila* with a pocketful of seashells and after some bartering, disappear with my skateboard and a huge piece of cardboard tucked under his arm. I knew from watching him that he used the cardboard as a sail, and sped down the oil tanker pier with the wind blowing him all the way. Often he fell and several times got badly grazed. It never stopped him. When the next southeaster blew I would hear him once again knocking on the hull and calling my name. While Alex was away skating I identified the shells using my new book. Then, as Eva had shown me, I copied out each shell's common and Latin names, and the date, place and habitat in which they had been found, onto tiny scraps of paper. This I wedged into each shell's mouth before adding it to my straw-lined grape box. Because Alex knew quite a lot about shells even if he didn't care much for them, I never got any particularly rare specimens from him. Still my collection grew. Alex gave me a *Conus litteratus,* or Lettered cone with lovely broad shoulders and rows of black dots against a white background. He had dived it himself from a sandy bottom in Mayotte and it was in excellent condition. Or so Eva Fox said when I showed it to her. Another day, in exchange for three hours of skateboard time, I became the owner of an Imperial cone, or *Conus araneosus,* as well as a white Inscriptus cone and two shiny Arabica cowries.

Stocked to the gills with sacks of potatoes and onions, our lockers packed to the brim with whisky, we left Cape Town on Easter Friday, 25 March 1978, nine months after we had launched our boat. If we hoped to finish our circumnavigation in two years, it looked as if we were falling badly behind schedule.

Leaving the coast of Africa, a test lay ahead for Dad's new navigational skills; we were aiming for Saint Helena island, 17 kilometres wide and

1 400 sea miles away in the centre of the South Atlantic Ocean. With a new ham radio aboard and a wind vane called Baruch to assist with the steering, we were hoping for mild weather and an enjoyable sail. On the day of our departure a light south-east wind blew, so light in fact that we could hardly get away from land and we had to motor around Robben Island. Nelson Mandela was probably there at the time, resting after a day spent breaking stones in the quarry with his pickaxe, but this was apartheid South Africa, so I had never heard of him. And if I had, I would have been told that he was a dangerous terrorist.

The night before we set sail, my mother fried chicken. We had a gas fridge aboard which did not work at sea because it wasn't gimballed and Dad had decided to switch it off a few days early to get us used to living without refrigeration. Mom kept the chicken pieces in a covered bowl overnight until she served them to us the following day for a late lunch. In the evening, as Table Mountain grew smaller and at last disappeared from the horizon, leaving *Vingila* beyond sight of land for the first time, the breeze freshened. The Cape of Storms had a parting gift for us: a final unexpected goodbye gale. The breeze grew into a full-strength blow. Wind astern, we lowered the mainsail and made eight knots under a working jib. By then Robert and I were heaving. We had never been seasick before, but while hanging out in the fort with the kids, seasickness was a frequent topic of conversation. Both Gary and Hudson were ill at sea and their stories were graphic and detailed. However, while there may have been an element of autosuggestion involved in our illness, I'm inclined to blame the chicken. Whatever the cause, for three long days, the gale blew and Robert and I vomited. As *Vingila* pitched and tossed, the table in the main saloon was again latched against the bulkhead and our family lived on the floor. Although living is probably too active a word to describe our state. After the first day Robert and I gave up removing our foul weather gear. I wanted my jacket off, because the smell was awful and it mixed with the pervasive odour of onions and green peppers from the sacks in the forepeak, but inertia engulfed me. I was too weak to undress myself and my parents, also unwell, were busy dealing with the storm. So Robert and I lay on the floor wrapped in crochet blankets, wearing our oilskins. We dozed and had fitful dreams and our days melted into night and back into day again. The only constant was the nausea, the crying of the wind in the rigging and the thud of waves breaking against *Vingila*'s hull. When we became too weak to climb on deck and be sick overboard, we sat in the companionway and vomited directly into the cockpit, which was full of water anyway. As the wind grew stronger, the storm jib replaced the working jib, and when the wind grew stronger still, we took down the storm jib and, under bare poles, covered 75 miles in 24 hours.

On Easter Monday, four days after our departure, the wind began to ease and we knew the gale had blown itself out. The main saloon table was set up and we got off the floor and gathered around it. My mother had a surprise for us – Easter eggs. Robert and I stripped off our foul weather gear and ate three eggs each; the type with a squishy yellow marshmallow yolk and a covering of thin, cracked chocolate. They were the first thing I had eaten in days and they tasted delicious. Surprisingly, they stayed down.

Then the wind died completely. After rolling on long swells for a few hours, a gentle fifteen knot south-easterly wind sprang up and blew away the clouds. It was a trade wind – a wonderful, mythical, trade wind – blowing from just the right direction. A wind we had read and dreamed about, but had nearly given up hope of ever encountering. Way back in Benoni, however, we had prepared our boat for such a wind; so we raised a pair of jibs on *Vingila*'s twin forestays, with whisker poles to hold them out, and we set our new self-steering device, Baruch, on course with the wind behind us.

Once the weather warmed, we removed our heavy clothing and packed away our foul weather gear. Dad went even further – he shed all his clothes. My mother was aghast.

'Frank,' she said, 'the kids ...'

But my father was set. While working in the hot foundries, wearing his dirty overalls, he had thought constantly of the yacht on the calendar, the yacht with white sails on a blue sea. And when, in his sailing dreams, he had pictured himself on that yacht, he was most decidedly naked. This was all new to Robert and me. In Benoni, Dad had been a shadowy figure, arriving home late at night, grimy and smelling of engine oil, to give us a goodnight kiss. Weekends, he was irritable and focused on *Vingila*. The little I had seen of him before we went sailing certainly hadn't been naked. It looked painful when his soft white buttocks sank into the crevices of the non-slip cork deck as he sat down to take sights, but it didn't bother him. Initially, he suffered sunburn on tender, previously unexposed skin but it soon toughened up. In the evenings when it got cooler and he felt the chill, he slipped on a T-shirt, allowing the tip of his penis to peep out from beneath its hem. I had never seen Dad so content. His unfettered scrotum, swinging happily back and forth to the roll of the boat as he pored over charts at the navigation table, distracted me as I tried to read in the main saloon. But you get used to anything eventually.

Around the time we stowed our foul weather gear away, we also vacated our beds on the main saloon floor. Robert returned to his bunk in the forepeak where, having grown accustomed to the oniony smell, he slept amongst sacks of vegetables. My parents and I returned to our respective cabins. My hatch was now kept open; at night the warm wind wafted in and I could lie in my bunk and watch the stars. I had never seen such stars before; they blazed across the dome of the sky and formed great clusters and nebulae, like luminous balls of cotton wool, and streaking vapour trails of light almost bright enough to read by.

Vingila rolled back and forth down the waves and Baruch, our new wind vane, went twang-thunk, twang-thunk as he steered our boat along, keeping the wind astern. We weren't sure we trusted Baruch yet. We were learning that mechanical self-steering devices make capricious, unreliable friends. Baruch was named after an Israeli man in Cape Town who had wanted to accompany us to Brazil. Dad explained to the man that he had designed a wind vane which was expected to be finished at a local engineering company any day, but if it didn't arrive, the Israeli could join *Vingila* to help out with the night watches. However, if we received our steering device, we would sail alone, as a family. When the wind vane arrived the following week we named it after our would-be crew member. The contraption had a canvas sail spread over a stainless steel frame, which was connected, via levers, pulleys and shafts, to an auxiliary rudder suspended from *Vingila*'s overhanging stern. To set the device (which, like others of his kind, seemed to have a life and personality of his own), we fixed *Vingila*'s own rudder and then tightened a screw on Baruch, which transferred the responsibility of steering the boat to the auxiliary rudder and maintained our yacht on a fixed course relative to the wind. With Baruch set on a broad reach, for example, *Vingila* kept to a broad reach even if the wind turned 180 degrees and she reached in the opposite direction. Setting a wind vane requires some skill to achieve the balance between sails, wind and rudder. We didn't always manage it at first. After a day or two, though, we learned to sleep with Baruch holding course, although it was a light sleep, alert always to changes in the motion of our boat.

At night, on the quiet waters of the South Atlantic, we felt safe enough with Baruch holding course to a steady wind that we didn't keep a constant watch, trusting the few ships in that empty part of the ocean to avoid us. Although my father and mother awoke intermittently through the night to check the horizon for stray lights before returning to bed, they never saw any. Apart from ships we had no other concerns; the wind direction was not expected to change and no shoals or reefs lay ahead. In the mornings I collected flying fish on the deck. If they were big enough, we fried them for breakfast. They were bony but delicious. We set fishing lines out as the sun rose into the sky. We baked bread. In the cockpit, under an awning, we ate long lunches of fresh fish and boiled potatoes sprinkled with olive oil and dehydrated parsley. Robert and I did school work while Dad navigated; the triangles of intersecting lines on the chart denoting our position became smaller each day and moved further across the ocean, away from the coast of Africa.

We read and had afternoon naps and Dad chatted to other yachtsmen on his new ham radio. His pilot friend Leonard, who had taught him to navigate, had urged him to buy the apparatus, saying all cruising yachts had them. At first Dad wasn't convinced because an operator's licence was compulsory and he'd had enough of tests and exams. But Leonard explained that if Dad was careful and didn't use the radio in busy ports where he could be tracked down, he could become a pirate operator with an illegal call sign, and in this way he could keep up with sailing news. We learned in Cape Town from Al and Eva Fox, who had sailed ahead on *Foxtrot*, that whisky was selling in Brazil for ten times the South African duty-free price and that the people of Saint Helena had run out of potatoes and onions because their supply ship had broken down. Which explained why *Vingila* sailed laden with hooch and root vegetables.

On the airwaves during the long afternoons at sea while Baruch kept course, Dad met Bill (ZD7 Silver Dollar) and Sybil (ZD7 Sugar Sugar), an elderly husband and wife who lived on Saint Helena and who had once, from their island, talked to an astronaut on the moon with their ham radio. As the warm wind blew steadily, our skies remained clear, but Bill reported daily that it was rainin', rainin', rainin' in Saint Helena.

Al Fox ran the radio group, or 'sched' as the jargon went, and he seemed to take a special interest in us, giving advice about anchorages, weather patterns and the highlights of the places we were about to visit.

'You guys are gonna love Saint Helena,' he said one day after Bill and Sybil had signed off. 'Except for one thing. Make sure the children don't see it.' And he went on to describe an activity so shocking that afterwards I felt sure I must have misheard. It could not have been true.

Pepe, who'd found his sea legs after the storm abated, strolled the decks, barking at the flying fish shooting over the waves. At night, the clear PVC tubing of the toilet glowed with green phosphorescence when we operated the pump. Day after day, the sun rose from the sea at dawn and dissolved back into it again in the evening when we hauled aboard our fishing lines to avoid catching the long-toothed, inedible wolf mackerel that came up at night from the depths to feed. If sailing was always like this, I thought as I lay in my bunk at night watching the stars, then everything would be all right. I wished I had my doll Patsy to talk to. She would really like this, I thought, as I drifted off to sleep.

Our perfect existence was marred only by dehydrated vegetables. We had cases of the stuff which Mom had bought after reading a book by Bernard Moitessier, a hero of the sailing world. Bernard, a Frenchman, was a major contender in the world's first solo, non-stop, around-the-world yacht race. Near England after many months alone at sea, and in the lead, he turned away from the finish line to sail halfway again around the globe to Tahiti. His book *The Long Way* describes the voyage and his mystical love of sailing and the sea. From his writing it is apparent that food wasn't a driving force in his life, and that while he may have been an excellent seaman, he wasn't much of a cook. For more than a year he survived on boiled rice, condensed milk and dehydrated vegetables. Inspired by the book, and not thinking that Bernard never stopped to buy fresh food and so was forced to eat whatever he could, Mom bought ten assorted cases of desiccated vegetables without first tasting any of them. Moitessier also drank a can of condensed milk a day; however we didn't see any of that. We only got the vegetables and they were horrible. My parents were children of the Second World War, however, and unable to waste food, so we had to eat them, somehow. 'Spinach' was a green powder which turned to a khaki sludge with the addition of water. 'Mixed Veg' – nubbins of yellow, green and white flakes – stayed hard no matter how long they were soaked or how vigorously they were boiled, but were nevertheless pronounced 'not bad' by my mother. Which even she couldn't say about the dried tomato paste; brittle maroon coils with a strong metallic odour and a taste that was simultaneously bitter and sour, and guaranteed to ruin any food it was added to. A better cook might have done something with these substances, like throw them overboard, but we were not good cooks – and on a tight budget besides – so we had to eat them. This was our daily trial. At least we had fresh fish.

When we weren't cooking, eating, washing up or sleeping, we read books. Mom had traded a whole stack of new paperbacks in Cape Town and I began working my way through them. There were the usual murder stories, and love stories, and murder-and-love stories mixed up together where sometimes people killed somebody they loved and other times a stranger did it. Then one morning I randomly picked out a book with a tattered cover and, retiring to my cabin, opened it at the first page and began reading about a hobbit called Bilbo Baggins who lived in a hole in the ground. Many hours later, after I had travelled through forests and over mountains, worked my way deep into caves via underground river systems and had survived an epic battle, a pale evil creature and a tetchy dragon, I reached the end. Outside I found my brother in the cockpit whittling a piece of wood with his penknife.

'Here,' I said, tapping him on the shoulder and thrusting the paperback at him. 'Read this.'

'What's it about?'

'A hobbit.'

'A what?'

'A hobbit. Look, just read it.'

A day later after Robert finished the book, I begged to read it for a second time and when I had finished my brother took it again and refused to return it.

'What is that you're reading?' Mom asked him.

'*The Hobbit*,' my brother said.

'The what?'

He didn't look up or answer.

Robert and I memorised Gollum and Baggins's riddles and chanted them at each other. We discussed the death of Smaug the dragon and the tactics and strategy of the Battle of Five Armies. We argued over which of the thirteen dwarves were bravest and what we would do with a ring that made us invisible. After *The Hobbit* the rest of the murder and love story books seemed dull and boring even if they had sex in them. I searched the bookshelves in hope of finding a story even remotely like the adventures of Bilbo Baggins, and found nothing.

At eleven o'clock in the morning on the eighth of April, fourteen days after leaving Cape Town, my mother sighted a faint blue smudge on the horizon off our port bow; it was land, and confirmation that the sights my father had shot and calculations he had made were true, for we had found Saint Helena, and a good thing too. Unlike the Pacific, islands are sparse in the Atlantic, and the next one along was Ascension, 700 miles away. After that there was nothing except the North Atlantic ocean.

We adjusted Baruch and approached the windward side of the island; a protruding tip of an ancient volcanic mountain rising sharply from the ocean floor. The map on the chart table showed a roundish blob labelled with names that might have come from Bilbo Baggins's home, the Shire. I found Half Tree Hollow, Deadwood Plain, Longwood Dairy, Barren Ground, the Briars and Breakneck Valley. Places that sounded wonderful and exciting and I imagined Robert and me having adventures. I imagined dragons and dwarves and tried not to think of what Al Fox had told us.

Slowly, like a polaroid image, the blue smudge on the horizon developed details and features; the colour deepened, becoming greener, the topography grew mountainous. With steep cliff walls plunging directly into the dark sea, the place had the guarded, unwelcoming appearance of a fortress or medieval castle. Such was the constancy of the trade winds that the island was clearly divided into two distinct sections: wet and lush on the windward side and dry and brown to leeward. At sunset we finally reached the anchorage – a poorly defined bay – on the leeward side of the island. Ignoring a friendly light flashing from shore, we tacked back and forth all night without sleeping. The next morning, after the sun rose, we motored straight in. A pair of polished basalt ridges rose high above us, compressing a small village into the narrow valley below. It was as if a slow battle was taking place between the rock and human habitation; the dwellings driving a wedge into the heart of the island, the mountains straining to push the buildings into the sea. We dropped anchor in four fathoms of dark blue water and watched our chain snake towards the sea floor and land in a puff of sand, where it was inspected by a few curious fish.

5

SAINT HELENA

Getting ashore in Jamestown, the capital of Saint Helena, proved tricky. After rowing to the landing and negotiating the pier – a slick concrete slab awash in surge – we scrambled out and hoisted our dinghy clear of the swell. Carrying several bags of potatoes and onions, and Pepe in his harness, we climbed a flight of green slime-slicked stairs. A small crowd gathered to watch us and at the top we were confronted by a fisherman in plastic boots.

'Why'd you stay out all night for?' he asked. ''Aven't you seen my light flashing to show you the way in?'

Mom and Dad had no easy answer for him because in daylight we could see how embarrassingly straightforward the approach was.

'We're looking for Bill and Sybil, but we don't know their last names,' said Mom. 'The ham radio operators.'

The man waved his hand over his left ear as if he were shooing a fly. 'Oh yes, on the hill, t'other side of the village.'

Bill and Sybil lived on a hill away from Jamestown, in an area of good radio reception and high rainfall. Dad said that after two weeks at sea, some exercise would do us good, but we didn't find walking easy.

The path was steep and the earth felt strangely unsteady beneath our feet; it swayed and gave way at irregular intervals, making us stagger. Our gait, too, had altered. We walked hesitantly, with our knees flexed, constantly prepared for unexpected waves. Slowly, we made our way out of Jamestown and began to climb the hill. The hot sun was soon swallowed by a cloud which – as we drew higher – thickened and sagged further under the weight of its vapour. At Bill and Sybil's home the cloud had grown so fat it could no longer support itself and lay draped over the tangled cables of their radio antennae. A steady drizzle began to fall. The house – a shack really – was painted a startling shade of pink.

A rotund, brown-skinned woman answered our knock. She wore her hair in a greasy bun and streaks of her scalp showed through the carefully combed strands lying flat against her head. Swollen ankles disappeared into sagging wool socks and a pair of misshapen slippers. Her eyes, arranged above a pair of generous cheeks, blinked in the drizzle. She smelled slightly sweet, of yeast and mildewed dampness.

'ZD7 Sugar Sugar?' asked Dad.

'Yes,' said the woman, eyeing Pepe, who was dripping wet and showing imminent signs of shaking himself dry.

'It's me, Frank Stilwell.'

The woman looked blank.

'ZS6 Foxy Fox,' Dad said.

A smile spread across the expanse of her face, beginning at the jowls and finishing around the eyes and forehead, 'ZS6 Foxy Fox!' she said. 'Come on in.'

Pictures of astronauts decorated the inside walls. Most of them had been torn from magazines but one, in a heavy official frame, was an original signed photograph. Lace curtains on the single window restricted incoming light, leaving the damp interior as grey as the cloud outside. Worn paths in the lino led to the kitchen and bedroom. Dominating the living area, a ham radio sat on a pedestal before a pair of empty but attentive chairs.

'Bill,' Sybil called, and an equally rotund man shuffled out of the bedroom. 'It's Frank Stilwell and his family.'

'Who?' said Bill.

'You know, ZS6 Foxy Fox.'

'ZS6 Foxy Fox! Well I never. Good to meet you at last.'

'We've brought these potatoes and onions,' said Dad, handing Bill the sacks. Bill thanked him before stowing them in the corner.

Sybil shouldered her way through a curtain of plastic beads to reach a tiny kitchen where she began to prepare tea; putting a kettle to boil and stacking chipped cups on a melamine tray decorated with space rockets and landing capsules. Dad and Bill admired the ham radio before going outside to inspect the antennae. When they returned, still discussing the benefits of different lengths of cable aerials, Sybil poured tea. I hesitated before reaching for my mug. I had never before drunk tea with anybody who wasn't white. In both of my two grandmothers' houses the maids had their own cutlery and crockery and Dad's 'work boy' who sat on the back of his bakkie wasn't even allowed into our kitchen. I watched Mom and Dad carefully to see what they would do. When, chatting away, they reached for their tea and began drinking, I did the same. The tea tasted no different than usual, and Bill and Sybil's voices were reassuringly familiar. They talked of the weather and the times and radio frequencies of various maritime talk groups where we could find other yachtsmen. They recommended that my father apply in Jamestown for a courtesy call-sign, which he could use in island waters. The people at the radio office, they said, never checked for licence papers. The talk was easy and relaxed and I realised that while chatting to Bill and Sybil on the radio, they had simply become our friends.

'Saints' as the islanders are called, are descendants of British soldiers, whalers, freed slaves, sailors and employees of the English East India Company. They've been living on Saint Helena since 1659 and not always voluntarily. However, over the past hundred years attitudes have changed and at the time of our visit, modern Saints were homebodies, not wishing to leave their island. About eight hundred people lived in the main village of Jamestown: two rows of Regency houses with verandas and iron fretwork arranged along a main road, flanked by a huddle of smaller dwellings, all squeezed into the narrow valley and in some places creeping precariously up its sides. In the centre of town we found the law courts, a miniature jail, a library, and a public park with benches and shady trees. A lady in a straw sun hat told us the trees were weepuls, from India. A whitewashed castle bearing the arms of the Honourable East India Company stood opposite the park.

'This reminds me of England fifty years ago,' Dad said.

Being in his thirties at the time, I wondered how he would know.

'Saint Helena is an island of history,' said the taxi driver – a withered man in a flat cap – when he drove us to Longwood the following day. He twisted around in his seat to face us. His mouth, when he smiled, was a dark cave inhabited by a few lonely teeth. 'Going to Napoleon's house, are you?'

Island speech was distinctive, with remnants of Cockney from the settlers who arrived after the Great Fire of London, the odd word of Malay and Afrikaans and traces of old English too, like the transposition of v and w I would later find familiar in Dickens' *Pickwick Papers*.

'No, not today,' said Dad. 'We're visiting Joyce and Eric Mercury at the dairy.'

'That would explain the taters, then,' said the driver who had eyed the bags closely while loading them into the boot.

Joyce Mercury, a friend of Al and Eva Fox, the shell collectors on *Foxtrot*, taught at the Longwood School and Al had asked us over the radio to bring vegetables from Cape Town because the school had run out. To reach Longwood we hired one of the island's two taxis and got a history lesson thrown in for free. The elderly vehicle, a Morris Minor, guided by an equally elderly driver, juddered up the steep ascent from Jamestown, passing a dry heart-shaped waterfall before reaching green hills. The roads were narrow, winding and bordered by hedges, much as I had imagined the Shire of Middle Earth and I caught myself looking out for furry-footed hobbits or at least the porthole-like doors of their burrows.

'Very hilly,' said Dad, looking out the window.

'Too hilly for an airport, they tell us, so we rely on the mail ship and now that's stopped too. But they've promised us a new wessel, running once a month from Cape Town and on to Ascension and England. The *RMS St Helena*. Just don't know when we'll get her, 'cause there's been a delay.' Our driver turned off the engine and freewheeled down an incline. He winked at Robert and me, 'Doing what I can to save petrol, I am.'

We rounded a corner.

'What's that?' asked Robert, pointing at a field of grotesque plants sprouting massive distorted flower heads. They looked monstrous and neglected and they lay toppled over, caught in coils of weeds as if they'd been wrestling. Trolls and orcs would probably live here, I thought, or perhaps goblins.

'New Zealand flax,' said the driver. 'Grown to make twine, but after losing the contract we stopped farming.'

He went on to tell us, as he probably told every visitor who hired his taxi, the sad story of Saint Helena's economy. How, for the first few hundred years after its discovery in 1502 by the Portuguese, the island had been an important stop off point for sailing ships, so much so that it was claimed by the English East India Company in 1659 as their first settlement. When sailing ships were replaced by steamers, coal stores were established near the harbour. But over the years, as first sailing ships and then steam ships declined, so too did Saint Helena's importance as a trading post and supply point. Once it ceased to be profitable, the East India Company gave the island to Britain and although the Union Jack flies at the governor's office in Jamestown, the island has slipped gradually into increasing poverty and isolation. In 1907, after several failed ventures, including a mackerel canning plant and an attempt to grow cinchona trees for quinine, not to mention a stab at whaling after the whales had all been whaled, the flax was planted and in 1951 for the first, and sadly last time in history, Saint Helena's exports exceeded its imports. But, the taxi driver told us, a few years after the island's economic triumph, the British postal service, the island's main and possibly only customer, decided to close its postbags with nylon string, thus shutting down the island's flax industry.

'So how do people make money around here?' Dad asked.

The taxi driver grimaced, showing his few last teeth clinging to a rim of red, decaying gum. 'Half of the folks work for the local government and the rest fish or make lace. For some, like me, there's work from tourists, but tha's been scarce since the ship broke down and all. For others there's aid from London. The young fellas, well, they go to Ascension.'

'To the north?'

'Oh yes,' said the driver, 'most of our boys go over to Ascension to work on contract at the cable station or at the American air fields for a year or two. But they all come back.'

'They do?' asked Dad.

'Well, they don't have much of a choice now, do they? The Union Jack may fly at the governor's office, but we can't live in England.'

'Why not?'

'Don't have English passports now, do we? Or any British citizen's rights either, for that matter. And that's in spite of the Charter. Odd really, 'cos the Falklanders and folks from Tristan da Cunha have passports. London can't explain that, so here we sit, looking for a living. They say there's work in Cape Town and some folks go there, but ...' his voice trailed off.

'You're from South Africa, aren't you?' he asked.

Mom and Dad nodded, perhaps imagining life on the wrong side of the colour bar.

'It's a beautiful country, South Africa,' said Mom.

'So I've heard,' he said, looking sideways through the window at the hedges, green hills and ruined fields of flax.

'Yes,' said Dad, 'one of the most beautiful countries in the world.'

In Longwood, the second largest settlement on the island after Jamestown, oak trees shaded a few whitewashed buildings. Joyce Mercury stood waiting for us at the dairy, adjacent to the two-roomed school. She was school principal and, before it had closed from lack of funds, her husband had run the dairy. Our taxi driver helped unload the sacks of vegetables, then he doffed his cap, scratched his head and asked for part payment of his fare in potatoes.

From the start I knew that I loved Saint Helena. The roads in Jamestown may have been too rough for skateboarding but the island held other attractions, like the four ancient tortoises from Reunion Island that roamed the grounds of the governor's house, munching his lawn and groaning hoarsely when they mated. The village bakery served fresh bread, barracuda fish cakes and tasty meat pies and at eleven o'clock each night the local bobby, a member of the island's police force, visited the pub to warn the patrons it was closing time. The handful of prisoners in the jail, most of them incarcerated for unruly behaviour and disturbing the peace, were let out each morning to swim in the sea, and later in the day all activity on the island halted for afternoon tea, which was usually served with cucumber sandwiches. Saint Helena was charming, out of date, very civilised and also oddly familiar. Although I failed to find evidence of hobbits or dwarves, the high teas with cakes and sandwiches, the cobblestones, the castle, the hills and hedges, the way the people spoke, all harked back to the mythical world of Enid Blyton. As a very young child, before we went sailing, I had read almost everything she wrote. The children in her books lived in a gentle green country and had never heard of peanut butter, government brown bread or boerewors. Growing up, I had been surrounded by Zulu miners wearing wood plugs in their stretched earlobes and women who walked with pots on their heads through waist-high grass in the harsh highveld sunshine, and when I read Enid Blyton stories I discovered a world as foreign and exotic to me as China and I failed to reconcile any of it with reality until I reached Saint Helena.

Jacob's Ladder in Jamestown, for example, seemed to have been lifted directly from the pages of a fairy story. A stairway of 699 stone steps (a century of use had trod the 700th step into the earth), led directly up Ladder Hill where, I imagined, it reached magical, forever changing lands where children could have adventures. In fact Jacob's Ladder was built in 1829 by the Royal Engineers for soldiers to carry ammunition and supplies to the fort on top where there are barracks, a signal station and an observatory. At the time of our visit the barracks and fort were quiet; lookouts were no longer needed to guard the coal supplies once held for passing ships, and Jacob's Ladder served as an occasional tourist attraction and as a giant slide for the local boys and girls who hooked their ankles over one banister and their elbows over the other to glide all the way down from the top. The morning we walked up the endless stairs to see the fort, Robert and I wanted to slide down. Mom however refused, saying she didn't want to deal with a broken leg.

Joyce Mercury at Longwood Dairy invited Robert and me to attend the Longwood School where she was principal. Robert was relegated to the woodwork shed with the boys, while I spent time in a big room with a coal fire stove, where I boiled potatoes and learned to bake tea-cake with the girls. Joyce taught me how to knot lace. I liked that. I sat with a special cushion on my lap and, using a paper pattern, pins, and thread wound around a set of bobbins, I twisted and plaited strands to produce somewhat lumpy looking lace. This, I thought, was how school should be.

'What's that?' Robert asked, showing interest at last.

The chalk-white object holding his attention was slightly smaller than a head and bore folded, human features.

'I don't know. It looks like some sort of a face,' I said.

The lady in a droopy floral dress, overheard us. 'That,' she said, 'is the ex-emperor's death mask.'

We were in Longwood, visiting the house of Saint Helena's most famous and least enthusiastic resident, Napoleon Bonaparte. Although smaller than I imagined, the bungalow was set in a spacious, beautiful garden and was painted the same startling shade of pink as Bill and Sybil's shack. I wondered if there had been an island special on paint. A French flag flew at the entrance.

'Welcome to France,' the lady in the baggy dress had said when we arrived at the front door after walking up the serpentine driveway. I wondered if she'd been watching us from afar because we hadn't even had a chance to knock before she'd opened the door.

'France?' said Mom. 'I thought Saint Helena was English.'

The lady gave her a triumphant smile. 'Not this part. Queen Victoria sold it to France.'

She said she was a volunteer from the local historical society and offered us a tour, leading the way through a series of gloomy wood-panelled rooms decorated with old pictures and busts. Mom and Dad spent forever looking at the display cabinets containing hanks of Napoleon's hair, medals and items of his underwear, while Robert and I, fighting a growing feeling of confinement, fidgeted and longed to be outside. At last we reached the emperor's deathbed, which was not grand at all. I had been expecting a four poster, swathed in yards of linen and muslin, and instead we were shown a narrow, knee-high folding metal cot. It looked very uncomfortable.

'Is this really his bed?' I asked, scanning the room for an alternative.

But apparently Napoleon, constantly on war campaigns, had lost the ability to sleep in anything else. I felt strangely disappointed. A great man, I thought, should have a great bed, or at least manage to die in one. I was glad to see that his bath, a stately copper tub with high, curved sides, looked fitting for an emperor.

Then Robert spotted the death mask and was intrigued. 'How did they make it?' he asked our guide.

'After he died, they rubbed his face with a greasy ointment something like Vaseline, and then poured plaster of Paris over it. They used the ointment so the plaster wouldn't stick and they could peel the impression off easily.'

Robert moved around the cabinet, viewing the object from different angles.

'Did all the people have one?'

'Oh yes, everyone who could afford it had a death mask in those days. You must remember that they didn't have photographs yet, so this was quite the fashionable thing to do. As soon as a person died they called for an undertaker and the mask maker.'

Robert and I leaned closer. In death, Napoleon's crumpled face looked grumpy.

'He doesn't look very happy,' I said.

'Of course not, stupid, he'd just died,' Robert said.

'I know that, Robert. What I mean is, apart from just having died, he looks as if he'd been unhappy for a while.'

I turned to the woman in the floral dress. 'Was he happy?'

'I don't suppose so. He'd been an emperor, you see, the most powerful man in the world, before he lost the war and was brought to this island as a prisoner. Of course we love Saint Helena, but it's hardly the centre of the universe. It was difficult for him. And he was sick. Also, he hated the rain here in Longwood and he wanted to move to the sunny side of the island.'

When Napoleon arrived his house had not been ready because the builders had fallen behind schedule. While waiting he had had to live in a small bungalow in town, in the same house that Arthur Wellesley, later the Duke of Wellington and the man who defeated him at Waterloo, had once stayed. After such an inauspicious beginning, his situation didn't improve and he spent the final six years of his life soaking in his copper bath and writing his memoirs, squabbling with the governor, who he detested, and searching the island for a suitable place to be buried. Then the governor, fearful the general would escape, forbade him to leave Longwood without an escort. Napoleon retreated to his bathtub. Depressed and in constant pain, possibly as a result of being slowly poisoned with arsenic, his doctor suggested that a bit of gardening might be beneficial.

'Napoleon loved his garden,' said the lady in the floral dress leading us outside.

A system of sunken paths intersected the overflowing flower beds. We were told that the emperor, annoyed by the guards – and other people – who peered over the hedges at him, instructed his gardener to dig down so that he couldn't be seen. Because he was so short, the task wasn't too difficult, and he was able to take his walks and tend his garden in peace. The lady in the floral dress pointed out the surrounding trees – they had been planted by Napoleon himself, she said, and so too the everlasting flowers which still germinated each year to bloom around us.

I thought Saint Helena and her Saints were gentle, friendly and generous. Years later Hans from the junk *Maria Jose* would tell me how he lost his virginity in Jamestown with a prostitute, but as a ten-year-old I never experienced that particular side of island life. As our stay continued I found it harder to believe the shocking warning Al Fox had given us over the ham radio. Everybody we met seemed so nice and normal. During our final week on the island I decided to broach the subject with Gary, Joyce's foster son. We were in the garden of Longwood Dairy one afternoon, admiring a shoo-shoo vine and its thorny pale green squash-like fruit, some of which we had just had with melted margarine for lunch.

'Is it true,' I said, 'that people here kill and eat dolphins?'

Gary was a plump child of eight, and he turned to look at me with languid brown eyes. He didn't appear at all shocked or offended by my question.

'My mother says that if God didn't want us to eat them,' he replied placidly, 'he wouldn't have put them in the sea.'

Fair enough, but I had seen Flipper on TV. He looked after Sandy and Bud and rescued people in trouble. I knew dolphins as playful, intelligent creatures who surfed our bow-wave and leapt from the sea with something that I liked to think was joy. I only hoped any slaughter would take place long after I had sailed away because I didn't want to see dolphins killed or eaten. One day, however, towards the end of our stay, we arrived at the concrete landing in our dinghy to find that a group of fishermen had harpooned a small pod of dolphins and were butchering them on the pier. Too intelligent to take fishing lures, dolphins, like other sea mammals, are usually speared to death. I tried not to look. The concrete was awash with bright mammalian blood and, in spite of my attempts to keep my eyes averted, I spotted several pairs of lungs set aside to be discarded. One of the dead dolphins had been pregnant because, curled amid the severed heads and entrails like an outsized jelly baby, lay a perfectly formed dolphin foetus. I thought of Gary and how he had gone on to say, 'But why are you so upset anyway? You eat cows, don't you?'

Slaughtered dolphins aside, I would have liked to stay longer on Saint Helena, baking tea cakes at school, knotting lace and drinking tea in the afternoons. While leaving was difficult, the actual act of sailing away was ridiculously easy. We simply pulled up our anchor, motored a short distance from the island's lee, and found the south-east trade winds waiting to blow us to Ascension. We raised our twin jibs, adjusted the whisker poles and set Baruch on course.

After only two weeks in port it was easy to slip back into the rhythms of sea life; mom baked bread, my father shed his clothes, and the sun – unimpeded by land – rose and sank each day from the sea. With us we carried parcels and letters for Saints working on Ascension. I had been given a parting gift from Joyce; a lace-making cushion with a set of bobbins and spools of bright turquoise thread and, in the afternoons while the boat rolled back and forth, I made lace. Mom left Nana's address with Joyce, and the two women began a correspondence that lasted until my grandmother's death. Long after I finished sailing I could still catch up on news from Saint Helena: a missing cow, two men arrested for having an altercation over a donkey, and an unusually good catch of tuna for March.

6

ASCENSION ISLAND

'Waddle it be?' Beneath his wedge of bristling hair, our waiter's features arranged themselves into an enquiring smile.

Fortunately, after spending time with American yachties, we understood him and knew exactly what we wanted.

'Four cheeseburgers and four Cokes,' Dad said with a tone that implied, 'and bugger the expense.'

'Yawl wand French fries?'

Of course we wanted French fries. This was our big treat. We wanted the lot. We were sitting on plastic seats in a hermetically sealed white box balanced on crushed volcanic rock and, after weeks of tropical trade winds, we found the air conditioning uncomfortably cold. A juke box played pop songs while beyond the permanently closed windows a moonscape baked in the sun. The scorched island of Ascension looked like nothing on earth. In fact, during the early days of space travel, astronauts had been sent to Ascension to prepare for the psychological shock of encountering the lunar landscape. Ascension, like Saint Helena, is formed by the protruding tip of an oceanic volcano. To the Shire of Saint Helena, black-rocked Ascension is Mordor, but with clearer skies.

The island – geologically new – arises from the very crest of an abyssal suture line, the Mid-Atlantic Ridge, birthing place of South Atlantic islands. Saint Helena, also formed here, has drifted south over the millennia, its cone becoming extinct on the way. Ascension's volcano is far from extinct. Its drowsy cone last erupted six hundred years ago and the island still slumbers uneasily; prone to occasional shudders, puffs of steam and belches of hot mud. Away from the few settlements there are only black volcanic rocks, cinder cones, outlandish lava flows and naked silence. Green Mountain – the highest peak – is barely green although the sprinkling of vegetation which grows on the windward side extends its range each year by a few metres. In several more centuries, if the volcano stays sleeping, Ascension may well become as green as its older sibling to the south.

Al on *Foxtrot* had told us about the cheeseburgers.

'The best greasy cheeseburgers in the South Atlantic,' he'd said over the ham radio. He was American and we trusted his judgement on burgers. These were pre-cooked and flown in from the United States on a plane.

On arriving at the island after a week at sea eating nothing but fish, rice, dehydrated vegetables and the last of our potatoes, a longing for cheeseburgers had been instilled in us too. We made our way directly to Cat Hill and the mess hall at the American air force base.

Ascension, barely 10 kilometres across, is even smaller than Saint Helena. After rowing over transparent water and beaching our dingy on a strip of salt-white sand that terminated abruptly in black rocks, we began walking along an unexpected broad tarred road. A stroll around the island, however, wasn't easy. After a week at sea we were prepared for unstable ground and a clumsy flexed knee gait, but we never expected to be stopped by so many Americans in air conditioned vehicles, all of whom insisted on giving us lifts. After several refusals and repeated explanations that we wanted to walk, we finally gave in and accepted a ride to Cat Hill. Besides, Ascension lies seven degrees south of the equator and inland, away from the cooling sea breeze, the sun and heat bouncing off the black rocks had begun to grill us.

From our chilly booth in the canteen we looked out on lava flows and a huddle of cuboid buildings baking in the sun. This island, it seemed, was either too hot or too cold. We listened to the juke box and exchanged smiles with young men, mostly Saints by the look of them, who all had cropped hair and drank Coke.

Our cheeseburgers arrived. Dad lifted the top off his and looked inside.

'Don't get much for the price,' he said.

The white bun dissolved in my mouth, leaving nothing but a thin film of sludge with a faint, slightly sweet aftertaste. The cheese, processed into a perfect uniform square, failed to melt, but succeeded in gluing the grey meat patty to the bun. Rolled into balls, I felt certain it would bounce like silly putty, assuming I could ever get permission to play with my food. I took a sip of cola so sweet it made my ears ache, and turned to the French fries which were every bit as greasy as I'd expected them to be.

After my encounter with American burgers and fries, I was upset when Mom refused to let me taste either the pina coladas or banana daiquiris. We were in a foreign country and I wanted to try everything. My mother refused because she said the drinks contained alcohol. Bonnie offered to make a pitcher of cocktails without rum, which sounded wonderful to me, but Mom told her not to worry, Robert and I preferred water. Then she felt remorseful and offered me a sip of her drink. It was sweet and slightly oily, with floaty bits of fibre and fruit pulp and an underlying aroma of rum which reminded me of diesel fuel. It was definitely the most exotic drink I'd ever tasted and I wasn't sure I liked it. Bonnie told us the canned pineapple juice came from Hawaii and had arrived on a ship from America. Everything in Ascension arrived either by ship or plane: the juice and tinned coconut milk, Bonnie's three bedroomed ranch-style house, and possibly even its surrounding swathe of green lawn. Mack and Bonnie, a couple from Florida, both had pale skin and sparse eyelashes and looked so alike they could have been brother and sister. She was prettier than he was though, with soft blue eyes and a nose garnished with freckles. She really was quite attractive, Dad said later in private, except for those thick ankles of hers. When it came to women's legs, Dad was an expert and frequently provided us with detailed leg reviews of women we met. We all knew Mom had great legs. She'd once won a Lucky Legs competition on Durban beach and as proof we had a picture of her in a bikini with a satin sash across her shoulder. My mother had more than great legs; she was patient, cheerful, easy-going, resilient and game for adventure. She could catch fish, bake bread, knit and crochet. She taught Robert and me. Only thing was, my father said, sometimes she knew just how to piss him off.

Bonnie's legs didn't seem to bother Mack, her husband. He worked as a supervisor for the undersea cable company which was, in pre-satellite days, the biggest employer on the island. We were discovering that supervisors tended to be British or American, while Saint Helena supplied the workers. Everyone, however, was on contract. Ascension was – and is – an island without any natives or permanent residents. We heard that even babies delivered in the tiny hospital couldn't be citizens of Ascension and had to take their parents' nationality. The British who own the island but lease most of it to America, hardly consider it to be a place. In an early inventory of the empire it was classified, along with a few other unpromising marine rocks, as 'a stone sloop of the lesser class' and for the first hundred years children delivered on the island were deemed to have been born at sea.

Mack, our cocktail host, was yet another friend of Al and Eva Fox, and a fellow shell collector. I wondered sometimes if we were taking the Al and Eva Fox tour of the South Atlantic. Bonnie and Mack were childless and he treated me uneasily, in the forced, condescending manner of somebody pretending to like children. He was disappointed, I suspected, to find that I was more interested in conchology than my father was, but while my parents sipped their sickly cocktails, Mack made the best of it and invited me to see his collection. The shells were kept in a spare bedroom, where a child would have slept if they had had one. Cabinets lined the walls, surrounding a central, sheet enshrouded table. We looked through all the shells in the drawers but I found myself enticed by the covered table.

'What's under here?' I asked, lifting a corner of cotton cloth.

Mack swept the sheet away like a magician.

'Just got back from a holiday in the Philippines, where I dived out these beauties.'

On the table were at least a hundred map cowries which I recognised from my shell book. 'Cypraea mappa,' – I had read in Sea Shells of the World – 'is a large, uncommon cowrie with distinctive markings like the map of a winding river on its dorsal surface.'

'Wow,' I said. 'So many mappas.'

And then I added, just in case he hadn't got the hint, 'And I don't even have one.'

He spent some time looking through the shells, picking them over.

'Well, now you do,' he said. 'This one's for you.'

The cowrie he gave me was a juvenile and, from a shell collector's point of view, almost worthless. I couldn't understand why he had even taken the shell, killing the animal before it had a chance to reach maturity. I took it and thanked him politely, hiding my disappointment. He looked at me speculatively.

'Come here,' he said. 'I want to show you something.'

He opened a book on his desk.

'Will you remember this?' he asked, showing me a photograph of a rust-coloured cowrie with white dorsal spots and well-defined orange teeth. I looked at the picture and nodded; I was quite sure I could remember the shell. Under the photograph was a name: *Cypraea surinamensis*.

'When you sail to a place in Brazil called Fortaleza, I want you to find the fishing boats, and look for one of these. If you post it to me, I'll send you twenty dollars.'

He gave me a sticker with his name and address and made me promise to do as he said, then we returned to the kitchen where Bonnie and my parents were still sipping their pina coladas and banana daiquiris.

The transparency of the sea around Ascension was heightened by the whiteness of the sand on the sea floor. The water looked perfect for swimming and snorkelling, except for a few ragged, mobile stains which, on closer examination, showed themselves to be tightly packed schools of black-skinned fish about 15 centimetres long. These, we were told, were blackfish. Their appearance was unremarkable but we quickly discovered that they made piranhas seem as docile and tame as goldfish. Blackfish were a type of trigger fish, thick-skinned grazers with a trigger-like fin on their back which, in other waters, swam in pairs or alone on tropical reefs and nibbled daintily at seaweed. The blackfish of Ascension, however, swam in packs and ate everything. Attracted by the slightest splash, they congregated in a heaving mass. They devoured anything we threw overboard, leaping into the air to consume apple cores, dehydrated tomato whirls, eggshells and onion peels. When we pumped the toilet, the water beside the hull boiled with deranged trigger fish fighting for the choicest bits – and they ate every last scrap of toilet paper too. Fishing was impossible. Well, fishing for anything other than blackfish, that is. As soon as our bait touched water the blackfish swarmed. Their jaws and teeth were so strong they often bit right through our hooks. And blackfish were cannibals. Hooked fish not lifted from the sea were quickly torn to shreds by their demonic fellows. When Robert landed a medium-sized blackfish and, on a whim, held an apple to its mouth, it lunged at the fruit, taking frantic mechanical bites, like a battery operated toy. Its jaws only stopped moving when it died.

When Mack offered to show my father how to dive for cowries, and said he would teach us how to clean them without damaging the nacre, I wondered how anyone could swim in the waters of Ascension with the schools of blackfish about. Mack said he would fetch Dad at five o'clock that evening. While we waited, Robert and I watched a newly arrived yachtie don a mask and flippers and jump into the water. A dark cloud of blackfish diverted its course and converged on him. Seconds later he leapt from the sea with a blackfish clamped firmly to his lower lip. A woman inside the yacht, alerted by the man's howl, rushed up the companionway to help him. From where we sat, it didn't look as if the fish was letting go easily.

'I don't know how Dad's going to dive here,' Robert said, dangling his own dead blackfish by the tail as he spoke. The movement dislodged a piece of apple – the creature's dying bite – from its mouth. Idly, my brother laid the fish on the bait board and slit it open. I almost expected to see circuits and tangled wires inside, but within the carapace of thick dark skin lay perfectly white fish fillets.

'What'll we do with this?' he asked.

'Bait?' I said.

'Don't need it. They take a bare hook.'

'We're not eating it, that's for sure.'

'Feed it to Pepe?' I suggested.

Pepe, at the sound of his name, lifted his head. In Benoni he'd been taken every few weeks for a 'lamb chop' trim and he had looked like a poodle. Now his fur, shaggy and matted with salt, hung down in clumps of thick dreadlocks. He peered at us from beneath the rough fringe my mother had hacked above his eyes.

'Nah, he won't eat it,' said Robert. 'He'll enjoy this, though. Pepe, come here boy.'

And my brother threw the butchered fish into the water where, in the churning water, it was immediately stripped to the bone by its mates while Pepe barked himself into a frenzy.

Blackfish had one redeeming feature, however, a feature which made it difficult for me not to believe in a god. Between five and half past five every evening, they all swam down to the seabed, anchored themselves with the trigger-like hook on their dorsal fin, and went to sleep for the night. This was when Mack arrived to take Dad diving, and Robert and I learned that we could throw in our fishing lines to catch some decent fish.

When Dad came back he handed me a pair of live *Cypraea lurida* – chocolate brown, glossy with a white band on their backs and creamy lips.

'Mack tells me they're a special variety of the lurid cowrie, found only here in Ascension. Do you like them?' he asked.

I nodded.

Mack showed us how to kill live shells. You can't boil them, he said, or they crack. And the flesh of the rotting animal should never be allowed to touch the surface of the shell or the glossy nacre turns milky and the shell becomes worthless. The best way, Mack said, was to put live shells in a small basin, on a wire mesh, and fill the basin with kerosene. The kerosene killed the animal and, over several days, dissolved its flesh which fell through the mesh, keeping the nacre clear and glossy. He showed us how to make wire hooks which he said we should use to pull out the scraps of remaining animal parts.

'We can be a team,' Dad said later after Mack had left. 'I'll dive shells, you can clean and identify them. I'm not so good with names, you know.'

When my father was affectionate he called me Nicholai Nickolia-novich and I sometimes found him staring at me as if he wanted to express something and was unsure how to proceed. I was sensitive, prickly and was quick to bear a grudge. His family were physically undemonstrative and when he tried to touch me, his attempts were awkward and often inappropriate. He nuzzled my neck or ran his fingers down my spine and around the whorls of my ears. When my mother saw him doing this, she told him to stop. Enough was enough, she said. When he was happy he sometimes also called me his blonde bombshell. I asked my mother what that meant.

'Someone who's pretty on the outside, but empty on the inside.'

'But why *blonde* bombshell?'

'Because that's how blondes are: stupid with nothing in their heads.'

Ascension, a dependancy of Saint Helena, belongs to Britain. The British maintain and run the main undersea cable company linking South Africa to England, the radio relay station for the BBC, and the military base and airfield which would later come in handy during the Falklands war. The island, always with a strong military presence, has remained strategically important ever since the English first set up barracks during Napoleon's incarceration on Saint Helena in an attempt to block the French from building a base from which to free their Emperor. For similar reasons a garrison was also established on Tristan da Cunha to the south.

Visitors to Ascension, although welcomed and offered cocktails by socially deprived American contract workers, are officially discouraged. There is no hotel on the island. Upon arrival, British immigration officials informed us we were to stay aboard our vessel from sunset to sunrise. So before we met Mack and Bonnie, and later the boys from

Saint Helena, we were led to believe that drinking daiquiris well into the night with the locals was strictly forbidden and that going to see nesting sea turtles was impossible. Apart from the immigration officers, we never met a single other Brit. They kept to themselves and never offered us lifts; if we walked the road to Georgetown and a car passed without stopping, we knew the driver was probably English. The Saints, however, were just as friendly on Ascension as they had been on their own island, and when we put the word out that we had mail and parcels, we soon met Joyce's relatives.

Perry, Hot Bread and Piece-a-Cake were in their twenties and worked for Pan Am at the refuelling station. They had the casual attitude of young men away from home who were somewhat lonely, but nevertheless enjoying their freedom. Hot Bread and Piece-a-Cake smoked incessantly and drank vast amounts of watery American beer from flimsy aluminium cans, but Perry said he hated smoke because it hurt his eyes and he didn't like the taste of beer. Shortly after meeting us, they announced it was full moon and we simply had to see the turtles. When Dad asked about the official curfew, they just laughed.

Armed with several six packs of beer, we made our way to a beach on the far side of the island one night. The Union Jack may fly over Ascension but we were discovering that the island really belonged to the wildlife: the seabirds, blackfish and green turtles. Perry told us that each year thousands of female turtles arrived from Brazil or further off to lay their eggs on the beaches. He said green turtles aren't green at all. Their shells and skin are brown and it's actually their fat that has a greenish tinge. Mariners found that green fat delicious. For a few hours we sat in the dark while Hot Bread and Piece-a-Cake drank and smoked. Then Perry, who'd been listening intently, hushed us. Over the sound of the waves I heard laboured, painful breathing.

'She's here,' whispered Perry.

'Yeeha!' shouted the other two and, turning on their torches, they ran to the ocean where a dark shape inched its way from the sea like a moving boulder.

The grand old lady who hauled herself out in front of us weighed about 150 kilograms and – by the sound of her – was feeling every one of them as she struggled up the beach. Turtles lack tear ducts and tears that are usually washed away by the sea, stream down their faces when they're out of water. I found our turtle's tears, slow progress and painful breathing heartbreaking.

'Can't we help her?' I whispered, tears welling up in my own eyes.

But Hot Bread and Piece-a-Cake laughed and shone their lights in the turtle's face.

'It's always like this,' Hot Bread said. 'It's nature.'

They offered to turn her over, so we could inspect her underside and when we declined, they did it anyway and then flipped her right way up again and took turns sitting on her back drinking beer as she struggled onwards, leaving a strange tractor-like trail behind her. At last she hauled herself above the high water mark, but her work wasn't done. Still breathing heavily, and using her back flippers, she began to dig. As the sand mounted in crumbling heaps, Hot Bread excavated her burrow and wedged his torch under her tail to illuminate the shiny, mucus-covered eggs pouring from her like ping-pong balls. After the flow of eggs ceased, leaving only a silver strand of slime connecting the turtle to her nest, she broke the connection with a covering of sand. Once she had finished burying her eggs, Hot Bread and Piece-a-Cake grabbed her front flippers and head, pulled her around and pushed her back to the sea. She reached wet sand and, when the first wave washed over her, heaved an extended sigh. For a few minutes she lay resting with her head on the beach but when the next wave broke, she pushed off with her flippers and was gone. Even Hot Bread and Piece-a-Cake seemed a little subdued after she left. But not for long. Soon more beers were opened and cigarette ends glowed red in the dark as they told stories about growing up on Saint Helena and how they had got their nicknames and all the naughty tricks they had played on their uncles and aunts when they were younger.

The night was warm, windless and clear. The moon laid a silver path across the sea as tiny wavelets nibbled the shore. The sand on which we sat, still carrying heat from the day's sun, glowed pale in the moonlight. It was long after midnight – the latest I had ever stayed up – and to the east, dawn began to glow. Stirred by the beauty of the place and the turtle's great struggle, we didn't want to leave. When we stood at last, brushing our clothes off, an odd thing happened; the beach beneath our feet began to boil. Dark heads the size of grapes thrust through the sand, followed by flippers attached to little heart-shaped shells. We'd been sitting on another turtle nest and the babies were hatching.

The shell of a fresh hatched turtle is velvety soft and the entire creature, which weighs around 25 grams, fits comfortably in a child's hand. The babies were so perfect it was hard to believe that fewer than one in a thousand would survive to adulthood. Young turtles make for the reflection of the moon on the sea which is why, Perry told us, they often gatecrashed beach barbecues, lured by the light of the fire. Hot Bread and Piece-a-Cake arranged turtle races using the light of their torches to guide them, thankfully in the right direction, and the hatchlings scrambled and collided with one another like a collection of clockwork animals, as endearing as the blackfish were horrible. I wanted my little turtle to save his or her energy for the big swim ahead and so, probably interfering irrevocably with its global positioning system, I carried it down to the sea where its best chance of surviving to adulthood was almost zero. When I got to the water's edge, I kissed it gently on its soft shell. I was thankful it had hatched at night, when the seabirds and blackfish were sleeping, and as I released it into the dark sea I wished, in the same way you wish upon a shooting star, that my turtle would survive and – if it was a female – come back again to this very beach as a heaving, sighing adult.

7

SALVADOR

In Brazil I refused to leave the yacht.

'Nicky, you can't stay on this boat forever, you know,' Mom said.

'Why not?'

'Because we're in a new country. You have to see it. Anyway, you're not staying here alone.' Mom was losing patience with me. 'Now get your shoes on.'

We were anchored beside the naval base in the fetid small-craft harbour of Salvador. Everything stank: the brown oily water in which we were anchored, the air, and the city itself. A French boat without a toilet lay next to us and in the morning, while officers in ornate uniforms paraded at the naval base, the French yachties hung their bums over the stern rail while drinking bowls of coffee. With their free hands, they waved greetings at us as they dropped turds into the water. Beyond the naval base, the city's buildings balanced uneasily on a hill mutilated by red mud slides. The multi-storeyed structures were ramshackle, unpainted and decaying. One building in particular was almost solely responsible for my refusal to go ashore. Though I tried not to look at it, I couldn't stop myself. Turning away and closing my eyes, I still saw its dark empty windows regurgitating foul mildew stains which dribbled like secretions down its facade. I pictured floors extending deep underground to passages as coiled as entrails, where, I imagined, unspeakable atrocities were committed. I feared that if I went ashore and approached the building, it would suck me in and swallow me. I wanted desperately to go back to Saint Helena or Ascension; I longed for clear blue water and the fresh clean smell of remote, ocean islands.

'I don't want to go ashore. Why can't we go back to Saint Helena?'

'Come on, Nicky, we don't have all day. Now get your shoes on.'

Mom and Dad had a bit of smuggling planned.

We had arrived in Brazil the previous day, 15 May 1978, less than two weeks after leaving Ascension and nearly a year since we had launched *Vingila* in Durban. Once again we'd sailed with the trade winds and made good time. Baruch and the twin jibs did their job and we had averaged 130 sea miles a day. As we neared the land mass of South America, the trades had shifted, giving way to variable north-easterlies. The blue of the open ocean became tinged with green, which darkened and grew cloudy. After we had sighted a thin strip of hazy mauve land that gradually took over most of the western horizon, the sea had grown muddy and clotted with rubbish. Dad's navigation was a few miles out and we made landfall to the north of Salvador, our destination. So we had turned south and sailed down the coast to reach the city and its putrid harbour.

'Get in the dinghy now, Martinique Stilwell, and I don't want to hear another word from you.' My mother lifted her hand but I knew she wouldn't really hit me.

We went ashore. On the choked streets, black smoke billowed from throbbing vehicles and the open gutters were clogged with iridescent mud and rotting vegetable matter. In side alleys strewn with faeces, animals barely recognisable as dogs roamed the pavements. They were emaciated, with pink, naked skins, encrusted with scabs. What little fur they had, adhered to their bodies in tattered clumps. They cringed and stared at us with beseeching eyes, before backing off to forage in the rubbish that people threw directly from the open windows above. Boys my age smoked cigarettes and sold marmoset monkeys from makeshift stands on the street. The tiny primates, with minute clammy fingertips and the white-fringed faces of distraught old men, were tied by the waist and swung through the air on strings to attract potential buyers. On every corner a woman squatted and fried a sort of corn cake in filthy oil. We watched in horror as my father bought one and ate it. He said it tasted better than it looked and offered to buy another for us but we refused.

On the street everybody stared at my waist-length white-blonde hair. They sidled up to touch my pigtails and stroke my arms. The build-up to the 1978 World Cup had begun and pictures of Brazil's hero Pele and his blonde barbie doll of a wife were plastered on billboards throughout the city, alongside photographs of other blondes selling soap powder, toilet paper and face cream. I, however, seemed to be the only living blonde on the streets, and the first fair child many Salvadorians had ever seen in the flesh. A pair of women with sticky yellow beehives and coarse black hairs sprouting from their forearms asked my mother, in sign language and broken English, what brand of dye she used on me. They looked disbelieving and suspicious when she explained that white hair grew, quite naturally, from my scalp and ran their fingers over my head to check for themselves. I shrank from the women's inspection. I hated the attention, the smell, the dirt and the crowds.

I begged again to leave for the islands but my parents had illicit business to complete. When we entered the country, we crossed our fingers and prayed that our boat wouldn't be searched, but we need not have worried. Salvadorian officials never boarded *Vingila*. We were simply directed to the customs office on the quay where Dad was asked to sign a form declaring our vessel clear of contraband. No cases of whisky and certainly no guns. He signed the form. Formalities completed, Mom and Dad were free to proceed with their smuggling.

Salvador fringes a wide bay and away from the congested city centre, overlooking the sea, the Bahia yacht club clung to a cliff face. We reached the place by bus. It was an architecturally ambitious building, blindingly white, glinting with stainless steel fixtures and cantilevered over a crystalline swimming pool of Olympic proportions. Our French neighbours in the small-craft basin had explained that it was impossible to moor near the club because it lacked a marina. They advised us to avoid the place. There were a few power boats tied to a jetty, they said, and, stowed under a canopy, some smallish sailboats which were never used. Getting through the door might be difficult, they warned, and inside the unfriendly members spent their time taking saunas or lying beside the pool, inhaling chlorine fumes and honing their suntans, while white-coated waiters served iced Coca-Cola and stuffed crabs. It's not a yacht club for sailors, they said.

Disembarking from our bus, we reached the portico of the club building. The doorman, protected by a glass cubicle, at first made as if he couldn't see us, but Dad pressed our Royal Natal Yacht Club cards to the glass.

'We want to visit your club,' Dad said. 'Do you have reciprocity?'

The doorman raised a careful hand and spoke into an intercom. After a short wait, a man we took to be the manager arrived and ran his eyes over our best – but slightly wrinkled – jeans, and dirty feet in open sandals. He inspected the cards, shrugged and let us through the door.

'This looks very expensive.' Mom took in the gleaming bar, partially covered pool, the row of sunbathing loungers and the staff picking discarded towels from the tiled floor.

'I suppose we'll have to order something. We can't just sit here doing nothing,' she said.

A waiter walked by, bearing a platter of crabs and frosted drinks tinkling with ice. In his wake he trailed the aroma of shellfish roasted in butter. I wanted to taste everything he had on his trolley and my mother saw it.

'Can't the children share a Coke, Frank?' Mom asked. 'I'll just have water.'

Dad nodded, his eyes on the sunbathers.

We sipped our drinks, and while the waiters admired and stroked my hair, Dad strolled the perimeter of the pool. He chose a caricature of a man wearing the tiniest of swimming trunks, with a gold medallion nesting like a bird in the hair of his chest between the oiled hairy hills of his belly, pectorals and jowls. Dad approached from the side, did the man perhaps want to buy a few cases of whisky? The answer was an immediate yes.

Once we'd established our contact, Dad packed a pair of duffel bags with bottles every day. These he carried through the naval base and past the customs office, before catching a bus to the club, where he sold our stock of Chivas Regal and Johnny Walker Black Label for ten times the amount we had paid in Cape Town.

When Dad had sold all the whisky, we left the city centre and made for Aratu Yacht Club, deep within the bay, which we had heard was a real yacht club. A yacht club for sailors. Surrounded by mangrove swamps and rain forest, it was accessible only by sea and a rough dirt road that turned to red mud when it rained, which was often. Motoring down the bay we missed a marker buoy and struck a reef. For a few terrifying minutes *Vingila* lurched and crunched on an outcrop of submerged rocks before Dad reversed her off. If she had been made of ferro-cement, it might have been the end of her, but she was strong steel and lost only a few layers of paint. In Aratu we hoped to meet Ari and his wife Rowena, South Africans of German descent, whom we'd got to know over the ham radio. As we sailed from Ascension, Dad's daily conversations with Ari on the radio had grown progressively more intimate and friendly.

Ari told us he was thirty-seven, wore a beard and hated cats. Rowena and he liked the name Sygun so much that they'd given it to their single child – a girl of seven – and also to their home-built, hard-chine steel boat. His daughter, he told us, was the most important person in the world for him and he was sure that Robert and I would love her. They couldn't wait to meet us and when *Vingila* arrived in Aratu, we would have a party.

Among a huddle of South African ferro-cement boats, many of which looked abandoned and sported 'for sale' signs, *Sygun* stood out in her ugliness. Painted prison grey, with mean piggy-eyed portholes, she rose from the water like a fortress. Ari appeared on deck. His teutonic beard, worn without the benefit of a moustache, sprouted from the outer reaches of his face, emphasising moon cheeks and a tiny lipless mouth, open in greeting. My heart sank.

The party, it was decided, would take place that night on *Vingila*. Robert and I hadn't been invited because Mom had generously suggested we babysit little Sygun onboard *Sygun*. That way the adults would be undisturbed, she said. Ari's yacht was as ugly below decks as she was from the outside. A weak fluorescent bulb trickled out a beam of attenuated light that left much of the cavernous interior in shadow and gave our skins a creepy corpse-like hue and emphasised the circles under our eyes. When we spoke, our voices echoed from bare steel walls. The air smelled of stale frying oil. Little Sygun, however, was pleased to have us. She wanted to talk and play but, young for her age and demanding in a single child way, she didn't interest me. When I asked her if she read, she shook her head. I'd forgotten to bring a book and, searching the shadowy recesses of the saloon, I found no bookcases. Across the water I heard the sound of adults laughing on *Vingila*. The evening stretched endlessly ahead and I wanted to be at home, in my own bunk.

'What time do you think they'll finish?' I asked Robert.

'How should I know?' Robert said.

He slouched on a bunk, picking at the nicks on his fingers. He yawned.

'Don't you have anything to read here?' I asked Sygun, who was swinging on the hand rails and not looking at all sleepy.

'My daddy has magazines,' she said, 'naughty magazines.'

My dad had magazines too. They were called *Scope*, and had pictures of women in panties with gauzy scarves around their shoulders posing with their backs arched to counterbalance the weight of their bosoms. Stars were pasted over their nipples, because naked women were illegal in South Africa. In Ari's magazines there were no nipple stars. My brother and I flicked pages in stunned silence. I felt sick. I knew about sex; I read adult books. The paperbacks I liked had pictures of women on the cover, their eyelashes weighed down with mascara, beige velvet roses drooping from satin ribbons tied around their throats. The women in my books had sex, but only near the end. If they had sex in the first few chapters somebody would usually kill them. They sighed a lot, and moaned; it felt so good it was unbearable and sometimes they fought with the men but afterwards they made up. In Ari's magazines, harsh lighting illuminated cold studios and men with tattoos and goose pimples stuck willies as long and pink as French polonies into women with heavy make-up and mottled legs. Sometimes there was just one woman, with a lot of men. Often, it looked painful. Little Sygun, ever helpful, asked us if we wanted to see more, because her father had lots of magazines, some of them with animals.

Much later that night we were retrieved by our parents. Sygun had at last collapsed on her bunk and gone to sleep, and Robert and I had curled up in the cockpit, away from the ghastly fluorescent light. The evening was over but the magazine images and my sense of shock lingered. Robert and I never spoke of the incident and I couldn't tell my mother because I felt that I had done something naughty and forbidden and if I said anything I thought I'd get into trouble, so for a while I walked around in a daze, looking at all the adults, particularly Ari and his wife, and picturing them in different poses: hanging backwards over the white plastic tables, on all fours in front of the bar, or lying entwined in groups on the rickety sun-loungers by the pool.

I don't think my parents' evening went particularly well either. They never said anything but I noticed that after the party, relations were noticeably cool between the yachts. They restricted themselves to drinks at the yacht club bar together, where, when it was Ari's turn to buy beer, he asked the barman to show him a selection of unopened bottles first, so that he could choose the fullest. One day Ari and Rowena caught a lift to the city and came back with a marmoset monkey for Sygun. The animal, which arrived with a strand of twine tied around its waist, was about the size of my fist – small enough to perch on the side of an empty glass without toppling it over. With bleary eyes and a tattered off-white ruff, it cowered and shivered, sometimes showing tiny, yellow teeth. They fed it potato crisps and encouraged it to drink beer from glasses on the bar, which they thought was funny. At night the little animal burrowed into Sygun's hair and they slept together. When she rolled over and squashed it to death a few weeks later, her parents bought her another because, as Ari said, monkeys were really quite cheap in Brazil.

On weekends, middle-class Brazilians arrived from the city to swim in the greenish pool, eat *churrasco* and watch soccer matches on a television bracketed to a concrete wall. Two brothers from the south ran the yacht club. They were gauchos from the cattle grazing plains and, the Salvadorians told us, practically Argentines. Pleased with his stash of American dollars under the mattress following the whisky sale, Dad said that we could eat *churrasco* too, but only once. Seated on white plastic chairs in our best jeans, we swung our legs and waited for the sweating gauchos to deliver swords of meat that had been cooked at an angle over an open fire, thus offering a range of very rare to completely overdone. They brought chicken first, then sausage and lastly beef. Bowls of manioc, a coarse flour made from cassava roots, were placed before us for sprinkling – Brazilian-style – over the meat to soak up the juices. Almost as an afterthought a table pushed against the back wall held rice, black beans and salads. Pepe especially loved *churrasco* and got to eat it every weekend by begging shamelessly and with great success. Despite mornings spent chasing crabs through the mud of the mangrove flats, he grew fat.

Vincent and the boys on *Dou-Dou Diop* never ate at the club. The night that they invited us to supper they borrowed most of the ingredients from Mom beforehand. The rest of what we ate, Vincent told us later, had been stolen from the grocery shop by Roland.

Roland was tall and lanky with stringy blond hair. He'd recently walked away from his wedding reception – and his new bride – with only a purple velvet suit and a pressure cooker. He admitted that the pot had been one of the wedding presents. His new wife got everything else, he said. Our supper of potatoes, onions and bacon was cooked by the boys in Roland's wedding pot. We ate in the cockpit. Over a bottle of *pitu*, the local fire water, Vincent, Roland and Jean-Pierre, who looked to be in their early twenties, told us they had sailed from Senegal via the Cape Verde islands. The boat, Vincent said, was named after his mentor, a Senegalese man who had shown him how to spear fish as a child while his parents taught at the village school. Growing up in Africa had made it impossible for him to go back to France, Vincent said. He had tried and failed, returning later to Senegal to buy *Dou-Dou Diop* with his friends Roland and Jean-Pierre. They planned to sail indefinitely by whatever means they could and had been joined by a Venezuelan woman named Soledad and Vincent's French girlfriend Nadine. Five adults on a 35-foot gaff-rigged wooden fishing boat was proving to be crowded. Jean-Pierre apparently thought so too because a few days later he left for another yacht.

'Nee-kee, Nee-kee,' Soledad called one morning across the muddy strip of water separating our boats.

'Nee-kee, I have a present for you.'

Soledad knew that I, like Vincent, collected shells and when she came aboard she unwrapped a bundle of cowries and cones, all in very good condition. I recognised them at once as being valuable.

'They come from my country,' she said. 'Venezuela.'

Soledad, short, curvaceous and chocolate-skinned, was the most recent addition to *Dou-Dou Diop*'s crew and had joined the boat in Brazil to comfort Roland after his failed marriage. She was wrong about the shells, though. *Cypraea picta*, of which there were four in the cloth bundle, are rare cowries from Senegal, not Venezuela.

Later I showed the shells to Vincent.

'Look what Soledad gave me.'

I unwrapped the bundle.

'Zat black beech,' he said. Apparently he and Soledad had fought that week, shortly before she visited me. Vincent picked through the shells, turning them over in his fingers. My father, who was with us, stayed mute. The three of us examined the spotted cowries and graceful cones ringed in black and tan. I knew I should give them back and was struggling with my conscience when Vincent shrugged, gave a wry Gallic smile and said, 'Now they are yours and I must go and speak with Soledad.'

A while later when we met up with *Dou-Dou Diop* again, on the island of Fernando de Noronha, Soledad was gone, and Jean-Pierre had moved back on board.

We left Salvador on 2 July 1978, two and a half months after we had first arrived and anchored in the dirty harbour and shortly after Brazil beat Argentina to win the World Cup. We had returned for a final time to the small craft harbour to clear out with customs, and on the night of the final match the city was silent, the streets empty.

We were woken from our beds when the city exploded in a storm of fireworks and bleating car horns. People poured from the buildings into the streets where they formed crawling samba lines that wound their way up alleys and through public squares. From across the water we felt the excitement and I experienced a fleeting urge to go ashore and join in. Subsequent to my first miserable days in Salvador, my feelings about the city had changed as I'd found places I enjoyed. Like the quiet central *mercado* where paddle fans stirred smells of leather and coffee into the warm air and stalls sold bags and sandals of hard pink cowhide. Outside, on the pavement beside the *mercado*, men with the bodies of ballet dancers performed *capoeira*, the graceful dance of self-defence created by African slaves brought to work in the sugar cane fields. After overcoming my initial shock and disgust at the filth and crowds, I had begun to think I might like Salvador after all but the feeling came too late, as we prepared to leave.

8

BRAZIL

In the city of Recife Mom gave Robert and me away to a stranger for the night. Afterwards, she regretted it. We arrived in Recife, which lay several hundred miles from Salvador, by sailing northwards along the bulging coast of Brazil for three days in a moderate south-easter. During this time it became clear to us that ocean passages with the trades were vastly preferable to coastal sailing with all its worries of variable winds, shipping lanes, shoals and hidden reefs. Before the invention of GPS, travelling within sight of land required constant vigilance. Anxiety, night watches and sleep deprivation replaced the peace and tranquillity we had found in the open ocean. Perhaps the promise of an uninterrupted night's sleep without children swayed Mom in allowing the stranger to take us home.

'At the time it seemed like a good idea,' she said later. 'It was only after you'd gone that I realised what I'd done. I didn't know the man from a bar of soap. Not his name, telephone number, where he lived, or anything.'

She didn't sleep much that night. Then again, neither did Robert and I.

The stranger who took my brother and me away introduced himself to Mom at the bar of the Recife Yacht Club. When she declined his offer of a sleep-over, he insisted, saying we would be company for his son, who was lonely. Over the evening and a few beers he wore her down and eventually, without thinking to consult us, she agreed to let him drive off with her children.

The man lived some distance away in a wealthy suburb. His house was stark and modern and appeared to be still under construction. The interior seemed barren and desolate and our voices rang and echoed from the bare concrete walls. A spiral staircase led to nowhere. The man – we never learned his name – said his wife and daughter were away in Rio. Or perhaps only his wife was in Rio and she had left to recover from his daughter's death from cancer or possibly suicide. The exact circumstances of his life weren't clear, his English was poor and he was very drunk.

He showed Robert and me our room; a cell of concrete with a strip of high windows beneath the ceiling, and then he left us alone with a pair of electric fans and two beds starkly made up with a single sheet each. The place had the feel of an abandoned hospital. On *Vingila*, Mom lay awake fearing she would never see us again, but our concerns were more practical.

'Where are the blankets?' I asked Robert. Beneath the sheets we found nothing but bare mattresses.

'Just sleep on the sheet, I think.'

I started to cry. 'I want to go home.'

'Don't be such a sissy, it's not that cold.'

We turned off the light and lay down in our clothes. But a swarm of mosquitoes, with whines like dental drills, bore down on us.

'Are you sleeping?' Robert asked.

'What do you think?' I was lying on my back, trying to swat each mosquito as it landed. The air above my face was thick with insects trumpeting their desire to suck my blood. I could feel the husks of their bodies when I waved my hands in the darkness in front of me. The insects were hungry and not to be deterred.

'We can't sleep like this,' Robert said after a while.

'What about the fans?'

We tried the fans; on low they blew the airborne invaders slightly off course and on high they chilled us till our teeth chattered. At last, in the early hours of the morning, we dozed on bare mattresses, cuddling our pillows for warmth, with fans turned to medium and mosquitoes biting us through the sheets. At dawn we gave up our efforts to sleep.

'When do you think we can go home?' I asked.

'I dunno.' Robert's voice sounded thick, muffled by tiredness, but as the morning light trickled through the strip of windows, I saw that his eyes were a pair of black slits in a swollen bowl of a face. His skin had the texture of oat porridge.

'Robbie, can you see? Something's happened to your face.'

Eyes blinking, he ran his hand over taut pebbled skin.

'My face feels funny,' he said, 'all hot and tight.'

'Jeez, you really got bitten. Maybe you're allergic.'

'I want to go home.' My brother sounded tearful, an unusual state for him.

'I hope you don't die. What will Mom say?'

'When do you think we can ask the man to take us home?'

Our host slept on for a further two hours. We crouched at his bedroom door and waited for him to wake. His son, tangled in a sheet, lay beside him and together they slumbered to the whirr of an oscillating electric fan. They were both naked. Twice, the father, who snored, fell from his bed to the floor but each time he climbed back without waking. Later, he opened a single eye, slowly focusing on us, but we took fright and ran away down the passage. He followed and found us in the kitchen where he seemed surprised by our presence, as if he'd forgotten bringing us home the previous night. He made coffee and asked vaguely about Robert's face. After a breakfast of coco-pops we drove in silence past acres of hovels to the yacht club where Mom stood waiting on the jetty looking pale and pinched beneath her suntan. I was so pleased to see her I forgot to be angry. She hugged us far too hard.

'I'm so glad you're back,' she said.

She kissed Robert on the head and held him at arm's length.

'Good grief,' she said, lifting up her glasses and squinting to see better, 'what on earth has happened to your face?'

After that I kept within the boundaries of the yacht club. While my parents shopped for food and explored the city, I swam lengths in the pool until my hair, stained by the water's chemicals, turned lime green and my nose reddened and peeled from sunburn. As far as I was concerned, Recife was just another squalid Brazilian city and I wasn't interested. I also decided that if my mother ever again suggested we sleep at a stranger's house, I would refuse.

When we left Recife to sail for the island of Fernando de Noronha, roughly 300 miles from the coast of Brazil, Emelio, Nina, Evandro and Joyce came with us. Dad had met this gaggle of Brazilian university students at the Recife Yacht Club one night and, in a burst of alcohol inspired generosity, had invited them to join us for a cruise. The next day they moved aboard and we sailed. Shortly after that relations on *Vingila* began to sour. My father had promised the young Brazilians a sunny two-day cruise, but *Vingila* was slow, the sun retreated behind a bank of cloud, and within a day everybody aboard was disappointed. The students, who Mom said were spoilt, crowded us out of the saloon. They withdrew behind a wall of whispered Portuguese, emerging only to ask for food. They ate constantly but were picky eaters, demanding cheese, quince paste and canned ham. At night, they refused to take watches, preferring an uninterrupted night's sleep. They were surprised to learn that if they wanted to wash, there was a bucket filled with cold sea water at the stern. Five days passed. Landfall, some spears of tapered rock pushing from the sea like growing shoots, was met with relief by all aboard and directly after anchoring, we lowered the dinghy and delivered the students ashore. Without a word of thanks or a glance backwards, the young Brazilians disappeared over the ridge of the beach in search of a hotel and we never saw them again.

We were not the only yacht in Fernando de Noronha. *Dou-Dou Diop*, the small wooden gaff-rig with its ragged crew of Vincent, Roland, Jean-Pierre and their assorted girlfriends, lay anchored in the turquoise water between the beach and the rocky islets guarding the seaward side of the bay. We had not seen them since the Aratu Yacht Club in Salvador when Soledad presented me with bundles of West African seashells, stolen from Vincent. Now Vincent appeared in the companionway of his boat and waved my parents over with an open bottle of *pitu*. He said *Dou-Dou Diop* had sailed directly from Aratu, bypassing Recife because they had heard it was a terrible place. Mom and Dad settled in with Vincent and the *pitu* bottle, and Robert and I made for the shore where a line of docile white breakers washed and rewashed sand that was already sparklingly clean. A brown-skinned boy of our age, with bleached saltwater hair and eyes that shone glass-green in the afternoon sun, helped haul our dinghy beyond the high water mark. He was alone on the beach and said his name was Roberto. He pronounced it 'Hobberty'. Having exhausted his English, he beckoned us to follow him.

The island was dusty khaki, with outcrops of reddish rock and flocks of goats roaming its hills. There was a shop, Roberto said in Portuguese, but no village. Some tourists stayed in the far hotel, near the beaches. This, I thought, was where our students must have gone. With Roberto we walked along a gravel road past some scattered bungalows. We climbed the crest of a hill and at the top, looking downwards and drawn by the slope of the road, we burst suddenly into a sprint. I ran until the air burned my throat, my stride lengthening with the angle of the decline, until we finished at last, laughing at the bottom of the hill, with the tension of our previous days at sea dissipated and our friendship with Roberto firmly cemented.

According to our family mythology, we spent four months on Fernando de Noronha, although, in the same way a childhood summer holiday stretches towards eternity, to me it felt longer. When I consult *Vingila*'s logbook – the official record – I see that we stayed on the island for only six weeks. During that time my brother's fate and the watery path of his life was sealed. Each day he and Roberto submersed themselves in the glassy water surrounding the island. Robert had a Hawaiian sling; a spear with a rubber loop on one end and a spray of tiny harpoons on the other. Roberto had a trident. At first Robert speared more rocks than fish, but within days his skills improved and I was able to order any fish I wanted to eat – a fresh sole for breakfast, a squirrel fish to poach for lunch, or a rock cod for supper. Most of the two boys' catch went to feed Roberto's eleven brothers and sisters who lived with his parents in a bare-floored, two-roomed house overlooking the bay.

Although Roberto spoke only Portuguese, day by day we understood him better. One morning he told us that the biggest octopus he'd ever seen lived in a hole in the reef near the headland protecting the anchorage. He had wanted to catch the animal for some time, he said, but it was very old and had grown very big and clever. Using mime to supplement his words he described its constricted cat's pupils and angry, flushing tentacles. How it lay coiled and brooding within its shell-strewn hole. How much he wanted it. Roberto and Robert often caught smaller octopi which we stewed with wine and tomatoes in our pressure pot, as Dad had learned from a cook in Mozambique. Although the little animals were delicious, Roberto wasn't satisfied. He wanted to catch the big old octopus. He spoke about it constantly, hatching plans for its capture.

Over the decades, my brother's attitude to octopi would change; their intelligence and the naked show of their emotions expressed by the changing colour of their skin as they blanched with fear or flushed with anger, would begin to move him. In later years he would lose all desire to kill them. But at the age of ten, he and Roberto took their spear and trident and battled it out one day with the wily old octopus Roberto wanted. The cephalopod put up a good fight; it took the two boys most of the morning before they finally had him writhing in the dinghy at my feet. Then Roberto killed the creature by turning his head inside out. This was an improvement on the method I had read about in a *Hardy Boys* storybook, which suggested biting the animal on the pea-sized swelling between the eyes, which they said was its brain. The big octopus was slow to die completely. Even chopped into pieces his skin continued to change colour in fluttering arpeggios of violet and brown, expressing, I fancied, the last show of his feelings. And after we'd cooked him, we found suckers stuck to the side of the pot as if he'd made a last attempt to escape.

On the rare days that Roberto and Robert didn't dive, the three of us roamed the island together, walking about or catching a lift with the milk delivery man on his donkey cart to visit the tourist beaches on the far side of the island, or the old man who kept a vegetable garden and who would, for a few cents, let us eat green peppers off the bushes. But mostly our days centred around the sea, which was warm, clear and teeming with fish and coral. Sometimes other boys joined us – friends of Roberto's. Roberto and Robert snorkelled from the rocks, or I took them in the dinghy to nearby shoals. I swam with them but got cold quickly and was afraid of sharks, so I liked having a boat to escape to. Dad speared fish and dived for shells on the outlying reefs and islets with Vincent, Roland and Jean-Pierre and they occasionally took Roberto and Robert with them. Daily, the men and boys grew leaner and browner.

Their hair bleached and coarsened and their skins, when out of water, carried a permanent dusting of salt which accumulated in concretions of crystals on their eyebrows and cheekbones.

The shells that my father dived out, cowries, cones, muraxes and whelks, I cleaned and labelled as Mack and Eva Fox had taught me. I identified those I could, and, for all of them, noted the depth of water and the habitat they had been found in. My collection was growing.

As the weeks passed our Brazilian visas expired. The local official, a corpulent man named Roosevelt, with a passion for samba, assured us it was not a problem. He was the island's only gendarme and we believed him. A few days after our first meeting Roosevelt arrived on the beach with several bottles of *pitu*, and his friends Bispo and Solange, and a live goat on a string. Vincent fetched them in his dinghy, and, after offloading the goat, rowed over to *Vingila* and invited us to join them for a sail to the other side of the island. Rooseveld had, apparently, become close friends with Vincent. Taking the goat we sailed on *Dou-Dou Diop* to the Bay of Dolphins, a place where waves like sheets of glass rose and fell on a crescent of perfect sand. Shoals of coloured fish milled about and chased each other around a massive coral head set in white sand that crawled with winged gurnet fish. While snorkelling I got trailed by a barracuda, its open jaw weighed down by a load of jagged teeth. It was almost a foot longer than me and I was terrified it would bite my leg off, but it merely accompanied me to the safety of the dinghy. While I hyperventilated and tried to keep from sobbing, it waited expectantly at the surface for me to return to the water.

Many years later the Bay of Dolphins beach would officially be voted one of the most beautiful in the world, and the bay declared a World Heritage Site and off limits to tourists on the basis of its ecological sensitivity. On our visit we paid no attention to its ecological sensitivity as we speared fish, caught crayfish, made a fire and killed the goat on the beach. After eating the seafood and most of goat we took a siesta under the trees. In the evening, as the sun set, we sailed back to the anchorage and Roosevelt, wedged into the cockpit of *Dou-Dou Diop* with red eyes and a bottle of *pitu* in his hand, assured us yet again that there was no reason ever to leave the island.

By the time we finally left Fernando, on 28 August, our boat was covered in blue blotches and looked as if she had contracted a strange tropical disease. Vincent was to blame; he'd given Dad a packet of blue powder and had told him that adding a tiny pinch made white paint brighter. On the day he had a tooth pulled out by the island's part-time dentist and then self-medicated with pain pills and half a bottle of *pitu*, Dad decided to follow Vincent's advice with the blue powder. *Vingila* had a few rust spots that needed touching up and Dad added what he thought was a pinch of blue to our last pot of white paint. Roberto had chosen that day to go to school and Robert and I went with Mom to buy a bag of rice at the island's only shop – a hut whose bare shelves smelled of Baygon – and when we returned later in the afternoon we found Dad unconscious in his bunk and *Vingila* covered in blue spots.

'If we'd done this,' Robert whispered to me, 'he would've killed us.'

Without other paint *Vingila* had to stay the way she was until we reached Fortaleza, our next destination. Vincent found the blue spots very funny. Nadine, his naked girlfriend, said nothing but she seldom spoke to us anyway, and usually shut herself in the forepeak whenever we came aboard. Mom thought Nadine might be friendlier if she had clothes to wear and decided to crochet a string bikini for her. When it was finished we rowed over as a family to present our gift. At Vincent's request, Nadine emerged from her cabin in the bow and reluctantly donned the swimming costume but when Roland and Jean-Pierre wolf-whistled she dived back into the forepeak, slammed the door and refused to come out again. Vincent gazed after her fondly, shaking his head.

'That Nadine,' he said, 'her whole body is covered with little blonde hairs, just like a peach.'

The following day she was naked again.

We didn't really want to leave but our expired visas were making my father nervous so we said goodbye to *Dou-Dou Diop*. We said goodbye to Roosevelt and Bispo, who urged us to stay another few days, or a week even. Robert and I said goodbye to Roberto. He presented us with a pair of miniature sandals he had made from red and blue card. Across their soles he'd written *Remembranca de Fernando de Noronha, Roberto*.

'*Saudades*,' he said.

Brazilians speak Portuguese but claim some words, like *saudades*, as their own. *Saudades* are souvenirs or mementos, but the word also describes a feeling; the bitter-sweet longing for something or somebody lost. I still have Roberto's paper sandals. And, when I look at them, the feeling too.

The immigration authorities in the city of Fortaleza didn't share Roosevelt's lenient view about our expired visas. Paging through our passports, they calculated the days since our visas had lapsed and issued us with a hefty fine. The sum was larger than the profits of our whisky smuggling.

'We can't pay this,' Dad said. 'We don't have that much money.'

The alternative, the officer explained, was jail.

Dad blanched. 'We can't go to jail. Please, we're a family.'

I held hands with Robert and tried to look as if I were part of a decent, happy family. Maybe blonde hair would help. Surely in this country, little blonde girls didn't go to jail.

'Alternatively,' the officer continued, after looking us over, 'we can make you temporary citizens of Brazil.'

The ensuing paperwork left very little time for sightseeing. We were photographed and fingerprinted, weighed and measured. Portuguese forms were filled out in quadruplicate.

'Jail would have been easier than this,' Robert muttered in my ear.

After three days of bureaucracy we were presented with our certificates of citizenship, valid for two weeks. To celebrate our new nationality we took a bus trip out of the city. We drove past the *favelas* – kilometres of crowded shacks and hovels without toilets, electricity or running water – which were broken only by the spires and domes of disintegrating cathedrals. The bus route terminated at an enormous new soccer stadium which stood stranded in a sea of mud. It had been built, the bus driver explained, for the World Cup and had cost millions. Nobody used it any more.

Then we went to the *poste restante* to pick up our mail. There were several worried aerogrammes from Nana, who wanted to know why she hadn't heard from us in so long, and even a rare letter from my father's mother, who urged him to write and tell her we were all well. There was also a note from Lynnath, the marine biologist we had met in Port Elizabeth, who had given me my plankton collection and who had showed me how to use my microscope. She wrote that in a few months she would be sailing from Cape Town to Punta del Este in Uruguay as the navigator on a yacht taking part in the South Atlantic Yacht Race. From Uruguay she hoped to join us in the Caribbean, and could we please send her the dates that we planned to be at certain islands. We should write to the *poste restante* in Uruguay.

'I thought she was joking when she said she would see us again,' Dad said, shaking his head slowly in surprise.

My mother answered all the letters, assuring everybody we were well and telling Lynnath that we were unsure about our itinerary, but that the first island we planned to visit was Grenada and we would let her know once we got there.

Of the Brazilian cities we visited, I liked Fortaleza least. Here the gap between rich and poor appeared even wider than it had in Salvador or Recife. At the yacht club overweight teenagers baked in the sun, ate shellfish and threw their bottles and glasses into the pool for the cleaners to retrieve at the end of each day. Boatmen prepared yachts for sailing and after the members were done they stepped onto the jetty, leaving the boat behind, sails flapping, for the workers to pack away again. There was more crime in Fortaleza too. We were warned about muggings and in later years the situation worsened considerably. When Hans, who grew up on the junk *Maria Jose*, visited the place as an adult on his own yacht, he was ambushed while anchored in front of the yacht club. He fought the attackers off with a gun. The following night, however, a crew member on the boat anchored alongside him was stabbed in the neck by men boarding the boat. He bled to death in the scuppers. Although Fortaleza wasn't quite as dangerous as that when we visited, I still sensed an undercurrent of menace in the way the rows of dark-haired men in the streets eyed us and I felt uneasy.

Fortaleza was nearer to the borders of the Amazon jungle and had on its congested streets distressing, open-air pet shops where baby alligators lay tethered in muddy gutters while toucans, marmosets, wild cats, macaws and owls crouched miserably in stacked, overcrowded cages. I saw groups of crusty-eyed wild kittens quivering in canary cages while an otter paced relentlessly beside them in another. The smell of rotting food, dung, and musky fear was intense.

'If I had enough money,' I said, 'I'd buy them all and set them free.'
Mom led me away.

'There's nothing you can do about it, Nicky,' she said.

We set sail from Fortaleza on 12 September, having spent four months in Brazil. In the drawer beneath my bunk, wrapped in cotton wool and enclosed in a small box, was a *Cypraea surinamensis*, the cowrie that Mack on Ascension had asked me to send him in exchange for the promise of twenty dollars. Dad and I had visited the fishing boats on the far side of the harbour where, for a few cruzeiros, I had bought the shell from a fisherman who told us he had found it tangled in his nets. With a deep, burnt-orange underside and spots of cream and brown on its dorsum, it was even more beautiful than the specimen I had seen in the photograph on Ascension island. I knew it was worth several hundred dollars and it would remain the star of my collection for years. I had no intention of ever posting it to Mack.

9

DOLDRUMS

The day after we left Fortaleza on 12 September a hurricane slammed into the coast of Venezuela a few hundred miles to the north of us. It was the seventh storm of the season and according to news reports caused 'less deaths than expected'. Because Dad was unable to receive weather warnings on the radio we had no idea that havoc raged ahead in our path and so we happily waved the coast of Brazil goodbye and set off in the direction of the storm. As the sea cleared and turned familiar open-ocean blue, we let fishing lines trail in our wake. The Caribbean island of Grenada lay 2000 miles away and we did not expect to meet land again for at least three weeks. Aided by a strong current flowing up the northern coast of Brazil, we were hoping the trade winds would help us on our way. Challenges lay ahead, however, because we needed to cross the equatorial doldrums where trade winds die and although nobody said anything about it, we faced the possibility of hurricanes. Ideally we should have reached the safety of the Caribbean before the hurricane season began but our timing was wrong; we had left it very late to leave Brazil, and staying on was impossible. In the North Atlantic the hurricane season extends from June to November, and September –

the very month we chose to cross 2000 miles of ocean – experiences the most frequent and severe storms. We couldn't have chosen a worse time to sail. Mom, unaware that hurricane season often goes out with a bang, thought we were safe because the season had nearly finished. Dad was more worried and aware of the risk he was taking, but he didn't share his fears with us. Sailing during hurricane season was risky enough, but the safest way to do it was to follow weather reports on the radio closely and work our way slowly up the coast, taking shelter in Belem near the Amazon, and in the harbours of Guyana and Surinam. Dad, however, still didn't feel confident enough of his navigational skills to visit these countries. Caught between our expired Brazilian visas and his own navigational shortcomings, and aided in his decision by our inability to receive weather reports because the radio wasn't working properly, he felt he had no choice except to take a chance and make for the open ocean, miles away from any shelter. Robert and I, unaware of the danger, had no say in the matter. We were in Dad's hands and, not knowing any better, we trusted him.

For the first three days after we left Brazil a 20 knot wind blew on the beam and, with the current behind her, *Vingila* sailed on a broad reach, maintaining an average of 150 sea miles per day, a record for her that would remain unbroken. As we approached the equator, the sun at noon took up position directly overhead and Dad found himself unable to shoot midday sights. My father's friend Leonard Pratt of *Betty-J*, hadn't prepared him for this situation and he was at a loss. Noon sights gave us our position in latitude and without them we could only guess where we were. My mother simply wrote in the logbook 'Navigation not working'. So one morning we decided that we were crossing the equator. We knew what to do. Back in Cape Town, Gary and Hudson, the brothers of *Scud*, had filled us in on equatorial lore. Robert and I were pollywogs – grossly inferior to shellbacks like Gary and Hudson who had crossed the equator by sea. When crossing the line, pollywogs were required to undergo an initiation ceremony performed by a certified shellback. Luckily, Dad had crossed the equator several times while in the merchant navy and had been properly initiated. So he dressed as King Neptune, complete with my brother's Hawaiian sling for a trident, and made us perform several humiliating, but essentially good-natured acts. We sipped seawater and were baptised with buckets of the stuff. Unaware of what lay ahead, everybody was happy, and my mother wrote in the logbook that night, 'We are all shellbacks now, including Pepe.'

Sea temperature is a critical factor in the development of tropical storms. To provide enough energy to spawn and fuel a full-grown storm, the seawater must be at least 26,5 degrees Celsius, and that warmth must extend to a depth of 50 metres. This usually occurs only at the end of a long, tropical summer. The South Atlantic Ocean, cooled by the Benguela current from Antarctica, never warms enough to brew giant storms and so is blessed by constant gentle trade winds. But the great swathe of hot, equatorial water in the North Atlantic that extends from the coast of South America, through to the Gulf of Mexico and as far east as the Cape Verde islands, provides a vast breeding ground for cyclonic tropical storms. The Caribbean and the coast of North America experience around ten per year, almost all in the June to November period. The storms begin life as tropical depressions – or pressure waves – near the equator, in areas of light breezes where wind shear will not disrupt the deepening low pressure. Invariably these pressure cells move north and westwards, fuelled by atmospheric heat, warm water and the forces of the earth's rotation. They grow into tropical storms, without a central characteristic eye, but with the shape of a hurricane, and wind speeds of 33 knots or 63 kilometres per hour. On average, six of the ten annual storms go on to develop a central eye and a wind speed greater than 64 knots, or 119 kilometres per hour, thus graduating from tropical storms to hurricanes. The same storms will be called typhoons in the North Pacific and cyclones elsewhere. Of the six annual Caribbean hurricanes, two will be extremely severe, ravaging the islands and coasts of the surrounding countries to cause significant damage, destruction and death. A full-grown storm, it is estimated, releases the same energy as 10 megaton nuclear bombs exploding every 20 minutes.

Sailing towards the outflow of the Amazon River, the sea was extraordinarily rich in life and we were often accompanied by pods of dolphins who surfed our bow waves and sent Pepe into a barking frenzy with their high-pitched whistles. One afternoon more than a thousand spinner dolphins spent several hours swimming beside the boat, leaping from the water in synchronised groups, somersaulting and tail-walking. I felt as if we were in the centre of an orchestrated marine extravaganza, with cetaceans extending to the horizon on all sides and I sat at the pulpit, with the afternoon sun on the sails, entranced by the show around me and half expecting to hear a suitable soundtrack.

Dolphins weren't the only creatures jumping from the sea. The following day a big Spanish mackerel startled us – and itself – by launching into the air and nearly landing in our laps. It missed the boat by centimetres to fall back into the water. It must have been part of a feeding school because seconds later we hooked another on the line trailing from the stern.

'Jeez, look at that,' Robert said, after he'd hauled in the fish and Dad had gaffed it.

Bedecked in vertical navy stripes, its gleaming, scaleless body was longer than my father's. Expressionless black eyes gazed from an armoured head as sleek as a jet plane.

'I don't even know why you lot were fishing anyway because we certainly don't need another fish,' Mom said. 'We still haven't eaten the two wahoo you caught yesterday.'

Dealing with quantities of fresh fish posed a problem. We couldn't afford to own or run a deep freeze and, at sea, our gas fridge didn't work because it wasn't gimballed. So the previous day's fish fillets lay in covered bowls in the galley, sweating in the tropical heat. And Dad refused to throw food away.

'Listen here,' he said to Mom, 'we're going to eat the lot, you'll see. We'll make fish biltong.'

'You can't make fish biltong,' Mom said.

'Why not?'

'Because biltong's made from meat, that's why.'

But Dad marinaded the wahoo and Spanish mackerel in salt and spices, and then hung strips of it beneath the mizzen boom like fragrant, bloodstained washing. We had long stopped using the mizzen sail because Dad said it gave *Vingila* weather helm, pulling her off balance, but we found the mizzen boom and mast useful for hanging things like flags, radar reflectors, radio antennae and now strips of drying fish. After several days in the sun and wind, the biltong was dry enough to pack into sacks. We stowed the strips in Robert's cabin, where anyone was free to eat them. Pepe was allowed a piece of his own a day but, after asking permission from my mother, preferred to select it himself directly from the drying lines. In damp weather the biltong tended to mould and the smell intensified although it remained edible, or at least Dad said so. Robert moved out of his cabin and began sleeping in the cockpit.

With the steady wind and strong current we continued to make good time. My parents estimated that about a thousand sea miles lay between *Vingila* and Grenada, but because Dad was still unable to navigate we weren't quite sure and sailed blindly on. In the logbook Mom continued to write 'noon sights not working'.

The steady wind was not to last. To begin, it slackened in the mornings, leaving us stranded until lunchtime when it would pick up again for the afternoon. One still morning we awoke to a thick mist and the sound of heavy breathing. A light swell was running, and without wind to fill her sails, *Vingila* wallowed and rolled. Outside, wallowing next to her in the grey ocean, was a group of unusual creatures.

'What are these things?' Robert asked.

'I don't know if I like the look of them,' Mom said.

One of the animals turned on its side, fixing her with a round, unblinking eye.

'I think they're whales,' I said.

'But aren't whales supposed to be big?' Mom pushed her glasses up the bridge of her nose to take a better look. The animals were about the size of dolphins, but their glossy black bodies were rounded and their truncated faces lacked snouts. They lay in the water beside us, exhaling loudly. I went below for our encyclopaedia of marine mammals. When I returned I found the creatures still in the same position.

'According to this book,' I said, flipping through the pages, 'they might be porpoises.'

'Nonsense,' Mom replied. 'Porpoises are the same as dolphins, only with longer noses. Anyway, dolphins are playful. They don't just lie around like this lot.'

'Well, in that case, they're either pilot whales or melon-headed whales.'

'I don't know about that. I only hope they're not dangerous. Keep away from the edge. If you fell in now, we don't know what they'll do.'

The creatures looked more lethargic than dangerous and when a gentle wind rose up and blew away the mist it seemed to breathe some life into our companions too, for they swam lazily away. I felt quite sorry to see them go. But we weren't alone for long. We caught sight of our next visitors from afar. They made straight for the boat, whistling and clicking. There were two of them and although they were the size of small whales, they looked and behaved like dolphins. Their skins were an unusual dusky brown splashed with irregular, creamy blotches.

'So if those other things were whales, what are these then?' Mom said with a now-I've-got-you look.

I paged through the book again.

'They might be beaked whales. Or very large dolphins.'

'Do you always have to be such a smarty pants?' Robert usually took my side, but not always. He would have carried on but his attention was diverted.

'Hey look there,' he said, 'that one's got a big remora stuck on its side.'

'Impossible,' Dad said. 'I've never heard of a remora sticking to a dolphin.'

Using the suction cup that grows on the top of their heads, remora fish attach themselves to sharks and other large fish, hitching a ride and eating the scraps that fall from their mouths.

The dolphins circled the boat once and were gone, leaving behind a single lonely remora trying unsuccessfully to attach itself to Baruch's rudder.

'They came to scrape the poor thing off,' said Robert, hanging his head over the stern to get a better look. 'Shall we catch him?'

'Why? We can't eat him and Mom'll just get mad at us.'

But Robert was already dangling a lure in the water and within seconds had pulled the fish aboard.

'He must have been very hungry to take a lure like that,' he murmured, half to himself.

We played with his sucker a bit, crouching down so Mom couldn't see us, and taking turns sticking him to our legs. When we tugged at his tail he was impossible to dislodge but he slipped off easily nose first, leaving red marks on our skin.

'Those dolphins must have known just how to get him off,' Robert said, throwing the remora overboard. Keeping close to Baruch's rudder, the fish followed us for the rest of the afternoon, but by evening it was gone.

The next morning we awoke to find ourselves surrounded by syrupy mud-brown water. Something was very wrong. Dad scanned the horizon.

'I can't see anything,' he said. 'Bring the binoculars.'

Around us the horizon was clear, unmarked by land or low lying cloud. We were confused. By all accounts we were in the open ocean and the water should be blue and clear.

'I don't like this at all,' Dad said. 'I think it's the Amazon River.'

He went below, switched on the depth sounder and twiddled the knobs. The screen's twitchy light settled with a purr at eight fathoms, or 16 metres.

Dad came back on deck with his lips compressed and a frown chiselled between his brows.

He turned on the engine, opened the throttle and spun the helm around.

'What's going on, Frank? Where are we going?' Mom stood in the companionway with a sack of half-dried fish she intended to hang in the sun. (At night we took the drying biltong inside to avoid the dew.) Dad didn't answer right away. With the binoculars, he scanned the horizon again. His lips sucked in air.

'We're getting out of here,' he said. 'If a swell picks up at this depth, we'll have breakers.'

Mom lowered her bag of half-dried fish.

'What do you mean?' she asked. 'Where are we?'

'Well, we don't really know that now, do we? But I know where I don't want to be and that's in the bladdy Amazon River.'

The Amazon, torn by currents and countercurrents and strewn with treacherous shifting mud banks, is so wide it's possible to be in the mouth of the river and still be out of sight of land. We were more likely in the river's vast outflow, which stretches far out to sea, but it had been days since Dad had last shot a sight and, as we were sailing in the presence of a powerful coastal current there was no way to be sure. We turned *Vingila* east, away from where we imagined land – and danger – lay. With sails raised and the motor on full throttle, we made for the open ocean. All that night, and into the next day, we motored through brown water. At noon we turned off the engine to eat lunch without the noise and smell of diesel fumes. To avoid a tangle, we pulled in our trailing fishing lines and while doing so caught a very unusual pair of fish. We often caught dorado in pairs, but we'd never seen fish like these before. Flat as serving platters, they weighed about 20 kilograms each. With green dorsal surfaces and dark spots on their tails, they certainly weren't fish of the deep sea. They looked as if they were overgrown freshwater aquarium specimens and there was nothing remotely like them in our fish book, but we ate them anyway. They were delicious. Their meat was dark and tender and tasted to us like fine fillet steak. We gorged ourselves that night and the following day hung up the remainder of our feast to dry with our other biltong.

Over the next days the wind that had blown us to the equator died completely. *Vingila*'s daily distances, of which we had been so proud, plummeted from more than 150 miles to less than 40. After nine days at sea, Dad estimated that 800 miles still lay between us and the island of Grenada. He was reluctant to motor because diesel cost money and running the engine was hot and smelly, and somebody needed to take the helm because Baruch didn't work without wind. But to make any progress at all, we were forced to spend at least a few hours each day motoring. At night, if the breeze blew strongly enough to fill the sails, we set Baruch on course and left *Vingila* to sail listlessly at one or two knots. In wind too weak to fill canvas, we simply lowered the sails and slept, leaving our yacht to drift with the current.

In the afternoons Mom began to read aloud from a thick paperback with a picture of half a butterfly on the cover. Sprawled on sticky vinyl cushions under the shade of an awning we tried our best to catch the faint cooling breezes. The book was about Devil's Island in French Guyana where Papillon, a man with a butterfly tattoo, was held prisoner. He'd been found guilty of manslaughter in France and had been sent to the worst prison in the world; a tropical island surrounded by man-eating sharks. Of course he was innocent, and from the start we all knew it was just a case of mistaken identity, and that it wasn't his fault he had such bad friends. But for thirteen years he was imprisoned unjustly which was why he never stopped trying to escape. Life on the island was hellish. There were brutal guards, torture and solitary confinement and wicked fellow prisoners with money and drugs stashed in special containers called chargers that they kept hidden in their bums. The food was terrible. To get away, Papillon made rafts which often didn't work and got wrecked in the surf among the sharks. People died, but not him. It was gruelling. When he couldn't stand it any more, he escaped to live in Surinam with a local woman and a hut that had a hammock.

Robert looked out over the ocean. Somewhere to the west, across the glittering water, lay French Guyana, too far away to be seen.

'Is Devil's Island really over there?' he asked. 'Are we sailing past it right now?'

'Yes,' said Mom.

'With sharks and everything?'

'Yes.'

'And prisoners?'

'Maybe, I don't know if they still have prisoners,' Mom said.

'Why can't we go there?'

'I don't think it's very safe,' Mom answered. Actually we couldn't go there because Dad's navigation 'wasn't working'.

'Pity,' said Robert. 'I'd like to see it, and I'm getting a bit tired of this.'

Later in the Caribbean we would meet several yachts, with crews more confident in their navigation skills than we were, who'd visited Devil's Island to inspect the derelict, abandoned prison and photograph the packs of sharks circling the island. They showed us photographs and said it was fascinating.

Robert stood up in the cockpit and stretched. He gazed far over the horizon in the direction of French Guyana where a cluster of nimbostratus gathered.

'I hope we get some wind,' he said.

The sun beat down, blistering the deck. Its intense rays – directly overhead – were scarcely filtered by the atmosphere. Such heat warms the sea and the moist air above it, causing up-draughts which form heavy clouds and deep low pressure systems where trade winds from both hemispheres converge and die. This is the inter-tropical convergence zone, a weather system which extends roughly five degrees on either side of the equator but varies its position according to the season. In September 1978 we found it just north of the line, or we guessed we did. Seafarers know this region as the doldrums; miles of light, erratic winds, interspersed with sudden squalls and downpours where a sailing boat may find itself fatally trapped for weeks. Sailors dreaded the doldrums, which sap their strength and spirits, and sometimes even took their lives. Over the years, the word has leaked out of sailing jargon and become synonymous with stagnation and depression, the very emotions the region induces. In the doldrums the air is muggy and hot, and the clouds heavy and purple. This is the birthplace of cyclones, hurricanes and typhoons: monstrous storms spinning around a vortex or a central calm eye.

We knew something was wrong. By day, although the sun shone above us, we were surrounded by dark clouds and lines of angry squalls. At night the stars twinkled merrily overhead but we were encircled by flashes of lightning and rumbles of thunder. The barometer began to fall and our mood followed the line of its descent. Although we didn't speak openly of it, dread settled on the boat like an unwelcome extra crew member. Dad renewed his efforts at finding weather reports on the radio and Mom, between taking hourly readings of the barometer and recording the atmospheric pressure in the log, began studying a tome entitled *Sailing in Heavy Weather*. The results of these activities did little to provide reassurance. When the barometer continued to drop, Mom packed the book away. I overheard her telling Dad that she couldn't read any more because it scared her too much. I went to look for myself. Within the book's pages I found pictures of tiny boats flattened and wrecked by enormous wind-strafed waves. With a thumping heart I read that in severe hurricanes, the exact wind speed couldn't be measured because all equipment was usually immediately destroyed. Heavy spray and driving rain blurred the boundary between air and water, causing zero visibility and making it impossible to breathe. Heaving-to, sea anchors and other survival strategies were generally ineffective in such conditions. One could expect the decks to be swept clean. The paragraph ended on a chilling note. It is best, I read, to avoid these storms by seeking shelter in a safe anchorage and not sailing in open water during hurricane season.

Dad's efforts at the radio produced even more unsettling results. In the evenings we gathered around while he searched the airwaves. Through an evil background hiss that sounded as if it were issuing from a giant cauldron in the depths of hell, and punctuated by nerve-racking staccato time bleeps, we occasionally caught fragments of a woman's voice. She sounded cold and stern, and as distant as if she were broadcasting from the moon. She seemed comfortable being the bearer of bad news and sometimes a certain smugness even crept into her tone, as if she were actually quite pleased that terrible storms were raging in the North Atlantic while she sat in the safety of her cosy broadcasting studio. 'Come out here,' I wanted to say to her, 'and see how you like it.'

Reports were transmitted hourly. Inevitably they began with a severe weather warning which the woman described in fine detail. Hearts in our mouths, we listened to her robotic recital of winds gusting to 90 knots and waves 20 metres high. She would then proceed to give the position of the gale.

'This severe weather warning,' she said, 'extends from –'

And each time without fail, as she gave the co-ordinates of the storm, her voice would be consumed by a barrage of furious hissing. We knew a deadly gale was raging somewhere. But where? Although with Dad still unable to take sights, we weren't quite sure where we were either. In frustration my father would turn off the radio and we'd troop outside to peer anxiously around at the stars twinkling overhead while thunder and lightning encircled us. Sometimes the moon shone through a hole in the sky above, its rays illuminating the dark backs of bedraggled, exhausted-looking seabirds that had started flying from the line of squalls to sleep perched on our stern davits.

My mother gave up on the barometer readings when they stabilised just below 1010 millibars, and took to counting down the miles to Grenada instead. Although we motored for several hours every day, using precious diesel, progress remained painfully slow. By 19 September, after a week at sea, 670 miles remained to Grenada. Three days later, working on dead reckoning – as my parents called it – there were still 600 miles to go. We'd made only 70 miles in three days. At this rate Grenada was still weeks away.

Day after day, the weather conditions remained the same; blue skies or stars above us and surrounding squalls with steely clouds so thick they looked like a wall. I found myself imagining that the only way through them was to find a key which would open a massive secret door. Slowly it became clear that we were in the eye of a tropical low-pressure wave, an embryonic hurricane, and like us, and at a similar speed, it was travelling in the direction of Grenada. As the weather system moved it would either pick up speed and develop into a fully fledged hurricane or – if we were lucky – it would run out of power and dissipate.

On the evening of our thirteenth day at sea, just before nightfall, the situation changed. Four days after we entered the low pressure system and began travelling in its eye, the storm overtook us. With our sails hanging slack, we watched black and purple anvil-shaped clouds approach. Until now they'd kept their distance, but spurred suddenly by unknown forces, they rose darkly from the ocean and raced to meet us. The light faded to indigo, irradiated by flashes of lightning that turned the sea a sudden luminous blue and caught our faces in startled flashbulb freezes. Over the water gusts of wind churned the sea from smooth grey glass to matt black and then white as it was whipped to foam. We took down the jib and were putting a final reef in the main when the wind slammed into us. The sea foamed and spume stung our faces. *Vingila*, sluggish and somnolent for the past week, leapt into action. Pushed over, she yawed and surged forward, her lee scuppers under water as she heeled, her rigging groaning. Dad took the helm from Mom and his white face was the last thing I saw as I retreated below with a quivering Pepe. The high winds lasted most of the night and fortunately our heavily reefed main held. The next day when the sun rose it was as if nothing had ever happened. The sky was blue, the dark clouds gone and we had a 15 knot trade wind from the north-east. That night a bedraggled seabird appeared from the sky to alight exhausted on our davits.

Our pleasure at meeting the north-east trade winds was short lived. They died shortly after they arrived and once again we were forced to use the motor and the dregs of our diesel. *Vingila* baked like a biscuit in the tropical sun. With no wind to cool us, and the sails down and unable to provide shade, there was no escaping from the blistering heat. We were, it seemed, still in the doldrums. Out on the deck the sun bored into the tops of our heads and glinted off the glassy sea, dazzling us and inducing headaches as we took turns at the helm, while down below the hot engine throbbed and roared in time to the surge of the swells. A miasma of diesel fumes exuded not only from *Vingila*'s exhaust which was placed directly outside the cockpit, but also from the panels of the engine room itself. It was difficult to decide if the smell was worse above decks or below. On our fourteenth day at sea, my father, who had obviously had enough and wanted to get to Grenada, motored for eight hours straight. At last, as the cool of darkness descended, he turned off the engine. Our ears reverberated with silence, broken only by the lapping of wavelets under the stern. Over supper we found ourselves shouting at one another as if we were hard of hearing. But at last Dad's noon sights were giving results, and they showed we were slowly nearing the Caribbean.

As the sun set the following evening, we spied the island of Tobago. Above our heads a mackerel sky bled pink, but on the horizon the hills of Tobago were black and overhung with sullen cumulonimbus. We welcomed the sight of land, but the island didn't welcome us. As citizens of apartheid South Africa we were forbidden to disembark on its shores and so we just sailed slowly past. That night its lighthouse kept us company until the morning when we left it on our beam. Two days later the lavender smudge of Grenada rose from the horizon and, after a day spent watching it enlarge with frustrating slowness, we anchored at last in Prickly Bay which was well protected, with clear, sun spangled water and a yacht club nestled among gardens of frangipani and hibiscus. We had been at sea for twenty days.

After a shower with astoundingly warm, fresh water, I sat on the club veranda watching the wind play in the palms and enjoying the feel of my salt-free skin while Mom and Dad ordered beers from the bar. A young woman holding a well-dressed toddler by the hand walked across the lawn and looked me over. She asked if I lived on a yacht. I nodded.

'Which boat is yours, then?'

Her hair was silky smooth and fell in a soft wave from her pink cheek. Her sandals were leather and she wore a well-cut dress. In spite of my recent shower I felt sticky again, aware of my salt bleached pigtails, my coarse bare feet and the peeling tip of my sunburned nose. I hesitated before pointing out *Vingila*. Our boat looked even more shabby than usual; her sails roughly folded, her hull streaked with rust and strings of drying fish hung above her decks like macabre prayer flags. At least she no longer had blue paint blotches. The woman and I contemplated *Vingila* for a moment in silence. Then she asked where we had sailed from.

'Brazil,' I said.

'That's awfully far, isn't it?'

'Yes, it is,' I admitted. I thought of the strange sea life we had seen. The muddy waters of the Amazon and the long squally days of the doldrums. I couldn't possibly explain to her just how far away Brazil was.

The toddler leaned forward to pick a crimson hibiscus flower from a bush while the woman sighed, lightly, in a contented sort of way.

'Tell me, how was your trip?' she asked.

'Okay, I suppose, but we were becalmed a lot and I worried about hurricanes.'

'Oh yes, hurricanes,' she said, gesturing toward a jumble of upended tree roots spoiling the otherwise ordered garden. 'We've had a few. In fact a little one came through just last week and tore up those trees.'

Part 3

CARIBBEAN

The Caribbean
British Virgin Islands
Anguilla
Puerto Rico
St Martin
Barbuda
Antigua
St Croix   St Kitts
Monserratt
Gaudeloupe   Marie Galante
Dominica
Martinique
St Lucia
Barbados
St Vincent & the Grenadines
Mapion Is.
Grenada

10

CARIBBEAN

Robert and I were struck by pirate fever in the Caribbean. Mom tore rags into strips for our bandanas, Robert used his machete from Brazil as a cutlass and the dinghy became our galleon. We attacked a nearby yacht owned by a photographer who, we understood, took pictures primarily of nude women. I'd heard Dad telling Mom that he had married one of his models. When we boarded we found the woman sitting naked on the deck, working at a sewing machine and fixing sails. She had wide blue eyes and freckles sprinkled over her whole body. After admiring her pretty curly pubic hair and deciding that I wanted some just like it when I grew up, I demanded loot. She gave a good performance of being frightened, perhaps because she'd noticed my brother's machete was real, and let out a few gratifying screams before saying that if everybody put down their knives, she'd give us juice and sticky buns, which she did. I liked being a pirate.

In Saint George, the capital of Grenada, my mother said she expected old pirate ships to sail into the harbour at any time. Luckily we were protected by the battlements and cannons scattered among the surrounding hills. Although *Vingila* was anchored in Prickly Bay we often travelled to Saint George by taxi to shop at the fresh vegetable market and walk about the cobbled streets of the old town. Before returning to the boat we got into the habit of stopping at an old bar with dark wooden floors and a view over the bay. Mom and Dad drank rum punches and Robert and I were allowed Bentleys, a mix of fresh lime and Angostura bitters. The barman dipped the rims of our glasses in sugar and garnished the cocktails with green leaves and sticky maraschino cherries. My brother said Bentleys were naff, but drink in hand, I felt grown up and sophisticated and it was one of the few times I stopped being a pirate.

The post office was in Saint George and when Mom went to check for mail, the woman at the counter handed over a stack of blue aerogrammes. Nana had written weekly, with news of her miniature pinschers, my young cousins who were growing up fast, and updates from the church where she was an usher. As always, she expressed concern for our safety and hoped my mother was taking care of Robert's and my spiritual education as well as our regular schooling. She longed to see us again. A letter from Lynnath asked for a detailed itinerary of our cruise through the Caribbean so that she could book her plane ticket.

'This Lynnath woman really sounds serious,' said Mom. 'What will we do if she comes?'

Dad shrugged. 'It probably won't happen.'

'What shall I tell her? We don't have an itinerary.'

'Just say we're not sure of our plans. We'll let her know as we go along.'

'My mother wants to visit too,' Mom said, casting a sideways glance at Dad to gauge his reaction. My father didn't respond.

'Do you think we can invite her over?'

'Your mother? On the yacht?'

'We won't be making any ocean passages, just a few day sails. She's desperate to see the kids again. You know how much she loves them.'

Dad sighed. 'I'll think about it.'

I liked Grenada. After the filthy cities of Brazil, the quiet island, planted with nutmeg, sugar cane and cloves, and overgrown with hibiscus and bougainvillea, was a relief. Part of the British Commonwealth, it had been independent since 1974 and was ruled by an eccentric despot, Sir Gairy, who was obsessed with flying saucers and the occult. Nevertheless, in spite of their crazy leader, the local dogs had fur and the people were relaxed and friendly, literacy rates were high and the supermarkets were well stocked. It was altogether a lovely place that looked nothing like the hotbed of repression and suffering the United States claimed it was when they invaded four years later.

For most of the southern Caribbean, Robert and I remained pirates. We lost interest somewhere around the Antilles when I found Jesus and my brother committed his life to spearfishing, but until that time – when I wasn't sipping cocktails – pirates were all we could think or talk about. Robert was Blackheart and I was Ursula, Terror of the Seas, although when the situation called for it, we sometimes represented entire crews of bloodthirsty buccaneers. We duelled with each other, and we invaded islands and other boats. We buried treasure on tiny islets and drew up maps with crosses detailing its position. We added Jolly Rogers and burned the paper's edges to make our maps look more authentic. In Grenada we turned eleven and playing pirates was the culmination of a series of generally violent and bloodthirsty games we had begun as pre-schoolers in Benoni: Cops and Robbers, Cowboys and Indians, and War. In those games too, players were armed with guns or knives and people got to choose if they wanted to be a goody or a baddy. I liked being a baddy because it was more fun although we all got to die horrible, protracted deaths. Dying was an art we practised – throwing ourselves to the ground, clasping our chests, or bellies, and moaning, writhing and gasping. Sometimes we rose up to die again, depending on how many children were in the game. In the Caribbean, although we played alone, our imaginations swelled our ranks to hordes of salty sea dogs and we possessed a boat and real knives and often had ancient cannons or deserted islets to ourselves.

In Grenada the days melted together in a peaceful haze, mellowed in my father's case by bottles of inexpensive rum. After our difficult sea passage we needed rest and a month passed before we felt ready enough to move on. We looked forward to a Caribbean cruise. Northwards of Grenada, a string of islands stretched all the way to Florida like stepping stones, each one separated by no more than a single day of sailing. We need never be out of sight of land again, or doubt our position. We could choose our weather and wait out unfavourable winds. Apart from the rare hurricane, from which we could hide, the weather would be mild and the sea calm. We expected sailing nirvana. As did the multitude of other yachts jostling with us for space in the anchorages. Some of them – a handful of long-term cruisers – we'd met before, but there were also bigger, smarter yachts on jaunts from America and Europe, and haughty racing boats en route to other places, and monstrous gin palaces: bloated motor boats with on-deck jacuzzis, jet-skis and helicopter landing pads. The most common craft were charter yachts, ranging from elegant fully crewed luxury vessels to Sunsail bare boats with all the soul of a rental mobile home. Interchangeably identical, with beige topsides and a maroon stripe wrapped around their hulls like a ribbon, they dribbled, in a seemingly endless stream, from an extensive, parkade-like marina in St Lucia. We liked to look down on these boats and their crew, calling them chocolate boxes and despising the holiday makers, usually American, British or German, who rented the boats for a week and followed a set programme from which few dared deviate. Their schedule was most apparent on Thursday nights when multiple barbecues were simultaneously fired up in the baskets suspended from the boats' rear ends.

Because the boats were leased without a skipper or crew, they were often sailed by people with very little experience or skill, and they collided frequently with other yachts, dragged anchor, and failed to keep a polite distance. They could sometimes be downright dangerous. But having sailors more bumbling than ourselves to sneer at was a change.

We would spend five months in the Caribbean and visit more than twenty islands: Grenada and the Grenadines, the Windward and Leeward Islands, the Greater and Lesser Antilles, the US and the British Virgins, but when I think back I can't remember making a single significant connection with a local person. *Vingila*'s visitors' book, full of the names of Brazilians and people from the Pacific, contains only a single entry from a Dominican islander by the name of Martin Romain, and I can't even remember who he was. Caribbean society, it became apparent, was sharply divided between tourists and locals. This was most apparent on Union Island, where an opulent hotel was fenced off from the local shacks. When we tried to go for a walk beyond its barricades, a group of local people followed us, hissing, yelling 'honkey' and throwing stones. Even within the tourist group there were divisions, particularly among the yachting community. We sailed and socialised with the cruising clan. The racers wouldn't have us and we, in turn, would have nothing to do with the chocolate boxes.

After a month in Grenada we made our way through the Grenadines north towards St Vincent, stopping briefly at Tobago Cays, a cluster of uninhabited coral islands. Arriving late in the morning at the cays we dropped anchor outside the anchorage to dive and have lunch. A few minutes later we were joined by a pair of chocolate boxes who anchored on either side of us and spent the next hour, while we ate, anxiously consulting their sailing directions. Then a man on the closer yacht leaned over and snapped his fingers as if my father was a waiter in a restaurant.

'You there,' he said, fanning himself with the folded sailing directions. He had a smear of zinc cream across his nose and wore a Hawaiian shirt over a pair of cotton pyjama pants. His arms were bright red and shiny and a pair of pink sunburned feet stuck out beneath the hem of his trouser legs. He was following another charter boat schedule, one as predictable as the set meal plans. Day one – white skin and bare chest; day two – blistered red flesh and long loose pyjamas. Sometimes by day six a few of the tougher skinned sailors would be tanned and back in bikinis and Bermuda shorts in time for the Thursday night barbecue.

'Is this the anchorage?' the zinc-creamed man called over to us.

Dad shook his head. 'No, it's not,' he said.

'What do you mean, it's not the anchorage?' The man consulted his sailing directions again. I wondered if – in addition to instructions for supper that evening – they included advice on treating sunburn. His face took on a crafty look as if we were keeping something from him. 'If it's not the anchorage, then why are you anchored here?'

Dad didn't have to raise his voice to converse because they were so close we could have handed them a sandwich if we'd wanted to.

'The anchorage,' said Dad, 'is through that passage.'

And he pointed the way to a well-marked entrance.

Giving us resentful looks, as if we'd deliberately mislead them, they raised their moorings and left.

'Idiots,' Dad said.

When Robert and I learned the chocolate boxes, unlike regular yachties, had money to spare we hated them even more. Then we learned some of that money could be ours. In Tobago Cays my brother speared a crayfish almost as long as he was. Mom refused to have the creature aboard. It was too big, she said, she couldn't be expected to cook a thing like that, we simply didn't have the pots. So after a photograph with his prize, Robert took the creature to the chocolate boxes. The people on the first boat were unwilling to deviate from their prescribed meal plan and told him as much, but the next group proved more adventurous and paid Robert fifteen US dollars – an unimaginable sum – for the biggest crayfish I ever saw. Robert quickly established a new source of income by selling fish and crayfish regularly to the charter yachts. Then our friends Vincent and the guys on *Dou-Dou Diop* arrived from Brazil and began extracting money from the chocolate boxes too. They sold the tourists seashells and trinkets they carved from bones and turtle shell. Sometimes they outright begged. At night, when they weren't swimming into the marine reserves to spear fish, they stole the charter boats' anchors which they later sold second-hand to other yachties. They were always kind enough not to set the boats adrift and, after releasing the shackles, tied the denuded chains to clumps of coral or rocks.

'It is most important,' Vincent explained, 'to be the first boat to leave the anchorage in the morning.'

Nadine had left him, temporarily, for another man, and Vincent had met a pretty young Swedish girl with magnificent breasts, a good all-over tan and a penchant for brushing her teeth frequently. Although they seemed happy together the relationship was doomed to fail. For a start, Vincent didn't even own a toothbrush.

From island to island we sailed together with a loose group of fellow yachties, meeting randomly in different anchorages as we made our way north. Like Vincent and Roland, Dad preferred wilder places, where the snorkelling and spearfishing were better. Our friend Tommy Tucker on *Spectrum* preferred history to nature. I had first seen Tommy's wife Maggie when Urbine pointed her out to me way back in Durban, over a year earlier when we were still anchored out on the moorings and thought the international sailors were remote god-like beings.

'Have you seen that woman's. . . ?' Urbine said to me with a smirk, his voice drifting off as he cupped his hands a considerable distance from his chest, weighing them up and down as if he were lifting hefty fruit.

Maggie Tucker's back was bowed by the weight of breasts so great that over the years her bra straps had cut chasms into the flesh of her narrow shoulders. She was English, fair skinned and approaching sixty. She had the profile of a chicken, with a beaky nose, narrow lips and an almost completely absent chin. The ten years she had spent in Australia had failed to acclimatise her to tropical weather and she was always hot and flushed, and fanning her great glowing bosom. 'Dear, dear, dear ...' she would say, flapping her hand ineffectually above her impressive cleavage. She was an unconvincing circumnavigator. Her husband, a retired major in the British army, she called Good God Tucker, although his name was Harold, or something like it. He always introduced himself as Tommy. He had a speech impediment and was unable to pronounce the consonant 'f', substituting it instead with 'th'. Pink wattles hung from his chin and quivered when he became indignant, which was usually whenever he talked or thought about 'the Thrench' whom he detested. The Tuckers' two sons had been raised in Australia, purging them of all English traits. Jock – tall, rangy and sunburned – had big gnarly hands on the ends of his skinny wrists and he liked grabbing Robert's and my ankles in a single paw and sweeping us up to dangle head down over the side of *Spectrum*. We never got to meet Stretch, he had stayed in Australia, but we were told he was even taller, thinner and rangier than Jock, whose real name – by the way – was Andrew.

Tommy, outwardly unmoved by his wife's generously proportioned figure, appeared driven by two forces in life; a dislike of all things French and an appreciation for young women in bikinis. Dad liked young women in bikinis too, he even invited one to live aboard with us in Salvador, but she didn't last long. Dad thought Bev and her selection of swimwear were great and said she could stay as long as she wanted, but Mom, who'd begun banging pots around in the galley a lot, said she didn't see the point of cooking food for someone who went and vomited it all up in the toilet just to stay thin. That, according to my mother, was a waste. Less than a week after arriving on *Vingila*, Bev declared that she couldn't ever be happy with us because our boat 'had an atmosphere' and announced her intention to move to *Spectrum*, where she had found Tommy and Jock to be very welcoming and friendly. She was right, they were friendly and if she'd asked around the yacht club she would have soon heard just how friendly the two men could be. Yolanda, who also wore a bikini, might have told her that Tommy was so friendly he'd offered her rowing lessons which included an unexpected rubdown of her bare legs while she received instruction on her strokes.

In Grenada, when we met up with *Spectrum* again, Bev was gone but the tensions she'd left in her wake lay just beneath the surface. We took care to avoid mentioning her name.

'I think Jock got lucky,' Dad said to Mom, 'but not without some stiff competition from the old man.'

There is a long history of animosity between the French and the English in the Caribbean; islands of each nation lie side by side and are littered with forts, emplacements and cannons. The skipper and first mate of *Spectrum* took us to inspect them.

'British, of course,' Tommy Tucker would say, pulling himself up with military pride if the rusty old armaments had the correct pedigree. If not, wattles aquiver and lips pursed in distaste, he would mutter, 'Bloody Thrench ...' To which Maggie, sitting on a nearby cannon and fanning her glowing bosom, would reply with a distracted 'Good God, Tucker.'

'This place is bloody unbelievable,' Tommy greeted us in Martinique, my namesake island. 'We've had the damnednest time with the bloody crowd at the *poste restante*. You wouldn't believe it. Typical ruddy

Thrench.'

They had tried to collect a letter addressed to 'Tommy, Maggie and Jock Tucker, Yacht *Spectrum*' and the woman at the counter had refused to give it to them because, according to their passports, their names were Margaret, Harold and Andrew. She finally agreed to hand over the letter if they could provide the passport of 'Yacht *Spectrum*', confirming everything Tommy believed about the French and providing fodder for endless wattle quivering diatribes.

Nana flew to visit us in Martinique, arriving from Johannesburg via Rio in a wash and wear polyester pantsuit she had bought specially for the flight. Chummy, my grandfather, stayed at home to look after the dogs. Anyway, he said, hell would freeze over before he got on a boat or a plane. My grandmother's plane was delayed for a day in Brazil, so Nana, in the same pantsuit – which held up well – took a trip to see the giant statue of Jesus with his arms outstretched and his back turned on the masses of poor people. She arrived in Martinique bearing a speargun for Robert and looking very excited and fresh, except for the back of her head, where her hair-sprayed curls had been squashed flat from sitting so long in the aeroplane. She hadn't changed since I'd last seen her in Alberton. She still had the same thick stumpy legs, crinkled smiling eyes and thin, disapproving lips.

Two days later she was lying face-down at the stern of our boat, crying and hugging a bollard with both arms, while I stroked her back and told her everything would be all right. Mom and Dad had decided to race *Vingila* against *Spectrum* to the island of Dominica. Sailing into the lee of the island, the wind funnelled through gaps between the mountains and pushed-up whitecaps, throwing our yacht over so far that her scuppers were submerged and water coursed along the decks. Ignoring Nana's sobs, Mom and Dad cheered and whooped when *Vingila* made ten knots. My father was pushing the boat hard in a way I'd never seen before. Sheets groaning and throwing spray in the air, *Vingila* juddered over the waves like a bus over a dirt road.

Nana wept and prayed to God. Her face turned scarlet and the sea spray dissolved her laquered helmet of curls into a sticky mass. I patted her back and spoke soothing, meaningless words of comfort. She refused to open her eyes or lift her head. She thought we were going to die. I squeezed her arm and told her we probably wouldn't.

My father didn't like my grandmother much; he thought she gave her husband too much lip. One thing he couldn't stand, Dad said, was a woman who gave a man lip. At least his own wife knew how to toe the line. Chummy needed to put his foot down and show Nana who was boss. As *Vingila* yawed over again and my grandmother let out a fresh sob, I saw Dad at the helm glance over his shoulder at the prone form clinging to a bollard, before he turned the wheel further into the wind, forcing the boat to heel over even more. It looked to me as if my father was putting his foot down and showing his mother-in-law who was boss. Making her toe the line.

Afterwards, once her holiday was over and she was safely back in Alberton with Chummy, Nana contacted a newspaper journalist who wrote a dramatic story about our dangerous trip around the world and the perils we faced on a daily basis. It included a big photograph of my Nana, with my young cousin on her lap, staring unsmilingly at the camera and looking very solemn and brave. She described big waves, strong winds, a boat out of control and how Pepe had nearly fallen overboard and drowned. She left out the part about fighting with my father afterwards.

Nana's trip to the Caribbean wasn't all bad. She loved the village of St Pierre which had once been the capital of Martinique. She thought it interesting that in 1902 when steam began issuing from the top of Mount Pele, a suspiciously cone-shaped mountain looming above the town, the local authorities confidently assured the residents there was nothing to be concerned about. After a week of grumbled warnings,

Mount Pele blew its top, burying the town in hot lava, cinders and ash, and killing all of its thirty thousand inhabitants except one. Nana liked the museum full of melted scissors and cutlery, and thought it fascinating that the single survivor of the devastation was a prisoner held in solitary confinement. He'd been locked in a tiny free-standing cell with walls as thick as a clay oven. She was sure there was a moral somewhere in the story, but was uncertain just what it might be. The highlight of her visit to the Caribbean, however, was an encounter with Tommy Tucker's naked buttocks in Dominica.

Dominica is more widely known for its numerous geothermal attractions; it bubbles and seethes with vents, springs and erupting mud pots. Its most spectacular feature is a boiling lake.

'Forget it,' Dad said. 'We're not going to the boiling lake, it's out of the question. They charge entrance fees. And we'd have to hire a car or take a taxi to get you lot there. I don't have the money for that.'

So instead of the boiling lake, we made do with a lukewarm pool, which was free and within walking distance. A handful of young boys, eager to earn a tip, led us and the Tuckers up the hill. When we reached the pool they stripped off their shorts and T-shirts and plunged in.

'Bloody warm weather, isn't it?' Tommy Tucker wiped his forehead with the back of a hand. He sat on a rock beside me, watching the boys in the water. The rest of our group had elected to rest above the pool, in a patch of shade.

'Hold this a minute, won't you?' Tommy said, handing me his shirt, and a few seconds later not only his khaki shorts but an enormous, baggy pair of Y-front underpants as well. Naked, he sat down to take off his socks.

'Tell me again . . .' Nana asked me repeatedly in helpless fascination for the rest of her holiday whenever we were alone. 'Tell me again how his bum looked.'

I never tired of telling her. 'It was soft and floppy,' I'd say, pausing for dramatic effect, 'and it looked like an octopus, slithering into the cracks of the rock.'

Nana had only seen Tommy's buttocks from the slope above the pool when Maggie, who'd been sitting in the shade trying to cool off, had suddenly blanched and then flushed again, her hand frozen in mid-flap above her bosom. Below in the water the children screamed for joy as Tommy, with his head extended, crawled into several inches of tepid mud. The water, the depth of which he had misjudged, was insufficient for full submersion and left the surface of his milk-white body exposed to the air and our interested stares. A withered turtle neck with a bald head on it, a slump shouldered back and – like an island separated from the mainland – a pair of pale, disembodied buttocks.

'Good God Tucker,' Maggie said, jolting up from her place in the shade and craning her neck over the edge for a better view. 'I don't believe it. He's in the ruddy nuddy!'

My grandmother's holiday passed quickly in a blur of day sails, nudist encounters, geothermal attractions and family turmoil. Near the end of her stay, Nana and my father reached a sort of truce and for a treat she took us out to a restaurant where we tasted butternut soup for the first time and callaloo – a slimy type of spinach. We sailed her back to Martinique two days before Christmas. The night before her flight home to Chummy, she bought a tiny leg of lamb which Mom cooked until it was grey through to the bone. Nana told us she could have got a whole sheep in South Africa for the same price. The following day, in spite of my tears, she got on a plane and flew away.

'Jesus,' said Jeff, pausing to take a sip of tea from his mug, 'is with us right now, sitting at this very table.'

A thrill coursed through my body. 'Really?' I said.

'Yes, really. He said so in the Bible: "Whenever two or three people are gathered together in my name, there am I in the midst of them." Can you feel his presence?'

At his words I felt a distinct tingle in my limbs, like a trickle of cold water, and I knew right away that it was Jesus, making his presence felt.

I nodded. 'Yes, yes, I can.' For some reason I found myself whispering.

Jeff smiled. He knew a lot about the Bible; he spent several hours every day reading it and could recite entire passages by heart. He wanted to know even more, however, and he and his wife Sue and her two grown daughters were en route in their trimaran from South Africa to America to enrol in Bible College. The purpose of their entire voyage, Jeff said, was to know the Lord better and to understand the wisdom of His ways. I wondered what the purpose of our trip was.

Above the rim of his mug, Jeff's eyes held an air of sweetly sad compassion. Sue's indistinguishable daughters sat pallidly next to us, strumming guitars and singing what they called contemporary religious songs in low, muted voices.

'Jesus wants to come into your life, Nicky,' Jeff said. 'Are you ready to accept him?'

After sailing northwards for some months we were in the Virgin Islands and I knew I needed Jesus – or something – in my life. I was suffering the first twinges of nascent adolescence, compounded by an acute culture shock which had been precipitated by Nana's visit. After a stable childhood in Benoni where alcohol was usually consumed discreetly, if not surreptitiously, and people always kept their clothes on in public, my world had changed. Some of the changes had happened so gradually that, with the flexibility of childhood, I had scarcely noticed them until Nana's arrival. My grandmother, a Calvinist, was an usher in the church and a member of the Alberton Methodist Women's Auxiliary Group. She was on first name terms with the minister and made stacks of pancakes at the church fête each year. She hated drinking and grudgingly allowed my grandfather two small shots of whisky every

Friday evening, although even that annoyed her. In the Caribbean she was horrified at my parents' behaviour. In South Africa only low-life coloureds smoked marijuana – or *dagga* as she called it – and anyone who did should be thrown in jail to rot, she said. Although she was too scared to say anything directly to my father, Nana held Dad responsible for our family's state of moral decay. When she and I were alone together she listed the sins my parents and their friends were committing. Failure to observe the Sabbath, immodesty, theft, fornication and, although she couldn't be sure, adultery too she suspected.

'The only thing for you to do, my girl,' she would say, 'is to pray to God and ask Him to make your parents stop all this nonsense and come home.'

My growing feelings of disapproval and despair climaxed soon after her departure when we sailed on *Dou-Dou Diop* to visit a remote anchorage for the day. All the women, including my mother, went bare-breasted, marijuana smoke filled the air and Roland speared a turtle and then cut its windpipe, leaving it to rasp for breath in the dinghy as it died slowly over the course of the afternoon. The final result of such protracted reptilian suffering was a single tough steak and a shell which after a quick scrape clean was sold to a passing chocolate box. That evening, overwhelmed by the debauchery and cruelty I had witnessed, I succumbed to a flood of tears and tried to swim into the bay to drown myself. Robert and my mother followed in the dinghy. She told me I was being silly and my brother told me to stop acting like a baby.

My friend Belinda also needed Jesus. Since our first days in Cape Town, when she had kissed Gary on *Scud* while the rest of us looked on, she'd grown into a sensible, slightly spotty fifteen-year-old. Her mother – the wild-haired Grace and skipper of *Antoinette* – was still in pursuit of the girls' father – the ex-husband who sailed forever out of reach on his yacht *Odette*. Grace had failed to capture her husband or resolve her chronic crew trouble. We'd seen *Antoinette* briefly in Fernando de

Noronha but they had been pushing for Grenada with a sulky crew member who insisted they get to the Caribbean so he could leave the boat. As we got to know the family better, it became apparent that Belinda and Kim's happiness depended almost entirely on Grace's fluctuating relationships with the series of young men who joined – and then left – the yacht. In Grenada, we thought the family might achieve some level of stability; their new crew member seemed reasonable, and initially the availability of cheap rum soothed Grace's temper. Even her hair seemed more settled. But as we sailed north through the Grenadines toward the Antilles and Virgin Islands, relationships aboard *Antoinette* began to deteriorate. As Grace's fondness for rum grew, so did her affection for the young man. When her feelings were not returned, she increasingly sought solace in rum and Belinda was forced to look after not only her younger sister Kim, but often her mother as well.

'Why don't you invite your friend Belinda to visit us sometime?' Jeff asked, putting down his empty mug. 'Jesus is waiting here for her too, you know.'

His stepdaughters stopped their strumming for a moment to smile gently and nod in agreement.

A few days later, over a cup of tea, Belinda and I accepted Jesus into our lives and we were reborn on the trimaran. To celebrate, Jeff invited us to share our rapture at the local church by attending an evening service that night. Our parents agreed to let us go. The church and surrounding houses were a little ramshackle but the choir in purple satin robes was more impressive than anything I'd seen at the Alberton Methodist church or Sunday school. I noticed that everybody except us was black. Ouma, my dad's mother, wouldn't have approved. Her Christianity was based in the secure knowledge that when she died she was going straight to the whites-only section of heaven. When the Caribbean choir sang, the congregation stood up, moaning and swaying their hips. They stamped their feet and clapped and said Amen a lot.

Then the preacher, a sweaty man with unstable eyeballs, stood up and told us we were all going straight to hell, where we would burn in eternal damnation. That wasn't fair, I thought. I could make a whole list of people who should burn in hell before me. And Jeff had told me I was saved. The preacher said that those who sat so smug and safe, believing they were saved, knew nothing. We were wicked. Wicked and evil and God could see right through us, into our black evil little hearts. There was no hope for us but for the love of Jesus. He went on. I started to believe that most of us were such sinners, not even the love of Jesus was going to help. He was so insulting to his audience I expected them to walk out, but the congregation seemed to agree with him, nodding their heads and murmuring words of encouragement and affirmation.

'Amen,' they said. 'Hallelujah!'

After a while I stopped listening to the preacher's words and watched the fountains of spit spray from his lips. In the light, the droplets became little shooting stars, before falling downward to disappear into the hair of the assembled. The preacher stopped talking only to swab his brow occasionally with a white cloth. After he had exhausted himself listing our moral transgressions and the punishments we were going to suffer for them, he sank into a worn red velvet chair, to a chorus of fervent Amens and hallelujahs. In the silence that followed Jeff stood up and asked if his daughters could sing a song. Pale and devoid of make-up they took to the stage with their guitars and murmured their way through 'Killing Me Softly With His Love', which I'd never considered a religious song. I had always thought it was about sex. The congregation seemed equally confused. After that the choir took over again for a few more rounds and then we all went home. On the way back Jeff looked uneasy and refused to meet our eyes at first. Then he sighed and explained to Belinda and me that Jesus really was very kind and very loving and infinitely forgiving and if we believed in Him we really were saved and we shouldn't worry too much about burning in hell.

For the time that I remained a Christian I tried to get Robert to see that our family needed saving from their sins, but he refused to be drawn in. He had found his own religion: spearfishing, which he worshipped daily at the great altar of the blue ocean with offerings of bloody piscean sacrifices, and he told me he had no wish to waste his time with Jesus.

At almost every poste restante in the Caribbean we found a letter from Lynnath Beckley. She wrote that she had quit her job in Port Elizabeth where she had been working as a junior lecturer in the marine biology department and after sailing to Uruguay on a race, she would be free to join us and sail the world for as long as her money lasted. In the letter she sent to St Thomas, in the American Virgin Islands, she mentioned that by following our progress through the Caribbean via my mother's letters, she estimated that *Vingila* would be in Puerto Rico in early March and that she had booked her plane ticket and would meet us there. At first Dad wasn't sure about taking on crew. He said we had become self-sufficient and other people just seemed to cause complications and tension. However Lynnath appeared so determined to join us, that we felt it would be rude not to welcome her aboard and we gradually grew to accept the fact that we would have a new crew member.

'It might not be that bad,' Dad said, 'to have another pair of hands on deck, someone to help with the night watches.'

'Yes,' said Mom, 'and maybe she could teach you some marine biology, Nicky. Remember how you loved that plankton?'

I just hoped Lynnath wasn't a vomiter like Bev because I knew how Mom felt about that.

Near the end of February, after cruising slowly north through the Caribbean islands, we anchored off the coast of Puerto Rico near the town of Fajardo, at Isleta Marina, a scrap of sand dominated by the towering stalk of a condominium. On the ground floor of the skyscraper there were warm showers, a laundromat and a cramped convenience store which was usually closed. On the rare occasions I found it open, it was presided over by an unfriendly old woman who refused to sell me more than a single loaf of bread at a time, forcing me to hang about the entrance and beg strangers to buy another for me. Outside, on the rim of land not consumed by condominium, there was a patch of unnaturally green lawn and a swimming pool which was usually deserted. On the weekends, however, it filled up with the fattest children I'd ever seen. They lolled in the tepid water like pygmy hippos, emerging only to make trips to the convenience store for cans of pop, packets of chips and endless ice cream cones.

While we waited for Lynnath to arrive, Dad had time on his hands to watch Robert and me more closely. He said he'd noticed that we had been slacking off. He set us to work sanding the grab rails and as we scraped away at the blistered varnish, he settled in the shade of the cockpit with a glass of rum and told us what was wrong with us. We were lazy, for a start. Some of us spent all day with their noses in a book. We gave him lip. Anything we did, he always had to come and do over. In that way we were like kaffirs – worse than kaffirs come to think about it – because kaffirs were cheaper to feed. He said there was work to be done on the boat and no excuse for people to lie around reading books. Any time one of us felt the urge to read they just had to tell him and he would find that person something useful to do. Another thing wrong with us, he said, was that some of us thought we were much smarter than other people. We might be clever, he said, but we weren't very bright. Our biggest problem was, we didn't know how to think.

On the day that Lynnath was expected to arrive, he and Mom went to the airport in San Juan to look for her but she wasn't there. They left Robert and me on the boat with no way of getting ashore. We were given a list of chores to complete; sand and paint the gas bottle; chip the port scupper; lift and clean the duck boards in the cockpit. When Dad returned – without Lynnath – he found the work we'd done in his absence to be lacking and unsatisfactory. There were some grounds for his dissatisfaction. Shortly after their departure I had sunk into a book and emerged hours later, to race through my tasks and it showed in the results. But something about Puerto Rico or Lynnath's imminent arrival irked my father, inducing rages and strings of abuse to pour from his mouth. I put my head down and took it. I was used to his insults, I'd been hearing them on and off since Durban and they'd lost the power to hurt me. Robert and I had learned to endure them in the same way we endured beating into a headwind, or other bad weather, as something that would pass. The next day my parents went to the airport and again returned without Lynnath. This time my father brought a cane home with him. It was as long as his arm and finger-thin, with knobs marking each bamboo joint. He picked it up and slashed the air. Let me introduce you two to the Whistler, he said. He tucked it into the saloon curtains. Where I can reach it quickly, he told us. And over the following weeks, months and years, Robert and I grew to know the Whistler very well.

Dad checked the date on Lynnath's letter again.

'We'll give her another week,' he said, 'then it's her tough luck.'

The next time my parents went to San Juan Mom persuaded Dad to take us with them. And so Robert and I got our first taste of America. On the mainland of Puerto Rico we wandered through supermarkets like alien visitors from another planet, our mouths agape at the aisles of glass fronted deep freezers. I had never seen anything like it. In South Africa I'd first tasted fruit yoghurt in a plastic cup when I was about eight years old. I can still remember the shop where it was on promotion and the lady explaining to my mother that yoghurt was a kind of sour milk, but you could eat it. With time, it became an exciting addition to our diet of meat, rice and potatoes. We bought no other processed food, unless you counted cheese. On the boat we ate fish, rice and vegetables from the local markets and I'd never seen a frozen TV dinner before, but in Puerto Rico there seemed to be little else. Robert and I pressed our faces to the cold glass doors, reading the labels aloud. Roast turkey with gravy and candied yams, meat loaf and mashed potatoes, crumbed steak burgers. Overwhelmed by the cornucopia of delights before us we approached a sales assistant and stated our hearts' desire (or at least the only one we felt we could afford). We wanted Marmite. They had never heard of it. We were led up and down vast aisles lined with jars of peanut butter and jars of grape jelly and jars where somehow the peanut butter and grape jelly had been miraculously packed together in great stripy swirls. But no Marmite and no real bread either, only packets of stuff called Wonderbread, a fluffy white substance which was difficult to stomach after our months on the French islands eating crispy baguettes and *pain de campagne*. Away from the American supermarkets, however, there was a Latin flavour to Puerto Rico. People spoke Spanish, and there were old forts and bald scabby dogs that reminded me of Brazil. Along the road to San Juan, in anticipation of Easter, people sold live chicks dyed garish shades of green, orange and pink. My mother bought a dead fowl from a woman who was selling them from her garage. Mom boiled the bird for most of the afternoon and although the meat tasted good, it was so tough that we found it almost impossible to chew or swallow.

The next day while Robert and I were at work scraping the cockpit lockers and giving them a new coat of varnish a Zodiac buzzed across the channel separating Isleta Marina from Fajardo; in the bow sat a familiar boyish figure.

'Well, look what the cat dragged in,' Dad said, looking up from the cockpit where he was sitting. 'A new brother for Robert.'

But when the Zodiac with Lynnath pulled up alongside, he took her bag, turned his smile the right way up to welcome her aboard and showed her the bunk in my cabin where she would be sleeping.

A few coconut palms grew on Isleta Marina, but between the well-stocked and plentiful vending machines and the convenience store nobody collected the coconuts.

'These people have food growing right under their noses,' said Dad, 'and they're too fat and lazy to collect it.'

He sent my brother up the trees to pick all the coconuts he could and we filled several sacks with nuts and stashed them away in the anchor locker. Then we turned our attention to the amenities on offer. My mother, who had been washing our clothes by hand for months, a chore that involved fetching jerry cans of water in the dinghy, was given money by my father and told to enjoy the laundromat. Each warm shower I took was such a pleasant and unusual event that I recorded it in detail in my diary. Then Lynnath and my mother discovered a beauty salon across the channel in Fajardo that gave haircuts for three dollars. Lynnath, boyish to begin with, received an Elvis Presley hairdo. After a disastrous haircut in Dominica which made my mother cry, I'd been nominated official ship's hairdresser, and after first practising on my brother, had been giving my mother what I thought were quite nice haircuts. With my mother now having found a new hairdresser, I turned my attention to the dog. I created increasingly elaborate poodle cuts, with a close-trimmed snout and pom-poms wherever I could make them, and then gave my brother a page boy like the one Trish had once worn. My father received the same haircut he'd been getting for the previous twenty years. Only my hair stayed uncut; waist length and worn in a pair of plaits that started at my ears.

Clean, groomed and having stockpiled a substantial stash of coconuts, we had no further need to linger at Isleta Marina and so, five months after first arriving in Grenada from Brazil, we raised anchor and set sail for Panama, leaving the Caribbean behind us.

11

PANAMA

During the years that we sailed I sporadically kept journals, my style and handwriting changing as I grew from a nine-year-old girl to a teenager of sixteen. My writing tools matured with me. In crayon, pencil, ballpoint and later, fountain pens with frivolous coloured ink, I described the islands we visited, my mother's experiments with Chinese cooking, and my first adolescent encounters with boys. The latter I encrypted, using an elaborate symbolic code that I quickly forgot how to decipher. In the cramped confines of a yacht, privacy is in short supply and I kept my diaries wrapped in plastic and hidden in the secret space beneath my bunk. Later, when I left *Vingila* so suddenly, I didn't pack them. My papers were discovered in due course and read aloud by my family to much mirth, not all of it kind. Then my journals, stripped of their protective plastic covers, were misplaced or simply disintegrated in the wet sea air. Only a few, scattered pages remain.

I salvaged a record of our voyage across the Caribbean Sea towards Panama. Some time in March 1979, about eighteen months after *Vingila*'s launching in Durban, I picked up a pencil and wrote in careful round letters: 'I feel as if I am living in a blue sphere. Same thing. Sailing at four knots. Doing school and eating coconuts.' We were midway to Panama and Robert and I had recommenced our school work after a break in Puerto Rico. The weather was wonderful. We had a steady wind, the sea and sky were clear and our chain locker was full to the brim with coconuts.

Lynnath opened the nuts by cracking them with the blunt side of a machete, a task that had previously been my father's. She had quickly found a place in the family. She wore cut-off denim shorts and liked dogs. She didn't own a bikini but even if she had, I don't think it would have upset my mother very much. She caught and cleaned fish, and was good with the helm and sails. Unlike Bev, our bikini girl, Lynnath ate everything and kept it down, and she never seemed to notice Dad's nudity. Robert and I liked her. She joined us in games and read stories aloud and later, at Mom's request to 'please teach Nicky some marine biology', gave me a series of lectures covering almost the entire syllabus of the first year of a Bachelor of Science degree.

For the first week after leaving Puerto Rico a beam wind blew steadily at 20 knots, filling our twin jibs as the sun's rays skittered off the surface of the water. *Vingila* seemed somehow lighter than usual, happy to be in the open ocean again and skimming over the sea like a large, ungainly butterfly. We imagined a string of similarly leisurely days ahead, each melting gently into the next. Seven hundred and twenty glorious miles lay between us and the San Blas Islands of Panama. With Dad's navigation back on track, we were correct at least about the distance.

On 25 March, ignoring a heavy groundswell building from the north-east, we had a party to celebrate our first year at sea since sailing away from Cape Town. I helped Mom bake a cake using oil in place of butter and we opened a bottle of bargain wine she had bought in South Africa.

'Doesn't the sky looks strange?' Robert said to me. 'See those clouds, all whipped up, like the tails on running horses.'

He was right, the upper level cirrus clouds had a certain flayed look to them.

My brother seemed anxious. 'Don't you think the waves are bigger than they should be, considering the wind?'

We were sitting together on the cabin top eating, Mom and Dad had the bottle of wine between them in the cockpit and Lynnath stood at the stern with a slice of cake in her hand, looking into the distance.

Mom's voice floated up to us.

'Another glass of wine?' she was saying to Dad. 'Not too bad for three rand, hey?'

We were too busy celebrating to notice all the signs of an impending storm. After the cake had been eaten, Mom put a whole fish in the oven to bake with onions and tinned tomatoes. A quarter of an hour later a heavy swell rocked *Vingila* on her side, exceeding the limits of the gimballed stove and forcing the door of the oven to fly open and send a dish of bubbling hot fish shooting across the saloon to collide with the opposite bulkhead. Tomato juice trickled down the cushions. Holding Pepe away with one hand, Mom scraped the fish back into the baking tray while Dad found a bungee to re-secure the oven door.

'Why's the sea's so big?' Mom said as she wiped up. 'It doesn't make sense. There's not that much wind.'

Dad, wrestling with the escaping tray of fish and the bungee, didn't even turn around.

Two days later, in a shaky pen, I wrote in my diary: 'The waves are now as big as houses.'

We were in the midst of a severe storm, the likes of which we hadn't seen since leaving Cape Town. Although I was trying to be careful, my handwriting wasn't nearly as neat as that of my previous entry when I had been living in a blue sphere. It was difficult to keep a steady hand with *Vingila* free-falling down waves. Often I found myself briefly airborne. After finishing my sentence I decorated the page of my diary with a row of huge curlers which I filled in with blue crayon. Looking closely, it's just possible to see the tiny speck of our boat perched on the lip of one of them.

From the previous evening the wind had grown increasingly stronger and we had spent a turbulent night under reefed sails. By dawn the swells were pushing 30 feet and *Vingila* was thumping along at ten knots on a run under just her mainsail.

'I don't like it,' Dad said. 'If we keep this up, we're gonna pitch-pole.'

Lynnath was standing beside me in the cockpit, ducking spray.

'What's pitch-pole?' I asked her, shouting above the wind.

I had, in fact, read about pitch-poling in our sailing books and it sounded so horrible I wanted to double check and make sure that I had got it right.

'See how *Vingila*'s scooting down the waves?' Lynnath shouted back.

I nodded.

'And how steep it is at the bottom?'

I nodded again.

'Well, if she goes straight down and her bow digs in, she'll stop dead in her tracks. Then the wave from behind will lift her up and throw her over, head-over-heels in a somersault.'

'And then?'

'Then we lose the masts, and pretty much everything on deck.'

'What happens to us?'

A strange look flitted across Lynnath's face as she stared at me beside her in the cockpit, holding onto the gas-tank lockers for support and wet with spray. It almost looked as if she was feeling sorry for me.

'The import thing,' Lynnath said, avoiding my question, 'is to steer her out of the dips, get her nose around a bit, so that she can climb the next wave at an angle and not dig in.'

We both knew *Vingila* was far too sluggish in her response to the helm for that ever to work. Anyway, nobody was even on the helm. Baruch, the self-steering, had been left to do his best while Mom and Dad had disappeared below for a pow-wow.

As the waves pushed her faster, *Vingila* began to hum, emitting a low throaty growl I hadn't heard before. It sounded vaguely threatening. Our placid, dependable slug of a boat seemed to have transformed into a monster and was charging out of control, hurtling down the swells with the momentum of a truck. Dad came on deck and said that even with the reefed main *Vingila* was carrying too much sail and we had to slow her down. Dropping the main and leaving her bare poled wasn't an option; she would loose steerage and the waves would swamp us. These weren't waves to be fooled around with. If we wanted to keep our course while staying above water, we had to lower the mainsail and raise the storm jib simultaneously, a task that required co-ordination and seamanship. He said he wasn't sure we could do it but we were sure as hell going to try. Everybody would have to help.

So Mom took the helm while Lynnath and I shared the sheets in the cockpit. Gusts of wind drove sheets of spray against the hull and the wind made a terrible racket in the rigging. On the crests of swells we were exposed to the full force of the storm, but the troughs were so deep we were sheltered from the blasts and our sails hung momentarily loose and shivering as globs of foam fell from the storm-whipped wave tops above.

With the wind in her sails, *Vingila* shuddered and shook, stays groaning. I thought I saw her mast bend. On the bow Robert and Dad hanked the jib to the forestay before groping their way back to the main mast where they began hauling up the halyard. As the jib clattered, jerking its way along the stay, Lynnath and I yanked the sheets around the winch and the storm jib stopped thrashing and caught the wind with a crack. But just as Dad was loosening the halyard to drop the mainsail, an immense swell rose up from behind, lifting our boat into the air and exposing her to the full force of the wind. I held my breath, expecting the sails to go, ripped from clue to tack. They moaned, but didn't give. With her sails near bursting, *Vingila* balanced on the summit, giving us a good – if very brief – view of our surroundings. In the dim haze, slanting rods of sunlight broke through fleeing clouds to illuminate a surreal scene of endless breakers with plumes of spray rising from their arched necks. I was reminded of a picture that my Ouma – Dad's mom – had hanging in her lounge in Benoni. It was a cheap print of swollen cumulonimbus clouds shot through with shafts of light falling onto an intensely troubled sea. The colour scheme of the print was the same as that of our current storm: grey, violet and blue-black – the shades of fresh bruises. But Ouma's picture wasn't only sea and sky, it also had Jesus in a robe standing barefoot on a cloud with sunbeams radiating from the back of his head and a sweet smile on his face. Ouma – when she wasn't shooing dogs out of the kitchen – told me that as well as turning water into wine, Jesus could calm stormy seas and rescue sailors and fishermen. As *Vingila* began to hurtle towards the bottomless incline, I glanced back at the receding sky, expecting to find Him reaching out a perforated hand to save me as we raced into the trough and an almost certain pitch-pole.

Vingila's growl intensified. The needle on her knot meter passed 11, her previous speed record, and lodged itself firmly in the bottom right hand corner of the dial, as far as it could go, at the 15 knot mark. A curled wake spread from the stern, similar to the one I'd seen trailing Chummy's speed boat on Germiston Lake when I learned to waterski. My thoughts flicked from Jesus to waterskiing and then back to the chasm below. My white-faced mother stood frozen at the helm. Any steering *Vingila* required to escape the trough, she'd have to do herself, I thought. Lynnath stood frozen too but her eyes were shining and a wild smile was stretched across her face as if she was enjoying herself. I wondered vaguely if I should be doing anything in particular to prevent our deaths, when the knot meter and its stuck needle caught my attention again.

'Hey, Robert,' I yelled to my brother on the cabin top, 'check this out.'

He was hanging from a halyard in a cloud of spray and didn't even hear me.

Vingila did not dig her bow into the bottom of the wave. Without my mother's help, she pulled herself around while, at the same time, we managed to drag the mainsail down. I learned later that high performance yachts race like this – sails up, surfing the waves, hull humming. It's called planing and *Vingila* never did it again. To plane, skilled sailors constantly trim the sails while a good helmsman keeps course and guides the boat through the troughs. We decided the whole thing was a bit much for us and hove to instead under the storm jib. Once we had *Vingila* facing the waves in a reasonably controlled manner, we retired en masse to the main saloon floor where Robert and I were reunited with our crochet blankets. They had been stowed in a locker for more than six months and smelled strongly of mildew and diesel; however, we were pleased to see them again.

'I've got a surprise for you, Nicky,' Mom said, handing me a new book. I almost never saw new books, ours were all second hand, swapped with the other yachties.

'James Herriott,' I said. 'The best.'

Mom said she'd bought the book in St Thomas and hidden it away for an emergency. I was delighted with my present; it was a treat to get something I actually wanted to read. I rolled myself in my crochet blanket, opened my book and within minutes was lying on a cold, cobblestone floor in Yorkshire with a vet who had his hand in a cow and was trying to deliver a stuck calf. I was brought back from Yorkshire only when especially large waves broke full force over the deck and sent water spraying through the gaps in the closed hatch and onto the floor. Mom piled old towels to soak up the wet and I returned to the barn. Dad said he reckoned the wind was gusting to 60 knots and he wasn't sure he had ever seen bigger waves. Robert, who didn't have a new book to distract him, wasn't in good shape. Between chapters on calving, old dogs, and cows dying of milk fever, I turned to my diary. I drew a few shaky navy blue waves and wrote, rather unsympathetically, 'I read my new book and Robert was sick every five minutes.'

Strangely enough, even in the midst of a storm that rattled the masts and made the shrouds sing, Dad was much less irritable than he had been in Puerto Rico. On the open ocean his mood improved; he relaxed and no longer found his family so taxing, even as the wind howled and waves crashed about us. I was pleased he was happier because then Robert and I got to feel less of the Whistler. However, I still kept a low profile with my father, and tried, as he said, not to piss him off too much.

'Today we picked our selfs up by the scruff of the neck and put up our sails. We were soon going along at six knots,' read my next diary entry. After lying battened down for two days, we were on our way again. Robert recovered and our usual activities recommenced; cooking, school work, catching fish, washing dishes and eating coconuts. During ocean passages we did the most school work, catching up on the time we had lost in port, when sightseeing, shopping for food at the markets and doing laundry took precedence. Because of all these other distractions my mother had, over the year we had been at sea, whittled down our syllabus until Robert and I were only doing maths and English, which we could cover in a sessions of an hour or two, three days a week. There were no exams to be written and no inspector to check if we were keeping up. It doesn't really matter, Mom and Dad agreed, because nothing beats the school of life.

During the long afternoons, when I wasn't reading trashy novels,

I paid attention to my shell collection. In St Martin, one of the Lesser Antilles, I had gone snorkelling with Belinda, my friend who lived on *Antoinette* with her little sister and their crazy mother Grace. Floating together over gardens of seaweed and colonies of tiny sand eels who ducked into their burrows as our shadows fell on them, I had found a big brown cowrie with white spots wending its way through the weed. It was a *Cypraea zebra*, one of the largest of the Caribbean cowries, and rather uncommon. It was differentiated from *Cypraea cervus*, a very similar cowrie, by the fact that the more lateral of its white dorsal spots were ocellated. I knew this because Dad had bought a wonderful new book in St Thomas. It was simply titled *Cowries* and had been written by Dr John Taylor of the British Museum of Natural History. Inside its hard blue cover was a colour picture and description of every known species of cowrie, and at the back was a price list, giving me an indication of their rarity. The *Cypraea zebra*, for example, was worth five dollars, while my pride and joy, the *Cypraea surinamensis* from Fortaleza, was worth three hundred and fifty. From reading the front section of the book, I learned that cowries had been a form of currency for thousands of years in places like China, India, the Pacific and Africa. Slave traders on the coast of Senegal had bartered in cowries, as did explorers like Livingstone and Stanley. The Chinese word for cowrie forms part of the written characters for wealth, preciousness and buying. In many cultures cowries are associated with life, birth and fertility and are thought to have magical, protective properties. When I read that I wondered if my cowries had protected us in the storm and kept *Vingila* from pitch-poling and killing us, rather than Jesus.

I asked Lynnath what she thought and she said she really didn't know and directed me instead to the pages covering the scientific description of the cowrie animal. This is more interesting, she said. So I read about how cowries are mainly nocturnal gastropods moving on a broad and extensible foot. That they have a bilobed mantle that builds and maintains their shell and they breathe through a siphon and eat with a proboscis. Instead of teeth, they have a radula, which is like a file. Some cowries are herbivores and live on algae, while others are omnivores. Dr Taylor dissected the gut contents of a *Cypraea cervus* in Florida and found calcareous sediment, green and red filamentous algae, large quantities of sponge spicules, tubes of polychaete worms, foraminifera, copepods, ostracods, bryozoa, and small gastropods. That particular cowrie sounded like quite an adventurous eater.

Cowries, I discovered, even had sex. Or as Dr Taylor put it, practised copulation, the male inserting his penis, which was about a third as long as the shell, into the genital aperture near the rear end of the female. Lynnath was right, the scientific parts of the book were interesting. The book also gave practical advice like keeping shells in the dark to prevent them fading and wiping off fingerprints which ate into the nacre of the shell, and took away the gloss.

After the storm, a week of uneventful sailing passed before we sighted the San Blas Islands. Sandy remnants of an ancient reef, the islets form a broken offshore chain to the south of the Panama Canal. The Kuna people live in palm frond huts on a few of the 365 islands, and tend groves of coconut palms on most of the others. They grow vegetables in gardens on the swampy mainland several kilometres away, which they reach by outrigger canoe. Lynnath's guidebook described the inhabitants of the San Blas as Dwarf Kuna Indians. The book has probably been updated to be more culturally sensitive, but the average indigenous adult still stands around five foot tall. And they are not Indians at all, just another group of South American people who fell victim to Columbus's poor geography.

We anchored in the lee of the main island of Porvenir. It differed from the islands of the chain in that, in addition to white sand, coconut palms and huts, it had a shop, an airstrip and a single clapboard hotel. Our anchor had scarcely touched bottom when *Vingila* was invaded by dugout canoes carrying unusually dressed people all wanting to sell *molas* – hand-stitched reverse appliqué cloths – and demanding to have their photos taken for money. English conversation was strictly limited to matters of finance. A bandy-legged man in a white dress shirt and faded shorts introduced himself as Mr Morris, took over negotiations on our behalf, and announced that he'd take us on a jungle tour on the mainland the following day.

'What time tomorrow?' Dad asked.

Mr Morris pointed towards a spot in the sky on the sun's trajectory and, squinting his eyes, said 'Ten-tirty.'

That night I went to bed breathing in the smell of palm trees, grass huts, wood smoke and coral exposed by the low tide. In spite of the *mola*-sellers and touts, there was something wild and unspoiled about the place that I found exciting. Something that the Caribbean islands lacked. I took out my diary and wrote: 'Went to sleep happy.' The next day, after an expensive and unsatisfying outing in Mr Morris's dugout canoe which ended in an unpleasant haggle, we left Porvenir and fled to the outlying islands of the barrier reef.

There Lynnath took me snorkelling to look for cleaner shrimps who shared their burrows with goby fish. We collected a sea sponge and dissected it to see its structure. From a book she had bought at the souvenir shop on Porvenir, she taught me some Kuna phrases.

'The Kuna word for American,' she said, 'is Murky.'

'Murky? Can we really call them that?' I said.

Lynnath thought for a moment. 'Probably not to their faces, I think,' she said.

We practised our new language on the people of the outlying islands who were friendlier and seemed genuinely interested in our family. They allowed Robert and me to sail their dugout canoes, took us to the mainland to see their jungle gardens and never forced us to buy *molas*.

After a week in the San Blas Islands I came to the conclusion that I didn't want to be a Christian any more. I wanted to be a Kuna Indian. The men in old shorts and T-shirts were not special. The women, however, were breathtaking. Being a Kuna Indian, I thought, just *looked* better than being a Christian. And they were all my size. As a member of the tribe I imagined that I too would wear a *mola* blouse of many colours, with a navy and orange patterned sarong and a red headscarf. I wasn't sure about the pot-cut hairstyles, but the beaded bracelets and anklets encircling my exposed arms and legs would be magnificent. Mostly I loved the black stripes along the length of their noses, beginning at the knife-edge of their fringes and terminating at the heavy gold rings dangling from their nasal septa. As Kuna women aged and accumulated wealth by selling coconuts, the size of their nose rings increased. The weight dragged their noses to meet their lips, interfering with the ability to eat and drink from a cup. I admired everything about the Kunas. Obstacles stood in my way to Kunahood, however. For a start, Mom forbade me outright to even think of piercing my nose. And although the local women on the remote islands were friendly and painted black lines on the bridge of my nose whenever I asked them, the clans were fiercely traditional and not open to outsiders. Marriage beyond the tribe was strictly forbidden. And we heard rumours of albino babies smothered at birth. A blonde like me would not be welcomed. I cobbled together an outfit anyway with a second-hand *mola* blouse, scraps of material for a sarong and headscarf (I made do without the beads or gold) and on the privacy of the boat, I practised being a Kuna Indian by myself.

'I've never read a book in my life,' Stuart said.

I found the concept impossible to believe. 'Not even one?'

'Nothing.'

Stuart sounded proud of his achievement. He was fourteen and good looking with dark blond hair and straight Californian teeth flashing from a tanned face. His smile reminded me a bit of Urbine, my skateboarding love in Durban. I felt an urge to flirt with him but I didn't know where to begin. He had never read a single book.

'So what do you do in the evenings?' I asked.

'Watch TV.'

'Here? In Panama City?'

'Yup. We're picking up an American signal from the canal zone, so it's just like home.'

Stuart was the youngest member of the family living aboard *Odyssey*. Mom, Dad, three teenagers, a pointer dog and a television set were all packed onto a narrow 36 foot sloop. They invited us over one night to watch TV. Crammed into the cockpit we craned our necks to a bluish image jumping in a snowstorm and strained to hear buzzy words. I watched Stuart. His mouth hung open a little, exposing his teeth to the glow of the screen. Nobody said anything. They were as silent and round-eyed as owls. When Dad tried to speak he was shushed. Even the dog kept her eyes fixed on the box.

'I don't know how you live without TV,' Stuart said the next day.

Stuart and his family had sailed down from California via Mexico. Stuart's dad Mike was also blond, with a trimmed moustache and hair that always looked neat. On several occasions I caught him checking his reflection in the portholes.

'Panama is as far as we go,' Mike said. 'We're already too far from home. Time to get back to the good old US of A.'

Dad's eyes narrowed, but he didn't say anything about the US of A which he hated.

We'd just come through the canal from the Caribbean side and Dad was still fuming because we'd had to pay so much for a pilot. No matter the size of the vessel, the man had told him, the rate is the same, and if you don't like it, feel free to go around Cape Horn.

Our pilot's name was Mr Hastings. He had pocked, greasy skin and soft breasts that moved under his white cotton shirt. He sweated a lot. Shortly after boarding, he made it clear that he preferred sailing on larger vessels, like oil tankers and cruise ships.

'The service on cruise ships is exceptional,' he said, accepting a cup of tea and a slice of banana bread from Mom, who'd baked it especially for him. Over the course of the day we negotiated the ascending and descending locks with their scary gates dripping swathes of slimy seaweed, and along the way, washed ourselves and our clothes in the freshwater of Lake Gatun. Dad would have liked to spend a few days on the islands of the lake, enjoying the sweet water, but overnight stopping was forbidden.

'Besides,' said Mr Hastings, 'may I remind you that I have a meeting in Panama City this evening? Is this really the fastest your vessel can go? I've been on a few boats this size before, and I really don't remember the others being so slow.'

That night in Panama City, Mr Hastings completed his paperwork, ate the last slice of banana bread, disembarked on a concrete pier and, with a sour look on his face, shooed us from the harbour.

'Was he expecting a tip?' Mom asked.

Beyond the breakwater we anchored near a group of yachts huddled together in dirty water a considerable distance from a stained brown beach. We had no sooner anchored when Mike the Californian roared over in a Zodiac to introduce himself and warn us that theft was rife in Panama City and we were not to leave our dinghy unattended on shore. Unfortunately the shore was very far away, which made calling for a ride difficult. Mike showed us his walkie-talkie.

'I use one of these,' he said, and showed us how it clipped to his belt. 'I got it in the States. Maybe if you looked in the duty-free shops ...'

'I don't need one of those,' Dad said. 'I can whistle.'

When Mike went ashore the next day two young boys hit him on the head and stole his walkie-talkie. With blood running into his eyes, he was unable to summon his family who were watching TV on the boat. When the show ended and they turned off the set, the dog heard him and raised the alarm.

'You see,' said Mom that evening after we heard the story, 'sometimes it's better to have nothing. We've nothing to steal, so nobody robs us.'

In a way she was right. After more than a year of travelling we were looking a little ragged and Robert suggested that maybe we should start stealing from the locals. When Mom found a place selling factory reject T-shirts from the local sweatshops we were able, within our budget, to renew our wardrobes. We bought two dozen shirts, enough for ourselves and for trading among the Pacific Islands. Some sported strange slogans that didn't make any sense. *Dear the Blue, our dreams remain unchanged* and *Love Cows*. In a small shop in the side street next to the shirt factory Mom discovered a red leatherette edition of Charles Dickens stories which she brought back and hid from me. Not everything went well for us in Panama City, though. Robert failed to tie the dinghy securely to *Vingila* one afternoon and it was swept away with the tide. Mike, still bruised from his mugging, zoomed out in his inflatable to retrieve it, revving the outboard more than I thought was necessary. Coming back with the wind in his hair, he looked happier than he had in days. We thanked Mike, but once he'd gone, Dad punched Robert in the face and called him a cunt.

'I think it's time to leave,' Mom said, holding a wet face cloth to Robert's cheek.

I wasn't sad to go. Except for the yacht club in the American Zone where you could put as much sauerkraut on your hot dog as you wanted and soak your popcorn in melted butter until it dripped from the bottom of the packet, I hated Panama. I thought Colon on the Caribbean side had been bad, but Panama City was worse; all the filth and crowding of the Brazilian cities but with far more menace. And there were ships everywhere, dirty ships and dockworkers and prostitutes. We left the mainland behind under its haze of smog but the water stayed dirty long after the outline of the city had slipped from sight.

The Shah of Iran was in exile at the Tropical Star Fishing Lodge on Isla Contradora in the Las Perlas Islands, together with a few drug lords and a collection of South American politicians having trouble with the law. Our new friend Christian Eckhoff told us that before he set sail for Ecuador. Christian was German by birth and South African by citizenship. He owned and captained *Donella*, a wooden sloop crewed by Heike, his oldest daughter, and her Swedish boyfriend Janie. He told us he had left Cape Town two years previously. His middle daughter Claudia had married a Brazilian and stayed in São Paulo while Hanelora, Christian's wife, was back in South Africa where Anja, their youngest, attended school. Christian spoke with a German accent, just like our friend and porn fan Ari in Salvador. He even wore the same style of beard. Unlike Ari, however, Christian was a Springbok spear fisherman who held several of the records in our book of South African fishes. I could tell just by looking at him that he was fit, strong and fearless and it would take more than a shark or two to rattle him. I wondered if he had dirty magazines on his boat too, although I doubted it. He had brown hair, brown eyes and brown skin. His beard jutted aggressively from his jaw and his face was composed of planes all set at determined angles. Even his hair looked confident. Heike and Janie were pinker and softer with limp locks of white, baby-fine hair framing their faces. Janie's lips cracked easily in the sun and he kept a tin of lip balm which he applied regularly. Christian, in Robert and Dad's eyes, was the perfect sailing companion. Before Christian left for Ecuador Dad made arrangements to chat to him every day on the ham radio.

On Christian's advice we left the moorings at the Tropical Star Fishing Lodge, a discreet high security resort where half the men wore

Bermuda shorts and golf shirts and the other half wore dark suits and sunglasses, and we sailed to the uninhabited isles in the island group. Although water visibility was poor – the muddy contamination of the mainland extended to the islands – the sea stirred with life. At night we were awakened by the splash of fish leaping from the water; by day, fins continually broke the surface. At lunchtime each day we went ashore with a pot of rice, a machete, matches and a fishing rod. While Robert made a fire and climbed a palm for coconuts, Dad cast a line in the surf and within an hour we would be sitting down to grilled fish and coconut rice. It was a bit like paradise, I thought, only muddier.

Several decades after our visit, 'Survivor', a reality TV series, would be filmed on these isles, with contestants battling it out in the heat while the producers and film crew stayed in luxury villas on the main island, conveniently out of sight. I like to think of Stuart from *Odyssey* still enthralled by television and watching the series as a grown man. Would he know, I wondered, that the events were filmed only 50 miles from Panama City, where he'd once crouched in the blue light of the cockpit of his parents' yacht watching old American sitcoms?

From Las Perlas we set sail for the Galapagos, 800 miles away across the Pacific. Dad said the trip would take a week and he couldn't have been more wrong. Although how was he to know what effect the soupy, rich waters of the Gulf of Panama had had on *Vingila*? Even Lynnath with her degree in marine biology never suspected what had happened to our boat beneath the waterline.

Part 4

PACIFIC OCEAN

12

ECUADOR

After we reached the Galapagos, Lynnath gave me a lecture on cirripedes, or barnacles. I learnt that unlike the sessile acorn barnacle, which cements itself to rocks, hulls and the skin of whales, the goose-necked barnacle is free to move a little. Twisting its long, supple stalk, it directs its bivalved head toward the current and extends its adapted feet, or cirri, to trap food. Its tubular neck grows long and muscular, and is thought by some – the Japanese and Spaniards, for example – to be a succulent delicacy. Unlike acorn barnacles who cling to rocks, goose-necked barnacles usually grow on wood. They sometimes accept pilings but prefer the driftwood of the ocean. Once the crustaceans take root, they multiply quickly to form a bristling carpet of coiling necks, pale snapping heads and grasping, retractile cirri. *Balenus*, the rock barnacle, annoys humans by fouling the hulls of ships and harbour structures. The goosenecks usually keep a lower profile, sailing the open seas on their wooden rafts like Thor Heyerdahls of the barnacle world.

In the warm, murky waters of Las Perlas, a swarm of cypri, or non-feeding larvae, collided with *Vingila*. Reaching out with the cement glands on their antenulles, they took hold. The copper oxide and other poisons in her anti-fouling should have provided some degree of protection, but the high level of pollution in the Gulf of Panama with its heavy traffic of passing ships, perhaps inured the larvae. Whatever the explanation, *Vingila*'s protective coating did nothing to stop the invasion.

We didn't know what was wrong. Our boat wasn't moving. The wind was on the nose, and there was a strong current, but still. Twenty-five miles in two days? Rain clouds obscured the sky and Dad couldn't always get a sight, but whenever he glimpsed the sun we hovered at the chart table, waiting for the results and hoping for better news which didn't come.

I found Dad outside one morning, staring into the pulling sails while *Vingila* jackknifed and stalled in the waves.

'What the hell is going on here?' he asked, but he didn't seem to expect an answer from me.

On the ham radio we heard from Christian on *Donella*. They'd arrived in Ecuador and taken a bus to Quito, the capital. A filthy place, Christian said. But the good news was that they had visas for the Galapagos. He urged us to do the same.

'I'm not going to some dirty city just to get visas,' Dad said. 'I don't believe in visas. If the crowd at Galapagos don't want us, then they can piss right off. We're going to Galapagos.'

Except we weren't moving. After a week we ran out of fresh food. The last of our withered apples from Panama City was eaten. Then our cabbages and potatoes.

'I'm sorry,' Mom said, 'I didn't think it would take this long, and there was nothing to buy in the Las Perlas. The Tropical Star Fishing Lodge didn't have a shop.'

We ate food from tins. Granular pink corned beef, and pale tinned pork sausages. We finished the eggs. As a treat, Mom brought out some American breakfast cereal – pillows of latticed wheat. But when we added powdered milk, weevils swarmed from the holes and floated on the surface like coarse ground pepper on soup.

'I can't eat this,' said Robert.

Even Dad didn't insist.

We started to develop strange cravings. One night I found Mom eating sugar from the pot by the spoonful. The next day she said, 'I feel like fudge.'

Dad let her make it, even though it needed butter. We had some in cans but we were supposed to be saving it. Fudge also used a whole tin of condensed milk.

The fudge was faintly gritty and so sweet it made my ears buzz. But I craved it and could think about nothing else, particularly at night when I had to take watch. Three days after we had finished the first batch I asked Mom to make more. My gums had started to itch.

'This fudge business is getting expensive,' Dad said, but I noticed he was eating it too.

But even fudge didn't really satisfy my cravings, it just left me with a sour mouth and a need for more. What I really wanted was an orange. I imagined the smell of its skin, the spray of its oils as I peeled it, the burn of its juice sliding down my throat.

'Don't tell Mom,' Robert said, 'but there was blood on the brush when I cleaned my teeth this morning.'

'Maybe it's from the fudge,' I said.

One night we went to take in the fishing lines. We had left it pretty late and in the darkness they felt strangely heavy, but without the tug of a fighting fish.

'Feels like a plastic bag,' Robert said.

The bag spat a jet of water at us, soaking our heads as we looked over the side, trying to figure out exactly what we had caught. A hefty pair of squid, taken on our lead-headed fishing lures.

'Well I never,' said Dad.

The next day Mom fried the squid in batter for lunch. Although the wind was still on the nose, it had picked up and we hunkered down on the main saloon floor with the table lashed against the bulkhead while *Vingila* threw herself at the waves. We ate the fried squid from bowls balanced on our knees. Something was wrong with Mom's recipe; the batter had fallen off in the oil and formed brown floating balls which she had fished out and served atop the pale, contorted curlicues of sliced hood and tentacle. Frying oil, which could have been fresher, collected in pools beneath our mounds of rice. Mom thought draining food on paper towels was wasteful. Pepe had his own bowl in the corner with oil and crunchy bits. When he looked up, his beard was dark with fat.

'Did you put lemon on this?' Dad asked Mom.

'Now tell me, where would I get a lemon?'

'Tastes like lemon to me,' Robert said. He was right. Perhaps it was because we'd been so long without lemons – or any other fresh fruit – but our calamari, although not too tender, had a delicate citrus aroma. It was delicious. After two hours of cooking and eating we were full and fell greasily asleep on the floor for the rest of the afternoon.

Some days later when Dad's sights showed we were being pushed towards the coast by the current he said, 'Why don't we go to Ecuador?'

We were all tired of sailing by then and Mom was hoping she could buy some bananas. We turned *Vingila* so that the wind hit her beam, and she increased her speed by a fraction as she made for the coast of Ecuador where Dad found Baia Pinas, a settlement so small it scarcely appeared on the chart. We were very far from Quito. In fact we were far away from almost everything. A ring of mountains in a thick coat of jungle formed a backdrop to a tiny cluster of dwellings. There was a wooden hotel on stilts and an airstrip, a few huts and a small but secure anchorage crammed with smart, new, recreational fishing boats. In the evening, after the boats came in, giant marlin and sailfish were hung bill down on hooks while the men who had caught them posed alongside for photographs. Once or twice I spotted bare chested jungle people in loincloths and grass skirts drifting out from the damp, liana draped trees to watch. They never spoke a word. Inside the hotel, the walls were covered with the pictures of men and their fish. There was a ten to one club, for those who had caught a hundred pound marlin on ten pound breaking strain line, and a twenty to one club. In the corner a glass case stood filled with trophies. Against the far wall a stuffed and painted marlin at least nine foot long swam against the grain of the wood.

After the first night the manager of the hotel asked us to leave.

'This place is for fishermen only,' he said, 'and we have a very exclusive clientele. I don't want any trouble.'

'What kind of trouble was he expecting anyway?' Mom asked. She was upset because she hadn't been able to buy any bananas.

'Drugs?' said Robert.

'Don't think so,' I said. 'Aren't drug running boats supposed to be fast?'

Dad gave me the evil eye then, so I didn't say anything more, though I could have.

Back at sea the wind had turned and the skies had grown clearer. We set our sails again for Galapagos. *Vingila* still wasn't moving and we still hadn't figured out she was dragging a carpet of writhing barnacles cemented to her underside. Around us, the sea teemed with billfish. Even at our low speed we caught a few, but they snapped our lines. We saw silvery torpedoes rocketing from the sea and tail-walking to the whirr and ping of our reels. We were fishing with 200 pound breaking strain tackle. We didn't even belong to the one to one club, I thought, no wonder the manager had asked us to leave. But what would we do with a fish that size anyway, Mom wanted to know, who would cook it? One morning Dad found a few marlin on deck. As long as his thumb, they were perfect copies of their elders, right down to the dorsal fins that slotted into pouches on their backs. Lynnath put them in a jar of formalin.

'As far as I know,' she said, 'baby marlin haven't been described. I'm going to write this up.'

'Another magazine article?' Mom said. 'That would be nice.'

When we started catching birds we knew we had reached the Galapagos. We had spent a month at sea crawling our way over 800 miles and even our onions were finished. *Donella* had arrived in the Galapagos a week earlier and Christian, over the radio, told Dad to clear in at Wreck Bay on Santa Cristobal before making our way to Isla Santa Cruz. Mountains rose from the sea like black teeth and the gannets wouldn't leave our lines alone. They dived like arrows and we kept pulling in soggy, yellow-eyed birds, avoiding their beaks and unhooking them as they vomited seawater over the stern. We threw them back before Pepe got at them but a few looked as if they wouldn't make it.

Mom came up with the pilot book.

'I've just read,' she said, 'that this entire area is a nature reserve. So I think you should stop catching these poor birds.'

Lynnath agreed and we took the lines in.

The *capitano* of the parks board wasn't pleased with us either.

'Where are your visas?' he asked.

Mom and Dad acted surprised. What visas, they said, we didn't know about visas. The *capitano* had shiny hair combed back from his forehead and a black moustache. He was unmoved.

'If you don't have visas, you cannot stay. Please prepare to leave.'

Then Dad launched into a story about how we had had such a long and difficult trip, and we had run out of food and that Robert and I, since leaving South Africa had only ever wanted to see the Galapagos Islands, which was why we had started the whole circumnavigation in the first place. We only bought this boat, he repeated, so that our children could see the amazing animals of the Galapagos. This was news to me.

'How can you turn them away now?' Dad asked, casting his hand towards the bunk where I was sitting beside my brother.

I saw the *capitano*'s moustache quiver a little. His eyes lingered on my blonde plaits, making me wish I had washed them more recently. I gave a small, unhappy smile, glancing at Dad to see if that was what he wanted.

'And we also have a scientist aboard,' my father went on, gesturing to Lynnath, 'who has come here especially to study the animals and write articles about them.'

Lynnath smiled at the *capitano* too. She wasn't looking particularly scientific. Her glasses were hazy and smeared with salt, her Elvis Presley hairstyle from Puerto Rico had long since outgrown itself, and her ragged cut-offs needed cleaning.

'This,' my Dad repeated, 'is our scientist.'

The *capitano* sighed.

'Give me your passports,' he said. 'I will allow two weeks. No more.'

'See,' said Dad once they had left, 'I told you we wouldn't need visas.'

Seals were swimming in the anchorage at Isla Santa Cruz and we saw *Donella* anchored in front of a house built on an outcrop of black rock at the water's edge. Marine iguanas were sprawled about on its roof, sunbathing.

'Annie, annie annie annie!' the owner of the house yodelled twice a day, and at his call they jerked from their torpor and came alive to be fed. It was surprising how fast they could run, slithering over one another down the walls and pouring through the door to his courtyard in a black scaly river to eat rice and lettuce from a bowl.

'Sometimes I give them a few dog biscuits as well,' the owner told us, grabbing an iguana at random to show us the third eye on the top of its head. In his hands the beast went limp, its black clawed limbs dangling, white membranes drawn down over its eyes like blinds. The man's name was Karl Angermeyer and he spoke German to Christian. He said he hadn't been back to Germany in more than twenty years but it was good to stay in practice. He had come to the island, he told us, with his three brothers to escape the war. The voyage over had not been easy; there had been a shipwreck he said, and one brother had died. The three survivors built houses on Santa Cruz. They had planned to stay only until the war was over but after a few years discovered that they did not want to go back to Europe. This place is my home now, he said, I couldn't imagine living anywhere else. As he talked the lizard stayed limp in his hands and his fingers flicked idly at the loose skin peeling from its body.

'Why Annie?' asked Christian.

Karl put the reptile down, brushing dry flakes from his hands. 'Oh, Annie was something my daughter started when she was just a baby. I don't know why. The iguanas are used to it now.'

Karl had two other brothers on the island. We didn't meet Fritz who was away, but the youngest brother stayed down the road. Gusch, a shirtless man with gleaming olive skin, told Robert and me to call him the King. He said that his wife Lucrezia, a tiny, snappy-eyed woman with long hair down her back, was a Peruvian princess. She lived in the main house while Gusch said he preferred the cave at the back of the garden. It was a fantastic cave, with walls of volcanic boulders and an entrance obscured by a thick curtain of creepers. The floor inside was smooth concrete, and in the gloom kerosene lanterns spread soft haloes of light. There were whale vertebrae to sit on and animal skins, plenty of books and bones, and a real human skull that the King said he'd stolen from catacombs in Peru. The King said his brother Karl was an artist, a finger painter, but that his own job, as king of the island, was to collect things. He had done well; in addition to the books, bones and skins that covered the floor and every surface, an entire whale skeleton swam suspended from the ceiling on ropes. Robert and I loved the place; we spent hours lying on the furs, reading his books, looking at stuff and listening to the King's stories.

Before leaving Las Perlas I had found a battered copy of *Kon Tiki* in Mom's locker which I read as we sailed to the Galapagos. Thor Heyerdahl was a hero. Norwegian – a Viking really – he sailed from the coast of South America to Polynesia on a raft with a group of equally heroic friends. They were all Nordic, good-looking men with red gold beards and brave-sounding names like Knut, Bengt and Torstein. They battled storms and killed sharks and didn't always have enough fresh water to wash their hair. Before they left people told them they were going to die but they went ahead anyway. In the black-and-white photographs in the book they grew wilder, more suntanned and better looking as the voyage progressed. I loved *Kon Tiki,* and while I lay in my bunk, sucking a piece of fudge to make it last, I thought about Thor and imagined him asking me to join the expedition. I could help them catch sharks and would make them fudge and they would all say how great I was. After we got to the Galapagos I was still thinking of him. On the floor of the King's cave I found another book by Thor. *Fatu Hiva* was about how he and his wife went to live in the Marquesas Islands which was to be our next stop after the Galapagos. I was a bit disappointed to find out that he had a wife, and an adventurous Norwegian one at that, but I read on. According to Thor, Fatu Hiva was dark, wet and spooky; full of taboo and tikis and people dragging huge, swollen elephantitic limbs around. There were also plenty of mosquitoes which drove Thor a bit crazy. After a month he began pulling them through the net by the snout, and amputating parts of them. Apparently, when you live on a rainy tropical island, you have time to do things like that. When he got to the stage where he was removing their mouth parts and watching them try to feed, he decided it was probably time to leave. I kept waiting for his wife to contract elephantiasis and get disfigured but she didn't. If his wife got sick, I thought, and I was there then I would nurse her and over the months while she worsened, Thor would see all my good qualities and fall in love with me. Because he was true to his wife he would only realise how much he loved me after the funeral. I would be taller then, and have breasts. I couldn't stop reading. Late in the afternoon, when the King strolled in and asked what I was up to, I lifted the book to show him the cover.

'Oh Thor Heyerdahl,' he said, 'you like him, do you?'

'I do,' I said, 'a lot.'

He told me that he and Thor were close friends and that Thor had spent many an hour in this very cave with him. Then he scratched around and pulled out a crumbling letter.

'Read it aloud,' he said.

It was from Thor. He wrote that he had gone to a ball to meet royalty and was expected to dance with the queen's cousin except he couldn't waltz. Some friends gave him an emergency lesson, but it didn't help. I got the idea that he preferred sailing across the ocean on a raft. That night I wrote in my diary that I had read aloud a letter by the great adventurer Thor Heyerdahl himself. And when I had finished I looked at my hands and said to myself, these hands have touched the same piece of paper that Thor's hands touched. I put my cheek against my right hand, which had had the most contact with the letter, and went to sleep.

Mom encouraged us to visit the King and spend as much time ashore as we wanted. I think that after a month at sea together she was pleased to be free of us for a while and after the episode with the goose-necked barnacles, I thought Robert needed a break too.

We first saw the barnacles when we launched the dinghy to go ashore right after the *capitano* stamped our passports. Mom screamed because she didn't know what they were. But Lynnath identified them immediately and even told us their scientific name: *Lepas*.

'I don't care what they're called,' Mom said, 'they give me the heebie-jeebies.'

Dad ran his hand over the side of the hull, reaching down below the waterline.

'Jesus Christ Almighty,' he said. 'No wonder we weren't moving.'

The crop covering *Vingila* was almost ten centimetres thick by then. A bristling forest of wrinkled, swaying necks and mouths that shut sullenly at our approach. Not an inch of our boat's underside appeared to have been spared. The crustaceans had even invaded her prop shaft and seemed to be working their way up the stern gland. I pictured them coming up the rudder into my cabin. I imagined waking up to find them growing on my face and arms.

'Don't be such a baby,' Robert said when I told him. 'You know they can't live out of water.'

Dad made Robert help scrape them off. Because the frigid Humboldt current flows to the Galapagos from Antarctica, the sea was icy cold, which explained why fur seals and penguins were living on the equator. Unlike my father, Robert didn't have a wetsuit but Dad said he'd warm up swimming. I sat inside in my cabin listening to the rasp of their scrapers against the steel hull and when I went up there were chunks of barnacles floating everywhere and marine iguanas and seals all swimming around having a look. When Robert came out his lips were blue and his teeth didn't stop chattering even after Mom wrapped him in his crochet blanket and made him drink hot Milo. Dad said the swim would make him tough and later, once he was warm again, Robert told me the one good thing about it was that the seals had been friendly.

Christian came over for tea and laughed at Robert's blue lips. He said Dad was quite right, swimming in cold water makes you strong. He told us that he'd been doing some research and that to see the real animals we had to go to another island but we needed a guide.

'Always the same bladdy thing,' Dad said. 'Pay, pay, pay. I got on this yacht to be free. First visas and now guides. What next? Chains of American supermarkets? Cruise ships?'

Mom said she had heard that a few years previously yachts could sail where they liked but then a bunch of French yachties arrived and collected tortoise eggs and ate all the flamingos.

'Flamingos?' asked Robert. 'Do they have flamingos here?' He was warming up a little because his lips weren't as stiff and he had started forming words again.

'Not any more,' said Mom, 'because the Frenchies ate them all.'

We decided that to save money we would share a guide for a day and sail on *Vingila* because she was bigger than *Donella*. So we went to Plaza Island, a shelf of brown rock with sandy paths and a few cacti growing from the cracks where we found giant tortoises and iguanas just strolling around. The iguanas, golden-orange with a spiny crest running the length of their body, stomped slowly, rolling their eyes as if they thought they were dragons. None of the animals or birds were the least bit frightened of humans. The seals tried to steal our dinghy and nearly sank it. After our walk, we found a group of them squashed between the seats and one in the sea trying to untie the painter. The gunnels were almost underwater beneath their grinning, whiskered heads. They didn't leave until Christian shouted and waved a stick at them. Apart from telling us twice not to leave the path, our guide explained nothing about the island or its animals. Later that night, as we lay in bed, Lynnath told me about Charles Darwin and how he'd visited the islands on the *Beagle* and noticed how the tortoises looked different from island to island, depending on what there was to eat. That got him thinking, she said, and he came up with the theory of natural selection. You see, she went on, everybody thought it was the finches that gave him the idea, but it wasn't. He just used the finches to confirm his theory. Then she reminded me again what natural selection was because I'd forgotten. I loved the theory of evolution. It all made perfect sense to me and took my mind off the goose-necked barnacles which had been giving me nightmares.

Santa Cruz, the capital, was half deserted. The dry, sandy ground and cactus plants gave it a sort of Wild West feel which was reinforced by cowboys strolling the streets and pushing through the swinging wooden doors of the dusty saloon on main street. There were no supermarkets but at the butcher shop on the hill they slaughtered a cow every morning and hung it from a hook in the ceiling. Only two cuts of beef were available; with bone or without, and in an unpainted concrete room a man in a bloody apron and boots hacked chunks from the warm carcass and wrapped them, still quivering, in brown paper. At the place next door we bought onions and hefty, earth-covered carrots for stew.

One morning I awoke to the lowing of cows in distress. The island ranchers were exporting animals to Ecuador, driving the creatures into the sea and swimming them out to an anchored ship in the bay where they were winched aboard by the horns. In the afternoon the crane got stuck, or the workers went for lunch or something, and for more than an hour a dangling steer was left to bellow and make runny shits into the sea. Although I didn't like what we'd seen, I kept eating meat.

A few days later we left Santa Cruz with *Donella* and sailed to Floreana Island to visit Post Office Bay.

'That sounds boring,' Robert said when he heard the name of our destination.

Lynnath explained that it wasn't boring at all; we were visiting a place where, for hundreds of years, buccaneers and other sailors had dropped their mail off in a barrel.

'And it's all still there, right?'

'Ha, ha, Robert. No, other people pick it up, of course, and take it to where they're going. That's how mail used to work. If we leave post there, someone might deliver it for us.'

Robert said it still sounded boring.

Post Office Bay had a hippy feel to it, with a few weathered stumps to which sailors had nailed boards with their boat names. Shells and pieces of bone and driftwood dangled on lengths of twine in the surrounding trees, and clanked quietly in the wind. The heat had cracked and peeled the bark from the trunks of the trees and only the cacti seemed to be thriving. Dad painted *Vingila*'s name on a plank and nailed it up while Lynnath sorted through the letters and left a postcard for her parents in the barrel.

The Galapagos with its unusually tame animals, I was learning, was a favourite destination for pirates and whalers. They came to hunt fur seals and collect tortoises which they took aboard two to three hundred at a time. Stored upside down in the holds and remaining alive for more than a year without food or drink, the reptiles could be slaughtered any time for fresh meat. In their free time, early sailors killed the other tame animals for fun. Darwin hated senseless killing but even he ate his fair share of tortoises. The younger ones in particular, he wrote, made fine soup. Over the centuries all that soup had taken its toll. We saw no wild tortoises at Post Office Bay, the Floreana species was now extinct and Darwin himself probably ate some of the last of them.

Post Office Bay was a lonely place with ice-blue water and a greenish beach. Dad and Christian went spearfishing.

'What about park regulations?' asked Mom.

'If you see anybody, then make sure you tell us,' Dad said.

Lynnath went snorkelling too, but she didn't take anything. Dad shot some fish and collected two excellent specimens of *Cypraea nigropunctata* which, like most of the other island creatures, were to be found nowhere else in the world. After cleaning the animals out, I hid the shells away, in case we were searched. Robert wasn't keen to dive, he said it was too cold without a wetsuit, so he walked around the island with Mom and me, looking at the cactus plants and enjoying the birds, who, like the other animals, showed no fear of humans, even though they should have. I liked the red-footed boobies, but the blue-footed ones were my favourite. They looked preposterous and unnatural; it was as if somebody had dipped their feet into bright, powder-blue paint, and they stomped about, taking exaggerated steps and waving their legs in the air as if they were trying to flick the colour off.

Our last stop on Floreana Island was at Ma Wittmer's place. Mom said she didn't want to go because she'd heard that Ma Wittmer had murdered her husband.

'How did she do it?' I had just finished reading a detective book where everybody had been murdered in a different way.

'Poison,' said Mom. 'So I don't think we should eat any food there. In case she tries to do it to us too.'

I felt a thrill run down my spine. A real life murderess was almost as good as the blue-footed boobies.

'I don't think it was her husband who died,' Lynnath said. 'I read that there was a German doctor who ran away to the island with one of his patients who was married, and then the Wittmers came and lived in pirate caves until Ma had her first baby, and then a baroness arrived with her three lovers. They called it the Galapagos Affair.'

'I'm not sure the children want to hear this story,' said Mom.

'Oh yes, I do,' I said. 'What happened next? Who died?'

'Well the baroness wanted to open a luxury hotel, but she shot at people and swam in the only drinking water on the island. That made everybody cross. Also, one of her lovers started beating up the other one.'

'And then?' This was even better than my detective book.

'And then she disappeared with her lover, the one who had been beating up the other one, remember? The Wittmers swore the couple had taken a yacht to Tahiti, but nobody on the island remembers seeing any boats that week. And they left all their stuff behind.'

'And what happened to the guy who kept getting beaten up?'

'Well, he asked a Norwegian fisherman to take him to Santa Cruz, but they never got there. Their mummified bodies were found on

Marchena Island.'

'Mummified bodies,' I said. I liked the sound of that. I also liked to hear Lynnath say the word 'lovers', mainly because I knew Mom didn't like it.

'Sounds a bit far-fetched to me,' said Mom. 'I thought somebody was poisoned.'

'Well, yes,' said Lynnath, 'the Gêrman doctor was.'

'Who was he again?' I was struggling to keep up with the plot.

'The one who ran away with his patient, remember? They were nudists and vegetarians, but I think they stopped getting on. Anyway, he was poisoned with a chicken and she went back to Germany.'

'I thought he was a vegetarian.'

'That's what's strange about it.'

'So only the Wittmers were left?' I said.

'That's right,' said Lynnath, 'and they had the island all to themselves after that.'

'I told you there was poison,' said Mom. 'And I still don't think we should eat any of her food. I don't want to be murdered.'

'I should be so lucky,' said Dad.

Ma Wittmer's long grey hair was twisted into a bun. Her cheeks were pink. She had smile lines fanning out from her eyes and a sweet, tinkling laugh. I'd never seen anyone look more like a granny. Her hotel and bar was on the damper side of the island and the evening we visited her a fire was burning, which glinted off the dark wood furniture and gave the place a cosy feel. She said she hadn't seen visitors in a long, long while and offered us home-made orange wine and cookies. We didn't ask where her husband was. Christian seemed very relaxed and chatted away in German. He said the orange wine was delicious and he finished all the cookies. I didn't eat a single biscuit and, after Robert ate one, I watched him closely for suspicious signs.

Ma Wittmer told Christian about the oranges. If you walk up the mountain you'll find them, she said. She was right. Once we were past the cactus and grey scrub, the air cooled and grew misty. Moisture dripped from the plants. There, amongst the indigenous vegetation, were orange trees, loaded with fruit. We filled several sacks. Three thousand miles non-stop lay between us and the Marquesas Islands; a month at sea in the best conditions, with a clean hull and good trade winds. I couldn't bear to think of such a long sea voyage without fruit. The oranges we collected were perfect; fresh and ripe. I picked one from the tree. Its skin sprayed fragrant oil as I peeled it and, when I bit into the flesh, juice spurted into my mouth, stinging the back of my throat.

13

THE MARQUESAS AND TUAMOTUS

Our journey from the Galapagos to the Marquesas took thirty days, all of them wonderful and very different from the twenty-four days we had spent sailing from Las Perlas to Galapagos. Sailing for the Marquesas we had a clean hull, wind on the stern and oranges – sweet juicy oranges – to eat every day. The north-east trade winds arrived as we set out, blowing the clouds and mist away from the harsh mountains that formed the backdrop to Ma Wittmer's pub and hotel. Raising our twin jibs, we left the rough, half-finished looking landscape of the Galapagos to be swallowed by the ocean, a volcano emitting one last puff of steam into the pale sky as if its fire had been extinguished by the rising water. From that moment, until we made landfall in the Marquesas a month later, the wind blew steadily, never varying its strength by more than a few knots. Other than a row of unkempt cumulus clouds slouching on the windward horizon and promising nothing more than a continuation of the trades, the sky remained clear. Sitting on deck in the evenings, watching the glowing ball of the sun melt into the horizon, I believed I could feel the world turning.

Vingila grunted and creaked contentedly, sighing as she descended the waves. With the wind behind her and twin jibs out on whisker poles, she didn't once argue or fight with Baruch who kept course for her without complaint. The temperature of the air was never too hot or too cold and I felt safe and completely content.

During the long afternoons Dad taught Robert how to navigate; to take sights with the sextant and make calculations from the sight-reduction tables. My mother was the timekeeper. We had long since discovered a cheap digital watch that outperformed Dad's brass chronometer on its bed of crushed velvet. When my father, with Robert at his side, focused his sextant on the sun and, using the index bar, measured the angle between that glowing orb and the horizon, he called out to Mom who sat below decks and recorded the exact time. Then Dad would come below and, opening the nautical almanac, would take out his pencil and begin the calculations Leonard Pratt, the retired pilot, had shown him back in Cape Town.

'Can I learn to navigate too?' I asked my mother.

'No, navigation's a man's job,' she replied.

'Why?'

'Because,' she explained, 'boys are better at maths than girls.'

Mom found scraps of material for me to sew a doll. I worked by hand with a needle and thread, my doll taking shape as the days passed. She had white skin, a red dress and long black hair hanging down her back. I wanted her to look like Snow White and onto her blank head I embroidered two long-lashed eyes and a pair of red lips. I didn't intend it, but her face emerged angry and wicked, with a sulky, twisted mouth and mad eyes looking in different directions. I felt shocked and disappointed at first, then, after some thought I decided that I could – with caution – still love her. I named her Lucrezia after the King's Peruvian princess wife, to whom she bore some resemblance. Once she was finished, we curled up together on my bunk in the stern cabin, and read the works of Charles Dickens which Mom had bought in Panama. Of the stories – *A Christmas Carol, A Tale of Two Cities, The Pickwick Papers,*

David Copperfield, and *Great Expectations* – only the *Pickwick Papers* bogged me down. I could see that Dickens meant the story to be funny, but I couldn't understand why men would want to start a stupid club and keep notes on their meetings. I loved all the other stories. *Great Expectations* I read twice; losing myself in the spooky cobwebby house with bitter old Miss Havisham, I ached with Pip's love for the beautiful icy-hearted Estella, and was torn by his terrible disappointment. Occasionally I came up for air, my head still on the moors and filled with the mournful clanging of the convict ships. Outside I would find the sun shining and Robert gutting a fish for lunch. There was no mist, no gloom, no unrequited yearnings. Dad hadn't even raised his voice for weeks. Mom baked bread daily and, on Christian's daughter Heike's advice, sprouted mung beans and alfalfa seeds in a jar. Heike, from *Donella,* was a vegetarian, the first one I had ever met. So was Janie, her soft-lipped Swedish boyfriend. They had lived in America where health food was the latest craze and from them we learned about ratatouille and brown rice. Through Christian on the radio, she gave Mom recipes and told us how to eat the sprouts. Make tuna salad, she said, with the next fish you catch, and eat it on bread fresh from the oven. Sprinkle sprouts on the top. Christian and Dad spoke every day. The crew and captain of *Donella* were also having a wonderful time and Christian told us they hadn't trimmed a sail or touched the helm for days. After a few hours of bright, tropical sunshine I'd be drawn back once again to the convict ships, filthy London and the closed-up, dusty house of heartbreak.

Over the days we grew so familiar with the predictability of *Vingila's* motion that we traversed the decks as if we were dancing; one big step, three quick ones and a rapid stop as she reached the end of her roll. We used our hands too, reaching for shrouds and swinging off in time for the next wave. Our movements became graceful, unthinking, and it seemed I could scarcely remember a time when I had plodded across solid ground, one dull footstep after the other. My body, unchanged as yet by puberty, felt exactly right and as it should be; my limbs and feet obeyed my commands and were the correct size, not too large, clumsy or far away as they would soon become, and my skin, soft, small-pored and fine of hair, covered all of me just as it should. I was as happy and comfortable with myself as I was with the wind and sea around me. A month passed like this before the faint outline of mountains appeared on our port bow, ragged as the backs of sleeping dragons. My heart sank. I didn't want to stop sailing. I wanted everything to stay as it was and I understood then how Bernard Moitessier, reaching the end of his around the world race, had turned his back on England and the finish line, to sail all the way to the Pacific and Tahiti again.

The mountains rising from the sea in front of us belonged to the Marquesas Group, and the names of the individual islands on the chart were confusing; Fatu Hiva, Ua Huka, Hiva Oa, Fatu Huku, Nuku Hiva and Ua Pou.

'Which one are we going to first again?' asked Robert. 'I keep forgetting.'

'Ua Hooker, isn't it?' said Mom. 'Or was it Hiva Poo or something?'

'Fatu Hiva,' I said, 'the one Thor Heyerdahl lived on. That's first.'

After reading Thor's book I knew exactly what to expect: gloomy jungle, mosquitoes and a morose population disfigured by the swollen limbs of elephantiasis. I couldn't wait. I discovered that his descriptions were fairly accurate. The Marquesas Archipelago was volcanic, gloomy and brooding, the islands draped in jungle, and the people, our first Polynesians, weren't very friendly. The mosquitoes on Fatu Hiva were as bad as Thor had described. I looked hopefully for elephantiasis sufferers, but there were none to be seen.

Fatu Hiva's silhouette, seen from afar, had suggested the backs of sleeping dragons. Up close, however, it became apparent that the dragons weren't sleeping after all, but were in fact long dead. All that remained were the remnants of their decaying carcasses. Black ribs of rock fell into the sea, shattered shafts of femurs and tibias poked through the slimy, green vegetation. Broken skulls had caves for eyes. Everything was smashed and rotten. A crumbling pillar cast long shadows across the anchorage and in some of the dank valleys the murk was so dense I doubted the sun had ever penetrated. The beaches were black too, composed of a fine sand that, when the sun caught it, gave off a toxic-looking, metallic gleam. In the black sand-bottomed bay, the navy blue water appeared impossibly deep. Taking off from the beach in a dinghy felt like dropping off the edge of a cliff.

Some years earlier, missionaries had built whitewashed churches. In the dampness, mildew had eaten into the plaster, turning it dark. Before the arrival of the missionaries, people worshipped tikis, snarling gods they chiselled from black volcanic stone. Tikis were everywhere. Over the years lichen grew into the stone, eroding it, although the carvings remained largely intact. Some of the bigger tikis stood out in the open, while other taboo tikis crouched in caves and the trunks of very old trees. Three young boys with flea-bitten ankles and coarse, horny feet offered to show us the forbidden gods for a fee.

'And bones too,' they said.

As we left the village, they warned us not to say a word to anyone or we would all be in trouble. We followed them up a slippery track to a place where a pile of rocks marked a cave from which the old god gazed. Beside him lay a heap of human skulls and long bones. The boys could not, or would not, say to whom they had once belonged, and after taking some money, turned and ran home.

On Sundays when the church bells rang, people wrapped in their best *pareos* of garish hibiscus-printed cloth, formed slow processions to worship. But it was clear who the real gods of the islands were.

Some people consider the Marquesas beautiful. I found them unsettling, like distorted visions of paradise. The palm trees were there, and the blue water and beaches, but somehow everything was wrong. I found the locals gloomy too. At night as we lay in our bunks Lynnath told me how relations between the Polynesians and visitors had, right from the beginning, been marked by misunderstanding and dreadful diseases. The islanders had done their best to counter the threat of the visitors by eating missionaries and skirmishing with buccaneers, but they had fallen to influenza and smallpox. From 100 000 strong, the population had dropped to a paltry 2 000 individuals. At the time of our visit fewer than 500 people lived on Fatu Hiva, in a squalid village pressed against the base of a dripping cliff. Thor had considered spending longer on the island, which he had envisioned as paradise, but I could understand him moving on after less than a year, worn down at last by mosquitoes, mud and hostility. Two days before we ourselves departed, I finally saw an old woman with elephantiasis. She crept from a hut, dragging her hugely swollen, deformed leg behind her, to stare unsmilingly at us.

'What on earth are those triangles?' Mom said, pointing to the muddy stream which trickled into the bay to form a half moon of brown water that washed against the beach.

'What triangles?' Dad asked. We were standing on a low hill looking down at the bay in which our boat lay anchored. After Fatu Hiva, my father said he'd had enough of people, and we had sailed to another island in the Marquesas group, Motane, which was deserted. Christian, the spearfisherman on *Donella*, had come with us. He said he felt the same way, and besides we needed fresh meat. Dad lifted his hunting rifle and put his eye to the sight.

'What are you talking about?' he said to Mom. He swept the rifle in an arc which encompassed the bay where our boat was anchored and back to the dry red hills behind us. He was searching for the wild sheep we had heard roamed the island.

'They're sharks' fins,' Christian said, referring to the black triangles in the muddy water.

He was standing next to Mom and didn't sound particularly concerned.

'Can't be,' said Mom. 'Not so many, surely.'

The black triangles patrolled back and forth and occasionally came together in splashy collisions, which made counting them difficult.

'Twenty-seven, I think,' I said.

The triangles kept to the brown water, which was roughly the size of the municipal swimming pool in Benoni.

'Impossible,' Mom said. 'I didn't see any when we came in. What're they doing there?' My mother still didn't want to believe that twenty-seven sharks were swimming less than ten feet from the beach. We looked to Lynnath for an answer.

'I've no idea,' she said, 'breeding or something, I'd imagine. I've never heard of anything like this.'

'So how are we going to get through the surf back to our boat?' I said.

'Well, for one thing, we can't tip over in the waves,' Robert said. 'If that happens we're dead.'

We had come ashore in Christian's Zodiac, and I got to wondering if a shark could bite its way through an inflatable dinghy if it wanted to. Then, leaving the sharks for later, Lynnath, Mom, Robert and I took a walk to investigate the headland while Dad, Christian and Janie went hunting. Motane was the only non-volcanic island in the Marquesas, and apart from the muddy stream which flowed intermittently, the place was dry and covered in sparse shrub which had been eroded to reddish patches by herds of feral sheep and goats. Beneath a stunted tree beside the stream stood the remains of an abandoned shack. It had been built by a Frenchman who had tried – and failed – to live on the island, Robinson Crusoe style. The Polynesians had never even bothered to settle on Motane.

From the top of the headland we looked directly down to *Vingila*, anchored in three fathoms of clear water on a sandy bottom. We could see the stream and the shack and the brown water near the beach, although it was too far to see the sharks. We watched the three men walk inland with their rifles and disappear behind a hill.

'Do you think we'll get back to the boat okay?' Mom asked Lynnath.

'I don't know, it depends how aggressive the sharks are.'

'I didn't like the way they were acting,' I said, 'and I wish we had the hard dinghy, not the inflatable.'

'I never thought of that,' Mom said. 'What if they bite a hole in it? Will it sink?'

'I hope not,' Lynnath said.

Robert wasn't listening to us, he was staring at *Vingila*.

'What's that?' he said.

There was a very long, dark shape beneath our boat that hadn't been there before.

'The shadow of the keel on the sand?' Lynnath said. She didn't sound convinced.

'So why is it moving around when *Vingila* isn't?'

Donella, anchored a short distance away, had nothing but clear water beneath her keel. From the hill we could see her bobbing on her anchor chain while Heike sat in the cockpit, drinking tea. As a vegetarian, she had declined to be part of the sheep hunt. The dark shape beneath *Vingila* swam to the stern to investigate Baruch. It was enormous.

'I think it's a shark,' Robert said.

'Not *another* one,' I said. 'I don't like this place.'

'It's quite big for a shark,' Lynnath said, 'and the shape's wrong. I guess we'll find out when we get back, if it's still there.'

I said, 'If we get past the other sharks first, you mean.'

'Shh,' Robert said. 'Listen.'

A gunshot ricocheted from the far hills.

We waited for almost two hours beside the stream before Dad and Christian came back. It was very hot and the air smelled of goat droppings and dust. Pepe panted in the sparse shade of the tree, rolling out a steamy, swollen tongue. I held him loosely by the collar because Mom asked me to keep him out of the sea, away from the sharks who were still patrolling. As the afternoon wore on our eyelids grew heavy in the heat. The arrival of the flies awoke us.

Dad and Christian walked ahead, each with a sheep slung across his shoulders. Janie came behind with the guns. Clouds of flies accompanied them and raced ahead to meet us; crawling over our arms and faces to drink our sweat, and burrowing into our noses and mouths. The men looked tired, blood smeared their clothes and their dusty faces were streaked as if they'd been crying. Dad's sheep was missing its head, the neck terminating in ragged flesh, a windpipe and shards of bone.

'What happened to your sheep?' Mom said.

'I think this hunting rifle,' he said, 'is for elephants, not goats. One shot took the head clean off.'

Christian's animal was lumpy, covered in multiple bulbous skin tumours.

'Can we eat that?' I asked. 'What if we catch something?' I pictured the lot of us breaking out in mobile, squashy bumps.

'I'm sure it'll be fine once it's cooked,' Mom said, waving a fly from her upper lip.

Pepe pushed forward and began licking the blood from the open neck of Dad's sheep.

'Get him out of here,' Dad said, sharpening a fish-filleting knife on a stone. *Donella* had a deep freeze and the plan was to freeze portions of mutton after Dad had butchered the carcasses. We would eat the liver for supper that night. I hoped there wouldn't be lumps on it.

'Don't let him anywhere near the sea,' Mom said. Pepe hadn't noticed the sharks yet and we didn't want him chasing after them.

Dad began by hanging the animals from a tree by their back legs. He made cuts around their ankles and pulled off their skins as if they were pyjamas. I was relieved to see that the lumps came off too, leaving the meat underneath looking normal. Dad had grown up on a farm and knew what he was doing. He slit open the abdominal cavities, catching the spilling intestines in a bucket. Rivulets of blood formed little dams in the dust as they trickled downhill. More flies came, crawling over the carcasses and drinking from the sticky red rivers of blood.

Dad sent Robert to fetch water to clean the meat. As scraps of gristle and fat washed into the stream and then the sea, activity increased in the bay. The black triangles began moving faster, swimming back and forth with a jerky urgency. Then one shark, obviously deciding he couldn't take it any longer, tried to invade the land, surfing up the beach on a wave which receded to leave him thrashing on the sand. The big fish was dark-skinned, without fin markings, and had a blunt, bullish face, quite unlike the white-tipped reef sharks we were familiar with. Pepe pulled free of my grasp and charged, barking his shrill, poodle yelps. Robert ran after him. I followed and got close enough to see a pair of piggy, unblinking eyes. The shark looked confused, torn between lunging for Pepe and making an escape back to deeper water. A wave rolled in and the big fish twisted, turning over and gaining purchase with its fins. Dragging Pepe by the collar, we retreated to the tree.

Hanging from a branch, the sheep were looking less like dead animals and more like meat. Janie carried the bucket of entrails, hooves and the remaining head to the beach and emptied it into the sea which erupted in fins, mouths and sleek, sinewy bodies.

Dad's eyes went flat. His lip twitched and tightened, made to turn down at the corners. 'Why the hell did you do that?' he said.

'For fun,' Janie said, returning the look.

Later, when the meat had been packed into buckets, we stood on the shore beside the dinghy and Christian spoke to us.

'I don't have to tell you,' he said, 'that we can't, under any circumstances, flip over.'

He didn't need to tell me we couldn't turn over. I knew that if we capsized we'd be floating in muddy water with twenty-seven overexcited sharks and two dismembered sheep. I tried to be brave. I thought of Thor: he wasn't afraid of sharks, he plucked them from the water by the tail as they swam beside the raft, and hit them on the head until they were dead. That was okay for him, another voice in my head said, he was on a raft, not floating in muddy water with a bucket of mutton parts. And his raft was made of wood, not rubber, which any shark could bite through, if it wanted.

'So does everyone understand?' Christian said. 'There'll be no silly buggers, okay?'

He looked at Robert and me first, then at Janie. I nodded my head, no silly buggers from me.

'This is how we'll do it,' he said, and gave us our orders.

'Nicky,' Mom said, 'just make sure you look after Pepe, okay? Don't let anything happen to him.'

My mouth felt as dry as the eroded earth beneath my feet. Ripples of heat and a rank goat-smell arose from the fly-covered meat. Then the light changed quality and became suddenly brighter and – momentarily – everything looked further away. A few lazy yellow spots floated up in my field of vision. I thought I was going to be sick.

'Mom,' I said softly so that the others couldn't hear, 'I'm scared. I don't want to do this.'

'Don't be silly, you can't stay here. Now take Pepe, and whatever you do don't let him go.'

We carried the dinghy to the sea, and packed the buckets of meat into it. Robert and I climbed in first with the dog while the adults waited and watched the wave sets for a gap. At the first lull, they grasped the inflatable by the handles on its sides and ran into the water, kicking off and jumping in quickly. Janie and Christian grabbed paddles and began stroking against the surge. We were using Christian's dinghy and he hadn't thought we'd need the outboard. As the dinghy hit the water and was carried out by the backwash, the fins all disappeared.

'Where'd they go?' I asked, looking around. I held Pepe by the collar, pressed onto the floorboards in case he decided to jump. He fought me, rolling his eyes and twisting his throat as if trying to choke himself.

'Look! Here they come,' said Christian, raising his paddle.

The fins approached, swimming rapidly, pushing up bow waves and leaving wakes in their trail.

Before I could scream, or rather squeak, because Mom didn't like me screaming, Christian smacked the first shark on the head with his paddle and, without missing a stroke, continued paddling. More sharks were shoved away by either Janie or Christian, depending on who was closest. Thor Heyerdahl himself couldn't have done a better job. Christian, I thought, could easily have made the Kon Tiki team. It took more than twenty-seven irritable sharks to scare him. Once we crossed the line, solid as a glass wall, that demarcated the brown water from the clear, we left the sharks behind.

Back at *Vingila* a very big, very old kingfish was waiting for us, casting the shadow we had seen from the hill. He kept close to the side of our boat, sidling up for protection or company, I couldn't be sure. His scales were almost the size of my hands, and his wide, thick-lipped mouth looked big enough to swallow Pepe whole. Filamentous parasites trailed from his fins and his opaque eyes appeared ancient and somehow sorrowful. His movements were slow and stately, no sinewy thrashing in the shallows for him. Later, once we had the dismembered sheep aboard, he refused the scraps of mutton I offered him, opening his mouth as he rose to the surface to ingest the globs of fat and muscle before fixing me with a reproachful eye and spitting them out. He liked fish biltong though, and over the course of an hour I fed him a bowl of it.

In the Tuamotu atolls the people ate dogs. On Takaroa atoll, Turoa, a round-bellied Polynesian man in a dirty *pareo*, told us he liked to kill dogs by stuffing them in a sack filled with rocks and throwing them into the lagoon. He said he fed the dog meat to unsuspecting tourists. I wondered where he found tourists. There wasn't a hotel on the island, or an airstrip and the crew and captains of *Donella* and *Vingila* were the only visitors I could see. We had stopped in at the Tuamotus on our way to Tahiti for the cyclone season, because Christian had said the diving was good. The Tuamotu islands are all coral atolls formed on the craters of volcanos lying beneath the sea. Seen from high above, they would look like a string of smoke-rings, with their circles of white sand surrounding bottomless lagoons.

Making landfall in the Tuamotus was tricky because the atolls were only as high as their tallest coconut palm. Robert perched on *Vingila*'s prow, listening out for the sound of breakers, which were usually the first indication of land. Almost every atoll sported the rusting remains of a Taiwanese fishing boat, stranded high on an outlying reef. Sometimes we saw these broken vessels first, before the reef or the palm trees.

'Why so many wrecks?' Robert asked.

'Probably can't hear the breakers over the sound of their engines,' I said, 'or maybe the navigators were sleeping.'

Turoa of Takaroa told us the Taiwanese boats fished for shark fin and *bêche de mer*, or sea cucumbers. He said that captains of wrecked trawlers, if they survived, were arrested by the crew of the next trawler and sent back to Taiwan to be tried for negligence. If found guilty, he had heard that they were executed. Sometimes they committed suicide before they were arrested. They can't take the shame, he said.

Making landfall wasn't the only difficulty in sailing the Tuamotus, the passages into the lagoons were equally hazardous; between tides, water rushed through the narrow openings at such a rate it formed standing waves, and our engine at full throttle was barely powerful enough to get us through. On Takaroa, we tied up to the concrete jetty at the entrance to await slack tide, before we attempted entering the lagoon. *Vingila* lay alongside *Donella* near the oily-smelling copra sheds and a pool with captive sharks cooking in the sun. From the pier, a road of crushed coral bisected a small settlement of lime-washed houses with roofs of steel. Shade was in short supply, provided here and there by a coconut palm or breadfruit tree. Hibiscus bushes, heavy with blooms, sprouted from gardens of swept beach sand. The sea, either the luminous turquoise of the lagoon or the deeper blue of the open ocean, was almost always within sight and the breakers on the outside reef sounded like traffic on a distant highway. The blinding glare, reflecting from every surface, made us squint. In addition to being a vegetarian, Heike suffered from migraines and a short walk into the village was enough to bring on a sick headache which drove her back to *Donella*, where she rested with a wet towel over her eyes. Lynnath was made of hardier stuff and, with her eyes protected by photochromatic lenses, which turned almost black in the glare, she spent the afternoon investigating the shark pool, showing me the males with their double penises, or 'claspers', as she called them, and describing their mating habits. They were small reef sharks with unhappy mouths of fine yellow teeth and skins that caught the sun like diamond sandpaper. That's where Turoa found us and introduced himself. When the next Taiwanese trawler arrived, he said, the sharks would have their fins cut off. Then he described how he killed dogs for eating and fed them to tourists.

'What about those dogs?' Lynnath asked, pointing at a couple of grizzled specimens sleeping in the shade of the copra shed. 'Would you eat them?'

'Of course not. Those are pets. We keep eating dogs somewhere else, and feed them only coconuts, for the taste.'

'Anyway,' he added, sizing them up with a gourmet's eye, 'those animals look too old.'

That evening, after the sun fell, we were visited by locals with guitars and gifts of shell jewellery. As the numbers of visitors increased, Dad sent Robert to the village to buy beer. After a while the singing started. People grew merrier as the night wore on. Then after midnight the mood changed and a certain melancholy pervaded. The songs became increasingly mournful. Women keened; men moaned. The sounds were of yearning, mourning and regret.

'I don't know if I like the music,' Mom said, 'but it is distinctive.'

I went to bed soon after that, drifting from sleep to catch snatches of music or laughter and the footsteps of people climbing on and off *Vingila* through the night.

On the atoll of Manihi, a secretive Japanese company had set up a black-lipped oyster farm and were cultivating pearls. The manager granted us a truncated tour of the fenced-in plant where masked women scratched the insides of live oysters and planted marble sized 'seeds' beneath their mantles. At the reception desk, oversized, fake-looking black pearls lay arranged in a glass case. We asked their price and were informed that nothing was for sale, the pearls were for display purposes only. At the end of our tour the Japanese manager bowed and thanked us, then suggested we move on to another atoll.

'Recreational snorkelling and diving here is forbidden,' he said. 'Our company bought the rights.'

Before my father could reply, the man said: 'We have patrol boats. I wouldn't recommend trying.'

In the village on the other side of the chain-link fence, we found none of the friendly smiles we'd received in Takaroa. People sitting on the steps of their houses lifted their heads as we walked through, then turned away quickly or looked down again.

On Ahe Atoll the people were as laid back and friendly as Takaroa.

Standing on the copra jetty we found the famous sailor Bernard Moitessier, who had eaten tins of condensed milk and dehydrated vegetables while racing his yacht non-stop around the world. *Joshua*, his boat, was anchored in the lagoon – looking just as she did in the book taking pride of place above Mom and Dad's bunk. Hard-chine steel and still the same shade of red but a little more weather worn. Bernard, wearing a pair of underpants and plastic sandals, looked a little more weather worn too. He had skinny, ropy-veined legs and when my parents approached him to say what an inspiration he was to them – and to all sailors for that matter – I saw a look of panic enter his eye. He didn't seem to like people much, which I supposed was why he'd spent months sailing around the world alone and was now lying low in Ahe. Still, he nodded politely and accepted my parents compliments and admiration with a dignified bow of his head and a shy smile. After a while he excused himself and left us to watch Polynesian men load rancid-smelling bags onto the copra schooner, which was taking the dried coconuts to Tahiti where their oil would be pressed out and turned into soap.

14

TAHITI

The ferry from Moorea capsized the morning of the storm. Laden with people and bananas, it turned over in the harbour entrance where the waves were breaking across the channel and the buoys marking the reefs on either side of the pass. In the white water, the dirty red underside of the ferry looked like the back of a bleeding whale. We watched a tug and two rescue boats go out and heard later on the radio that four people had drowned. The harbour master issued a heavy weather warning and advised all anchored yachts to evacuate to the far side of the island which was less exposed. Papeete harbour, in addition to offering poor protection, was also very crowded and hundreds of yachts were slotted stern to shore in an accordion-sweep from the inner concrete pier to the outer reaches of the beach. The boats deep within the bay were slightly more sheltered than those of us anchored further out where mooring was cheaper.

As the day wore on, the storm worsened. An onshore wind tore straight through the channel towards *Vingila*, held by a single anchor at the bow and a pair of stern lines tied to bollards on the shore.

'When are we moving?' Mom said after the harbour master's

announcement.

Vingila tugged and jerked at her moorings like a disobedient dog on a leash. Behind the stern, rising breakers threw tantrums on the dirty sand and dissolved in spumes of foam.

'Moving where?' Dad said.

'To a safer anchorage. I thought you said there was a hurricane hole somewhere.'

'And how are we going to get through that pass? Tell me that, then we'll go.'

'Well, what about the evacuation then, like the harbour master said?'

'Are you out of your tiny, cotton-picking mind?' Dad snorted. 'We're not going through that pass. Didn't you just see what happened to that ferry? Can't you see we're stuck here?'

I retreated to my cabin. From the porthole I watched the breakers on the beach. If I really had to, I could just about swim ashore, I thought, wondering where the life jackets were. I couldn't remember seeing any since Durban.

I lay on my bunk feeling sad. Some weeks earlier Lynnath had announced she was leaving us. She had run out of money, her mother wanted her to come home and the University of Port Elizabeth had offered her a post as a lecturer.

'I have to go, the job's too good to turn down,' she had told me, 'and I can't wait here for the whole hurricane season.'

She had bought a plane ticket back to South Africa and now a huge storm had blown up on the day of her departure. To take my mind off Lynnath I picked up the book my new friend Barbara had loaned me and I tried to read. Beneath the curly script of its title, *Sweet Savage Love,* a woman in a silk dress with streaming hair rode a horse at high speed. Her tight bodice was cut very low at the neck and it looked as if her breasts were about to fall out at any moment. At first Mom had expressed some half-hearted reservations regarding the book's suitability for a twelve-year-old but when I told her Barbara had read it and she was twelve my mother gave in. There was a lot of sex. Ginny, the woman on the horse, burned with passion for Steve Morgan although it took her most of the story to accept it, because they fought so much at first. In the beginning he had to force himself on her. For a while she also became a prostitute but they found true love in the end even though he called Ginny a whore and was fooling around with a slave girl on their wedding night.

Barbara, who was from America and lived on a yacht called *Barnacle Bill*, had told me there was another book after *Sweet Savage Love*, called *Wildest Heart*, which was just as good and I could read it as soon as I finished the first. However, distracted by my sadness, the swaying curtains and the stern smashing down and sending up sheaves of spray, I found reading difficult. The rattle of the halyards and the rising whine of the shrouds protesting against the gale didn't help. Flecks of froth, blown by the wind, stuck quivering to the portholes. After a while, Lynnath came through to the cabin and began to pack. It didn't take long; her books and clothing fitted easily into one small rucksack.

'What time are you leaving?' I said.

Vingila heaved, nearly throwing Lynnath off her feet.

'After supper,' she said.

Dad had agreed to take her ashore that evening – after that she was by herself, he said. She put her passport and plane ticket to one side, with her camera. Then she looked out of the porthole to where rain had begun to mingle with the spray of the waves.

'They said the sea will be even bigger later,' I said. 'Will you make it in the dinghy?'

Lynnath was quiet for a time, her gaze on the sea outside, one hand on the grab rail for balance. I waited for her to say she'd changed her mind and decided not to go, that she wanted to stay and keep sailing with us, teaching me marine biology and helping us catch fish, but all she said was, 'I hope *Vingila* will be okay tonight.'

Later that afternoon the harbour master closed the port of Papeete. All vessels were forbidden to leave or enter the channel, except in an emergency. Rain fell and the sea was so rough we couldn't get ashore. We settled in to await the evening and Lynnath's departure, hoping the storm would ease off. Mom cooked an early supper and we gathered in the saloon.

'Do you think the waves look like they're getting closer?' Robert said. 'I mean, are we getting nearer the beach?'

'Have some more soup,' Mom said, pushing the pot over.

Dad reached into the pot for the Swedish ham bone Heike had given us after Christian ate the meat off it. So far Mom had made three batches of ham-flavoured soup by adding new vegetables from the market daily.

'Nah,' Dad said to Robert, waving the bone at him. 'When the waves are bigger they just break further out. That makes them look closer.' He patted my mother on the leg. 'Nice soup, Fatso.'

As *Vingila* dragged her anchor slowly and edged towards the shore without us realising it, Mom cut a pineapple for dessert. We ate pineapple every day. It was the cheapest fruit. Often, after shopping at the local market for our daily soup greens and pineapples, we walked through the Bon Marché to look at the cheese and expensive apples and peaches on display. We never bought any.

'Pineapple, anyone?' Mom said, as if it were a treat. She had even started making beer from the peels. When I told her that it sometimes made me feel drunk, she said I had a vivid imagination. When we ate too much pineapple we got mouth ulcers, then we stopped for a few days.

'I'll have a slice or two,' Lynnath said. 'My last piece of Tahiti pineapple. I'll probably miss it when I'm gone.'

'If the weather clears tomorrow,' my father said, 'I'll check out the wharves and look for work.'

Even on a diet of soup and pineapple, we were digging into the last of the whisky smuggling money. Tahiti was expensive and soon our funds would be finished.

'Yes,' said Mom. 'A little cash would be nice for Christmas. I never thought everything would cost so much, and we're stuck here for the rest of the hurricane season.'

I was finding that it was much easier to be poor on the islands than in a city with bookshops and supermarkets and rich people on other boats who all seemed to have better clothes and nicer food to eat than we did.

After supper, Lynnath wrapped her camera and passport in a plastic packet and hugged me goodbye. We went outside to see her off. It had stopped raining but the gale was still blowing strong. She ruffled Robert's sun-bleached hair and punched him on the upper arm.

'Look after your sister,' she said, 'and both of you, try to be good. Don't make your Mom cross. And, Nicky, keep up the shell collecting, you're getting so good at identifying them now, and don't forget to record the data. That's the most important bit.'

'Have you got the newspaper article for Nana?' Mom asked.

In October, just after Robert and my twelfth birthday, a journalist heard about my shell collection from the captain of another yacht who also had an interest in shells. The journalist had visited *Vingila* together with a photographer and shortly thereafter my face appeared on the front page of the Papeete daily. *Le petit musée flottant de Nicky*, ran the headline. Nicky's little floating museum. After two years at sea and several months in the Pacific, my collection had grown considerably. Boxes of shells, wrapped in toilet paper and cotton wool, filled *Vingila*'s cupboards and the empty spaces under the bunks. Larger shells were tucked away in barrels in the bilges. The photographer wanted to see them all and took pictures of me posing seriously with my favourite cowries. The journalist marvelled that I knew their Latin names and ended his article by writing that I would like to exchange specimens from my collection with local collectors who could find me on *Vingila*, which was moored at Paofai, opposite the pizzeria. In the days that followed, a stream of shell collectors, mostly middle-aged men, came aboard to trade with me. I parted with one of the rare *Cypraea picta* from Senegal that Soledad had stolen from Vincent in Brazil, and in exchange received some equally rare deformed cowries from New Caledonia. One man offered to buy my *Cypraea surinamensis*, but I refused.

'Are you sure you've got the article?' Mom asked Lynnath again.

Lynnath threw her rucksack to Dad in the dinghy.

'Yes, I do,' she said, 'and I'll post it to Nana as soon as I get back.'

She gave me a final hug.

'Now, Nicky, don't cry. I'll see you again one day when you get back to South Africa. It's not so far.'

I knew she was just saying that. South Africa couldn't have been further away. Lynnath herself had pointed out that it lay exactly on the other side of the earth. I felt more tears rise in my eyes. I was losing my teacher and friend. And with Lynnath around, Dad didn't hit Robert and me so much. Lynnath lowered herself into the lurching dinghy which Dad was struggling to keep beside the boat. The wind was too strong for rowing, so the old Seagull had been brought from its canvas wrappings in the chain locker and screwed to the back of the dinghy. My father primed the engine, wound the cord and gave it a yank. It sputtered a bit before coughing into life. In the dark we could see the white heads of the breakers.

'How will you get past those waves?' Mom shouted.

'The harbour will be more sheltered,' Dad said. 'We'll tie up there at the dock.'

We watched him and Lynnath motor away into the night, the bow of the dinghy rising and falling in veils of spray. I could see they were taking on water. I hoped they'd turn around, but they didn't.

'She'll be soaked when they get ashore,' Robert said. 'And I hope the plane can fly in this weather.'

The dingy became smaller and smaller until it was lost at last in the hazy, uncertain line where the sea met the sky. I watched until it was out of sight and then I went into my cabin, lay down and – trying not to look at the empty bunk opposite mine – I closed my eyes.

The roaring of *Vingila*'s motor woke me and I knew something was wrong. Dad never over-revved the engine because he said it caused damage. I groped my way from the cabin, fighting against *Vingila*'s lurching and a strange, unnatural angle she'd adopted. In the radio room I found Mom. Water ran from her wet hair and mingled with the tears streaming down her face. She was wearing only a pair of panties and stood sobbing into the VHF radio. I couldn't see my father. Robert was next to Mom, bracing himself against the tilt of the passage.

'Mayday, mayday, mayday!' Mom cried. 'This is *Vingila, Vingila, Vingila*.'

Her only answer was an unconcerned swish of static.

My mother dropped the microphone, leaving it dangling in the air as she scrambled up the companionway stairs. The engine gave another anguished whine. I followed Robert into the cockpit, my feet slipping on the wet steps.

'What's going on? Where's Dad?' I yelled.

Outside spray drenched me. The air was thick with the stuff, and *Vingila* was jolting and banging so much that I could hardly make out what was happening at first. Then it became clear that our boat had dragged anchor and was lying in the breakers, nearly on the beach. Submitting to the force of the waves, she had rolled over on her side like a dog. White water pushed her hull closer ashore and sluiced the decks, swamping the cockpit. Her masts, glowing in the light of the street lamps, tilted over to almost touch the sand. Waves banged her hull against the ground in a series of crunching blows.

'God, no, help us!' Mom screamed as *Vingila* struck the beach again.

I thought it was the end of our boat. I couldn't see her making it through the pounding she was taking and I couldn't see how we'd ever get her off the beach. This, as far as I could tell, was a shipwreck. *Vingila* would break apart and soon the main saloon and cabins would be flooded and I would lose everything. My clothes, my red leatherette Dickens compendium and all my journals. Everything.

'Nooo! I can't steer.' Mom spun the helm. She revved the engine again and the propeller chopped foam. Hair blew over her face. Her glasses teetered askew. Her mouth formed an 'O' of distress in the white mask of her face. Abandoning the helm, she groped her way back downstairs into the tilted radio room, where she grabbed the mike and fell to the floor.

'Please, somebody, come and save us,' she moaned.

I thought we were about to die. Leaving my mother to sob into an unresponsive radio, I went outside and curled into foetal position on the cockpit duck boards because I couldn't think of anything else to do. A wave breaking over the hull brought me spluttering to my feet. Robert poked his head from the companionway.

'What do you think you're doing?' he said.

Before I could answer that I was preparing to die, we were distracted by the sound of a Seagull engine at full throttle. I looked up to see my father surfing towards us on the back of a fresh roller. Now at least, I thought, we'll have an adult to help.

The wave carrying my father rose up and broke, collapsing and taking Dad and the dinghy with it and burying them in several feet of tumbled water. When the breaker sucked back, we made out the overturned dinghy with the Seagull prop still spinning in the sky, but no Dad.

'Where's he gone?' I said.

'I dunno,' said Robert. 'It's hard to tell, it's so dark.'

We crawled uphill to the stern for a better look. A black blob, which might have been a head, surfaced and was then swallowed almost at once by the next wave. The blob resurfaced, nearer this time.

'It's Dad, he's swimming over.'

We were perfectly placed to see the breaker that lifted my father into its barrel and threw him against Baruch's rudder with such force that it jolted the transom. His head was sucked under again, but his hands, like those of a horror movie monster refusing to die, rose up from the black water to cling to the self-steering device.

I heard voices calling then and, looking up, I saw that a few men had waded into the surf, fighting the waves to get closer to the boat. Between breakers they were able to stand, holding their arms open.

'Jump,' called one man, 'jump and I'll save you.'

So I jumped. My rescuer was big and soft, with a full beard. I wrapped my arms and legs around him and buried my face deep in his hairy neck, and he waded to shore through the breakers. Twice he nearly lost his balance to the surge of the waves, then he caught his footing and we continued on. A white VW Beetle was parked on the road running parallel to the beach. He left me there on the lap of a young woman sitting in the passenger seat. I shivered and she hugged me against her bony chest. Her neck was marked by a string of purple bruises and her hair smelled of cigarette smoke. A few minutes later my rescuer came back with Pepe and Robert who were soaking wet and shivering. Pepe climbed onto my lap. Robert crawled into the back seat where he sat cradling his left arm. His face looked oddly yellow.

'Robbie, are you okay?' I said.

He nodded.

'And the arm?' I said.

'Sore,' he said, 'but okay.'

Since tumbling from a frangipani tree several days earlier he had been complaining of a sore arm. He'd scaled the tree to pick flowers for Shannon, a pretty American girl he liked. When a police car with flashing lights delivered my brother to the moorings after his fall, Mom's first thought was that he had been arrested for stealing. New Louis L'Amour novels had been turning up lately in his cabin and we knew he couldn't be buying them. When my mother paddled ashore in the dinghy, the policeman told her my brother had been found lying on the pavement in front of a small, concerned crowd; he was injured. Back on the boat, Dad, wondering if Robert's shoulder might be dislocated, had given the arm a hard yank, draining the blood from my brother's face and eliciting a surprisingly shrill scream. We found out much later that his humerus was broken in two places, but initially my parents hoped his injury wasn't serious and would heal on its own. It's pointless taking him to a doctor and paying good money only to find out nothing's wrong, Dad had said.

In the back seat of the VW, Robert rubbed his arm cautiously.

'Are you sure you're okay?' I asked.

'I'm okay.'

After a while I reached for his hand and said, 'Oh Robbie, I'm so scared.'

I knew *Vingila* couldn't go on pounding against the beach for much longer. I felt as if I was watching my house burn down. Our boat lay on her side, pinned to the sand by the wind and the waves. Dots of people trying to help clung to her sides like ants. She looked helpless and ungainly, like a fat woman collapsed in the street with her skirt wedged up to show her underwear. Our boat was pathetic and also somehow shameful and embarrassing; a public testament to our incompetence and carelessness. I started crying again. I thought about what a good yacht she was, not too lively or quick, but solid and dependable. It seemed she'd taken care of us when we needed her and now we had let her down. The girl with the cigarette hair put her arms around me again, murmuring French words into my ear. Pepe pushed against my chest, nudging my arm with his damp muzzle. Robert reached over to pat my shoulder.

'Nicky, don't cry,' he said. 'At least it's sand, not rocks and the hull's steel, that makes a difference.'

People kept coming to the window to ask if we were okay. Then somebody brought news that a rescue tug was on its way. He told us that some yachties – rich ones with a car – had heard Mom sobbing on the VHF radio. When the harbour master didn't answer her distress call they'd driven around themselves to see what was going on and had found the emergency people asleep in their compound with the radio turned off. It had taken quite a lot of shouting to wake them, the man said. Anyway, they'd dispatched a tug. He patted our hands through the window.

'It will be all right,' he said.

'Where's Dad?' Robert said. 'Can you see him?'

Vingila had worked her way sideways up the beach, with her tilted deck facing us and her masts horizontal. Several human shapes clung to the rails at the bow, but I couldn't see my father. Then a fresh gust hit the Beetle, driving rain against the windscreen and obscuring our view.

I began crying again.

'I can't see properly, but I think that's him on the bow, with Mom and some other people,' Robert said. 'And look, here comes the tug.'

The rescue boat threw *Vingila* a line and within minutes had pulled our boat, anchor and all, off the beach. Then it towed her to the far side of the harbour where she disappeared from view. The crowd on the beach started walking towards the road.

'What now?' I asked Robert.

He shrugged. We looked at the girl with the cigarette hair but she didn't know either. She had come to the boulevard to watch the storm and kiss her boyfriend in the dark; she'd never expected to pick up a pair of damp kids and a poodle. The crowd on the beach drifted up to stare at us. Mostly they were fellow yachties I'd seen on the pier. After a huddled conversation, a woman stepped up to the window.

'Do you remember me, children? My name's Mrs Kiefer.'

I knew her. On yachts nobody called anyone mister or missus. She made a point of it, though. She was American and she lived with her husband on an elegant schooner at the expensive walk-on moorings, closer to town. She was rich and stingy and she usually greeted me with a hint of pity, looking sorrowfully at my bare feet and grazed knees. I got the feeling she thought Robert and I were neglected and needed to be taught some manners. It was true that we usually looked scruffy and I had recently spent some weeks with my nose covered in yellow impetigo crusts. Mom had hoped they'd get better by themselves but they didn't. At the height of my skin infection when the scabs had spread to my chin as well, Mrs Kiefer had found me at the Bon Marché staring at the imported fruit. She was wheeling a loaded trolley and the expression on her face made me flush with shame. I wasn't averse to sympathy but Mrs Kiefer irked me because I suspected that she enjoyed feeling sorry for us. It confirmed the image she had of herself as a caring, morally and materially superior person. I hated her for it.

Her concerned face pushing in through the window of the Beetle made the hair on the back of my neck stand up.

'I suppose you two will have to come with me,' she said, sighing, 'and we'll get you back to your parents in the morning.'

'And Pepe?'

She sighed again. 'And the dog, of course. Come along, be quick now.'

When I got out of the car I saw that I was wearing only a pair of old panties and the torn T-shirt I had been sleeping in. Robert at least had had the sense to get dressed in a pair of shorts before abandoning ship.

Mrs Kiefer's 72-foot teak schooner was immaculate; all polished brass, varnished mahogany and tasselled lampshades. Every surface was clean and uncluttered and Persian rugs were scattered over the gleaming floorboards.

'What lovely carpets,' I said.

'Rugs,' said Mrs Kiefer, 'we call them rugs. Now I'm going to find you something dry to wear. Wait here, you two, and please try not to touch anything. And don't drip.' Looking pleased with herself, she trotted away in the direction of the forepeak.

The largest, most intricate carpet lay on the main saloon floor and had a golden tree embroidered on its surface. Hanging from its branches were fruits of different colours. Little birds sat in the tree, their beaks open in song. Pepe sniffed around with interest before walking to the centre of the carpet where he squatted down and deposited a coil directly onto a singing bird. A hot wave of shame and disgust swept over me. I felt sick.

'Quick,' said Robert, 'she's coming, do something.'

I picked up Pepe's poo in my bare hands, ran up the hatch and threw it overboard. I'd never touched a poo before and the bulk and steamy warmth of it surprised me. I could still feel it on my hands after I'd tossed it in the sea.

Downstairs, Mrs Kiefer held out an old shirt of her husband's.

'Try this on, dear.'

I can't wear that, I thought. Mr Kiefer was even creepier than his wife. He smelled sweetish and strange and so did the shirt. How could I wear a strange man's clothes? I looked at Robert. If I have to wear Mr Kiefer's shirt I'll never be able to sleep, I wanted to tell him. I'll have nightmares.

'Put this on,' she said. 'I don't have any underwear your size so you'll have to do without.'

I had survived a shipwreck only to sleep without underwear on an unfamiliar boat with the Kiefers and an incontinent dog. Tears welled in my eyes and my throat closed in painful spasm. I knew one thing,

I wasn't going to sleep without panties with those creeps around. I'd keep my own panties on, even if they were torn and wet.

'Can I wash my hands first?'

'Whatever for? You're wet enough already and we can't go around wasting fresh water.'

The next day, while we waited for our parents to find us, Robert slipped on the dock and fell onto his sore arm. He returned to the schooner where I was lying low in Mr Kiefer's shirt, too embarrassed to go out and see my friends. He told me he had heard a crunching sound when he fell. He had tears in his eyes. I didn't know what to do.

'Just sit here quietly with me,' I said. 'It will get better.'

'A bunch of bladdy rats,' Dad said that afternoon when Robert and I saw him again.

'Rats deserting a sinking ship. That's how you acted. Because that's what you are. A useless pair of bladdy rats.'

He spoke slowly, taking shallow breaths between words and he sat bent over in the main saloon, a frown of pain stamped on his face. His ribs, he said, had been broken when the wave threw him against Baruch. Mom sat beside him stroking Pepe. She didn't look up. Dad was angry with her too. He said she should have raised the anchor and motored away from the beach. He said that most likely she'd had the motor in reverse and not forward. There was no excuse for what she'd done. She hadn't been paying attention and she'd panicked. She was just as bad as us two kids. Useless.

'Get out of my sight,' he said to me. He reached above his head for the Whistler and was brought up short by his painful ribs.

I ran to my cabin. Dad didn't look quite up to using the Whistler although I thought it best not to hang around and find out. We were back at the same mooring, having re-anchored securely further from the shore. The storm was over and the harbour had reverted to its placid self. *Vingila* was missing nothing more than a few layers of paint on the port side of her hull. The dinghy had been retrieved and even the Seagull engine, after a little cleaning, still worked. I lay on my bunk, fuming. I wanted to tell Dad that while I hadn't broken any bones, my night hadn't exactly been easy either.

I could hear my father's voice in the saloon as I lay sulking in my bunk. I wanted to say to him that I had been brave. I had thought I was about to die. Waves had broken over me, and I had been carried through a stormy sea to be abandoned with strangers. I was only twelve years old anyway. And what about picking up dog poo with my bare hands? What thanks had I got for that?

Dad's voice rose. He was talking to my mother.

'I didn't ask for any bladdy tug,' he was saying. 'Who the hell's idea was it to ask for a tug? I could've got my own boat off the beach, I didn't need their help. And now they want me to pay for it. Where's the money going to come from?'

I was trying to picture Dad getting *Vingila* off the beach without a tug when I heard a knock on the hull. Outside a rough-hewn man and a pretty woman with short, dark hair and a heart-shaped face were standing in a red dinghy. Years later we would get to know them as friends and discover that they were from Marseilles where the man had worked as a truck driver.

'I'm Jean-Marc, from *Cipango,* and this is Dominique. We have to speak to you, can we come aboard?'

Dad invited the couple in and, over a cup of coffee, they told him their warp had been swept away by *Vingila* the previous evening and that they wanted compensation. Which was when the conversation really heated up and Jean-Marc put to use some of the hand signs he'd learned as a truck driver in Marseilles.

Later, after the French couple had left and Dad had taken some painkillers and we had all lain down and taken a nap, we were awoken by another knock on the hull. Outside, in another dinghy, was another couple.

'Hi,' said the man in an American accent. 'I'm Don, and this is my wife Muriel.'

Don was tall, with wide hips, narrow shoulders and heavy rounded buttocks. He had a dark red, spade-shaped beard and kind, crinkly eyes. Muriel was compact, with prematurely grey hair and prominent teeth. Later we would learn that her close friends called her Beaver. Something about Don looked familiar.

'What's your name?' Don asked me.

'Nicky.'

'Well, Nicky, we just came over to see how you and your brother were doing today. Last I saw you, you were shivering in that Beetle with your brother and the dog.'

Then I recognised him. Don was the man who had waded into the surf the night before and carried me to the shore in his arms.

'You feeling okay now?' he said. 'We just wanted to check. You were pretty scared last night.'

'Yeah,' said Dad, 'scared as a rat. A rat deserting a sinking ship.'

Don and Muriel were from Montana, although they had lived in a log cabin in the wilds of Alaska for several years before buying *Aries* and beginning their slow circumnavigation. Although I would never admit it publicly, Don became my hero. Over the days following his rescue of me from the surf when *Vingila* foundered, it became clear that not only was Don a kind and brave man, he was a tactful one too. He quickly sensed both Dad's anger and my embarrassment about the rescue. After all, I was twelve and had wrapped my arms around a total stranger's neck and snivelled into his shirt, behaving – as Dad continued to point out – like a total coward. Picking up on the tension in our family, Don never mentioned the incident again, and took to pretending that we'd met under perfectly ordinary circumstances. Barbara, my friend, also liked Don. A few days after the Tahiti beach event, once *Vingila* had been restored to her moorings, Barbara and I found a stray kitten cowering beneath a bush beside the main road, which we presented to Don as an expression of our gratitude for rescuing me. Don and Muriel were childless and lavished attention on the scrawny pot-bellied animal. They named her Jib and she quickly grew into a spoiled, overweight and vicious cat.

At the beginning of December my father found work in the docks dismantling a gas carrier for scrap and we were able to plan a modest Christmas celebration, one that did not include pineapple. Most of the money my dad earned was put aside to see us through a few more years of cruising; nevertheless our tight budget eased a bit and Robert and I even received a little pocket money. Mom and Dad went with Robert to the hospital where the doctor took X-rays and told them my brother's arm was broken in two places. He then proceeded to wrap most of Robert's upper torso in plaster of Paris.

A few days before Christmas, Shannon helped Dad cut off Robert's cast with a pair of side cutters. The doctor had recommended the plaster stay on until mid-January but Dad said he couldn't take the stink any longer. I had to agree with him. I could smell Robert from his cabin in the forepeak. At night the ammoniacal odour of his discoloured bandages crept into my dreams as I slept, forming images so unpleasant they woke me up. After my father cut through the plaster, Shannon got her fingers under it and they broke the dirty shell open like an egg. Under the cast, Robert's skin was dirty-looking, and as dry and cracked as mud on the bottom of an empty lake. Shannon fetched a bowl of water and scrubbed my brother's back and arms with a sponge, rubbing and mopping until the wash water looked like soup. She dried him with a towel and asked Mom for moisturiser which she smoothed into his skin. Her movements were slow and languorous. I noticed that she was leaning against him with her bare legs pressed against his body. And he wasn't moving away, he leaned against her and pressed back.

For Christmas my brother spent half his pocket money on a fake gold chain for Shannon and the remainder on a Granny Smith apple from the display I'd been admiring in the Bon Marché. He wrapped the fruit in coloured paper and placed it on the chart table with the other presents and on Christmas day we exchanged gifts. The apple was for me and when I bit into it, its crisp sour flesh tasted as exotic and exciting as mangoes had once seemed in Benoni.

15

SOCIETY ISLANDS

In Moorea, we anchored in the shelter of the outer lagoon. Behind us steep slopes rose from white beaches. Before us, turquoise water stretched out to the thin line of breakers marking the reef and, beyond that, to the contours of Tahiti's mountains on the far horizon. Moorea, I thought, could well be the most beautiful island in the world. A pair of deep bays lay side by side, separated by a forested tongue and overlooked on each side by green mountains. A fringing reef created a calm, clear lagoon around the island, like a moat around a castle. A few hotels lined the shore, their discreet buildings lost in gardens of hibiscus and frangipani. When it rained in the afternoons, the warm droplets left the narrow island roads steaming and the damp air smelling of flowers.

Because he hoped Shannon and her father would arrive from Papeete, my brother's eyes often swept the horizon, searching for a set of sails belonging to the wooden sloop with a pretty eleven-year-old aboard. He was distracted and dreamy. He told me often how pretty he thought Shannon was, and how sweet and kind. It was true that she had sparkling eyes and a quick bright smile. Robert asked me if I thought she liked him. Yes, I said. I'd seen her scrubbing dead skin from his arm, and I couldn't imagine liking any boy enough to do that. While he was waiting for Shannon, however, my brother French-kissed my friend Barbara Hearn from *Barnacle Bill*. Who – he told me afterwards – he didn't even like that much.

I suppose it was my fault in a way. I probably started it all by kissing Barbara's older brother Michael. He was fourteen, about to turn fifteen, and he had glasses, bushy brown hair and milky white skin entirely unsuited to a tropical climate. His teeth stuck out a little at the front and had wide gaps between them. His stepfather, he said, had promised him braces when they reached Australia. Michael often annoyed me with stupid jokes and general teenage boy boorishness but he could also be funny and clever and sometimes we got along. One afternoon we were sitting in my cabin looking at a book together when he asked me if I'd ever tried French kissing. When I said no, he admitted that he hadn't either ... and would I like to give it a go?

From reading *Sweet Savage Love* and its sequel *Wildest Heart* I knew a lot about kissing. For the perfect kiss it was best to have both a full bosom and full lips. I had neither. Galloping horses were good too. The man you loved, even though you didn't think so at first because he made you so angry, should chase you. Preferably on horseback. It worked best with two horses. If there was only one horse, the man should ride it. Once he'd caught you – or your horse – the man, who was very strong and lean in an open-necked shirt which revealed his hard flat muscles that gave you a tingling feeling whenever you saw them, would sweep you up, or down, depending on how many horses there were, and press his lips to yours, thus causing an even more tingling feeling to course its way from your lips to your loins. I wasn't exactly sure where my loins were but all in all kissing seemed a thrilling business. If you had a horse, that is, and a full-lipped man in a silk shirt.

'So,' said Michael, leaning towards me. 'Do you want to kiss or not?'

'Well, okay,' I said. 'I suppose so.'

It wasn't very nice. His peg-like teeth clashed against my lips and his thrusting tongue, coated with oddly cold saliva, felt big inside my mouth. When our noses collided I thought I would suffocate.

'How was that?' he asked, after I pulled away. I felt an urge to run outside and spit overboard, but forced myself to swallow. I wiped my mouth and took a deep breath.

'Weird,' I said.

He nodded. 'I thought so too.'

When Robert heard what we'd done, he went and kissed Michael's sister Barbara.

'I thought you liked Shannon,' I said, 'and she's prettier.'

'I do, but she's not here, is she?'

'So how was it then?'

He shrugged. 'Okay, I guess.'

We were finding the Society Islands to be quite sociable. In Tahiti there were hundreds of yachties – long distance cruisers – not racers or tourists on charter boats. Sailors filled our visitors' book with entries and every night there were drinks or dinner invitations. *Wotan*, the converted Danish fishing trawler, threw huge parties and had a foredeck big enough for dancing. Julie and Dancha Papazov, the Bulgarians, supplied the vodka. They received endless deliveries of bottles in wooden crates from the Russians – a shadowy crowd from a ship in port. Julie, with an explosion of peroxide hair, claimed to be a concert pianist while Dancha, stumpy and thick-lipped with heavy spectacles, said he had once been a composer and conductor before turning his attention to science and research. In our visitors' book, they wrote their names and address in Cyrillic. They added rare stamps celebrating a voyage that the two of them had made, rowing across the North Atlantic in an open boat for three weeks, eating nothing but plankton which they had caught in a trailing net. Then Dancha presented Dad with a card, signed by the *Director General of Bulgarian TV* and the *Chairman of the*

State Committee for Science and Technical Progress – a certain Nacho Papazov, – who may have been a relative. The card, embossed black on white, commemorated the *PLANKTON expedition which is of lasting and fruitful importance* and proclaimed itself to be *a modest expression of the deepest respect for Frank's attention, assistance and simpathy.*

The Papazovs weren't eating plankton in Tahiti. In addition to delivering regular crates of vodka, their Russian friends provided them with jars of caviar.

Mom didn't enjoy it. 'Too fishy,' she said, 'and I don't like how it pops in my mouth.'

Dad, who hated the commies and thought they were trying to take over the world, found these two, the first he had ever met, to be quite likeable, although he was puzzled by certain details.

'So if you're communists,' he asked, 'how did you get a yacht like this?'

Dancha explained that private ownership being illegal in Bulgaria, their lovely wooden sloop with varnished topsides belonged to the state and was in fact on a government sponsored expedition to cruise the world. Even their life rafts, of which they had several, had been donated by the Russian space agency, and one calm afternoon they opened one up to show us. We took turns sailing the orange inflatable with its stumpy, gaff rigged sail, in slow circles. It came fully stocked with cans of dehydrated astronaut food. In a gesture I found difficult to interpret, the Papazovs donated a selection of unlabelled tins to *Vingila*. Our breakfasts became a lottery. The dried strawberries were tricky to identify, but delicious. The desiccated rice pudding was almost completely unrecognisable as a foodstuff by either its appearance, smell or taste. Even Pepe wouldn't eat it and I could understand why the astronauts had given it away. After several months of partying, vodka drinking and strange tinned food in Papeete my parents said they needed a break and sailed to Moorea. Which was when Robert and I became more involved with Michael and Barbara.

'Maureen,' Michael said to my mother the day after we had kissed, 'I want to take Nicky on a date.'

Mom looked mildly surprised.

'Where to?' she asked.

'Just ashore, to the jetty. But we want to go at night.'

Mom looked doubtful.

'You'll have to ask her dad.'

My father agreed to a date as long as Robert went along too, and Barbara as well. I couldn't quite understand his logic. If he thought my brother would keep an eye on me with Barbara around he was wrong. Barbara and Michael's stepfather Jim told them they had to be back by nine and because we didn't own watches, Jim said he'd flash the light on *Barnacle Bill*'s masthead to let us know our date was over. That evening, after supper, Barbara and Michael rowed over and took us ashore. After securing the dinghy to a post, we spread towels over the rough surface of the wood jetty, lay down and got in about forty minutes of French kissing before the masthead light flashed. While I still wasn't sure I enjoyed kissing Michael Hearn, I felt that with practice I could get used to it and that perhaps both of us would improve. For a start, we'd learned to tilt our faces slightly rather than coming at each other head on and I found breathing through my nose to be helpful. Robert, substituting vigour for feeling and expertise, kissed Barbara so hard that he split her lip. It was still swollen and bruised the next day.

Going on dates was all right, but I preferred swimming from the boat with Barbara – diving down in the clear warm water, holding the anchor chain and screaming our heads off together. We also liked sneaking into the island hotels and swimming in their pools. A fellow yachtie told us that if we wandered along the beach in the morning it was possible to follow the Club Med holidaymakers into the dining hall and partake of their breakfast buffet.

'All for free,' the yachtie said, 'just make sure you don't get caught. Act casual.'

Each day, after finishing our boat work and an hour of school work Robert and I were allowed to take off and do whatever we liked as long as we returned home by sundown. We roamed the island, getting about by hitch-hiking and visiting all the hotels and beaches in turn.

'Of course I don't worry about those two,' I overheard Mom telling someone. 'What could happen to them here?'

Barbara and Michael usually joined us on our outings around the island and we often split off into pairs, which made getting lifts easier. Sometimes Michael and I stayed together, and at other times he went with my brother. Barbara and I, when left alone, took to washing our hair and shaving our legs at the tap beside the road, and trying out new ways of wearing our *pareos*. We decided that it was time for us to be more like women and less like girls. Ever since I had discovered Dolly Parton back in Benoni, when I was very young, I knew just what kind of woman I wanted to be. Her high, sweet voice warbling 'love is like a butterfly, as soft and gentle as a sigh' entranced me. I thought it the loveliest song I'd ever heard and convinced Mom to buy her record. When I saw Dolly on the cover, with her fantastic chest, mounds of candy floss hair and sticky black eyelashes, she looked even more beautiful than her voice sounded. I decided immediately that when I grew up I would have breasts just like hers. Barbara, with a freckled face beneath a wedge of frizzy ginger hair, also liked Dolly Parton. She confessed that she wanted big breasts too and her period. When we shaved at the tap, we compared recent changes in our bodies and discussed our impending metamorphosis into beautiful, curvaceous women.

Robert and Michael – more interested in shoplifting than personal grooming – stole sweets, books and pens almost daily from the local store until the shopkeeper got wise and refused to let them past the door. Our weekly dates continued, developing from straight kissing sessions to fish barbecues followed by making out. Kissing non-stop for forty minutes could get boring, we were discovering.

Then Shannon arrived. One day the set of sails that my brother had stopped watching for appeared on the horizon and made their way through the pass to anchor between *Vingila* and *Barnacle Bill*. Shannon, sitting on the fore-deck of her father's sloop, gave us a shy wave.

'So what are you going to do now?' I asked my brother.

He shrugged. 'I dunno, go spearfishing I suppose.'

Which he did, ignoring both girls and going off in the dinghy to the outside reef with Dad instead.

'I don't think I like your brother any more,' Barbara said to me that afternoon when we met at the tap with our razors. We hadn't asked Shannon to join us because Barbara didn't want to, but we could see her sitting hunch-shouldered in the cockpit of her boat watching us on the shore.

'Well, I don't like yours either,' I said, which was true. Michael had begun to repulse me. I disliked his pale skin and bony chest, his peg-like teeth and the way he breathed through his mouth when he read. I didn't like the teenage boy smell of him, or his dorky glasses. I wanted a boyfriend who was strong and suntanned and preferably blond. Somebody who looked and acted a bit like Thor Heyerdahl or a more polite version of Steve Morgan from *Sweet Savage Love*. Michael wouldn't even go spearfishing with Robert because he was scared of sharks and he lacked the strength to load a speargun. He was funny though, and clever, and he knew a lot about music and Fender Stratocasters and Jimi Hendrix, but that didn't count for much if I was going to be as glamorous and buxom as Dolly Parton. I wondered if Estella had felt the same way about Pip in *Great Expectations*, who might also have had strange teeth and an irritating personality and who may have looked at her with begging puppy eyes. If Estella had met a man like Thor or Steve Morgan she might not have been so cold and haughty. Being around

Michael made me act cold and haughty and, like Pip, instead of driving him away it had the opposite effect. I'd had enough. Besides, I was cross with Barbara for saying she didn't like my brother; I wasn't sure I always liked him much myself, but somehow that was different. We soaped our legs in silence.

'I don't feel like trying on *pareos* today,' said Barbara.

'Me neither,' I said. 'I think I'll just go back to the boat and read.'

'Oh well, see you sometime then.'

'Yeah,' I said, 'sure.'

'You're back early,' Mom said. 'Want to help me make supper?'

Ever since our Chinese banquet in Papeete, Mom had been cooking more adventurously – with mixed results. That night, over an experimental stir-fry of bully beef and bitter cabbage dripping with soya sauce, Dad announced we would be sailing the next day for Huahine. I didn't hear him at first because I was trying to feed Pepe my supper under the table without anyone noticing.

'I suppose you'll miss your friends, specially now that the little girl Robert fancies has arrived,' Dad said, 'but we can't stay here forever.'

Robert swallowed, an unreadable expression crossing his face. 'What's that?' he said.

'We're off to Huahine tomorrow. Don't you ever listen?'

Pepe shoved a greasy chin onto my thigh and gazed up with imploring eyes for more bully beef. Robert scratched the last grains of rice from his bowl and looked relieved.

'That's okay,' he said, 'we can always make new friends.'

As if we found friends our own age on every island.

The next day we left Moorea to visit the other Society Islands, stopping first at the twin isles of Huahine Nui and Huahine Iti. Then we visited Raiatea and Bora Bora, an island even more beautiful than Moorea. And although we found a yacht club on Bora Bora and met several other yachts, none of them had children our age aboard and so

Robert and I didn't make any new friends. After a week we left Bora Bora with plans to anchor at the island of Maupiti. The wind, however, was so favourable that we chose instead to sail past Maupiti and make for Penrhyn, the northernmost of the Cook Islands, where Robert and I, although we didn't dare say it aloud, thought perhaps we would meet other kids.

16

PENRHYN

In Omoka village on the island of Penrhyn, while opening oysters in search of pearls for the premier of the Cook Islands, I found a whopper.

'Take it for you,' the man sitting beside me said, 'it's a *poe pipi.*'

He spoke in an offhand, casual manner. I had seen him in church, handing out hymn books and leading the choir, which in my eyes gave him some authority. I examined the oyster in my hand again. I hadn't done a very good job at slicing it apart; the bivalve looked as if it had been smashed by a rock. Shards of broken shell sprinkled the pinky-grey flesh and floated gently in the juice. My neighbour's oyster was cleaved cleanly in two. If I had been working in a restaurant shucking oysters, I would have been fired. Luckily, I wasn't planning to eat the oyster in my hand. My attention was focused on something else. A pearl. I scooped out the gem with the tip of my knife, and dried it on my T-shirt. In Brazil, the Caribbean, Panama and the Tuamotus we had dived for the oysters and always, before opening them, I had said a little prayer. *Please let this one have a pearl.* None of them ever did. I had started to believe that finding a pearl seemed about as likely as discovering a diamond or a bar of gold on the beach. Then we arrived in Penrhyn, an atoll famous for its natural pearls, where every sixth or seventh bivalve held a gem. Although to be truthful, most of them were disappointing; small and misshapen, and more like grains of faintly nacreous sand than honorary gemstones. Now, I had opened an oyster to find a real pearl at last. It was perfectly round and the colour I had heard the islanders call silver, or *poe pipi,* which wasn't silver at all, but more like a mix of colours that drifted and changed with movement. Golden-sheened with tones of black, pink and greenish-blue, it was as beautiful and mysterious-looking as diesel floating on the sea. I wanted it more than I could remember wanting anything.

'Take it,' the man said.

'Aren't all the pearls today for the premier?'

He shrugged. Reached for another oyster, opened it, gave it a cursory stir with his knife, and tossed it onto the pile behind him.

'That's for you to decide,' he said.

We reached Penrhyn twelve days after leaving Bora Bora. Unlike the Society Islands, whose volcanic peaks could be seen from 30 miles away, the coral atoll of Penrhyn lay low in the ocean, its coconut palms scarcely higher than the waves. Like the Tuamotu Atolls, the place only became visible when it was dangerously close. However, we had grown more experienced and knew now to send a lookout to the bow to spot white water and to listen for the sound of breakers above all the other sounds of a yacht at sea. After spotting the line of breakers, we began searching for the entrance to Penrhyn's lagoon. With *Vingila* tacking back and forth, Dad flipped through the pilot book and peered at the chart, then raised a pair of binoculars and stared at the line of the reef.

'Over there,' he said.

We didn't believe him.

'Can't be,' said Mom. 'That's not a pass – the waves are breaking across it for goodness sake.'

'So find me another pass and I'll take it,' Dad said.

Mom reached for the binoculars.

'It can't be right,' she said, 'look at the white water. How can anyone expect us to sail through that?'

We edged closer for a better look, trawling back and forth on the shoulders of meaty, curling swells. I squinted into the sun. Using my imagination, I could just about see a break in the reef just beyond some darker water where rollers were closing out.

'If you want to visit Penrhyn, we've gotta get through that pass,' Dad said.

We didn't particularly want to go to Penrhyn, it was more my father's idea. The pilot book described the place as seldom visited. Apparently the airstrip had fallen into disrepair and a freighter only passed by once every three months or so. Even visiting yachts were rare. To Dad, that had sounded ideal. Looking at the pass, I could think of one reason at least why visitors were scarce.

'Speed got us through the entrance to Manihi,' Dad said. 'Remember, back in the Tuamotus? Seems to me, the faster we go, the better steerage we'll have when we get into the breakers. Which means less chance of landing up on the reef. What do you say?'

We didn't say anything, just took our positions with quiet, fatalistic acceptance. There was no arguing with the old man. He took the helm which confirmed just how serious things were.

In 1805 the Beaufort Scale was devised for grading wind and sea conditions. It ranges from 0 (calm), through 3, 4 and 5 (gentle, moderate and fresh breeze) all the way to 10, 11 and 12 (storm, violent storm and hurricane). The sea is described at each stage too, from flat, to ripples, to completely white and the air filled with foam. I reckoned that on *Vingila* we had the Dad Scale to measure the severity of the situation at any given time. It was much simpler and just as accurate.

Level 1 – Dad reading or sleeping in his bunk.

Level 2 – Dad still in his bunk, but head cocked to one side and listening.

Level 3 – Dad sticking his head out of the hatch.

Level 4 – Dad standing in the cockpit.

Level 5 – Dad at the bow.

Level 6 – Dad at the bow and Mom crying on the helm.

Level 7 – Dad at the helm.

We'd never reached Level 8, but I imagined it would be Dad on his hands and knees inside with the rest of us while *Vingila* rolled around with her keel in the air and water poured through the hatches.

The entrance to Penrhyn's lagoon was a solid level 7.

My father gave the wheel a spin and grinned. I noticed that he had donned a pair of underpants and was no longer naked.

'Are you ready?' he said. 'Let's take on this pass.'

We trimmed the main and jib sails, switched on the motor, and took our run-up. As we sailed closer and the waves grew steeper *Vingila* began surfing. A wave reared behind us, its toppling front threatening to swamp the stern. As the crest collapsed in froth, the bulk of the wave picked our boat up by the tail, and thrust her forward. A steep drop opened beneath the bow, brown coral flashed past on the sea floor and a high, feathery wake spread out on either side of the hull. With *Vingila* humming so loudly I thought she might break into song, we shot through the passage and into a calm, wide lagoon. We were through.

To the right of the pass lay Omoka, the nearest of the atoll's two villages. Wind-burned and crusted with salt, we anchored before a huddle of low, steel-roofed houses. They had colourful, well-tended gardens, with coconut palms, morning glories and hibiscus bushes. Instead of lawn their yards were spread with bleached coral. Everything looked quiet and peaceful. We folded the sails, raised our yellow quarantine flag and, while Mom made tea, sat down to wait for the customs and immigration men before we could go ashore.

Within days of arriving in Omoka, Mom had enrolled Robert and me in the local school. I was nervous because I hadn't been in a classroom since Saint Helena almost two years earlier, so my new best friend Tepou promised to go with me. She agreed to meet me on the beach and in the morning I found her waiting under a palm tree. Unlike me (skinny, with a perpetually sunburned, peeling nose), or even my old friend – poor freckle-faced Barbara with her ginger frizz, Tepou was beautiful. She looked nothing like either of her parents, a pair of heavy limbed, unexceptional broad-faced Maoris. Tepou had smooth dark skin and straight white teeth. Her oiled hair smelled of coconut and lay in a heavy plait down her back. Her lips looked as if they'd been painted with maroon lipstick, except it was natural. She was so pretty she made me feel awkward, gawky and unsure of myself. I could hardly speak properly around her. Like the other Omoka scholars, she wore a white shirt and blue skirt. I didn't have a skirt – blue or otherwise – so I had just pulled on shorts and my best T-shirt. I hoped that would be okay. Both of us were barefoot. Seeing Tepou's feet made me feel a little better about her otherwise intimidating beauty. She had island feet as flat and broad as my own, and her ankles were scarred with sores.

Robert trailed behind us as we strolled along the crushed coral road to the far side of the village. Tepou and I talked. She could speak Polynesian, catch fish, weave hats from coconut fibres, open oysters and hold a baby so that it didn't throw up. She told me, and the other children would later confirm it, that I'd only get bitten by a shark in the lagoon if I swam on a Sunday or wore a revealing swimming costume like a bikini. As long as my family obeyed these two rules we were safe. Her mother and aunties always wore long dresses when they collected oysters, she said. Sunday swimming and bikinis made God mad and then His sharks would bite you. A few years back a boy had been eaten by a shark on Sunday. That proved it. Sunday was for church and singing hymns.

The school building, sitting near the beach under a grove of palms, was split into two sections by a drywall partition. One room was for secondary school students and the other for primary school children like ourselves. Robert and I followed Tepou to meet our teacher, Mr Dunn. He was Australian and had yellow hair, yellow skin and yellow eyes. He looked tired. Tepou was still talking about sharks as instruments of God and I could tell from his face that he didn't agree with her but all he said was that one should always be careful when swimming, and keep a constant eye out for dangers.

Mr Dunn gave me a seat in the front row beside Tepou. A boy with long plaited hair and a huge ulcer on his shin sat behind us. Almost all the children in the class had ulcers. I even had a few myself, although they were still quite small. They started as blisters which burst and grew crusty. Swimming washed away the crusts, making the sores itch and ooze sticky yellow water.

Gusts of wind blew across the lagoon, making the palm fronds scratch loudly against the tin roof, so that the noise nearly drowned out the voices of the children reciting their times tables on the other side of the partition.

Mr Dunn cleared his throat. 'Today, children, we're going to start with maths homework. Please open your books.'

He nodded at Robert and me. 'You can share with your neighbour.'

The boy behind me waved away a cluster of flies that had gathered on his ulcer. They rose in a cloud before settling back again.

Through the open door I could see the bright water of the lagoon and the beam of sunlight that reflected from it to form a rhomboid on the floor. As the morning wore on, the rhomboid flattened into a rectangle which tracked across the cracked concrete and crawled slowly up the wall.

Shortly before break time, when I leaned closer to read Tepou's textbook, I noticed something moving in her hair. It was an insect. She reached up, plucked it out and absently crushed it between her fingers, before flicking the corpse to the floor. The realisation came to me that my new friend had lice. Trying not to be obvious, I made a study of my fellow pupils' heads and came to the chilling conclusion that each one of them was infested. In Benoni nobody had lice, at least nobody I'd ever met. Nana said lice were for dirty people.

At break time we walked down to the lagoon and sat on the beach in the shade. I couldn't stop looking at Tepou's hair. Eventually she asked me if anything was wrong and I confessed that I'd never seen a louse before. She shrugged and said that on Penrhyn everybody had them. A thin, sharp featured girl with long pigtails told me that when she lived in New Zealand with her father, she never had lice. She thought it was because in New Zealand she washed her hair with hot water. Did I wash my hair in hot water? No, I washed my hair in cold water like everyone else.

Once they had finished eating their lunch, my friends began searching each other's heads for the parasites, which they collected in a cup. There was a flat rock near the sea, and they drew a starting line on it and lined up the lice they'd caught and proceeded to hold a louse race. As each soft-bodied insect crossed the finish line the girl with the long pigtails crushed it with a stone.

After break, we had a writing lesson and then we wove mats from coconut fibres. For phys-ed Mr Dunn took us outside to play volleyball on the beach. The boy with the ulcer on his shin didn't join in. He sat under a palm and watched us, and every now and then a school mate ran past and called him a *le-le*. Mr Dunn told them to stop it but they didn't listen to him and after a while he went inside, leaving us to play by ourselves. The boy with the plaits got up, dusted his shorts off with stubby-fingered hands and followed the teacher. I asked what a *le-le* was and everyone went silent except for one girl who burst out laughing. Nobody would tell me. Then the bell rang and we went back for the next lesson.

As we walked into the classroom, Tepou sidled up to whisper in my ear that *le-le* wasn't a nice word and that the boy was an *akava'ine* – a boy like a girl – which was why he wore his hair in such long plaits.

When I got back to the boat that afternoon, my mother was drinking tea in the cockpit with a visitor. Mom introduced him as Gunter, from the German yacht *Ghost,* which was anchored alongside *Vingila*. He was wearing a Speedo with a string vest and his bony feet were thrust into a pair of ugly German health sandals. Folds of shrivelled turkey skin hung from his neck, and his eyes were small and suspicious. They fixed on my ulcer-dotted legs.

'This is the problem with the atolls,' he said, 'everybody is eating too much coconut here. It's too high in cholesterol, and you get tropical ulcers.'

'I thought they were sand-fly bites,' Mom said.

'No. It's the cholesterol.'

When my mother asked me about school and I told her about the *le-le,* Gunter said that it was common in Polynesia for boys to be raised as girls, particularly if there weren't enough women in the family.

'Yes,' said Mom, 'I heard something like that in Tahiti too. I know certain yachties had trouble in the bars there with lady-boys.'

'What sort of trouble?' I asked. 'And what's a lady-boy?'

Mom was vague. 'Oh, just thinking they were girls and getting confused,' she answered, before adding, 'you have to watch out, you know, they can be very beautiful.'

But the boy with the ulcer on his leg wasn't beautiful, he had muscles and broad shoulders and a flat, fleshy nose and he didn't look as if he much liked being a *le-le*.

After a while Gunter stood up to leave. He wagged a finger at me. 'Stay away from those coconuts,' he said, before rowing back to his own boat.

Sitting on the cabin top eating my lunch, I identified Tepou's house by the size and whiteness of its crushed coral yard. Her yard was bigger than any of the others because her father was the chief. The building, surrounded by an airy veranda, was perched on stilts and the hibiscus bordered garden extended to the lagoon where a couple of small boats were bobbing beside a concrete jetty. I watched several other boats arrive. People converged on the jetty to unload great hessian sacks which they dragged into Tepou's yard.

'What's going on?' Mom said, staring at the shore. 'What are they up to?'

'Only one way to find out,' Robert said.

We woke Dad from his nap and piled into the dinghy with Pepe taking his usual position at the prow, with his tail up, mouth slightly open and the wind blowing back his ears as Robert rowed. Once ashore, we made fast beside the other boats. Tepou's family and most of the village were sitting on pandanus mats in the shade of the hibiscus bushes, around the sacks which we now saw were filled with oysters.

Tepou's father waved a short knife at us in what I supposed was a welcoming manner. 'Join in,' he said. 'Help us open. We're looking for pearls, but you can eat too, if you want. As much as you like. Tastes real good with coconut and a bottle of beer.'

For the next hour we opened shellfish. I found two knobbly pearls the size of rice grains and after a while worked up enough courage to nibble at a piece of oyster. It tasted like the inside of my cheeks when I bit them accidentally, only a bit more fishy. Dad was eating heaps of the things, and even Robert and Mom were scoffing a few. I tossed the rest of my oyster on the discard pile.

'Why don't you come diving for pearls with us tomorrow morning?' Tepou's dad said.

Mom sucked an oyster from its shell and swallowed uneasily. She looked at my father, who nodded. 'We'd love to, thanks,' she said.

'Isn't pearl diving dangerous?' I asked Tepou. 'I thought pearl divers dived very deep with heavy stones tied around their legs. Don't you need to be able to hold your breath forever?'

Tepou shook her head. 'My aunties do it all the time and they can hardly swim.'

'Do people ever die?'

'No.' She thought a moment. 'Well, maybe if you went on a Sunday and a shark ate you ...'

The next day we went pearl diving. In the calm of the lagoon, oysters grew on coral heads in sea so shallow that the fully clothed female members of Tepou's family stood waist deep in water and scooped the shellfish into baskets by the handful. Wearing suitably modest clothing, Mom donned her mask and snorkel and plunged in alongside a bevy of Tepou's aunts. Setting her basket within arm's reach on the coral, she began loading bivalves. When a bronze-backed shark sidled up to see what she was doing, she screamed into her snorkel, making Tepou's mother and aunties laugh.

'It's okay,' said a fat aunt, gathering her floating skirt and wringing it out. 'You're safe. Nothing to worry about. He won't do anything to you.'

Tepou's father oversaw the operation from his boat. He collected the full baskets which he stacked in the bow.

'Oysters are women's work,' he said to my father. 'Come fishing with us tomorrow. We'll fetch you in the morning.'

The next day, when Dad returned from his fishing expedition, his hair stood in wild peaks and his glasses were smeared with salt. As he climbed aboard I caught the coppery whiff of fish blood. He held a pair of coral trout tied through the gills which he tossed on the deck.

Mom looked up from a hand rail she was varnishing. 'So, how was it?'

'Never seen anything like it,' he said.

He told us they had gone through the pass – the same one we had surfed through – in an open boat.

'Waves breaking right over us, I thought we were gonna die.'

Once the men had made it through the narrow passage to reach the open ocean, they had anchored near the outside reef, bowed their heads and prayed. Then a man – quite an old guy, Dad said – had stripped off, donned a mask and filled his mouth with coconut. The men all handed him their baited hooks and he jumped from the boat and dived down, disappearing into blue water. The sea was so clear, my father told us, that if he leaned over the side of the boat he could see the old guy on the bottom, spitting out chewed coconut and dangling hooks in the cloud of fishes that had gathered before his face, picking the ones he wanted to catch.

'He held his breath for four, maybe five minutes. Then he came up, gave me a nod and told me to pull my line in. And this was on the end of it.' Dad gestured at the bigger coral trout. It was a fine specimen.

The days slid by. I walked to school with Tepou, recited my times tables, played volleyball on the beach and walked home again at lunchtime. In the afternoons we usually found Tepou's mother in the shade of the garden, weaving a hat or working her fingers through the hair of a sleeping toddler as she searched for lice. For lunch we helped ourselves to cabin bread – hard, white-flour crackers that were kept in a big silver tin in the kitchen. We ate them with Vegemite and brick margarine or tinned butter. Sometimes there was a block of processed cheese from New Zealand. After lunch, we ran around the village playing with the other children until the fishermen and pearl boats chugged in and my parents came ashore to help open oysters. I thought if Mom and Dad decided to stay forever on Penrhyn, that would be okay with me.

One afternoon, Tepou asked my mother if I could sleep over at her house. It was a warm evening and, together with her parents, little brother and some other children, we spread our pandanus sleeping mats over the coral near the lagoon. Like the members of Tepou's family, I used my *pareo* as a nightdress and a sheet. Later that night a squall swept across the atoll. We awoke to our *pareos* snapping in the gusts and fat raindrops splashing onto our faces and Tepou's mother, cradling the baby in her arms, herded everybody indoors where we fell into the great double bed. I snuggled against the others, listening to the palms thrashing in the wind and rain driving against the tin roof while Tepou's dad snored on the floor beside the bed. As I drifted off I felt a sudden anxious urge to check the anchor, before realising I didn't have to – I was sleeping in a house which was fixed firmly to the earth and I didn't have to worry about a thing.

In the morning Mom and Dad came ashore with Robert. My mother said their night had been horrible; with the wind blowing across the lagoon, *Vingila* had been on a lee shore and they'd stayed up checking the anchor and taking bearings every thirty minutes. Luckily the mooring had held, although they hadn't got much sleep.

Robert gave me a sheepish grin. He had a woollen hat pulled low over his forehead and I saw that overnight he had broken out in impetigo. Yellow scabs festooned his nose and chin. He said that his ear was sore. Gunter walked over carrying a jerry can. He stared at my brother's face.

'Not enough fresh vegetables,' he said, giving the word vegetables four syllables. Robert asked what kind of fresh vegetables he had in mind and where did he think we could find them, because he hadn't seen any for sale. I said that I didn't think fresh vegetables would be nearly as effective as antibiotic ointment because as far as I understood it, impetigo was a bacterial infection. The pharmacist in Tahiti had told me so. Gunter, pretending he hadn't heard me, turned and asked my father where we were headed next. He and Dad began talking about Suwarrow, an uninhabited island about 400 miles away.

Tepou's mother came outside with a rolled-up sleeping mat under one arm and a baby under the other. She gave the mat a shake and spread it over the coral. Sitting with the baby stretched belly-down across her lap, she asked Mom how much longer we planned to stay because the premier of the Cook Islands would be visiting Penrhyn the following week. The people of Omoka were planning a celebration, and they hoped we would join in. Later that day, she said, the men would begin by fetching very special oysters, from the best beds in the lagoon, and we were invited to help them when they collected pearls for the premier.

The sky was enamel blue and a light south-east wind blew across the lagoon the day the premier and his wife arrived in Omoka. In loose, cream-coloured suits and matching hats, they looked like African explorers on safari. She held a sun umbrella, and a crowd of children formed; reaching out to touch her dress and admire her shoes. Everybody pointed out how lovely and light-skinned she was.

The premier and his wife started their tour of the village at the school, where Mr Dunn conducted while we sang songs and waved cut palm fronds in the air. All the children looked neat and were wearing bright, well ironed shirts. The *le-le* boy had a clean new bandage over his ulcer. After our dancing and singing, we followed the premier in a procession to the church where the elders prayed for Penrhyn and the Cook Islands and the choir sang Polynesian hymns in high, shaky voices. Outside the church hall, a table was set with cakes and sweets and metal pots of tea. Mr Dunn told us the treats were for the adults but if we sat very quietly there might be something left over for good children at the end. There wasn't. Once the food had been eaten, the speeches began and gifts were exchanged. Black-lipped oyster fans, hats and place mats woven from white coconut fibres, and carvings and bolts of fabric were heaped on the table in front of the premier. The gift-giving ceremony climaxed with the presentation of a glass bottle completely filled with pearls. The premier thanked everybody and said what a pleasure it was to visit Omoka. He talked about Penrhyn's importance in the Cook Islands, even though it wasn't very populous and lay so far to the north. He spoke about the pearl industry and the copra and how they hoped to repair the airstrip one day which would bring in tourists. After he had finished speaking almost every other adult in the village had a turn to talk too. There was a lot of religious talk and some people said that even if Penrhyn was far away and didn't have a big population like Rarotonga, an airport would be a big help. Also, if the freighter came more often they wouldn't run out of supplies. The church elder I'd opened oysters with, spoke for the longest. While he spoke I crept closer to the presents, eyeing the bottle of pearls. I looked for the *poe-pipi* which I had found, but couldn't see it. I wished that I had kept it. The church elder talked at length about the fishing industry and its importance not only to Penrhyn's economy but also to that of the Cook Islands and I found myself wishing that he would mention the premier's gifts, particularly the bottle of pearls. I imagined him saying that, buried among all the other pearls, was a particular pearl. An extraordinarily rare and completely perfect *poe-pipi* that was far better than any of the others. A pearl which had been found by the blonde girl on the visiting yacht, and put in the bottle when she could have kept it for herself. Of course I knew he wouldn't say anything like that at all.

When we sailed from Penrhyn, an old man called Coaa offered to pilot us through the terrible pass. Tepou's father led the way in his boat with a few other men. With his strong hands on *Vingila's* helm, Coaa squinted at the breakers curling across the passage and told us not to be afraid. The pass was treacherous he said, but over thirty-five years he had delivered far bigger boats than ours in and out of the lagoon. It had been his work before he retired. He usually charged for his services but, because we were friends, he was helping us for free. If we ever came back to Penrhyn, he said, we just had to call him on the VHF radio and he would come out in the skiff to guide us in again. Once *Vingila* had made her way past the breakers and into open waters with Coaa on the helm, Tepou's father pulled his boat alongside and Coaa jumped into it. The two men bowed their heads in a prayer for our safety, and then waved us goodbye. We switched off the motor, trimmed our sails and set Baruch on course for the deserted atoll of Suwarrow, the most westerly of the Cook Islands.

Tepou gave me some pearls when we left so that I would not forget her. Among them was a *poe-pipi*. Small and egg-shaped rather than perfectly spherical like the one I had found myself, its colours were as lovely as diesel floating on water.

17

SUWARROW

While Robert and Dad dived with Lily's husband Dave, we took an afternoon walk along one of Suwarrow's beaches, just us girls. The sand was as soft as baby powder, and the sky as iridescently pink as the slices of smoked fish I'd seen in the pages of a *Bon Appetit* magazine I had flipped through aboard Lily's boat that morning. Across the pass the water was dark blue, lightening near the shallows towards Gull Island, where a cloud of frigate birds wheeled and soared, bullying the terns and tropic birds into giving up their food. The beach and sea stretched ahead of us, folding in on themselves like a mobius strip. Pepe trotted at our heels, sniffing at the seaweed and lifting his leg on the scattered piles of beach debris. Mom reached for a cowrie lying on the tideline and passed it to me.

'Have you ever felt depressed?' Lily asked Mom.

'Not really. Actually never. Why do you ask?'

I threw the cowrie into the sea, trying to make it skip. My mother looked at me with surprise.

'*Arabica*,' I said, 'beach worn.'

'Never even felt low?' Lily asked.

'No.'

I knew my mother was telling the truth. Sometimes Dad made her miserable – but not for long – and of course she sometimes got irritable with Robert and me and was scared in storms and poor anchorages, and panicked in the face of shipwreck, but I had never seen her depressed, or even slightly blue.

'I've been feeling a bit down lately,' Lily said.

'Whatever for?' Mom asked. 'It's so beautiful here, just look around.'

Lily gave a twitchy sort of half-smile and bit her lip. She had long bleached hair and the skin over her nose and cheeks was red, with rather prominent pores. She had a full cleavage and her arms wobbled a little when she walked. She was roughly the same age as Mom, late thirties, early forties perhaps, and she sailed on *Liberty*, a trim little boat, with Dave, her New Zealander husband. We had met them shortly after anchoring in Suwarrow and had quickly become friends. They owned a sophisticated music system, the entire set of Encylopaedia Brittanica and several shelves of gourmet food magazines filled with interesting recipes. The cushions in their saloon were covered in pale blue canvas and, unlike our boat, everything looked clean and pretty.

Lily, Mom and I walked on in silence except for the squeak of coral sand under our feet. I wanted to say something about how being on a beautiful island might not cheer you up. I had felt very sad in the Caribbean when I had tried to swim into the bay one night crying and half hoping I would drown, and I knew how lovely surroundings could make feeling sad worse because they didn't give you any excuses. You couldn't say: 'If only I wasn't in this horrible city, if only it wasn't cold and rainy, I know I'd feel better.' Lovely surroundings had a tendency to mock and belittle your misery and made feeling sad worse. It was like having a voice in your head saying, admit it, if you can't be happy here, you're never going to be happy, are you? I was thinking this as we walked, but I didn't say anything because I couldn't talk to an adult like that, and anyway the words wouldn't have come out right.

When we reached the end of the beach Lily said, 'Do you know that Robert Louis Stevenson's wife Fanny thought Suwarrow was the most romantic island in the world?'

Six days of unpredictable winds interspersed with frequent rain squalls had brought us to Suwarrow, the most westerly of the Cook Islands. It was yet another low-lying atoll with a central lagoon, and making landfall in poor visibility and heavy rain was almost impossible. Dad sent Robert to the bow, where he sat in a dripping oilskin to listen for the sound of breakers, although he failed to hear the surf above the noise of falling rain. When we saw the reef it was only a stone's throw from the boat and fortunately we were quick to come about or *Vingila* would have joined the old wreck of a Taiwanese fishing boat we saw minutes later sitting high on the coral. After some searching and tacking back and forth we found the entrance to the lagoon. Piyades Pass was a wider and easier passage than that of Penrhyn. Unfortunately, it led into a far more dangerous lagoon: a veritable booby trap of poorly charted coral heads and random reefs rising unexpectedly from deep water to nearly break the surface. Dad ordered Robert – still in a dripping oilskin – up to the spreaders to look sharp and shout directions. The squall blew over and the sun came out, its glare reflecting from the sea, blinding us and obscuring the subtle colour variations which gave us clues to the depth of the water.

'Can I come down? I'm getting hot in this raincoat,' Robert said from the spreaders.

'Too bad, *boetie*,' Dad said, 'you're not going anywhere until I say so.'

Vingila inched forward with her mainsail luffing to spill the wind. We wanted to go as slowly as possible. At speed a collision with a coral head would have sunk us (or at least caused considerable damage to the hull), and making repairs on Suwarrow would be almost impossible. Edging past the maze of reefs, we picked our way across the lagoon. The anchorage lay to the right of the entrance, tucked up against a small island where palm trees leaned attentively over a white beach and cast their shadows into the crystal water. Two yachts lay at anchor. *Ghost*, Gunter's red steel sloop we recognised from Penrhyn. Tugging on her chain beside *Ghost* was *Liberty*, Dave and Lily's ketch. Apart from the two yachts we had the lagoon and the surrounding isles of Suwarrow to ourselves. Robert and I lowered the dinghy right away and went to explore Anchorage Island with Pepe. Inshore, a short walk from the beach, we found the remains of a derelict house. This, we would learn, was the home of the late Tom Neale. Some broken chairs surrounded an open-air fireplace of coral blocks. The rusted water tank was full of rainwater, and its tap still worked. When we wedged open the warped door to the house a stream of big black rats poured out and scampered over our feet before disappearing into the palms with Pepe in pursuit.

Lily didn't mention being sad again. She certainly didn't act depressed. She cooked elaborate meals and invited us for dinner. We had frequent fish barbecues on the beach. And she organised the coconut crab hunt and the gull-egg collecting expedition. Catching coconut crabs proved more difficult than we expected. For a start, none of us had seen a live coconut crab before, although we had heard a lot about them. We knew that they were very big and weighed up to six kilograms, and that they had an arm span of five feet across which was tipped at each end with pincers strong enough to snap steel bars.

Lynnath had told me that they started out life as hermit crabs in the sea and then came ashore and outgrew their borrowed shells. Soon after taking to land they lost the ability to live in water and became prone to accidental drowning. (For females, returning to the sea to lay eggs was a hazardous business which often resulted in death.) Adolescents sometimes carried broken coconuts to protect their soft underparts, but adults were far too big for that. Grown crabs went naked and the plates on their bellies thickened and grew hard. Islanders called them Robber Crabs because of their habit of breaking into dustbins and houses. They were hunters and scavengers and were rumoured to ransack graves. During the day they dozed in burrows, emerging at dusk to hack into coconuts for the meat. Apparently they were strong enough to carry a nut up a palm and drop it repeatedly until it shattered. Once they got a grip (on a finger for example), they didn't let go unless they were gently tickled in just the right spot on the underside of their segmented abdomen. Which would be a difficult task to perform – I imagined – while having one's digit crushed and simultaneously dancing away from the other snapping claw. We had heard that their flesh was richer and sweeter than the finest lobster, which did much to explain their rarity on some populated islands and their extinction on others. What we hadn't heard, however, was how difficult they were to catch and keep captive.

There were no crabs left on Anchorage Island so the evening of the crab hunt we crossed the lagoon in Dave's Zodiac. After half an hour of high speed motoring, we reached an outlying islet where we beached the dinghy near a thicket of shaggy palms. A rustle in the undergrowth was followed by the sound of something heavy falling.

'Shh!' said Dave. 'What's that? A crab or a coconut?'

'Don't know, but it sounded pretty big,' Robert said. He scooped up his machete, a pair of diving gloves and a coil of line.

'Come on,' he said, 'let's go. Can't you hear them, they're every-where.'

Then I saw something moving over the ground. The crab stood knee-high, with a great scabby back, segmented legs and a strange, triangular little head, with beady eyes on close-set stalks. It waved a pair of insectile feelers. When Robert approached the creature, it turned and fled, with him following after it.

'I'm not going,' I said. 'It's getting dark and I don't have proper shoes. I'm scared I'll stand on one. I think I'll just wait in the dinghy.'

'What makes you think you'll be safe in the dinghy?' Dave said. 'Sitting here alone in the dark, they'll sniff you out and find you.'

'Why do we have to do this at night anyway?' I asked.

'You know why, stupid,' Robert called from the gloom of the palms, 'because they're nocturnal.' He said nocturnal as if it were three separate words.

'I knew I should have stayed behind on *Vingila*,' I said.

'Too late for that now,' Dad replied, securing the dinghy's line to a palm trunk.

For the next five hours I kept as close to my father's heels as I could, doing my best to avoid making contact of any sort with a giant crab. Actually, making contact wasn't that easy. Robert, Dave and my father were making active efforts and it wasn't working. The crustaceans were faster than they looked, and sneakier. We chased them with sticks and palm fronds, and threw chunks of coral at them. We tried to lure them into buckets using open coconuts as bait. We attempted to herd them into an empty tin drum we found rusting on the beach. Our efforts were not successful. The animals were skittish but curious; they seemed drawn to us. They swarmed around on their clicking legs, always keeping frustratingly out of reach.

'Maybe one of us should lie down and pretend to be dead,' Dave said. 'That'll bring them over. Any volunteers? Nicky perhaps?'

Robert, who had been reading a lot of Westerns, came up with the idea of using a lasso. Surprisingly, it worked. The lassos didn't so much catch the crabs, as tangle their legs and slow them down. Actually capturing them entailed buckets and oars and sticks and plenty of hopping about and swearing. Once we had three coconut crabs in buckets, we loaded them into the the dinghy and returned to Anchorage Island. It was past midnight when we got back to the campsite and nobody felt much like eating, particularly not coconut crab. That's when we discovered they weren't easy to keep captive.

They were strong and easily lifted the metal buckets we placed over them. They showed amazing climbing abilities. We resorted to bondage. Beads of sweat shone on Dave's face and a maniacal gleam had entered his eyes. His stringy grey hair stood in salty spikes.

'You hold him,' he said to Robert, 'and I'll tie him up.'

While the other two crabs scratched and threw themselves against the inside of a pair of overturned buckets which Mom and Lily were using as seats, Robert got an oar on the creature's back and Dave once again eased a line around its claws and legs.

'I've done this plenty of times with lobsters in Canada,' Dave grunted, 'and it worked there.'

After the knots had been tied – as tightly as possible and with considerable difficulty – the crab wriggled free as effortlessly as Houdini from a coffin. I thought Dave was about to cry.

'Maybe we should just cook them now and eat them cold tomorrow?' Mom said.

Her bucket lurched, nearly tipping her off. She gave it a kick.

'Stop that!' she said to its occupant, as if it could understand English. My mother looked tired and disinterested. She muttered something under her breath about how she preferred a nice piece of fish and when it came to eating strange creatures, she could take them or leave them. Lily, however, inspired by her food magazines, had ambitious plans for supper the following night.

'I'm worried they might go off if we cook them now,' she said, 'and they say you should starve them overnight in case they've been eating poisonous plants.'

'Anyway,' she added, 'even if we had a fridge, they'd be far too big to fit in it.'

'So are you planning to sit on that bucket all night?' Dave said. 'Because I'm not tying up this fellow again. I'm sick of it and I want to go to bed.'

In the end, we put two crabs in an empty drum with a sheet of plywood to keep them apart and prevent fighting and the third – and largest – crab in Tom Neale's old bathtub in the house, with a rock and a piece of corrugated sheet iron on top of the tub to stop it escaping. And then we went to bed.

Somehow, the great Polynesian migration that swept across the Pacific, from Hawaii to Tahiti, the Cook Islands and on to New Zealand, missed the atoll of Suwarrow, and so it had never known Polynesian habitation. In 1814, when the Russian explorer Mikhail Lazarev discovered the isle and named it after his ship, the place was deserted. Over the years Suwarrow became home to more than a few castaways and a couple of recluses. Tom Neale was the last of them, and the most tenacious. He was responsible for most of the crumbling structures on Anchorage Island. For a period of thirty years on and off until just before his death, he'd lived on Suwarrow, wandering around in a suntan and skimpy loincloth, spearing fish and enjoying being by himself, except for the short period when he put his back out. He wrote a book about living on Suwarrow called *An Island to Oneself* which Lily had aboard and lent me to read. It was all about finding the right island on a limited budget, stocking up, arranging transport to the place and how wonderful it felt when he was finally left alone and took his shorts off.

As we walked back to the beach and the dinghies, away from the ruin of Tom Neale's old house, we could hear the crab in the bath banging away at its tin roof.

'Tomorrow night,' said Lily, 'we'll make heart-of-palm salad to eat with our crab.'

In the morning the crab in the bath was gone, having dislodged the rock holding down the corrugated iron sheet.

Robert gave a low whistle – something he had been doing often since he'd started reading the cowboy books. Sometimes he even talked like a cowboy.

'Well lookit that,' he said, 'the bastid got hisself free.'

'Will it be all right on the island by itself?' I said. 'What if the rats get it?'

'Jeez, Nicky,' Robert said, 'it's a coconut crab, it probably eats rats. Can you believe it lifted that rock? And the steel sheet? I could hardly do that.'

'I read the buggers can carry up to 24 kilograms,' Dave said, coming up behind us and scratching the stubble on his chin. He looked tired. None of us had slept much the previous night. We'd been up until three in the morning restraining coconut crabs and had woken a few hours later to the tropical sun blazing down the hatches. After breakfast Robert and I rowed ashore, curious to see how the crabs were doing. After discovering that the crab in the bath was missing, we checked the two in the drum. They had pushed aside the barrier separating them and the smaller one was missing a couple of legs.

'Spirited little bastids, ain't they?' Robert said. He was still excited about the hunt the night before and the thrill of having used a lasso. We leaned over the edge of the drum. The crabs looked up at us, rubbing their hairy legs together and twitching their antennae like a pair of cockroaches.

'Jeez, they're ugly,' I said. 'See how they're looking at us? I don't like it. And why are they waving their feelers like that? Maybe I'll just eat salad tonight.'

'Probably smelling us out,' Dave said, 'by waving their feelers around. Or cleaning themselves.'

He yawned. 'I need another cup of coffee,' he said and wandered off in the direction of the beach.

Robert stretched over and tried – unsuccessfully – to flip the biggest crab on its back with the blade of his machete.

'Let's go,' I said. 'They give me the creeps and anyway, Lily asked us to chop down a palm tree.'

On atolls fresh vegetables were always scarce. In Penrhyn, the shopkeeper at the local store had been waiting for three months for the freighter and his shelves were empty except for some cans of cabin bread and a few boiled sweets turned milky-soft in the humidity. Vegetables had been sold out for months, he said. Some of the villagers grew bananas, but the mango season was over and the trees were bare and so, like the islanders around us, we lived on fish, breadfruit, coconuts and rice. Breadfruit, which grew on huge green-leaved trees, tasted very much as its name suggested – starchy, and bland, like a fibrous potato or washing-up sponge. We ate breadfruit boiled, before it ripened into a tangled mass of slippery, choking fibres. Although we ate breadfruit often, I hadn't learned to love it as some of the islanders did. To vary our diet, Mom sometimes opened a tin of peas or mixed vegetables, and occasionally we found a ripe pawpaw. Our biggest treat, though, was heart of palm. It was delicious – snow white, tender and crunchy. Lily said it tasted even better than fresh asparagus. I had never tasted fresh asparagus. I knew asparagus as pallid, sodden fingers that we hauled limp and dripping from a can. I couldn't imagine anything better than a heart of palm. Unfortunately, to make the smallest salad, a fair sized palm had to be felled. On inhabited atolls, where every last coconut was collected and sold for copra and each grown tree had a designated owner, for a yachtie to fell a palm was unthinkable. On inhabited islands we had to rely on rare gifts of heart of palm to eat something crunchy and fresh. However, on Suwarrow coconuts fell to the ground and sprouted unchecked in wild profusion, resulting in hundreds of adolescent palms for the taking. For the crab feast, Robert and I felled two.

Later that night we sat around the fire in the campsite, watching the crabs boil in a half-drum. Getting them into it had not been easy. Tom Neale's house lay beyond the ring of light cast by the fire and our kerosene lamps. If I looked hard, I could make out a steady procession of rats coming and going through the half-open front door. More rats rustled in the undergrowth behind us. Occasionally, one or two of the braver rats trotted over to inspect our feet. Pepe, exhausted from days of fruitless rat chasing, had given up. He lay at Mom's feet watching the rodents, growling on and off, but too tired to do more. The rats ignored him.

'I heard,' said Robert, stirring the fire, 'that the best part to eat is the belly.'

Light from the flames flickered across his face as he spoke. On a makeshift table to one side, Lily had spread a tablecloth and arranged a dish of palm salad, a pot of rice and two bowls of sauce, one pink and creamy, the other green. The sauce, she said, was for the crab. Dad had brought a hammer and a couple of pairs of pliers from his tool box.

'This isn't actually too bad,' Mom said after Dad had used the hammer to crack an oversized leg which he'd then dropped on her plate. She'd declined the sauce: 'No thanks, I prefer my food plain, nothing fancy for me.'

I excavated a gargantuan claw and ate its contents between bites of the palm salad which Lily had sprinkled with lime juice. The flaky crab meat was sweet and butter-rich. I tried both sauces. They were good; tart and a little spicy.

'What about that belly then?' Dave said to Robert. 'Are you game?'

'Of course.' My brother was about to turn thirteen and the muscles on his shoulders and arms had undergone a recent growth spurt. He spent several hours in the water each day spearing fish and he had developed a new, cocky attitude and an almost complete lack of fear for sharks. His skin, unlike mine, never burned. He was always deeply tanned and his hair was wild and sun-bleached. Girls would begin finding him irresistible. He reached into the drum for a crab carcass and wrenched off the abdomen. It was bulbous and segmented, with stiff hairs sprouting out at uneven intervals. Its cavity brimmed with a curdled, khaki-coloured soup of sorts.

'What about you?' Robert said, holding the abdomen out to Dave like a goblet.

Dave swallowed and shook his head.

'Not me,' he said. 'It looks like part of Shelob.'

'What's Shelob?' my mother asked, wiping her chin and hands with a rag.

'You know, that giant spider-thing in *Lord of The Rings*,' I said. 'The one Frodo stabs in the belly and then all that stuff oozes out –'

She interrupted me. 'Okay, okay, I get the picture.'

'Yuck. Are you really going to eat that?' My brother didn't reply. Lifting the broken-off abdomen to his mouth, he tilted back his head and took a few big swallows. When he'd finished drinking, he wiped a greenish smear from his upper lip and grinned at us.

'How was it?' asked Dave, with a mixture of awe and disgust on his face.

'Not bad at all,' said Robert, 'actually quite nice.'

'So what did it taste like?' I asked.

Robert thought for a moment.

'Mmm …' he said. 'A bit like salty, curried condensed milk.'

A few days after the coconut-crab feast, Lily organised a bird's egg hunt. If Lynnath had been there, she would have told us that tiny Gull Island housed three per cent of the world's red-tailed tropic birds, creatures as beautiful as they are rare. She would also have identified the different types of gulls and terns on the isle and described their nesting habits. She would certainly have given several reasons why we should leave the birds undisturbed to raise their young, but she was in South Africa, lecturing at the University of Port Elizabeth and we wanted to eat eggs.

Well, Lily wanted eggs. I wasn't sure if I did. Eggs made me squeamish. Even back in Benoni I couldn't eat lightly cooked white without feeling ill and I hated the thought of them sliding out of a bird's bum. On the boat it was worse. Mom bought eggs in bulk and rubbed Vaseline over the shells to keep them fresh without refrigeration. We stored them for weeks, eating progressively older eggs – eggs with blood spots and broken yolks that stuck to the inside of the shell. The last few would always be rotten, their cloying, sulphurous smell permeating every part of the boat.

'Fresh eggs would be so nice,' Lily said. 'I'd love *huevos rancheros* and we could even bake a cake or something.'

Lily talked so much about eggs and how long it had been since we had eaten any, that when we went to Gull Island, in our greed, we filled two buckets. The birds wheeled and screamed and dive-bombed our heads. Pepe went wild, barking and chasing the fluffy chicks and lifting his leg on the nests.

'Fantastic!' said Lily, hoisting her bucket into the dinghy. 'Now for breakfast on *Liberty. Huevos rancheros* it is.'

Lily cooked rice and made a pot of spicy tomato sauce.

'Now,' she said, 'we fry the eggs.'

We discovered then that we hadn't been very successful at collecting fresh ones. Once we'd sorted through the rotten eggs, and those containing foetal chicks in various stages of development, we worked out that there were two sorts fit to eat. One type had a normal-looking yellow yolk, although its white part, while setting firm with cooking, remained clear. The second, with a normal white, had a yolk the colour of fresh blood. Both kinds tasted strongly of fish.

'Not bad,' said Dad, 'if you put enough of this hot sauce on them.'

After tasting a bite from my mother's plate, I decided to eat my *huevos rancheros* without eggs.

'I don't know what we're going to do with the rest of these,' Mom said after breakfast, stowing the bucket of eggs on a shelf in *Vingila*'s forepeak next to Robert's bunk.

That night a storm blew in. It arrived abruptly at three-thirty in the morning and took us completely by surprise. Gusts blasted across the expansive lagoon, quickly building up ranks of steep, choppy swell. Our boats swung on their lines, to face the wind. Anchorage Island lay abeam on the port side, and the reef directly off *Vingila*'s stern. Before the storm woke me I had been having troubled dreams in which I was frying eggs which kept hatching into chicks that hopped and squawked in my pan. Crawling from my bunk I found Mom, Dad and Robert in the main saloon. The motor was on. Above the engine noise and the whistling of the rigging, the clatter of the halyards and the rattle of hastily stowed objects about the boat, I could hear the dull boom of breakers on the reef.

'We've got a problem,' my father said. 'For a start, we can't leave. We'll never get out the pass in the dark. In fact, it's unlikely we'd even make it across the lagoon.'

Robert nodded, wet hair plastered to his forehead.

My father continued. 'The reef's behind us now, and if the anchor goes, that's where we land up.'

Vingila gave a sudden lurch, jerking us off our feet.

'If she keeps doing that, we'll break the chain,' Dad said.

'Wind's picking up – waves as well,' Robert said.

He looked keen, up for the challenge. I wondered how he could feel that way. It was almost as if he were enjoying himself. I wished the storm would just disappear and let me sleep, even if it meant another baby chick nightmare.

As usual we had our plough anchor out on chain at the bow. It was a standard CQR with a hinged shaft, good for most bottoms except mud. And as he usually did in coral anchorages, Dad had hooked a heavy nylon spring line into the anchor chain and taken up the slack with it, creating an uneasy compromise. Coral cuts through nylon, but chain lacks give. If our chain wrapped around a coral head and *Vingila* jerked her head back, as she was doing in the chop, the chain could snap. A nylon spring line had stretch and give, and protected the chain from sudden, jerky movements. Our chain snapping could spell the end of *Vingila*.

'What we're going to do,' my father said, 'is motor slowly forward, keeping the bow into the wind to take some strain off the anchor.'

'You, on the wheel,' he said to my mother. 'I'll keep lookout at the bow and watch we don't override. Robert, you come with me. Nicky, you relay messages between your Mom and me.'

He'd barely finished his sentence when we heard the shocking thwang of the spring line snapping.

Outside it was as dark as the inside of a cow. Anchorage Island had disappeared in a fug of rain and we couldn't even make out the shapes of *Liberty* and *Ghost*. The wind ripped the breath from our mouths. Even with the motor running, our boat jerked and pulled with such force that our heaviest warps lacked enough give to absorb the shock. Over the next few hours, three spring lines of braided nylon as thick as my wrist were broken. *Vingila* simply threw back her head and snapped them like string.

'Damn it! Keep her head into the wind!' Dad shouted.

'I'm trying!' Mom yelled into the rain and spray.

Vingila, heavy and unresponsive as usual, ignored subtle turns of the helm. When my mother, in desperation, turned the helm hard over, our lug of a boat veered wildly, forcing Mom to overcorrect in the opposite direction. We zigzagged back and forth, overriding our anchor, often on just the single chain because the spring had snapped. Pepe didn't like being below without Mom and tried repeatedly to climb the stairs, getting thrown off by *Vingila*'s lurching, to fall clattering to the floor. After a while I helped him into the cockpit, where he sat at her feet, his damp hair blasted back from his face as if he were taking a car ride. At five-thirty the wind was still blowing. My father took the wheel and Mom made coffee. When the hot drinks were ready, we abandoned the helm and went inside for a brief pow-wow.

'If the chain gives,' Dad said, 'we're finished. It's impossible to hold steady in this sea. I can't see a damned thing to take a bearing and we can't go anywhere because of the coral heads. If we go, we'll take *Ghost* with us. And if *Liberty* loses her anchor she'll take both of us.'

'Then it's onto the reef,' Mom said.

'What about another anchor?' Robert said. 'We've got the Danforth. Can we row it out in the dinghy, maybe?'

He was referring to our seldom used fluked anchor, a heavy old thing best suited to mud bottoms.

Dad shook his head. 'A Danforth won't hold on a mixed bottom. You know that, and besides it's only got five metres of chain and then nylon. The coral will slice through it in a second. Anyway, who do you think you're fooling by imagining anyone could row in this?'

He drained his cup. 'Come on, outside again. Everybody.'

An hour later as dawn broke the wind stopped. It ceased abruptly, as if somebody turned it off. A pink sun rose from a silver sea. In the first light of morning, the clouds fled to the horizon, disappearing like vampires. The waves died.

Mom made another pot of coffee and set about heating leftover rice for breakfast.

'What's that pong?' Robert said.

An awful smell was drifting from the forepeak. During *Vingila*'s lurching, the bucket of gull eggs had been thrown from a shelf, to land upside down on the floor. Broken eggs – some rotten – seeped out, oozing towards the carpet. Pepe, walking up to investigate, gave a sniff and recoiled. Breakfast was put on hold while we cleaned shell fragments and pools of bloody slime from the floorboards.

'At least we don't have to worry about cooking them any more,' Mom said.

'I want to leave,' Dad said from the stove, where he was stirring rice in a pan. 'We can't spend another night in this anchorage. We made it through by the skin of our teeth this morning.'

Mom looked up from the floor, damp rag in her hand, and nodded.

'Are you crazy?' Dave said later, when we rowed over for tea on *Liberty*.

'Leave today? Look what a lovely day it is, and besides, you haven't had any sleep.'

I looked around. It was lovely. The palms, washed clean by the rain, trembled and shone in the light breeze. Wavelets nibbled the shore. The sky and sea shone as brightly as ship's brass after a good polishing.

'Stay another day,' said Lily. 'We'll have a fish barbecue on the beach later, and tomorrow, after a good night's rest, you can leave.'

'Go on,' said Dave, 'don't leave on a low note. You might not get a chance to visit a place like this again.'

'I suppose you're right, a night's rest won't hurt,' Dad said.

Against our better judgement we stayed another day. At three-thirty the next morning I woke to *Vingila*'s lurching and the sound of the engine starting up. I hoped at first it was a nightmare, my subconscious replaying the trauma of the previous night's storm. Unfortunately I wasn't dreaming. A second, equally intense, squall had struck. Outside, in the cockpit, I found my family.

'What the fuck are we doing here?' Dad said. 'We should have left yesterday.'

I performed a quick survey. Short, steep waves, blasting wind,

Anchorage Island to port, and the reef with its booming breakers directly off our stern.

'Get ready with the spring lines,' Dad said. 'We'll be needing a few, if last night was anything to go by.'

We took up our positions again: my mother at the helm, zigzagging and overriding the chain; Dad and Robert at the bow, replacing spring lines as they snapped; me mid-decks, relaying messages while Pepe cowered next to Mom. I cursed Dave and Lily for making us stay. If we were at sea we would just reef the sails and heave-to, which was better than being trapped amid reefs. The wind pressed against my chest, squeezing the air from my lungs. Rain stung my legs.

'How many hours has it been now?' I called to my mother.

'Two.'

'Which means,' I muttered to myself, 'that there's only an hour to go, if last night was anything to go by.'

It was strange how something could be so tedious and terrifying at the same time. Then our anchor worked its way past a coral head and lost hold.

'Frank!' Mom shouted. 'What's going on? The anchor's not working.'

No longer restrained, *Vingila* heeled over and began sliding downwind.

'Push up the revs! Keep her facing the wind!' Dad's hair whipped into his face.

'I'm trying, I'm trying.' Mom gunned the motor and spun the wheel, with no visible result. Behind, a dark form came into view through the haze, taking shape as it rapidly grew closer. A yacht.

I ran to the stern for a better look.

'Over here,' I yelled. 'It's *Ghost*. She's at anchor.'

Ghost's heavy bow was slicing through the waves like a chef's knife chopping onions. Gunter, her skipper, was nowhere to be seen

'*Ghost*'s gotta let out chain,' Dad panted behind me. '*Vingila* will only stop dragging if we let out more chain – the weight helps the anchor grip. But we need space. *Ghost* must let out chain too. Where the fuck's Gunter? If he doesn't get up here, we'll smash into him and drag him along with us.'

Mom revved the engine and tried to turn *Vingila* into the wind but it was no good. Our boat swept backwards. *Ghost* grew closer. We shouted for Gunter, but nobody responded. How could he sleep through this, I wondered. Without Gunter's help there was nothing we could do. Then all 17 tons of *Vingila* collided with *Ghost*'s chopping prow. The crash of his boat hammering repeatedly into Baruch, brought Gunter outside pretty quickly. He looked sleepy and confused.

'Let out chain!' Dad screamed at him. 'Now!'

Gunter fell to his knees and fumbled with the anchor locker while *Ghost*, having pretty much demolished Baruch, set about destroying our transom.

'Fend off,' ordered my father, a wild look in his eye.

I ran to the rail and reached out to fend off just as *Ghost*'s bow struck our stern again. Several tons of steel narrowly avoided crushing my hands. I stepped back. Maybe fending off wasn't such a good idea after all. Gunter loosened a catch on the anchor winch – finally! – and chain rattled from *Ghost*'s locker. She faded back into a haze of murky rain.

'Okay,' said Dad, 'now we let out chain.'

Our anchor, weighed down with an additional 50 feet of chain, caught against the bottom and held. Dad and Robert set out another spring line.

At dawn somebody switched off the wind yet again. The sun peeped over the horizon, pink as a rose. The waves gave up and died, the clouds put themselves to bed.

'I hate this place,' I said, sucking a finger tip, bruised during my ineffectual attempt at fending off.

'At least this time we don't need to clean up rotten eggs,' said Mom.

We didn't leave that day. We were too tired and the thought of sailing without a wind vane was worse than risking another squall in Suwarrow. Dad brought out his tool box and set about fixing Baruch, and hammering the dent from our transom rail. When he'd finished helping my father, Robert went spearfishing with Dave and came back with a couple of grouper for supper.

'So you're staying another night, are you? Dave asked. He had dark rings under his eyes and a pallor that showed through his tan. He looked as if he hadn't slept in days.

Dad nodded. 'Call us stupid, but yes, we're here for another night.'

'Anyway,' said Mom, 'what are the chances of it happening again?'

I went to bed that evening with a lump of anxiety in my chest and in spite of my exhaustion I had trouble falling asleep. How could a place so pretty and calm during the day turn so wild at night, I wondered. At last I dozed off. A few hours later I awoke to the hammering of my heart, which felt as if it was diverting blood from my hands and feet, directly into my eardrums. I lay for a moment, listening to the whoosh in my head and somewhere – far beyond that – to the sound of gentle waves lapping against the hull. A warm breeze wormed its way into my cabin through the open port holes, but the palms of my hands felt cold and damp. Climbing quietly through the hatch without waking my parents, I found the night sky thick with stars and blinking planets. They formed veils and vapour trails and shining clumps like candyfloss so bright I could have read by them. *Ghost, Liberty* and *Vingila* lay parallel on the still water, floating above their reflections, noses pointing towards the strip of land and its untidy palms. I sniffed the air for a storm. Nothing – except for Anchorage Island which was exhaling a warm, vegetable smell of humus and fermenting coconut. I searched the horizon for the smear of an impending squall and saw only clear sky. I sat awhile to enjoy the stillness and warmth but I couldn't relax. With my parents asleep, I felt somehow responsible for the fate of the boat in an anchorage that could turn on us at any time. To distract myself, I played a game in which I attempted to remember my old classmates in Benoni, but my memories were shadowy; their faces lacked details and I discovered that I couldn't recall a single name. I realised with a shock that they would be finishing primary school soon and would be preparing for high school. I tried to imagine what sort of clothes they were wearing and what hairstyles they found fashionable and found it impossible so I thought instead about sailing to Samoa, our next stop. After that we were going to Tonga and then Fiji and New Caledonia. And at the end of the Pacific lay Australia, where Dad hoped to find work and Mom said we might even go to school for a while. Thinking about all those islands made me drowsy and I returned to my bunk and fell quickly into a dense, dreamless sleep.

In Fiji, a few months later, we heard the news about Lily. At the time Robert and I were celebrating our thirteenth birthday at the Suva Yacht Club, eating Chinese stir-fried noodles with Don and Muriel, our friends from Montana who sailed *Aries*. Ever since he had rescued me in the surf when *Vingila* stranded herself on the beach in Tahiti, Robert and I had grown close to Don, and – to a lesser extent – Muriel. They had no children of their own and in Don, with his spade-shaped beard and gentle, crinkly eyes, I found a friend who was always available to listen. After Suwarrow we had been happy to see them again in Tonga and had arranged to sail to Fiji together. Don often spoiled us and in Suva, on the day of Robert's and my birthday, he promised us jelly-tipped ice lollies for dessert. *Donella* with Christian, our spear-fishing, shark-fighting friend who we had first met in the Las Perlas islands off Panama, was also on Suva. Christian had now been joined by his wife Hanelore and their youngest daughter Anja who had flown to Tonga from South Africa. Anja was fifteen, tall, blonde and suntanned and while sailing the islands of Tonga together I had got to know her quite well. She was a disco dancer and had been teaching me some of her moves. I felt I was coming along quite nicely and could almost spin my hands while doing pelvic thrusts at the same time. I thought pelvic thrusts were rude, but Anja told me everybody did them and boys really liked girls who were good disco dancers.

I never expected death to be a topic at our birthday celebration. I didn't know anybody yet who had died, although that would soon change. Usually people who die on yachts do so by drowning. In fact, of the group of yachties gathered together on the yacht club veranda that afternoon, two would be lost to the sea. Little Nathan from *Xyphius*, who was asking Don if he could also have an ice cream, had only six months left to live. He was a pale child of three with such transparent eyelashes and long white hairs on his arms that he made me feel all strange, especially when he chased me around the veranda telling me how much he loved me. In New Zealand while *Xyphius* was at anchor he would fall overboard and drown in the bay. Don too would one day drown by falling overboard at sea.

When Dad gave Mom the news about Lily, he spoke softly because he didn't want me to hear, but of course I did.

'You know the Kiwi boat that arrived yesterday, the one with the family?'

Mom nodded.

'I just met the father in the bar and he told me they were in Rarotonga a month or two after *Liberty*.'

'And,' said Mom.

'And the story is that one afternoon Dave came back and found Lily swinging from the shrouds by the neck. She'd hanged herself.'

Mom's face sort of crumpled.

'Are you sure?' she whispered.

'Well,' said Dad, 'it might just be a rumour.'

I thought back to the day on the beach when Lily told Mom she was depressed and how I wanted to say something and didn't. I remembered the coconut crab feast and the gull egg expedition and I thought about how neat and pretty *Liberty* was, with her pale cushions and the tidy shelves of Lily's gourmet food magazines. I wondered if Dave had had anything to do with it, or if saying something to her the day on the beach might have helped. I couldn't imagine Lily dead. I decided it was best to hope that the news was a rumour, distorted along its passage like a game of Chinese Whispers, and that Lily and Dave were healthy, well and living on their boat together in New Zealand, eating *huevos rancheros*.

18

SAMOA

From our anchorage in the harbour in Pago Pago, American Samoa, I couldn't make out what the man with the loudhailer was shouting. He stood on the back of a truck, leaning his elbows on the cab roof for balance and his voice emerged ardent and distorted from the cone, ricocheting off the buildings and bouncing off the hills. People on the streets were stopping to listen and I assumed he was campaigning, or announcing a rally. I decided to ignore him, turning my attention back to an English exercise I wanted to finish before I went to play with Barbara. After our split in Moorea, and a break of three months while we were in Penrhyn and Suwarrow, we were friends again. My brother Robert and her brother Michael were now our enemies. We were horrified that we had ever kissed them. They had decided that they hated us as much as we hated them and we avoided any contact except for the occasional exchange of vicious insults. Most afternoons Barbara and I visited a nearby shop that sold cheap jewellery and browsed through their wares. Then we wandered about hoping to see Shaun, a good-looking older boy who never paid us any attention. After exhausting the attractions of Pago Pago, a muddy town with lots of traffic, we usually landed up on *Barnacle Bill* where we read, talked about boys and prayed for further development of our still flat chests.

I turned to my English lesson. Mom had run out of schoolbooks from her sister Annette, and I had found an English textbook on the shelf. Nobody knew where it had come from, and with nothing else to do, I had tackled the first few exercises. 'Read the following passage, underlining the adverbs in red and the pronouns in blue before rewriting the text using the pluperfect tense.'

I wondered if the book was for adults. I had never heard of the pluperfect. When I asked my mother about the pluperfect tense, she told me, without looking up from the hand rail she was sanding, to 'look it up somewhere'. While I was searching for a red pen we were interrupted by a knock on the hull. Don and Muriel, our American friends from Montana were in their dinghy. *Aries,* their chunky, full-keeled sloop lay anchored beside us.

'Have you heard the news?' Don said. He stood in the centre of their dinghy, one hand holding a dripping oar. Several bags lay heaped in the prow and Muriel crouched in the stern with a cat basket on her lap. Through the zippered mesh panel I caught a glimpse of Jib's evil yellow eyes. Were they taking her to the vet, I wondered? Jib, possibly as a result of her traumatic early days under a bush, usually refused to leave *Aries.* On dry land she 'freaked out', as Muriel described it.

'What news?' Dad asked.

'A tsunami's on the way,' Don said.

'A what?' my father asked.

I half hoped Don would tell us a tsunami was a traditional Samoan festival with dancing and free food.

'A tidal wave,' said Don. 'The man with the loudhailer's warning people. There's been an earthquake near Japan, six point two on the Richter Scale and they're predicting a tsunami.'

'Oh,' said Dad, not looking too impressed.

'They're advising everyone to leave their boats and the low-lying houses and shops. They want us to move to higher ground. Didn't you hear?'

'I didn't,' said Dad.

'What's going to happen, Frank?' Mom said.

Dad shrugged. He surveyed the harbour.

'I dunno,' he said, 'looks pretty flat to me.'

'Anyway,' he added, 'I'm not leaving the boat for any tidal wave.'

Don's eyes widened, 'What?'

'I'm not a deserter. If my boat goes down, I go with her.'

'I don't know about that,' Don said. 'I've seen a tsunami once before, in Alaska. I'll never forget it. An oil tanker was on the wave, broken in half, with all the oil spilling out. Then it caught alight – the oil I mean – and the wave was burning – burning and carrying these two broken halves of oil tanker churning around in the white water like a pair of corks. There's nothing you can do against something like that.'

'Besides,' Muriel said, 'when it comes to tidal waves, this harbour's particularly bad.'

'I thought it was a good harbour,' Mom said.

The place was like a fortress, surrounded by high mountains and accessible by a single, long, narrow entrance. It was one of the best harbours in the South Pacific, a perfect hurricane hole.

Muriel glanced at Don, who nodded encouragingly for her to go on.

'It's good for wind,' Muriel explained, 'but there's only the one narrow entrance for all this water to get in and out. That'll cause big problems.'

'First the water sucks out,' said Don. 'This whole bay, for example. Sucked dry.'

I pictured the boats on their sides, a few fish flapping on the stinking mud.

'And then?' I said. Even Robert was listening. We were all there in a line, hanging over the side looking at Don.

'And then the wave comes in,' he said. 'A wall of white water carrying – I don't know what – yachts, bodies, wrecked infrastructure, broken oil tankers, burning oil.'

I looked around the harbour of Pago Pago again; placid greyish-brown water, surrounding mountains, a group of yachts in various stages of repair, all tugging gently at their anchors. I tried to imagine the scene Don described, first when the water drained out, and then when it came back and wrecked everything.

'When did they say the tsunami was coming?' I asked.

'Don't really know. Could be an hour, could be more.'

'Let's go then,' I said.

'I'm not going anywhere,' Dad said. 'If I need to fight for my boat, I will.'

Around us, people were throwing bags into dinghies and rowing to shore. Mom looked at Dad and opened her mouth to speak. I thought she was going to ask him if he'd lost his mind and turned stark raving mad but instead she said, 'Okay, then I'm staying with you.'

Don and Muriel swapped looks of disbelief.

'If you want to survive a tsunami,' Don said, 'you should get as far out to sea as you can, way past the entrance passage, that's the most dangerous place to be. I don't know if you've got enough time for that.'

'Then we'll sit it out right here,' Dad said.

'I'm not staying,' I said.

Dad turned to Robert. 'And you? I suppose you're turning tail and running away too?'

My brother looked torn, but only for a moment. Perhaps he was remembering Tahiti, and our reception back onboard after *Vingila*'s beaching.

'If you need my help, I'll stay,' he said.

'Good boy,' said my father.

'I'll just grab some stuff,' I said to Don and Muriel. 'Can you wait for me?'

'Sure, get your things.'

I fetched my most important possessions; a tiny crochet bag with a few pairs of earrings I'd bought using my pocket money. I didn't pack a passport – I didn't have one. Robert and I travelled on Mom's because Dad said it was cheaper that way, and I didn't pack any money – I'd spent it all on earrings – or any clothes. Mom stayed on deck with Dad so I had nobody to supervise my preparations for orphanhood or make any suggestions regarding the practicality of my choices.

'Is that all you're taking?' Don said when I came outside, swinging my little bag.

I nodded. If I was going to lose my home and family, at least I'd have a decent selection of earrings.

My mother appeared to be having second thoughts. She turned to Dad, with something beseeching about her posture, and it seemed that she was about to open her mouth, but my father stopped her with a cold stare. She sighed and looked back at me again.

'Nicky,' she asked, 'will you take Pepe?'

'Okay, if I have to.'

'Thanks,' Mom said. 'I wouldn't like him to die.'

From a suitably high spot on a hill Don, Muriel, Jib, Pepe and I sat in the shade of a tree and watched the harbour. We had a good view of *Vingila* and my family who would drown when the tidal wave surged into the bay. Pepe panted in the heat. Jib was mostly silent but every now and then she'd hiss or give low, rumbling growls. While we waited for the tsunami, Don and I talked about Robert Louis Stevenson and how when *Vingila* and *Aries* got to Western Samoa we would visit his house and his grave together in Apia. Don asked me if I liked Pago Pago and I said yes, I did a bit. But I didn't like that there was so much traffic and that the water in the bay was dirty and that we had to eat frozen turkey legs and lamb flap because it was the cheapest and Dad boiled the lamb flap in water with too much salt until all the grease ran out and formed a thick layer on the top. That made me sick, I said. But I liked the shop that sold earrings and having Barbara as my friend again. And it was fun when the Taiwanese fishing boat got wrecked on the rocks at the entrance and Dad and Robert went out along with a bunch of Samoans to dive for stuff. They came back with jerry cans full of soya sauce and tins of miniature boiled eggs and strange mushrooms which Mom said she wasn't sure were edible. I told Don that they also found enough poly-filament fishing line to last us forever.

He asked me what I thought of the Samoans. Big, I said, and with those amazing tattoos covering half their bodies. I told him how one Samoan swimming at the wreck had been wearing only a *pareo* – which in Samoa were called *lava-lavas* – and when he dived down we had got to see his whole tattoo which was like a swirly pair of blue pants reaching from his waist to his knees. Don said that was interesting to hear, he'd only seen the bits of tattoo sticking out above the *lava-lavas* and had no idea that they covered everything to the knees. It must be pretty sore, he said, to get a tattoo like that. It was, I agreed, but I'd heard Dad saying how it was a test of manhood and that the most beautiful girls in the village held the young men down when they were tattooed because that way they'd be too ashamed to struggle or cry. And then we talked about the fourth of July celebrations and how it had rained and the Samoan dancers had had to sit on the wet field as part of their dance, which had made their pretty yellow *lava-lavas* all muddy. But we didn't speak about the party at the barge afterwards with the other yachties and the Danish woman in a dress and no panties who got drunk and sat with her dress hiked up and her legs apart. And we didn't talk about how quite a few men, including Don, had gathered around her and had found everything she said very interesting. We didn't say anything about that. We also didn't say anything about the huge tidal wave that could come crashing into the harbour at any minute and how, if it did, we might get to watch *Vingila* sink and my family drown. After a while we stopped talking and sat in the shade just watching the harbour and I thought about where I would go if Mom, Dad and Robert all died and who would look after Pepe and if perhaps Don and Muriel would adopt me, seeing as they didn't have any children of their own, and if that meant I would become American. I thought about how glad I was that the tsunami warning had come when we were in a harbour, so I could leave the boat instead of going down with her and my family. Even though I loved *Vingila* – she was my home – I didn't want to die for her. You could always build another boat and I didn't understand why Dad couldn't see that. Then after a while I stopped thinking about my father and I got to wondering about Muriel's teeth which were big and a strange pinkish colour with a black line at the gum which didn't look natural at all.

At about four o'clock that afternoon the man with the megaphone came around on the truck again, announcing that the tsunami had passed. I did not know how we had missed it, but later when we met some yachties in the bay, they told us that the water level had risen and dropped again ever so slightly. That was all. Which was a good thing, Don said.

When Dad heard me climbing onto *Vingila*, he stuck his head out the hatch to look me straight in the eye. I checked for the Whistler but he wasn't holding it.

'So,' he said, 'the rat's come back, has it?'

I took a chance. 'Better a live rat than a drowned one,' I said, preparing to duck if he came for me. Sometimes, when he didn't use the Whistler, he hit us across the head instead with his hand. But Dad's hands stayed down and although he tried to hide it, I saw the beginning of a smile at the corner of his mouth and his eyes crinkled slightly.

While he was talking to Don, I went to my cabin to change earrings. I brushed my hair and looked at my reflection in the square of mirror stuck to the bulkhead, turning my head this way and that to view myself from different angles. I was glad to be back and glad not to be an orphan. I wondered if Mom would let me go ashore again because I wanted to see Barbara and find out what she had done all afternoon while waiting for the tsunami to strike.

Dad wearing shorts in the Caribbean

Robert and Pepe at the bow

A sample of my shell collection

Photos by David Harrison

Frank and Maureen Stillwell and twins Nicky and Robert, 10, on board their steel Lello 48 ketch *Vingila* which is now cruising in the West Indies. They plan to be away two years. They bought their boat in Benoni, then finished it in Durban. Photo: J.L. Moss

A family photo in the June 1978 edition of *SA Yachting*

Sailing with Dad

Vingila (left) anchored with another yacht, somewhere in the Caribbean

Dad and Robert opening coconuts

Coming in to anchor, Caribbean

On the way to the lukewarm pool on Dominica Island

Robert at the helm, before I learned to cut hair

Fellow French yachties, becalmed

Me gaffing a dorado on the stern

Lynnath in the Panama Canal

Passing through the locks of the Panama Canal

19

BRISBANE, AUSTRALIA

After two weeks on at sea we sailed into the port of Brisbane as night fell, gliding past the docks and ships without starting our engine. Dad's celestial navigation was so accurate that we scarcely needed to adjust Baruch, sailing from the Coral Sea past Stradbroke Island, into Moreton Bay and from there straight between the buoys marking the channel to the harbour in the mouth of the Brisbane River. Once in the harbour, we sailed further up the river, searching for the quarantine jetty. *Vingila* flew her mainsail, stained now in places with rust, and – at the bow – a yellow and green drifter that my father had bought second hand in Fiji. The drifter was sewn of light-weight spinnaker cloth, with a similar baggy cut, and it caught soft winds on the beam beautifully, billowing gently as we sailed up the river. We had come from Noumea in New Caledonia, and in the months before that, the islands of Fiji and the kingdom of Tonga, and before that Apia in Western Samoa. The Pacific Ocean now lay behind us. It was 1980, just before Christmas, and we had once again made an open water passage in hurricane season, although possibly only my father knew that. I was certainly unaware, and apart from light winds interspersed with heavy squalls, we had had no trouble. Robert and I were thirteen years old, and our family had been living on *Vingila* for three and a half years.

We were broke. The money Dad had made the previous Christmas working in the dockyards of Tahiti had been spent. My father had a contact in Brisbane, a big-bellied Aussie with a red face called Ray, whom Dad had met on the gas carrying ship he had helped to dismantle in Papeete. Ray had been working as a ship's engineer, but he owned a maritime engineering works in Brisbane and had promised Dad a job if we ever got to Australia. My father hoped to work in Brisbane for the rest of the hurricane season and thought we would leave after five or six months with enough money to keep us cruising for at least another year or two, which would take *Vingila* across the Indian Ocean.

Tying up alongside the quarantine jetty under the yellow sodium lights of the docks, I never imagined that over two years would pass before *Vingila* left the muddy waters of Brisbane River and encountered the open water again.

In the morning the customs officers came aboard and confiscated our food.

'It's forbidden to bring any fresh fruit or vegetables, or meat in any form into Australia,' said the officer. He was neatly turned out in a white shirt and it seemed as if he had been trained not to smile. He ordered in a crew who searched our boat far more thoroughly than the pair of Tongan officers who had clambered aboard *Vingila* in Nuku'alofa, sniffing Mom's bottles of dried herbs and missing the cases of contraband whisky stacked on my cabin floor that we were carrying for Christian on *Donella*.

Dad, deciding it best not to take any chances with the Australians, turned in the guns.

Mom watched as our varnished cans of bully beef and Gant's chicken curry from South Africa were packed into boxes and taken away.

'What are we going to eat now?' she asked.

The official shrugged. 'We'll give you a receipt,' he said. 'You'll get them back when you leave.'

'As for that dog,' he said, 'it's not allowed ashore under any circumstances. If that animal is seen ashore, it will be shot and you will be fined, and possibly sentenced to jail.'

Pepe, salty and matted, sighed and moved closer to Mom, shrinking from the officer's gaze.

'Can't we just leave?' Mom said to Dad later, after the customs and immigration officials had left.

'Can't afford to,' said Dad. 'We can live on next to nothing, but we can't live on nothing.'

So we made our way further up the river, under the great arch of Story Bridge and past a huddle of shiny skyscrapers, to reach the botanical gardens where we tied up on the pilings, nose to tail with some other yachts.

Later that day, after Dad had gone ashore to telephone Ray, he sat for a while on a park bench in the shade of a giant-leafed tropical tree, looking down at the muddy river flowing past the tethered yachts. An Aboriginal woman ambled over to sit beside him.

'G'day mate, how ya doing?' she said. 'Name's Jane. What's yours?'

'Frank.'

Jane's skinny legs and arms were attached to a bloated ball of a body. Her face was shiny, her lips swollen. Her smile, however, was kind.

'You new here?' she asked.

My father nodded.

'St Vinnies serve coffee and rolls at the gate at seven, Frank,' she said.

'Take care with sleeping in this park, but,' she continued, 'they close the gates at six and if the divvy van finds you after that they'll lock you up. You can sleep at the shelter, St Vinnies, again. Or I could show you a good spot.'

Jane was referring to St Vincent de Paul, the charity organisation for the homeless.

'Any questions, just ask me,' she concluded. 'Hope you're happy here.'

The months passed quickly. Dad started working for Ray's engineering works and after a while Robert began working there too. Ray wasn't too worried about contravening Australia's child labour laws. We had tourist visas and Dad himself was working illegally and being paid under the table. We saved money and lived frugally on lamb's liver, which Mom curried, and lamb's tongues, which she boiled. I was given a crab pot by a departing yacht and, baiting it with catfish that I speared from the dinghy with Robert's old Hawaiian sling, I added the occasional mud crab to our diet. Dad hid the cash he was accumulating around the boat, until Mom, tired of finding wads of cash in socks and other unlikely places, convinced him to open a bank account. Dad was content. He liked tinkering on ship engines and working on the machines. He got on with Ray, who also had a yacht, and the two men went racing on Ray's boat when work was slow.

Ray who did not mind contravening the child labour laws, had a girlfriend who did and after a couple of months Robert was told he had to leave. During the day while my father was away at the engineering works, Mom spent her time doing laundry and sanding and varnishing the hand rails and the duckboards in the cockpit. Robert and I, who now got five dollars a week pocket money, spent our days hanging around the city after we had finished our daily chores. Robert favoured a place called Las Vegas where he played Space Invaders, while I preferred the public library which had a young adult section, with beanbags on the floor and shelves and shelves of books where I discovered fantasy novels and science fiction. Once or twice we saw our old friends Barbara and Michael from *Barnacle Bill* with whom we had spent so much time in

Tahiti, Moorea, and American Samoa. They had also sailed to Brisbane, but *Barnacle Bill* had been left at the Maloolloba yacht club and their stepfather, who had decided to settle in Australia, had found a good job and had bought a house for the family. Barbara and Michael had been enrolled in high school, so they were seldom free.

The cyclone season passed and Dad showed no signs of leaving Brisbane. After six months of living on the river, my mother decided that Robert and I should also go to school like Barbara and Michael. Mom said she was worried about us. We came and went as we pleased, staying out late at night. I had a seventeen-year-old boyfriend who lived on the yacht next door and who collected the dole and stole things, and Robert spent all his money on video games in the dimly lit rooms of Las Vegas, which Dad had taken to calling Lost Wages.

In South Africa, my brother and I would have been in our first year of high school. On the yacht our home schooling had ground to a halt. Mom said she was stuck, she wasn't a high school teacher and she didn't have a syllabus. She wasn't sure that, as non-residents, we were entitled to attend an Australian school; however my father told her to take a chance.

'You know my motto,' Dad said. 'Fortune favours the brave.'

The vice principal of Brisbane State High, a burly man named Mr Brennan who looked as if he played rugby, wasn't sure what to do with us either, when my mother arrived at his office.

'You don't have any school records at all?' he asked Mom, a frown wrinkling his brow.

'Nothing,' said Mom.

'But you say you've been home schooling these two?'

Mom nodded emphatically.

'Covering all subjects?'

'Well ...' said my mother. 'We do maths and they love reading, and I'm sure they've learned a lot of geography. And Nicky here has an interest in marine biology. She knows the Latin names of a lot of shells.'

'Hmmm ...' The vice principal appeared to be at a loss.

'Let's go over this again,' he said. 'You've been living on a yacht for the last four years during which time these children haven't been to school or taken any tests.'

Mom nodded again, less certainly this time.

'And the yacht is now moored at the botanical gardens? And you're all still living on it?'

Mom smiled. 'That's right.'

We waited for him to ask if we had Australian residency, but he didn't.

'This is a very unusual request,' said the vice principal. 'Brisbane State High is a highly regarded school, and we usually only accept students with B aggregates, or those who excel at sport or music. Still, we keep a few places open for local children and you are in the general feeder area, although we haven't ever had pupils living in the botanical gardens before.'

He eyed my brother's broad chest and muscled arms.

'Do you play any sport, young man?'

'He rows,' said my mother quickly.

'Ah, rowing. We have fours and eights here at BSHS and we thrashed the other schools at the last GPS regatta.'

We had no idea what he was talking about.

Mr Brennan stood up. 'I'll just have a quick talk to Mr Mason, the head, and see what he has to say.'

'Sit up straight,' Mom hissed at Robert after the vice principal left the room. 'Try to look keen.'

After a while Mr Brennan returned with a handful of papers.

'The headmaster says that if Robert and Martinique take IQ tests and their scores are above average, we'll accept them.'

Some time later, after our tests had been marked and the results delivered to Mr Brennan, he smiled at us and said, 'Welcome to Brisbane State High.'

'Robert and Martinique can join classes in year 9, with their age group,' he told my mother. 'I know you said that in South Africa they would be in the equivalent of grade 8, but us Aussies start earlier here and I think it's best if they're with children their own age. If they don't cope, they can always repeat the year. Hopefully not, their IQ scores are solid. They'll be in different classes. Although the school's co-ed, we keep the girls and boys separate. We find they're a lot less distracted that way. Well, Robert and Martinique, I hope you'll be happy and productive here. And Robert, I suggest you try out for the rowing team.'

'That's good news,' my mother said after we left. 'I can't believe he didn't ask to check our immigration papers.'

Brisbane State High was a big school with sprawling grounds, sports fields, a music block, a separate library and several swimming pools. There was a headmaster, a headmistress, four deputy heads, 120 teachers and almost 2000 pupils. After my mother took us shopping for our uniforms, Robert and I were slotted into our classes, where we attracted very little notice.

Shortly after our enrolment, my brother and I each came home with a note from our teacher suggesting we have our eyes checked because it seemed we needed glasses. In fact the blackboard was a blurry haze for both of us. Mom and Dad were both myopic, Mom more so than Dad, so it shouldn't have come as a surprise that our vision was weak. Robert's eyesight was even worse than mine and I wondered how he had ever managed to helm *Vingila*, trim sails or see fish to spear them. Dad took the news better than I expected. I thought he would moan about the expense. However, all he did was hand Mom a wad of cash and tell her to get us sorted out.

Robert took physical education as a subject and tried out for the rowing team where he was quickly accepted. I chose art and speech and drama because Mom said I was artistic and those were good subjects for girls. I also took German, and both my brother and I had physical science, geography, biology and maths.

In my second week at school my biology teacher talked about Darwin and his finches on Galapagos. I raised my hand.

'I sailed to the Galapagos,' I said. 'It's amazing. The birds have no fear of humans, and if you stand still enough, they'll sit on your head. It was the tortoises though, that inspired Darwin to think about evolution and natural selection.'

There was a moment of silence, then the teacher said: 'Thank you for sharing that with us, Martinique. Shall we get on with the lesson?'

At the end of the period when I went to fetch my bag, I was followed by a thickset Greek girl who was called Hamburger by the others on account of her unpronounceable last name. She thrust her face into mine, close enough for me to see her blackheads.

'I've sailed to the Galapagos ...' she said in a high, sing-song voice.

She thrust her face closer. 'If you ever show us up again like that in class,' she continued, 'I'll snatch those glasses off your face, break them, and flush them down the toilet. You hear me?'

I kept her gaze, forcing myself not to back down or look scared. She was a lot bigger than me, although she had a softness to her arms and legs that led me to believe I might stand a chance if she tried to fight me. After some minutes of silent, face to face staring, Maria spun around, picked up her bag and walked away to the next lesson. I followed at a distance, thinking it best to keep my mouth shut about sailing experiences from now on.

A few months into school, as we approached the end of the academic year and Robert and I turned fourteen, I came to accept that, contrary to my mother's perceptions, I was not artistic, and that the subject of speech and drama was not easy for me. Nor did I like it. My interest and ability lay in maths, geography and physical science.

In geography we learned about weather, about how warm air at the equator rises to create low pressure systems, and cools and sinks to form high pressure cells further south or north and how the air rushing between them is deflected by the Coriolis forces of the spinning earth and forms the endless cycle of the trade winds. We studied cold and warm fronts, tropical storms and ocean currents. And although I kept it to myself, I was able to add to what I learned at school by what I had absorbed, overheard and observed while sailing. Suddenly everything made sense and the feeling was as thrilling as being able to identify the shells I collected.

Dr Schollery, a pretty young woman, took my class for physical science. From her I learned that the world around us could be described using the simple, beautiful formulas of Isaac Newton. Rather than feeling constrained by this new knowledge, I felt the universe crack open and blossom. While I didn't always like school with its rules and uniforms, I loved learning.

Mom announced that with Robert and me at school and Dad at work, she was tired of sanding and varnishing woodwork all day, and she got a job at a pub where she sat behind a hot glass box at lunchtime and sold customers pies and chips and other deep-fried snacks. It was nice to have some money of her own for a change, she said. The only problem was Pepe, who cried whenever she was away.

Robert and I passed our exams at the end of the year and moved into year 10. We were happy. Our friends Don and Muriel had arrived in Brisbane, and *Aries* was moored on the pilings near *Vingila*. Since our first meeting in Tahiti when Don had rescued me from *Vingila*, we had spent so much time with Don and Muriel Border on various islands, that Robert and I had started to think of the Borders as members of the family; our own patient, interested and caring Aunt and Uncle.

Although Nana still wrote regularly to Mom, we seldom heard from our other relatives in South Africa and I could hardly remember my real aunts and uncles any more. We saw Don and Muriel every day and they always wanted to know about school, and our friends, and how Robert's rowing training was progressing. When Dad got me down, Don told me how proud of me my father was, and how much he loved me.

'Your Dad just finds it difficult to show you,' he said. 'That's the way he was brought up. He's raising you in the only way he knows how.'

I don't think he suspected that my father still brought out the Whistler from time to time.

Our school friends thought it was cool to visit us on the boat in the river. Climbing down the river bank into the dinghy and rowing against the tide to *Vingila* was exciting. We often had visitors. At school Robert played rugby and had made the first four rowing team, and I had the tops marks for science in my class and had taken up the 'cello. The school provided the instrument and weekly individual lessons free of charge. My 'cello lived on my spare bunk where Lynnath had once slept, and every Friday I loaded it into the dinghy – where it interfered with Robert's oars as he rowed – before dragging it up the slippery ladder propped against the riverbank, and carrying it into the centre of the city where I caught the train to school. I didn't have much musical ability, but I loved the shiny varnished body and elegant arched neck of the first instrument I had ever been responsible for. Somehow, I still loved my 'cello even after I saw The Great Rock and Roll Swindle with the Sex Pistols and decided to become a punk rocker by cutting my hair off and wearing only black. Together with my school friend Melinda, who was also good at maths and science, I began skipping school, or wagging as the Aussies called it. Michael, my old boyfriend from Moorea, had taken to wagging school a lot too. While Mom worked at the pub, we hung out on the yacht, or visited the art gallery or library.

Even as I skipped school I continued to learn and in spite of my nihilistic punk rocker appearance, I began thinking of my future. I imagined going to university and becoming some sort of scientist, maybe like Lynnath. If we stayed in Australia I could do that. Living in a house would be nice too, with hot running water where I could shower every day.

Dad also began talking about staying in Brisbane. He announced that he would take the exams which would enable him to register as an electrician and if that went well, we would apply to immigrate. My father booked the test and, as the weeks passed and I waited for him to start studying I began to worry. Long before starting at Brisbane State High I had found a pamphlet with tips on how to study. Read the headings first, then read any questions to find out what the examiners are looking for, make summaries and write out all the important facts in point form. Then write out the important facts again. The weekend before his exam, Dad lay listlessly on his bed, head turned to the side, staring alternatively at the open book on the pillow beside him and the porthole above the opposite bunk. He didn't make any summaries, or write anything down in point form, and I didn't know how to tell him to do that. When the test results were mailed to us, my father had failed.

'I'm not staying in this stupid country with its stupid bladdy rules and regulations,' he said.

But stay on we did, renewing our tourist visas every six months as they expired. Robert and I finished year 10 and began year 11. I started thinking seriously about university. And then, at the end of our first term, when Dad went to renew our visas, he was told that there would be no further renewals and we had two weeks to leave Australia. Robert resigned from the rowing team, I handed back my 'cello, and we said goodbye to our teachers and all our friends. According to my father, we had no other choice.

Part 5

CORAL SEA

20

VANUATU AND THE SOLOMON ISLANDS

In May 1983 we left Brisbane and sailed back to Noumea, the capital of New Caledonia. Dad said that from New Caledonia we would make our way through the archipelago of Vanuatu to the Solomon Islands, which would take about nine months, and after that we would look for a safe place to spend the following hurricane season.

In Noumea the Kanuks were rioting against the French administrators and they had looted shops and defaced the town's statues, so we didn't stay long, and instead sailed south to Île des Pins, a tiny island clad in pine trees, and through the Réserve Yves Merlet to the beautiful Loyalty Islands of Maré, Lifou and Ouvéa with their blue lagoons. At all these islands Pepe, after his long incarceration in Australia, was free again to run along the beaches, sniff about the vegetation and lift his leg pretty much wherever he wanted to. After the Loyalty Islands we turned north towards the archipelago that Captain Cook named the New Hebrides in 1774, but since achieving independence from its twin colonial masters of France and Britain, had taken on the name Ripablik blong Vanuatu. Or Vanuatu for short.

On Efate island in Port Vila, the capital, we discovered Vincent in a supermarket. Our French friend from Brazil and the Caribbean, who we had not seen for five years, was eyeing a counter of cheeses. With a plaited leather thong around a tattooed bicep, and new gaps between his teeth, he looked as wild-haired as ever. We were surprised because we hadn't noticed *Dou-Dou Diop* in the harbour, and told him so.

'Ah, now we are on *Amulet*, our second boat since *Dou-Dou Diop*,' he said.

Nadine and he had left *Dou-Dou Diop* in the Caribbean, he explained, because they wanted a boat of their own. In exchange for keeping *Dou-Dou Diop*, Roland and Jean-Pierre had helped find Vincent another yacht. Well – *steal* another yacht actually – because none of them had the money to actually buy one. In Venezuela they came upon the perfect sloop. Customs officials had impounded the vessel after its original owner, a American single-handed sailor, had been run over and killed by a passing car. The yacht was kept tied to a jetty.

'It was so easy,' Vincent said, 'we just untied her and sailed away in the night.'

After taking off with the sloop, which they painted green and re-christened the *Rio Grande*, Vincent and Nadine sailed through the Panama Canal to the Pacific Ocean. Old mariners would have told them it's very bad luck to change a ship's name or paint her green. Although, to be fair, it wasn't as if Vincent had a choice about changing the name.

Less than a year later the *Rio Grande* was wrecked.

'She was a very, very good boat,' Vincent said, his hand absently caressing a wheel of wax-covered cheese, 'a good size and so fast and obedient.'

The *Rio Grande* had been swept onto the reef one night on Suwarrow in the very same anchorage where we had nearly lost *Vingila*. Vincent told us a horribly familiar story. A violent squall had ripped across the lagoon and conditions in the anchorage deteriorated so quickly that

Vincent realised immediately they risked losing the boat. He didn't have to describe the wind ripping across the lagoon and building up sharp, choppy swells, the chain-snapping coral heads, and the wicked reef to lee, because we, of course, already knew all that. The trouble was, the *Rio Grande*, unlike *Vingila*, did not have an engine. Vincent urged Nadine, who was then seven months pregnant, to find her mask and snorkel and get ready to swim through the dark, shark-filled water to Anchorage Island when he said the word. They stayed aboard, hoping to ride it out, until their anchor chain snapped and the wind began driving the *Rio Grande* towards the reef. Then they jumped off and swam. There was nothing else he could have done, he said. The boat had no engine and any sails would have been shredded in that wind. His rope for spring lines was finished, it had all been snapped to pieces. That same night four other yachts were also driven onto the reef and wrecked. In the morning Vincent and Nadine set up camp on Anchorage Island beneath a grove of palm trees near the remains of Tom Neale's old house. Unbelievably, the fresh water tank still functioned. From the remains of the *Rio Grande*, Vincent salvaged some supplies, and his dinghy and speargun. Food, he said, was not a problem. There were coconuts and the lagoon was full of fish.

'With our suntans, why did we need clothes?' Vincent said, slipping the cheese into his bag and walking towards the exit of the supermarket. 'I like Port Vila,' he added. 'Every day I come to this shop for cheese, and not once do I pay.'

On Suwarrow he and Nadine had eaten palm hearts, coconut crabs and sea bird eggs from the outlying islets. Apart from a few disputes with another group of castaways who objected to their growing of marijuana, Nadine and Vincent had lived comfortably for over two months, until the Cook Island authorities forcibly deported them a week before she gave birth.

Vincent invited us to his new yacht *Amulet* to meet Nadine and his son Ramone, a toddler with matted dread locks and a full body suntan just like his mother.

'I delivered him myself. In a hut in the jungle of Fiji,' Vincent said.

Nadine gave us a shy smile, before slipping away below decks.

'She still doesn't like to speak English,' he said, lifting the boy to his lap to kiss his head. He confessed that Ramone had no passport or birth certificate. He and Nadine had decided he wouldn't be schooled. He doesn't need to read or write, Vincent said, I'll teach him to sail and spear fish. I thought back to the Klaars on the junk *Maria Jose*, and how Ernest had said all his sons needed to know was how to sail and navigate. I wondered what had become of them.

'You still haven't told us how you got this,' Dad said, gesturing to the boat under our feet.

'Beautiful,' Robert said, 'what a classic.' He seldom complimented yachts.

'From the moment I saw her, it was love,' Vincent said. 'We found her hiding under tarpaulins in New Zealand, and after some negotiations, tidied her up. At night she sails like a moth, so quietly.'

Amulet, their graceful schooner, had been built in 1895 in Auckland, from the finest New Zealand white pine. She carried sails of canvas and had magnificent lines. Vincent's mother, together with a few of her friends, had bought the boat for him on the loose understanding that he would one day pay them back – somehow. He said his mother refused to have him living in a hut in the jungle of Fiji with her new grandson and had sent a friend to take Vincent, Nadine and the new baby to New Zealand where she hoped they would find work. He found the *Amulet* instead. Vincent's mother was generous, but even so, could only afford to buy half the vessel. The schooner's original owner had agreed to a co-ownership system, with alternating years of occupancy. Nadine and Vincent had taken the first year, after which they would have to move out.

'We have not yet decided what we will do,' Vincent said with a shrug. 'Perhaps it's back to the jungle of Fiji for another year.'

Away from Port Vila, the islands of Vanuatu were wild, with frequent rainfall and heavy jungle where semi-naked people with woolly hair lived in grass huts. The men wore penis sheaths, or *nambas* as they were called in pidgin, which were oblong woven purses that they slipped over their private parts and secured around their waists with twine. The women had bare breasts and muddy feet. Although they looked fierce, everybody we met was friendly and welcoming. Some islanders spoke a little French or *Bislama*, the Vanuatu pidgin. Many, however, spoke only their native tongue. We communicated with gestures and swapped fillets of dorado for mangoes and bananas, or taro pudding cooked on the fire.

On tiny Nguna Island we met missionaries who were translating the Bible into one of the four local languages while trying to get the islanders to change their ways. (With an average of 2000 speakers for each of the 113 indigenous languages in Vanuatu, Bible translators had their work cut out for them.)

Tourists were non-existent away from the few hotels in Port Vila and after we left its busy harbour, we only saw one other yacht: *Cipango*. As we sailed north through the islands we often found *Cipango* at anchor, or she would arrive soon after us. At first we ignored Dominique and Jean-Marc, the French couple who sailed her. Ever since our first meeting in Papeete several years previously, relations between our boats had been cool. The antipathy had started the night *Vingila* dragged anchor and beached herself, when they accused us of losing their warp. They had demanded compensation. Jean-Marc, a truck driver from Marseilles, didn't speak much English, but his gestures were eloquent. And now, it seemed, our old enemies were the only other yacht sailing with us.

When we arrived at the anchorage in Emae, *Cipango* was there.

'We can't keep on ignoring them like this,' Mom said. 'Why don't we invite them for supper?'

That afternoon, a man in a dugout canoe arrived with a dead chicken and four red-lipped olive shells, which he wanted to trade for a can of paint and a T-shirt. This was a windfall. I knew the olive shells were worth a hundred dollars apiece and fresh chicken was a rarity. We offered the man one of the T-shirts Mom had bought in Panama City and Dad gave him a can of paint, then we invited Dominique and Jean-Marc over to celebrate. The fowl, hunted in the forest with a bow and arrow, had been shot several times and was full of holes. Prior to its death by archery, the bird appeared to have lived an active life in the wild which had toughened its muscles, but we cooked it slowly in a cast iron pot with rice and olives.

'This food is good,' said Jean-Marc. 'Strange, because we always thought the English were unable to cook.'

My father told him we were not English.

A few weeks later on the island of Espiritu Santo – named by the Spaniards who discovered the place in 1606 – Dominique traded two T-shirts for a live hen, which Robert and I offered to kill for her. After I had given a demonstration on how to put a chicken to sleep by tucking its head under its wing and stroking it soothingly for a few minutes while murmuring pleasantries, we took the abject bird to the beach where Robert decapitated it with his machete. Dominique stayed on the boat and refused to hear our story of how the headless body had run into the sea and performed backward somersaults in the waves. That night we ate *coq au vin*, the second of many shared dinners. The next day Dominique called Robert and me over and taught us how to play Tarot, a French gambling game. As we sailed through the northern islands of Vanuatu, to the even wilder Banks Islands, and on towards the Solomons, our friendship with *Cipango* grew. We met up with them in anchorage after anchorage and occasionally also with Vincent and Nadine on *Amulet*. We dived with Jean-Marc and Vincent, and spent hours playing Tarot with Dominique. Nadine, as usual, kept to herself.

In October we arrived in Santa Anna, the easternmost of the Solomon Islands, where a pair of missionaries were living in a sago-palm hut in the local village. After we anchored, dozens of brown-skinned children with mops of shaggy sun-bleached hair swam out to swarm over *Vingila*. They swung from the shrouds and jumped into the sea from the prow. They ran through the cabins, fingering the sheets and curtains. They screamed at the sight of Pepe. The missionary couple rowed out to visit *Vingila* too. They told us they were translating the Bible and had built a church.

'Slowly, we're seeing some change,' the woman said. She had a pale, pinched face and wore a long, sack-like dress with a print of faded roses. 'These things take time. You realise, of course, that these people were cannibals not so long ago.'

When we went ashore, the adult villagers glared at us from under their dusty Afros. The bare-breasted village women wore grass skirts and had bones stuck through their noses. The men were in tattered shorts and had thick, scarred feet. Unlike Vanuatu and the Banks Islands, there were no smiles or offers to trade.

'Seems like there's quite an atmosphere here,' Mom said as we walked along a muddy track, dodging stray pigs.

'Yeah,' said Robert. 'I wonder when the locals will decide they've had enough of the missionaries and eat them.'

'The woman looked a bit tough and stringy,' I said. 'Maybe that's why they're holding back. Just not hungry enough yet.'

'If there's one thing I can't stand it's a missionary,' Dad said.

We decided to sail west to Guadalcanal where Robert and I

celebrated our sixteenth birthday with Myfanwy and her husband Charles Humphreys, an elderly couple who lived in an A-frame house on the tiny island of Tavanipupu, a safe distance from the malarial main island of Guadalcanal with its villagers and missionaries. The Solomons, equatorial and cloaked in dripping jungle, were riddled with treponemes and filarial parasites. Even on breezy Tavanipupu the Humphreys said they occasionally succumbed to fevers, while across the channel on Guadalcanal, villagers regularly took to their huts to lie shivering and dull-eyed on the floor. We had been warned about malaria in the Solomons and Mom had stocked up on prophylaxis, although on arrival in the islands, Dad and Robert refused to take medication. Dad said it wasn't necessary, if he got sick, that was that. Robert said he felt the same way. After two weeks of swallowing bitter pills, Mom said she couldn't handle the taste and stopped. Which left me dutifully swallowing tablets twice a week. I didn't want malaria.

It wasn't easy living in Tavanipupu, the Humphreys told us. Nevertheless, they were happy. Myfanwy told me their story. They'd met during the Second World War when Charles was in the airforce. As a fighter pilot in the RAF, a much younger Charles had inspired intense interest among the Wrens. But, she said, her eyes still dreamy at the memory, 'I was the one who got him.' Four decades of marriage and life on a remote island apparently hadn't dulled the satisfaction of winning her husband from the Wrens. After the war, Charles worked for the British Colonial Service before retiring to Tavanipupu with his wife. Advancing in age, he was still good looking and very charming. For my birthday he presented me with a ripe tomato from his vegetable garden. As he did so, his fingers brushed mine and his blue gaze was a little too prolonged. Picturing him in a raffish pilot's hat, I suddenly understood why the Wrens had got excited.

An optimistic Spanish conquistador hunting for King Solomon's gold named the 992 volcanic islands and coral atolls of the Solomon Islands. Four hundred years after their discovery, the gold has still not been found. The islands lie wedged against the equator, more than a thousand miles north-east of Australia. The climate is tropical. From March to November, trade winds cool the air to an almost bearable average of 27 degrees Celsius. From December, the winds die, temperatures rise and the rainy season begins. Showers pour daily from towering cumulonimbus clouds; part of the great monsoon weather system which later moves north to India. The rain is hot, the land steamy, and humidity levels hover above 90 per cent. Here we encountered our old friends, the equatorial doldrums, the birthplace of hurricanes.

As the cyclone season approached, we were the last sailors to leave the Solomon Islands. Heralded by a slackening of the trade winds and the gathering of clouds like strings of bruises along the northern horizon, the weather changed earlier than usual that year. Most boats had already moved on to Papua New Guinea which, like the Solomons, provides shelter and lies close enough to the equator to avoid full-strength storms. However, we were unable to follow them. During the years of apartheid, Papua New Guinea didn't recognise South African passports and – our Solomon Island visas exhausted – we had no choice but to return to Australia, a thousand miles away across the Coral Sea. In Guadalcanal, even if my father didn't share the urgency of his fellow sailors, I did. I remembered our sail to Grenada in hurricane season; the days of being becalmed, the squalls, the brewing hurricane. We had been lucky then, but I was worried we wouldn't be again. I began nagging Dad to set sail for Australia while the trade winds still blew.

'We're not leaving yet,' he said, sitting at the Honiara Yacht Club bar and sipping a beer. 'We haven't even seen New Georgia.'

The islands of New Georgia lay 105 sea miles to the west, in the direction of Papua New Guinea. People said that Marovo had the largest coral-fringed lagoon in the world, and that the diving was excellent. The villages scattered around the edges of the lagoon were difficult to visit, except by yacht. My father said that with a decent wind *Vingila* could cover the distance from Guadalcanal to New Georgia in under twenty-four hours. So what if our return to Australia was delayed by a few days, Dad said, a chance to visit the lagoon was a once in a lifetime experience. We just couldn't miss it.

We weighed anchor early, hoping to make landfall in Marovo the following morning, but without wind our boat sat within sight of Honiara for a full day. The hot air felt too heavy to move itself, let alone several tons of steel. That evening, using some of our precious diesel, we motored back to the yacht club, undoing twelve hours of sailing in fifty minutes. Robert and I were pleased. While we didn't care much for Honiara, a ramshackle town with a miserable market and broken roads stained with orange betel-nut spit, we liked the yacht club. The bar, beneath an airy thatched pavilion, served free ice water. There was an ablution block with cold showers and a place to wash clothes. After months of remote islands, a shower was heaven. And on Friday nights, jumpy movies were projected onto a fluttering screen. Although the soundtrack issued from a pair of crackling speakers and was further obscured by waves breaking on the concrete pier, we didn't miss a show. None of the yacht club members – a few ex-pat Australians – owned boats. They congregated at the bar to drink beer and gaze at the dirty beach. The only sailors at the club were fellow yachties like ourselves; deeply suntanned, wearing plastic sandals and living long-term on tight budgets with boats as old and battered as our own. The waiters, at least half of whom had proposed to me, all had betel-stained teeth. It never happened but Robert and I remained confident that we would, one day, meet a group of good-looking teenagers at the bar.

When we dropped anchor in Honiara after our failed attempt at sailing to New Georgia, the yacht club lights were ablaze and Robert and I felt certain the teenagers had arrived at last and were sitting at the bar drinking Coke with ice and slices of wild Solomon Island lime.

'Nobody's going ashore,' Dad said. 'We're leaving again in the morning and the dinghy stays up.'

We kept our hard dinghy hoisted on davits off the stern when we sailed. Also at the stern, beneath a covering of palm fronds, lay my new dugout canoe. I'd bought it from two young boys for ten dollars, the low price partial compensation for its extreme instability. I considered paddling to the club, but in Honiara's polluted anchorage where the bloated carcasses of pigs floated amid the other muck, black shark fins sometimes broke the surface of the water. I didn't want to capsize at night.

Sharks in the Solomons were plentiful – in many anchorages one had only to empty a pail of water overboard for dark, circling shapes to appear. 'Plenti tumas saks hea,' we were told by locals who explained that it had been so ever since the Second World War when many ships sank, often with a full complement of crew. The sharks, feasting on the corpses, had developed a taste for human flesh that was assumed to have been passed on to subsequent generations.

The six-month battle of Guadalcanal had been a turning point in the war. On this wild and previously unknown island, an American victory had been won over the Japanese at the cost of 30 000 lives. Henderson battlefield lay a short, reggae-blasting taxi ride from town, and we had been dropped off to walk on soil crunchy with the bones and teeth of soldiers dead forty years. In the Solomons war and death were everywhere. Iron Bottom Sound – the channel out of Honiara – was named for all its sunken ships. We dived on wrecks whenever we found them in shallower water, searching for rust-stained cowries that I knew would fetch a good price. Always, we looked out for sharks. Like the local people, sharks had entered our psyches.

I'd heard that on Malaita Island north of Guadalcanal, the people of

Auki lived on man-made coral islands and believed themselves to be the descendants of sharks, which they worshipped. If an Auki man's canoe capsized, he could call on a shark to carry him to shore, and unless it had been slighted or angered, the fish would oblige. But for relations between man and shark to remain amicable, sharks needed regular appeasement. So, summoned by a designated shark caller, they were fed the bodies of great chiefs and – more frequently – unwilling sacrificial victims. Missionaries and the government later discouraged the use of human flesh, suggesting roasted piglet as a substitute. Usually black and white-tipped reef sharks answered the call, but occasionally a tiger shark arrived, scattering the others. Big, aggressive, and responsible for most fatal attacks on humans in these isles, this was the shark to appease. Tiger sharks could eat a piglet in a single bite.

Looking first at the canoe and then at Robert, I considered my chances of overturning. If there were sharks about, I wondered if a sacrificial poodle would appease them. I decided probably not. In spite of the sharks, I still wanted to go ashore and meet the teenagers.

Robert read my thoughts and shook his head. 'Don't even try,' he said. 'Dad will kill us.'

A wave of laughter rose from the yacht club. I pictured the teenagers: clever and funny, joshing each other and ordering rounds of Cokes in the flickering yellow light. Then I went to bed with a book I'd read before, knowing that I'd never meet them.

The following morning, with a light wind ruffling the surface of the water, we set sail again. The breeze soon died. It took *Vingila*, and her following entourage of pelagic sharks, over sixty hours to reach the New Georgian archipelago. I was tense, the trade winds had died and I knew that we had missed the best weather for getting back to Australia. I kept hoping Dad would see the signs and forget about New Georgia. I kept dropping hints until he told me that a boat has one captain, and that captain was him and if I didn't shut the fuck up he would get out the Whistler.

I waited until I was alone with Mom.

'Can't you ask Dad to forget about New Georgia?'

Mom sighed. 'Since when has your father ever listened to me, Nicky?'

After that I was quiet about Australia, but I couldn't relax. To pass the time as we sailed, or rather drifted, Robert and I made lures from the silvery liners of wine boxes, which we hung from the stern to tease the trailing sharks. *Vingila*'s followers – with their attendant pilot fish and remoras – glided in blue space, barely moving a fin to keep pace with our boat. Sporadically they'd break from their torpor to attack our lures. The graceful blue-sharks, with dark, fathomless eyes, flashed their white bellies as they came at the lures side on. When they twisted their heads for the bait, we pulled the line from their mouths. We didn't want to catch blue-sharks, they were too pretty. The big makos, whose mouths spilled untidy teeth, attacked the lure directly. We let them bite, giving slack and enough time for the bait to be swallowed, before we hauled them in, fighting. After gaffing and beating them on the head until they were still, we sliced out their jaws and set them to dry in the sun.

'We'll sell these in Australia,' Robert said.

'Haven't you got enough now? How many do you need, anyway?' My mother sat beneath an awning in the cockpit with one hand on the helm and Pepe at her feet. Reflected sunlight from the sea played patterns on the underside of her jaw. Pepe raised his head to watch us with interest. He barked fiercely at each catch, but ever since a previous encounter with an energetic dorado had turned nasty, he declined to visit the stern while we were fishing.

My mother wiped the sweat from her glasses. 'Okay, you two, I think it's time to stop now. And make sure you wash every bit of blood off the deck. Use a scrubbing brush. And then what about some school work?'

She had enrolled us in an Australian correspondence school developed for the kids in the outback and we were meant to finish projects regularly and post them away for marking. Months sometimes passed, however, without us finding a post office.

In Marovo lagoon, we were greeted by the curio-laden canoes of Bislama village. The paddling salesmen wore salt-faded shorts and told us they were warriors; in the old days they had set out in war canoes for the surrounding islands and villages within the great lagoon. Sometimes they crossed the ocean, going as far as Santa Isabel and even Guadalcanal. They returned with heads. They also brought body parts, which they ate. But of course missionaries find cannibals irresistible. The men of Bislama explained, in pidgin: 'When the first missionaries came, they told us to stop. Our ancestors ate some of them, but later when we became Christians, the British government forbade us to hunt heads and eat men any more.'

This, oddly, was the same government who rekindled head hunting among the Dyaks of Borneo, encouraging the tribesmen to go after the Japanese during the war. As a rule, the Solomon Islanders stayed out of the war, and were merely bewildered observers of bloody battles fought by strangers on their own land.

'Where are the missionaries now?' Dad asked.

The men told us that after converting almost the whole village and building a church, the missionaries had left. Now they had their own pastor.

In New Georgia the local god, or Nusa-Nusa, adorned the prows of canoes. Salesmen scrambled in their hessian sacks for other Nusa-Nusas, which they wanted to sell us. The god was usually carved from ebony and inlaid with mother of pearl. It had a nose like a ski jump, with great flaring nostrils. Under the nose, tiny hands clasped a shrunken head. Sometimes, the hands held a bird. *'Dispela nusa-nusa he likum pis.'* This version, then, was the god of peace, carved primarily for the occasional squeamish tourist it seemed, for I never saw it on the prow of a canoe.

After the returning warriors had finished feasting on body parts, we were told the severed heads were deposited on an island in the centre of the lagoon. An older man pointed it out to us. When Dad asked to see the skulls his request was denied. *'Dis ples tumas taboo.'* Nobody went there nowadays.

'If nobody's going there,' my father said later, when we were alone, 'the diving's got to be good. Maybe a dive tonight?'

'I'm not sure that's a good idea, Frank,' Mom replied. She confined her snorkelling to shallow lagoons in the daytime, and she said it worried her when my brother dived at night. I was forbidden to go on nocturnal expeditions, she said she couldn't stand the thought of it.

Blackie Stephens, the headman of Bislama village, came to trade hand-carved fishing lures for spools of our Taiwanese poly-filament scavenged from the wreck in Pago Pago. His people, he told us proudly, were the blackest on earth. Visiting scientists from America had taken biopsies to prove that the skin of the Melanesians of New Georgia had higher melanin levels than the skin of the darkest person in Africa. When we told Blackie we were African, he looked at Robert's and my blonde hair and shook his head sadly. His colouring was impressive; not blue-black like the *National Geographic* pictures I had seen of equatorial Africans but matt-black like carbon paper, with deep orange palms and soles, stained darker in the creases. The whites of his eyes were orange too and when he smiled he showed gums the colour of molasses. John Wayne, the man sitting next to him on the deck, was equally dark but less talkative. After writing his name in the visitors' book, he ate a handful of popcorn before leaving in his battered canoe. Blackie, however, visited daily for the remainder of our stay, bringing gifts of bananas, purple fleshed yams and swamp-taro pudding. He drank tea and had long discussions with my father about fishing, seamanship and the possibility of exchanging Pepe for a wood carving. Weddings were never mentioned. In Bislama nobody wanted to marry me, for fear, perhaps, of diluting the melanin levels. The morning we left, Blackie gave my father a intricately carved ebony fishing spear. The attached tag – made from exercise book paper covered in clear tape – read: *Presented to Frank's family from Blackie's family, Bislama Village, Marovo Lagoon, Western Solomon Islands.*

After leaving Blackie we sailed across the lagoon to Tongoro passage, where we found *Cipango* in a deep bay, beside a chain of wooded islets. In Honiara we'd made loose plans to meet up in New Georgia, and we were pleased to see them again.

'*Salut*,' said Jean-Marc from the deck of his boat. 'The diving here is superb.'

While Mom, Dominique and Pepe wallowed together near the beach in a lukewarm soup of electric blue minnows, the rest of us went diving at the sea wall.

Napoleon wrasse bigger than our main saloon table swam past ornate coral formations while schools of barracuda played in the bubbles way above my head. We used the hooker – a compressor with twin air hoses – for shell diving; our scuba tanks were kept for emergencies. Robert seldom looked for shells; he preferred spearfishing and refused supplementary air, believing it was unsporting, so I dived with Dad. Our hoses snaked past the snouts of barracuda to the dinghy on the surface, as distant as an object viewed through the wrong end of a telescope, where Robert sat tending the air-pumping compressor. The paddles of his oars dipping sporadically into the sea disturbed its surface from the underside, as he followed the trail of our exhalations. Descending further, my father's red shorts turned purple and then deep maroon, as each frequency of light was absorbed in turn by the water. As we dived deeper and the water became darker, the coral trout, groupers, parrot and trigger fish grew bigger. I kept close to my father and whenever I saw a shark, I held his hand. Wearing gloves, we turned over rocks and poked in crannies with metal prods and our fingers. When Dad found shells he showed them to me and asked, with his thumb, yes or no. Thumbs up, the shell went into the mesh bag at his waist, thumbs down, it was returned to its place. *Conus geographicus* we never put in the mesh bag because of its fatally toxic harpoon. We carried it immediately to the dinghy in our hands, holding the widest part of the shell, while the harpoon waved energetically from the other end. Once in the dinghy, we confined it to a bucket until death. I never gave an adult *geographicus* the thumbs down; they were collectors' items and good for trading and selling.

After Dad and I had finished looking for shells, he and Robert went spearfishing with Jean-Marc. Then we gathered around a plastic basin of fish in *Cipango*'s cockpit for lunch.

'The season has changed,' Jean-Marc said, looking about at the still water. He spoke through a mouthful of *poisson cru* – snapper marinated in lime juice and coconut milk. His tanned, weather-beaten head looked as if it had been inexpertly carved from a block of wood. Dominique, with short dark hair and a heart-shaped face, sat next to him, like the sad queen in the deck of Tarot cards. An awning shielded us from the sun, but not the sight of the shockingly blue water and the strip of white beach trimmed with green palms. The colours were as strident and garish as those of a travel brochure, but we'd stopped noticing the features of our surroundings, except in terms of shelter, or as a source of food. Robert slouched to one side, fiddling with his speargun. I noticed a few dried fish scales stuck to his hands and saw tidemarks of salt that ran like snail trails down his brown arms and back. He'd speared and cleaned the snapper for lunch and also the fish for our supper that lay in the dinghy off *Cipango*'s stern. We were such unlikely twins. He was stoical, muscular, suntanned, and happiest in the sea, while I, nervy, scrawny and pallid, read books in my cabin. He read a bit, and I snorkelled, but we both knew where we belonged.

'It's time for leaving,' Jean-Marc continued, looking up at the sky. 'The trade winds have died. Soon, perhaps, we'll have the first cyclone.'

His face became thoughtful. His tongue roamed his mouth, searching out a fish bone.

'*Putain!*' – he spat the bone out.

He picked at a front tooth with his thumbnail. 'For us there are only two days of sailing to Choiseul and Papua. But you have two or three weeks to Australia if the winds return. If not, maybe more.'

Dad snorted. 'I'm not scared of a cyclone,' he said, spooning the last of the *poisson cru* from his steel plate and tipping the dish to his mouth to drink the juice. I *was* scared of cyclones but I knew better than to say anything. Robert, busy with his speargun, also stayed silent. Mom looked out over the dazzling water and sighed. She stretched her arms above her head. 'I wish we had some bread to eat with this fish,' she said.

The next day when we sailed from New Georgia, Dominique gave us a deck of Tarot cards, and to Robert and me a bar of chocolate and a small box of orange juice each.

She kissed both of us on the cheeks.

'*Au revoir, mes petits,*' she said. '*Bon courage.*'

Robert consumed his juice and chocolate immediately while I kept mine, thinking ahead to the voyage to Australia. In a hurricane, perhaps chocolate would cheer me up. And although we were leaving New Georgia, Australia wasn't on the cards yet, for Dad had noticed the speck of Bellona on the chart and read in the pilot book that it was inhabited by Polynesians.

'We can't miss that,' he said, 'and it's close, only a day or two away.'

At least this atoll lay to the south, in the direction of Australia. After four days of light winds which often faded away completely or alternated with gusty rain squalls, we reached Bellona.

There was no safe anchorage, only the calmness of the sea that day allowed us to drop anchor on the western side. Within minutes of anchoring, the chief of Mata-Moana settlement with all his men had paddled through the surf in their dugout canoes to welcome us. At least a dozen climbed aboard and introduced themselves with nods of the head and grave handshakes. Naked children swam out and climbed the sides of the boat to sit dripping and giggling on the cabin top, staring through the hatches, aghast at the sight of Pepe. I roasted popcorn, lifting the lid to dramatic effect while the kernels still jumped. A small boy, nudged on by the older children, fought back tears to take a handful which he ate reluctantly, while his friends laughed. Mr Rolf Teikangei, a village elder, removed a pair of one-armed sunglasses and wrote his name in the visitors' book before asking my father for the poodle. He'd never seen such an animal before, he explained. My mother declined. For months we'd received similar requests throughout Vanuatu, the Banks Islands and the far eastern Solomons. Pepe was her beloved companion, her ally, foot warmer and source of comfort. She would sooner have parted with one of her children than her dog.

Matthew Tamotai, newly returned from the Honiara Technical Institute in the capital, drew palm trees in the visitors' book with a ballpoint pen. After shading them carefully with fine cross-hatching, he invited Robert and me ashore in his canoe. The children watched us go – a few leaping into the sea from the bow and holding on to the dugout with clinging hands which Matthew removed, finger by finger, leaving them to swim to *Vingila* and pull themselves back aboard. Beaching on a strip of white sand, our new friend led us past frond huts where women with long hair sat in the shade on pandanus mats. Pigs foraged beneath the mango trees behind them. I felt as if I were in a painting by Gauguin.

'We are Polynesians,' Mr Rolf Teikangei had said while writing his name and address in the visitors' book. But they didn't look like the people I knew from Tahiti and the Society Islands, who were bloated and overweight, with swollen ankles and decaying teeth. Too much white sugar, we'd been told. Diabetes was rampant. Polynesians in the Solomons were a further anomaly, because we were in the heart of Melanesia. We hadn't seen a Polynesian in years. Mr Rolf explained: 'When our ancestors arrived on this island in their canoes, there were other people living here. Black-skinned people, but we killed them.'

Matthew led us away from the village. 'This palm,' he said, 'has the best drinking coconuts on Bellona.' Like Mr Teikangei, he spoke English, not pidgin.

'*You-fella no likum spik pijin?*' I asked. I'd been speaking pidgin for several months and, with teenage confidence, considered myself quite fluent. At first the language shocked me; it sounded as if it had been invented by supercilious colonists for conversing with golliwog dolls. The word for broken was *bagarup*. After I noticed that nobody else seemed embarrassed, I'd begun speaking with more enthusiasm than any real skill, and often made it up as I went along.

'Of course I speak pidgin,' Matthew said, 'but I also speak English. I learned it at school.'

That made him part of the one per cent of Solomon Islanders who spoke the official language. The rest spoke pidgin, introduced by the British to fill in the gaps between the seventy-one indigenous tongues and their multiple associated dialects.

Matthew climbed the palm quickly, followed by Robert who wanted to show that he could do it too. Both made the ascent look far easier than it was. I had climbed a coconut palm once, on Islas Las Perlas near Panama. I reached the top sweaty and shaken, my hands bleeding from the sharp bark. Looking down, with the potential for a deadly fall a quivering handhold away, I had resolved never to do it again. From that time on I waited below, well out of range of falling coconuts. Matthew opened the nuts with his machete. He was right, they were delicious. After five years in the Pacific, Robert and I knew our drinking nuts.

'I was born here, and I'm back on holiday.' Matthew said. 'But I want to live somewhere else. I'm looking for work and a wife.'

He ran appraising eyes over my skinny arms and legs, and flat chest. I was accustomed to rejecting marriage proposals, especially in Honiara where all the taxi drivers were from Malaita, an island to the north of Guadalcanal. On Malaita wives were bought for lengths of handmade traditional shell money, measured out in fathoms. Modern drills made the process easier, but it still took several months to make enough beads to buy a standard wife. Malaitan men often migrated to Honiara where women were free. This was the *kastom*.

'*Wea nao yupela stap?* . . . where are you going?' taxi drivers in Honiara asked me before flashing their betel-stained tooth stumps and enquiring, '*Yu marit nomoa?* . . . You married already?'

Western women were not only free, they usually came with appliances, like outboard engines or gas fridges. At least this is what the men in search of wives believed. In the smaller villages, men negotiated directly with my father. They wanted both Pepe and me.

But Matthew didn't propose, he asked for my address. Although his feet were rough and splayed from climbing coconut palms, he had lovely teeth and the drawings he'd made in the visitors' book had impressed me with their attention to detail. I said that if he wanted, he could write to me care of the GPO in Brisbane.

Back on *Vingila*, negotiations were taking place over fruit. With twenty-five watermelons and fifty pawpaws in the forepeak, and a mound of pineapples and cucumbers on the floor, my brother's cabin and bunk had become inaccessible.

'It's okay,' Mom told Robert, 'because at sea you usually sleep in the cockpit anyway.'

She had also given away most of our shoes.

'They asked me what I wanted and I said a bit of fruit, and then they came with so much and kept bringing it, that when our trading T-shirts were finished, I gave them our shoes.'

'We'll buy more in Australia,' she added.

Men in ragged shorts, with ledges of salt-stiff hair extending from their foreheads, crowded around the main saloon table, drinking tea and listening to our cassettes. They smelled briny, of fish blood and coconut husk smoke.

'If we start this lot on rum, they'll never leave,' my mother whispered. The cassettes were old and had stretched in the equatorial heat, distorting the music. The men preferred Aa'pa, our wailing Samoan music, to Mom's Neil Diamond or my Sex Pistols. They hummed along with the Samoans, swaying to the rhythm. My father made a note in the visitors' book: make and send a copy of Aa'pa to Bellona Island. Mr Teikangei described how they sailed their dugouts a hundred sea miles to Guadalcanal to trade copra, navigating only by the pattern of the sea and clouds. At dusk they departed in their canoes.

'Tomorrow,' Matthew said, 'we'll hunt a pig.'

'Great,' said Robert. 'What will we use?'

'Anything you like. Sticks, spears. Do you have a bow and arrow?'

'No. What about a speargun?'

'Okay, bring a speargun.'

But later that night we left without saying goodbye. When the wind changed, the sound of our mooring chain breaking coral on the sea floor had dragged us from sleep. A few firm wave-slaps under the stern roused us from our bunks. The wind was blowing onshore and we knew couldn't stay. We raised anchor in the dark, without turning the engine on. Robert pulled the chain up by hand, shunning the winch which he said was too slow. The moon, escaping for an instant from the clutch of a cloud, illuminated the bent backs of a line of palms, bowed over a strip of beach as curved as a nail paring. Above the rustle of the wind in the palm fronds, we heard the hiss and crash of distant breakers. The village, a few huts beneath the coconut palms, was dark;

the drums silent. Night air brought the smell of cooking fires, drying fish and smoked coconut. Working soundlessly, we raised the mainsail and hauled our bow away from the island. Then Robert raised the jib while I sheeted in, setting the sail. Dad sat on the cabin top, looking ahead. He hadn't given a single order; after seven years at sea, he often didn't have to any more. When the billowing sails caught the wind, our loaded boat yielded slowly, bowing over in supplication, as if she knew what lay ahead and didn't want to be part of it. Below decks, the cabins were packed with drinking coconuts, pawpaws, yellow watermelons, pineapples, seashells and cockroaches. Villagers had brought the fruit and – hiding within its crevices – cockroaches undeterred by repeated salt water dunkings, who had swarmed out to join our thriving resident population.

We were on our way back to Australia at last.

21

CORAL SEA

The wind that forced us to leave Bellona blew until dawn. The atoll, a dark smudge against a darker sky, dissolved into the sea, taking with it the smell of land and leaving a feeling of loneliness and vague expectation. The rise and fall of surf on the shore faded, replaced by the gurgle of waves against the hull. With a steady breeze and moderate sea, *Vingila* settled into a broad reach, cantering over the easy swells. The following morning the sun rose into a clear sky. The 18 knot breeze teased the scattered tops of wavelets into white frills. A group of cirrocumulus clouds above the north-east horizon suggested the wind would hold. The mood aboard lightened. Perhaps, after all, we weren't too late to catch the last of the trade winds which, if they held, would carry us across the Coral Sea to safety.

'What about pawpaw for breakfast?' Mom asked.

'I'm sick of pawpaw,' Robert said, walking to the stern for his morning pee.

Dad came up the stairs with a pot of coffee.

'Well, too bad, it's what we're having,' he said.

'So why ask me if I don't have a choice?'

'Dad's right,' Mom said, 'we can't let it go to waste.'

My father handed out mugs. 'Nicky, what about you?'

At sea, it was our habit to gather for early morning coffee in the cockpit. With warm mugs in our hands, we'd watch the sun rise while the decks were damp with dew and dead flying fish from the night before still lay in the scuppers. It was my favourite time of day. Since finding a drowned cockroach in the bottom of my cup, however, I'd gone off coffee. The roaches used the narrow ledges of the hand rails as thoroughfares to get about the boat. At night they could be seen marching along in glossy-backed single file, and sometimes – if an unexpected wave struck – tumbled off to land on the bunks, the chart table, the stove or the open book of a reader below. We'd been infested with cockroaches for years, but never to this degree. It was something about the Solomon Islands, Mom said. She had wanted to fumigate in Honiara, but the one shop in town, Joy Supermarket on Mendana Street, only had sacks of rice, cheap tinned fish and a few cans of Chinese duck. Pesticides were out of stock. Like new footwear, arthropod genocide would have to wait until we reached Australia.

For twenty-four hours after Bellona slipped from sight, the wind blew steadily on the beam and the ocean, superficially ruffled by the breeze, remained calm within its deeper layers, soothed as it was by the preceding months of light airs. *Vingila* made six knots, which was fast for her.

'A good week of this'll get us to Australia,' I said to Robert as we brought in the fish biltong that evening.

The next morning, the wind died, leaving our sails hanging limp. *Vingila* – a lump of steel – sat motionless on a sea of slate, beneath thickening clouds. The heat was suffocating. By noon the clouds were the colour of lead and sweat trickled in rivulets between our shoulder blades and down the backs of our knees.

'What about a watermelon for lunch?' Mom said, rising from the companionway with a long knife in her hands.

Dad looked up from his book. 'Don't ask them, tell them,' he said.

I reached over and dug my knuckles into my brother's ribs.

'I think Robert wants pawpaw.'

My brother made a face, grabbed my wrist and twisted it backwards.

'You're hurting me,' I said.

'Stop it,' my mother said. 'Let's eat some watermelon.'

We lowered the sails – without wind to fill them they were chafing against the shrouds – and we sat in a row on the cabin top eating watermelon and spitting the pips into the sea. Ripples spread from the floating seeds, fanning out and radiating across the still water. In air humid enough to drink, breathing felt like drowning. The safety of Australia seemed a million miles away. I pictured the ripples from our watermelon seeds spreading out in ever widening circles to arrive at the coast, weeks ahead of us. My watermelon rind looked like a fake smile. I stretched and threw it into the water to join the seeds.

'God, I'd like to feel those trades again,' I said.

Mom reached for the knife and stabbed the watermelon, splitting off another chunk. The flesh in the centre of the fruit was pale orange, almost white.

'Strange,' she said, 'I've never seen watermelon this colour before.'

I looked at the sky. To the east, a squall was trailing a veil of rain.

'I just hope we don't get a hurricane,' I said softly to Robert. Dad overheard me.

'You and your hurricanes,' he said. 'You're like a goddamn broken record. Always the same bladdy thing, isn't it?'

Lightning showed in the distance and the accompanying roll of thunder brought with it the faint smell of gunmetal.

'If it rains,' Mom said, 'at least we can have a wash and collect some drinking water.'

I ate another slice of watermelon and moved to the shade of the cockpit with my book. Sweat dripped down the backs of my knees and the bare flesh of my thighs stuck to the vinyl cushions. Mom and Dad went below. With *Vingila* drifting there was no reason to take the helm, no sails to adjust, no wake to watch disappear from the stern, and no comforting sense of motion. Being becalmed is, in many ways, more difficult than dealing with a gale because there is nothing to react to, no urgency, just a slow frustration mixed with mounting apprehension.

'Don't you wish sometimes we could just be normal and go to school and stuff?' With Dad below I could speak to my brother.

Robert looked up from the watermelon rind he was whittling with his pocket knife.

'What's wrong with you now?' he said. 'I thought you hated school.'

'I do. I just don't want another trip like the one from Fortaleza to Grenada. Remember? Becalmed, becalmed, becalmed and then a hurricane.'

Robert threw the rind overboard and leaned over to punch me lightly on the arm.

'You worry too much,' he said.

'And if it's worse than Grenada?' I said. 'What then?'

'Well, there's nothing we can do about that now, is there?'

I thought we were sailing – however slowly – for Australia. Dad, I discovered, had other plans.

'Look here,' he said, tapping the chart with the back of his pencil, '*this* is where I want to go.'

The reef he pointed at looked like a pale water stain on the white expanse of the map. Tiny black numbers, fine as hatched spiderlings, charted the shallows and the coral heads which extended from a central circle into a long, north-reaching arm.

'Where's the land?' I asked.

'Here.' Dad's finger jabbed at a tiny spit of yellow. A sandbar. I leaned closer. Elevation two metres, I read. The island looked about 300 metres long. The arm of its reef stretched out for 30 or 40 miles.

'Is there anything left at high tide?' I pictured white waves washing over the reef and sandbar. I saw the sheltered water lost in a swirl of currents and rip tides.

Dad shrugged. 'Who cares,' he said, 'the diving's got to be good.'

'But the anchorage won't be,' I said.

Dad ran his callused finger over the chart, absently following the convolutions of numbers and black lines marring an otherwise unblemished stretch of ocean. I leaned closer to read the name of the place: Chesterfield Reef. Where he saw pristine diving conditions, I saw disaster. Most of the submerged reefs would be visible only once we were on top of them, particularly if we made landfall at night. We would have to find a passage which led to an anchorage that looked almost non-existent, and was probably scattered with coral heads which could snap our chain like wet wool should the seas rise. A two-metre high sandbar would provide protection from neither waves nor wind. Getting out at night if the weather turned foul would be impossible. In a storm we'd be much safer on the ocean, far away from reefs. I was wary of atolls with extensive fringing reefs and poor land protection. Nadine and Vincent had survived the wrecking of their boat in Suwarrow, but Chesterfield, this new reef that Dad proposed we visit, would have no abandoned settlements or water tanks. In fact I expected to find nothing more than sand. What's more, the reef lay hundreds of miles from the nearest land; if we survived a shipwreck, we couldn't expect to be rescued.

My father bent his head over the chart, a pair of callipers in his hand and his mouth slightly open in concentration.

'Dad,' I said.

'Yes?' He looked up from the chart.

'Do we have to go there?'

'What is it you want, Nicky? No wait, don't tell me. You want a shopping mall where you can steal stuff. You want a yacht club with a bar and a city with movie houses that stay open till midnight where you can hang out with your good for nothing pals. Isn't that right?'

His lips tightened a little more and against the pale background of his blue eyes, I thought I saw his pupils constrict.

'I just don't like the look of it,' I said.

'Nicky, how many captains on a boat?'

'One.'

'That's right. So do me a favour, okay? Leave the sailing to me.'

So it was decided; we would sail to Chesterfield, except of course we couldn't get there without wind. The air was still. The sea stayed smooth and unmarked in the pre-monsoon heat that choked us and sent a panting Pepe to sprawl flat-bellied against the floorboards. At night he woke me with his whimpers and scratching and restless search to find somewhere cool. Day after day the sea remained calm; a hot, polished disc with us in its centre. The water was so flat that in the evening we ate our meals sitting at the table, from open plates instead of the bowls we generally used at sea. We might have been at anchor.

'Wind would be nice,' Mom said.

Sometimes, at night, we were awoken by the the sound of wavelets lapping against the hull, and a subtle change in *Vingila*'s motion.

'Wind,' Dad would grunt.

Pulling ourselves from our bunks, we'd go outside to raise the sails. The night breeze cooled the sweat on our bodies, bringing hope.

'Look, we're sailing,' my mother would whisper, pointing at the knot meter where the needle jerked from its resting place of zero to point hesitantly at one knot.

'Two knots now,' she'd breathe, stretching the truth. Dad would set Baruch and we'd fall back into our bunks. Drifting to sleep, we'd be reawakened, this time by the slapping of empty sails against the shrouds. Climbing on deck, we'd lower the main and genoa again to stop them chafing, before returning once more to our airless bunks and fractured sleep.

In the afternoons I listened to weather reports on the short- wave radio. An extensive low pressure system was building in the north of the Coral Sea. Water and air temperatures were high; squalls and rainstorms frequent. At least the Australian announcer sounded sympathetic. *Vingila* crawled slowly southwards, away from the low. The barometer hovered steady at 1012 millibars and the sky's tones deepened to shades of tarnished pewter. It rained almost every day. Sunsets, when we saw them, were crimson; sunrises, diluted bloodstains seeping through the sky. Dusk was brief and it stayed hot until after midnight. We ate pawpaw for breakfast, watermelon for morning tea, pineapple and cucumber for lunch and watermelon again in the evening. The fruit pile in Robert's cabin showed subtle signs of diminishing but still it crawled with roaches who marched in single file at night on their secret missions throughout the boat. A week passed.

'Walking would be faster than this,' Robert said, watching bubbles sliding slowly past the hull.

I started drinking vodka. Dad enforced an alcohol ban at sea so I pilfered from the liquor cabinet while my parents slept. Vodka allowed me to drift off and deadened both the hope and disappointment of getting and then losing wind in the night. Mom and Dad didn't notice that I wasn't always sober. The first night I mixed vodka with the box of orange juice Dominique had given me as a parting gift. I'd hidden both the juice and chocolate under my bunk to keep them away from Robert. I opened the juice as a kind of private nocturnal party for one, and decided to also allow myself a piece of chocolate. I planned to eat it bit by bit over the nights, but when I tore open the wrapping, a stream of cockroaches poured out. They had burrowed through the foil wrapper to nibble circular depressions in the surface of my chocolate bar.

'Serves you right,' Robert said the next day when I told him. 'You wanted to keep it all for yourself.'

At least the juice had been spared. A bizarre, neon shade of orange, it tasted far too sweet, although the writing on the box proclaimed at least six per cent natural fruit ingredients. After the juice was finished, I drank vodka straight from the bottle, pulling out the chart table quietly to reach Dad's booze stash. Two quick glugs were usually enough.

We were a hundred miles from Chesterfield when the wind finally picked up. One afternoon *Vingila* came alive as if she had been released from a spell. With the breeze in her sails, she shook herself and fairly scampered across the water. Charcoal clouds dispersed to reveal an evening sky the pale yellow of under-ripe mango. It was the first untroubled sunset we had seen in days. Baruch was put back to work, and the sound of his twang-thunk, twang-thunk and the other familiar sounds and rhythms of our boat making her way steadily across the sea, soothed us. And with *Vingila* moving, we could trawl for fish again. We set out fishing lines and caught a tuna for supper.

Bracketed to the wall of the radio room was a satnav, an early precursor to GPS, which Dad had bought in Australia for several thousand dollars. It had changed our sailing completely. Unlike the early days when we relied on celestial navigation, we now had a chunky black box which magically gave us our position every four hours.

As we sailed toward Chesterfield, Dad plotted the satnav's readings, tracing our progress. With the good wind, we reached the tongue of the reef the following evening as the sun was setting. The satnav confirmed our arrival, but there was no land in sight, just a long line of white breakers stretching ahead to the horizon. This was the reaching-out arm I'd seen on the chart. Taking readings from the satnav we sailed down the arm in the darkness. The moon came out. We took watch, keeping the silver line of rollers within view, to windward, on the starboard side. The roar of waves hurling themselves against the outside of the reef kept us company through the night, but the arm sheltered the sea and over the flat partially sheltered water, *Vingila* picked up speed. The wind rose. To ensure landfall at dawn, we dropped the jib to slow the boat down. Daybreak found us at the bow, searching for a sandbar in a sea dotted with whitecaps and foamy breakers. With each minute the wind strengthened.

'Typical,' Dad said. 'For weeks we haven't had wind and now when we don't want it, we get it in buckets.'

Mom went below to boil water for coffee and came back on deck looking pale.

'Frank,' she said, 'there's something wrong with the barometer. Come and see.'

Our brass barometer was mounted next to a matching clock on the bulkhead leading to Robert's cabin. They looked smart together like that, nattily nautical – particularly when we remembered to polish them. Dad stepped up to the barometer and tapped the glass with his finger. The needle juddered a little before returning to its position: 1005 millibars. I'd never seen a pressure reading so low. For weeks the needle had been hovering between 1012 and 1013. Now it appeared to have developed a sort of dropsy and was falling unsteadily even as we watched. By the time we had finished our morning coffee, the needle tip pointed tremulously at 1003 millibars. This was not a good sign. Low atmospheric pressure represents a void which air rushes in to fill. Rushing air is, of course, wind. The faster the fall and the lower the pressure, the stronger the wind blows across the gradient.

From geography lessons I knew that weather maps represented

pressure variations using isobars – lines on a chart joining areas of equal pressure. The closer the lines and steeper the gradient, the more violent the storm. Over the ensuing fifteen minutes we watched our barometer fall to 1000 millibars. Plotting these isobars on a weather map would be almost impossible, they were so close together.

'What the fuck's going on?' Dad muttered. 'Nicky, you're always listening to the weather reports. What does your clever man have to say about this, hey?'

I shook my head. 'Nothing. Just that big low building in the north, it's been there for weeks.'

I tapped the barometer myself. 'This doesn't make any sense.'

We were interrupted then by Robert shouting from the bow where we'd left him on lookout. His voice was barely audible above the wind, and Mom relayed the message down the hatch: Robert had seen land. The island he had seen lay so low in the water it was visible only from the crests of the waves. Joining my brother at the bow, and straining to see above the swell, I glimpsed a scoop of yellow sand and a single adolescent coconut palm cringing in the wind. It was more than I had expected. The anchorage, however, was every bit as terrible as I'd feared; there was no shelter at all, and short, choppy waves broke and foamed everywhere. In bright sunlight, through the water, we saw endless banks of coral. To anchor we needed sand, somewhere we could let out a length of chain to absorb the repeated shock of *Vingila*'s bow yanking against the choppy waves. Closer to shore we found a patch of sand, but a yacht was anchored there already. We dropped our mainsail and motored around the boat, yelling greetings. She was a small vessel, about 30 feet long, and her hatches and sails were battened down. A dinghy lay lashed upside down on her foredeck. Waves broke over her bow as she rode at anchor, jerking back against the chain as showers of spray drove against her sun dodger. Nobody responded to our calls.

Dad went below to make contact on the VHF radio.

'They're not answering. I tried the ham as well. I wonder if it's been abandoned. And the barometer's fallen to 998 millibars.' He looked around. 'Maybe we could anchor over there, in front of them.'

'To 998 millibars?' Mom said. 'We can't stay here.'

Robert came from the bow. 'What's happening?'

'Barometer's fallen to 998,' I said. 'We're in for something big and I'm not looking forward to tonight.' I turned my face into the wind and spoke into his ear. I was close enough to see how salt crystals had formed along the tiny hairs sprouting from his ear lobe.

'Dad wants to stay here,' I said.

'Why?'

'Frank ...' Mom said.

'What is it with you lot?' Dad's sweeping, exasperated hand gesture encompassed us all, including Pepe, who was cowering in the cockpit keeping clear of the spray. At the sound of my father's voice, Pepe winced. Robert and Mom were quiet; I had the feeling they were waiting for me to speak.

'Dad, if this wind picks up we'll never get out at night,' I said.

'Can't you see we'll never get the chance to come here again?'

Dad's voice took on a wheedling tone. 'Imagine the diving. Think of all the shells.'

I thought of the reef, the coral, the fish, the sharks and all the shells. I thought of the hot yellow sand and the single stunted palm. I thought of the dropping barometer and the rising waves. I didn't want to stay.

'What's here anyway? One frigging palm tree,' I answered. I waited for the old man to slap me, but he turned his attention to my brother, who was at the helm, keeping *Vingila*'s head into the wind.

'Robert?'

'Aw, Dad.'

'Well, I don't like it,' Mom said. 'I don't want to stay.'

'I didn't ask you, Tubby,' Dad said, staring at Robert.

Mom squatted next to Pepe, running her hand along his back. He heaved a sigh and shuffled closer, resting a damp chin against her leg and looking up at her to show the stained whites of his eyeballs. I noticed then how he had aged; his muzzle was grey and his pupils looked milky. Something in my chest clenched. I remembered a time when I too could be calmed by a word or pat from my mother and I envied Pepe his ability to still be comforted. I also envied the dog his ignorance of the barometer's falling needle.

Robert, who seldom voiced an opinion, did so now. '998 millibars doesn't sound good to me,' he said, holding Dad's stare. 'I think we should go.'

We circled the unresponsive yacht once more, blowing our horn and shouting, and then we left; picking our way through coral heads and a building sea, under a small mainsail. Robert looked sharp at the bow, standing on the pulpit with a hand behind him on the forestay for balance. By lunchtime we were clear of Chesterfield and the sea was so rough we could barely eat lunch.

'I'm sailing with a bunch of bladdy rats. Always ready to give up, always ready to leave a sinking ship,' Dad said, scooping cold fish and boiled yam into his mouth.

Which is when I started thinking that if we reached Australia alive, perhaps it was time for me to leave the yacht.

'So I'm a rat,' I said. 'I left the boat on the beach in Tahiti and I left in Samoa for the tidal wave. Well I'm sorry. I was only twelve at the time.'

'A twelve-year-old rat. And now you're sixteen and nothing's changed.'

At the sound of my father's voice Pepe shivered and tried to make himself smaller in a corner. Dad didn't generally forgive and forget except in a few, exceptional cases. After five years he no longer mentioned the line that *Cipango* claimed we had lost when *Vingila* was beached in Tahiti, but he could not forget my desertion that same night. He had made up with *Cipango* but he often reminded me of my lapse in courage. Then of course there was the tidal wave incident in American Samoa, and now a mutiny in Chesterfield, all of which confirmed my lack of bravery and loyalty. I couldn't see him taking my decision to leave the yacht very well and decided for the time to say nothing of it.

Dad's analysis of our character deficiencies was cut short when the gale intervened and kept us busy. First we went on deck to reef the mainsail and later – as the wind intensified – we were forced to lower the main and raise the storm jib. All this was done as the sun set and darkness fell. With an unabating soundtrack of wind screaming through the rigging, we bellowed at each other, even as the storm swept the voices from our mouths. The spray was so heavy it felt as if we were working under water, and all the previously inanimate objects on deck – the sheets, the winch handles, the helm, the boom – seemed to have come violently alive, to twist and fight in our hands, and to lash out vindictively. The sails we lowered refused to be restrained and tried to escape and take along anyone foolish enough to try to stop them. The halyards tried to whip us, or wind themselves around our legs. Everything was a fight. Once we finally got *Vingila* hoved-to under the storm jib, we went back inside, tired and hungry. We couldn't eat a proper supper – the sea was so rough we lay on the floor, gnawing fish biltong and black strips of dried banana while *Vingila* lurched and bucked like a bull at a rodeo.

Some hours later Mom made tea, serving careful half-cups. Outside where our storm jib strained in the darkness the sea had been churned to white foam. I wanted to sleep in my own cabin, as far away from my family as possible, but repeated wave blows under the stern threw me from my bunk, forcing me to return to the saloon floor where I spent a resentful night near Dad. The barometer – at least – was rising. At midnight the atmospheric pressure read 1002 millibars and, six hours later, 1008. It was clear that the blow, intense though it was, wouldn't last long. By morning the gale had eased, although the waves were still high and confused. At least we had wind again which we hoped would persist and blow us all the way to Australia, but it didn't. As the sun moved through a smeary sky, making its way between tattered clouds, the wind eased off and simultaneously inched around degree by degree until by late afternoon we were facing a light headwind. A breeze on the nose was the last thing we expected. Close-hauled to the wind, we set *Vingila* on a port tack. She responded sullenly, jackknifing into the waves. The satnav spat out the latest co-ordinates; Chesterfield now lay 120 miles astern. Thanks to the storm we had at last made some progress toward Australia.

Dad plotted our new position on the chart, measuring the distance we had covered with a pair of callipers.

'We're going back,' he said.

Mom's head snapped up from the book she was reading. 'What?'

'I said, we're going back.'

Mom looked confused. 'Back where?' she said.

'Chesterfield,' said Dad. 'Do you have a problem with that?'

That night when Mom made her daily entry in the logbook, in addition to the usual notes about wind speed and direction, the log reading and the co-ordinates of our position, she added an unusually personal line. 'This is a very sad boat,' she wrote.

We never reached Chesterfield Reef. First the south-west wind weakened and then it died. When it picked up again, it blew from the north. Dad wanted to beat again, this time away from Australia, but our lack of enthusiasm had worn him down, so we turned about and set *Vingila*'s course south. We were within 38 miles of Chesterfield at the time, and too far to see the palm tree.

Later, that same afternoon, Dad cheered up.

'Look at this,' he said, pointing to something small on the chart. 'Here's a reef I never noticed. We'll go there instead.'

I examined the tiny mark next to his finger. Bird Islet was smaller than Chesterfield and without the extensive fringing reef, which could possibly make the anchorage safer, or not. The entire place looked minuscule and I doubted palms fringed its tiny shore, but at least it lay in the right direction. In light winds *Vingila* might take several days to reach Bird Islet. During that time, much could happen. Dad could even forget about the place.

Over the following days the wind remained weak – around ten knots – which was just enough to keep us moving, although progress was painfully slow. We caught wahoo and tuna, and made biltong from their flesh. A school of bonito swam beside the boat for most of a morning. We began to spot seabirds. To the north, the low pressure system gradually intensified.

Bird Islet was roughly the size of a rugby field. Composed of nothing more than yellow sand sprinkled over a crown of coral, it rose incongruously above the waves in an otherwise empty stretch of ocean. Without the satnav we would have sailed blindly past, or right into it. The place lacked even the single, clichéd palm of Chesterfield, although it did have a lot of birds and in the light winds the anchorage was protected by a close ring of reef. We took Pepe ashore where he disturbed the colonies of nesting frigate birds, gannets and fairy terns which, until then, had thought they were safe from land-based predators. Having no desire to eat gull-egg *huevos rancheros* ever again, we didn't collect any eggs. Pepe sniffed at the fuzzy chicks, ignored the screaming adults and, after failing to find anywhere suitable to lift his leg, squatted near the high-water line to pee on a heap of drying seaweed. Dad and Robert snorkelled on the reef and speared a couple of coral trout, which we ate for lunch together with our tenth last pineapple and a slightly shrivelled cucumber. After we finished eating, we cleaned up, had a rest, and then raised anchor and sailed away.

'That wasn't so bad now, was it?' said Dad, giving me a playful cuff on the ear.

That evening the sympathetic Australian weatherman announced that the low pressure system lying to the south of the Solomon Islands had deepened further and was growing more organised. The system was now officially classified as a tropical depression. He seemed vaguely apologetic, as if he were in some way implicated in the recent developments. Within the depression, winds had begun gusting to 39 knots, or 63 kilometres per hour and, although it still lacked a central eye, it was showing signs of developing into the first tropical storm of the season.

Robert and I lay together at the back of the boat, spitting water melon pips into the sea and watching small fish dart from beneath the protection of *Vingila*'s hull to investigate the floating seeds. I lowered myself off the back of the boat, holding on to Baruch's rudder. It was cooler there, closer to the water in the shade of the overhanging stern.

'Watch out for Dad,' Robert said.

'It's okay, he and Mom are busy inside. He said not to bother them for a while.'

I sat on the part of the rudder above the water.

'What do you think they're doing?' Robert said, smirking.

'You know, the usual.'

I dipped a finger into the impossibly blue, impossibly clear water. It felt as if we were floating in space. Bending my head over, blood pulsed in my ears. The sun's rays refracting through the depths fell on long, silvery shapes swimming below. I trailed my finger in a circle. The bravest of the small fish darted out and took an experimental nip.

'Ouch.' I pulled my finger from the water to suck it and bent my head over again.

'What are you doing down there?' Robert asked.

'Just having a closer look.'

Above the abyss, *Vingila*'s deep keel looked small and toy-like. Her red anti-fouling paint flashed dull purple in the blue light. Leaning over, I could see her rudder and the brassy glint of her prop as she rose and fell on almost imperceptible swells. I straddled Baruch, dragging my feet in the water. The fish fled, then turned back on themselves, lured by the promise of something to eat.

'How's the hull?' asked Robert.

'Clean. No barnacles.'

'Remember the Galapagos?' Robert asked, hanging his head over the stern and looking at me upside down with his blond hair falling over his face.

'Yup, and all the goose-necked barnacles.'

'If we had them now, I'd have to jump in and scrape them off.'

'I'd watch out for sharks,' I said, 'but don't expect me to get in with you.'

'That feels like years ago.'

'Because it was, stupid. We were eleven then and we're sixteen now.'

We were quiet for a while before I said, 'Robert, don't say anything to Dad, but when we get to Australia – I mean, if we get to Australia – without a hurricane or anything, I'm thinking of moving out.'

'Leaving *Vingila*?'

'Yes, leaving the yacht, and Mom and Dad. You too, I suppose, if you don't come with me.'

Robert looked at me and shook his head. 'What do you want to do that for?'

'Because I can't sail like this any more.'

'Jesus, Nicky, it's not that bad. Just relax a bit for a change.'

After a while he said, 'Is it Dad?'

'A bit. Don't you hate it when he hits us?'

'He only does it when he has to.'

'And when he calls us cunts?'

'Well, sometimes we are.'

'And when last did we see kids our age? Apart from Matthew, I mean. All we do is go to stupid desert islands with nothing on them.'

'Desert islands aren't that bad.'

'Robert,' I said, 'don't you want your own boat one day?'

'Of course, don't you?'

'Yes, you know that. Thing is, how will you get one?'

'I dunno, I'll make a plan I suppose.'

'What sort of plan? Steal one like Vincent did? Because unless we get decent jobs I can't see any other options.'

'What's got into you?'

'I'm sick of desert islands and sailing with a fucking hurricane breathing down the back of my neck, that's what. And I want to be the captain of my own yacht one day, and right now it's not looking likely.'

My brother stood up and stretched.

'You're crazy,' he said. 'I'm going back to the cockpit, it's too hot out here.'

I didn't answer. My feelings were contradictory and difficult to put into words. I wanted to leave because of my father – who still kept the Whistler handy and who told me I couldn't think – and I wanted to leave because I hated taking chances with the weather and not having a say about it. I loved *Vingila* but with the love came a feeling of responsibility that I didn't want any more. The night I had watched our boat rolling in the breakers on the beach in Tahiti, she had become something more than an inanimate object to me. I began thinking of her as a protector with whom I'd formed a pact. She kept us safe in storms and heavy seas, and we in turn looked after her. In fact Dad expected us to defend her with our lives, thus making me responsible but powerless, because of late it seemed that I needed to save her from my father himself. Everything I had was invested in our yacht – my family, my possessions, my options, my future. And sometimes I suspected that my father was quite ready to sacrifice his family's safety in the pursuit of adventure.

I was also tired of not having friends my own age and not having money. Not all the yachties we met lived like us, scrounging and bartering. Many had lovely yachts with good food and decent clothes. For me, the freedom of sailing was, in a way, a false freedom. A trap of poverty and endless moving on. I feared living the rest of my life like Vincent and Nadine.

Robert, halfway to the cockpit, turned back and swung his head over the stern where I was still sitting on Baruch's rudder.

'So,' he said, 'what are you planning to do?'

'Go back to South Africa and live with Nana.'

'And then?'

'Well,' I said, 'I think I want to be a doctor.'

I had just finished a book about a pathologist who solved crimes. It sounded interesting, there were dead bodies and you got to look down a microscope, and find out how people died and sometimes who killed them. And the few doctors we had met sailing all had very nice yachts. Also, I thought, if I were a doctor it wouldn't matter if my family or I got sick or hurt at sea or on a desert island because I would be able to fix them.

'We don't have enough money for that,' Robert said.

'Nana might help and maybe there's something in Benoni from the houses. I'll take some cowries to sell. The *guttata,* and a few others like the red-lipped olives.'

The *Cypraea guttata* was my most valuable shell; a rare, deep-water cowrie usually discovered in the stomachs of fish, as the specimen I owned had been. I had bought the cowrie in Honiara with the pocket money I had saved in Australia. Even though I had always wanted a *guttata* I felt I couldn't rightfully keep the shell in my collection, because I hadn't found it myself or traded it with a local person; however, I knew I could sell it again for a profit. To comfort me for the impending loss of my *guttata*, I had a lovely golden cowrie or *Cypraea aurantium*, which I had traded for a T-shirt. The shell was not quite as rare as the *guttata* but just as beautiful and collectable. The waters of New Caledonia, the Banks Islands, Vanuatu and the Solomons had been rich in unusual shells and my collection had grown even further. In addition to knowing the names of every species of cowrie, I also knew their current market price and I regularly traded and sold duplicate specimens to other collectors whenever I met them.

'You'd sell the *guttata*?'

'For five hundred US dollars, I would. Just don't say anything to Dad yet, because I'm scared he won't let me go.'

'You're crazy,' said my brother.

'Am I? Then tell me something. What's more important to Dad? Us or the boat?'

'I'm not even going to answer that,' Robert said.

'Yeah, because you know the answer. And it's crazy.'

Over the following days, I took to spending time alone at the stern. Lines of drying fish sticks tangled in my hair when I stood up and the scuppers stank of dog piss, but at least I could be by myself. For comfort, I dragged over a cockpit cushion. It had been with us since Durban and, during seven years of life at sea, had not aged gracefully. The bleached vinyl had split in places, taking on the colour and texture of peeling, sun-burned skin. The mildewed foam interior bulging through the cracked surface had grown flabby and waterlogged. Dragging the cushion felt like dragging a corpse. I spread my *pareo* over its vinyl cover, rigged another cloth for shade and lay for hours with my chin on the stern toe rail, looking over the edge at Baruch's rudder slicing through blue infinity.

I completed my school exercises at the back of the boat too, working my way through the modules of the Australian correspondence course. When we reached Australia I planned to post the chapters, and I expected a written response from a faceless teacher within a few weeks. I sometimes finished several weeks of maths in a single morning. At sea, I found science and biology difficult because I couldn't always set up my experiments properly if the water was rough, and the lenses of the microscope I had bought in Durban had, in the humid air, become overgrown with black fungus.

Usually Robert and I did school work together at the saloon table, but as the tropical depression slowly intensified I did all my work alone, lying on the scabby cushion at the stern. Once I was done, I read books or just lay quietly, looking into the water and thinking. I thought about Jean-Marc and Dominique on *Cipango*. I imagined that they would have reached Papua New Guinea, and I wondered how they were liking it. I thought about Nadine and Vincent and how we'd met up again in Vanuatu. The last time we'd seen them was in an anchorage on Guadalcanal when Vincent invited us to dinner. He served us boiled yams and purple sweet potatoes from wooden bowls he'd carved himself. We ate with wooden chopsticks because Nadine preferred not to have metal aboard, except for a few essential tools like pots, spearguns and fish hooks. That night she couldn't join us because she was too ill. While we ate, she lay in pain in the forepeak with an abscess the size of a grapefruit on her thigh. She probably needed urgent surgery to drain the pus, but Vincent declined my mother's offer of painkillers and antibiotics, telling us Nadine refused to take anything unnatural. Ramone had watched us from under a tangled fringe with animal eyes. I thought about his future and my own. I thought back to the beginning of our voyage and about Ernest on the junk *Maria Jose* in Durban and how he believed his sons didn't need schooling because they could sail and navigate. Opting out of a conventional existence was all very well, I decided, as long as it was voluntary and I couldn't see any evidence that any of these children had been given an option.

My thoughts were interrupted by Dad shaking a fist in my face.

'You!' he said.

'What?' I ran through all the things in my head I might have done wrong. Had he found out about the vodka?

'You did this!'

'What?' I knew I should have topped the vodka level up with water, but because he never drank at sea I didn't think he'd check.

'You thought it up.'

So it wasn't the vodka.

'Dad, what is it?'

'All that worrying and fussing. Before we even left Marovo you were at it. Always talking about hurricanes. Always going on and on. Well, now you've got one.'

He thrust his face into mine. 'Jonah!' he hissed. 'You thought this up!' and he stalked off to the cockpit.

I lay back on my cushion and looked around. The wind blew from the north-west at about 15 knots, *Vingila* rode small, even swells and the sky above was scattered with benign white clouds. Where was the hurricane?

The Australian weatherman confirmed my father's news. Cyclone Winnie, with wind speeds of 150 kilometres per hour, had formed in the Coral Sea, south of the Solomon Islands. Meteorologists label each year's hurricanes alphabetically from January to December, which made Winnie the twenty-third storm of 1983. Apparently Cyclone Winnie was very unusual because, in terms of the calendar year, she was the latest severe tropical storm on record. Which also made her the earliest storm ever to appear in the Coral Sea's hurricane season. And according to my father, I had thought her up.

'At least now you can stop waiting for it,' my brother said when he

339

joined me later at the stern, where I sat brooding. Then he went to help Mom with supper while I sat hugging my cushion until after the sun had set and the sky had turned dark.

Part 6

SOUTH AFRICA AND THE INDIAN OCEAN

22

ALBERTON

I wept on the plane from Brisbane to Sydney. In Sydney I changed planes and stopped crying and remained dry eyed for the duration of the eighteen-hour flight to Johannesburg. As the aircraft ascended into the sky, pushing me back into my seat, my emotions drained away as if they had been left behind on the ground. I felt calm, and strangely empty, like a shipwreck survivor who, after a good pounding by the waves, has been washed up on a quiet beach. Outside the plane's porthole, a frigid wind screamed and lumpy clouds wallowed above the red earth of Australia. At unpredictable intervals stewardesses delivered trays of alien food and brittle cups of orange juice and, apart from mumbling thanks in the general direction of their stiff, painted faces, I spoke to no one. We landed in Johannesburg just before New Year, bumping along the runway as the captain told us to stay in our seats until the seat belt signs went off. When the plane stopped I collected my bag. Everything I owned fitted into a day-pack; a pair of rather worn school shoes, one pair of jeans, five T-shirts, six pairs of panties and a sweatshirt. I'd also packed a selection of rare cowries, including the *Cypraea guttata* which I planned to sell so that I could buy some clothes and shoes. Slinging my bag over my shoulder I made my way from the arrivals terminal. A pair of automatic doors opened with a sigh and I spilled into a white hall. When I spotted Nana and Chummy waiting behind a waist-high barrier I began crying again. Sobs welled up and shook my body. Nana waddled over and took my hand in both of hers. The sobs intensified. A few late-night stragglers paused to stare at me. Chummy, who was probably expecting a slightly larger version of a nine-year-old girl, made eye contact and looked away again, alarmed. The spiky punk hairstyle I'd cultivated when we had left Australia to sail to the Solomon Islands had grown out, but I still wore my antique spectacles with tiny, twisted arms and round, telescopic lenses. I had holes in my jeans, an image of Johnny Rotten on my T-shirt, and a pair of plastic lace-up shoes on my feet.

My grandfather moved forward awkwardly, approaching an unfamiliar teenage girl with caution. I hadn't seen him since 1977, the day my mother had packed Robert and me into the back of her blue Peugeot 404 together with Pepe, seven years earlier.

'Please, Nicky, don't cry,' Chummy said, reaching into the pocket of his sports coat for a neatly folded tissue and handing it to me.

His gesture elicited a fresh burst of sobbing. As he searched for words of comfort, his hand reached up to my shoulder, stopping before it got there. He looked bewildered.

'Please don't cry, we'll get you a new pair glasses,' he said.

'Don't bother the child like that. Maybe she likes her funny glasses.' Nana appeared to have shrunk. Her head barely reached my shoulder. Around us people waved Happy New Year signs at arriving passengers. In spite of my tears my grandmother looked determined to remain upbeat.

'If we hurry,' she said, 'we can watch the end of the New Year party on television. Chummy watches it every year, so we mustn't dally, he doesn't like to miss it. And there's a surprise for you at home, Nicky.

Somebody's waiting to see you.'

The smell of Nana and Chummy's house hadn't changed since I was nine. Walking through the door I inhaled the familiar mixture of lavender floor polish and fried chicken. The decor hadn't changed either; green lino in the kitchen, brown carpet in the lounge, the long parquet-floored passage leading to an aqua tiled bathroom with frosted windows and net curtains. Even my bed still had the same candlewick spread, its tassels hanging neatly in a row above the floral patterned rug. And yet everything was foreign.

'Look who's here!' Nana said, taking me over to the spare bed. 'See, here's Lulu, and Sharon and here' – she lifted up a familiar figure – 'is Patsy!'

She handed me my old doll, the one with a bald head as big as a baby's, still wearing her frock and frilled bonnet of gritty, blue fabric.

'See, I've kept her for you. Doesn't she look pretty?'

Patsy's dimpled plastic arms had faded somewhat but otherwise she was unchanged, just a little more artificial than I remembered. I tipped her over and her stiff eyelids with their bristled lashes clicked closed, releasing me from her glassy stare. A pain shot through my chest with such force it made me gasp. The abstract thoughts I had once had about leaving *Vingila* had now become a reality. I was in Alberton and my family were in Australia. I pictured my mother and father sitting around the main saloon table drinking coffee and eating rice for breakfast with my twin brother. Pepe with his chin on Robert's thigh, begging for food. Dad on the fishing box, which was also the best seat. My place empty. Sacks of tuna biltong and dried bananas in the forepeak next to my brother's bunk, their smell mixing with that of the early morning coffee. I saw my bunk in the stern cabin, near the sail locker and the workbench with the vice and I wanted nothing more than to climb into my own bunk, the one I had slept in for the last seven years, put my head on my pillow and go to sleep. When I woke up I'd find that the plane flight, Johannesburg, Alberton, Patsy and my grandparents were nothing but a dream.

'Come on,' Nana said, 'let's watch the end of the TV party, it's fun.'

For three weeks I walked around with a constant pain in my chest. It was worst in the evenings after we'd finished supper, which we ate on trays in front of the television, and when I helped Nana with the dishes. As I dried plates and cutlery, tears ran down my face, dripping onto my chest. Outside, African birds sang in the dusk. Everything was both familiar and simultaneously alien. Often there were thunderstorms with lightning and strong gusts of wind and although I no longer needed to worry about the anchor dragging or taking down sails, I was thoroughly miserable.

Nana enrolled me in my new school and had taken me to buy my uniform, a shapeless dress of sky blue, and a bag to carry my books. We decided my old school shoes from Australia would do. The first term would start in mid-January and I had been taken to meet the vice principal who had told me that because Alberton High was small, I couldn't expect to take German or several of the other subjects I had studied in Brisbane State High.

After three weeks, as I stood drying the dishes and crying one night, my grandmother asked me if it wouldn't be easier to return to my family. I shook my head. I couldn't explain how much I needed to finish what I had started, how I could never go back to *Vingila*.

'No, Nana,' I said. 'I'll feel better soon, I promise. I'll get used to it.'

At night I dreamed I was sailing. *Vingila* with her main and jib trimmed, heeling over in a broad reach, pushing up a bow wave. Pepe strutting the decks, barking at schools of flying fish bulleting from the swells. When my dreams woke me, I lay in the dark and thought about Cyclone Winnie trailing us across the Coral Sea before turning away and dying. She never caught *Vingila,* although for a time it seemed she would. In the days before she dissipated, the winds of her outskirts pushed *Vingila* to Brisbane. You see, my father had said to me, you always worry for nothing. A week after we arrived in Australia, Mom had gone behind his back and bought me a non-refundable one-way ticket to South Africa. The day before my flight I told him I was leaving. I expected my father to be angry, instead he looked hurt and surprised.

'Why do you want to leave, Nicky?'

I couldn't bring myself to tell him the whole truth, so I said, 'I want to finish school and go to university and I'm the right age now.'

'School can wait. We still have the entire Indian Ocean to explore, and you might never get a chance to do that again. Think of all the islands.'

'I've seen a lot of islands already,' I said, 'and I want to study.'

'It would just be a few more years,' he said. 'What's a few years in a lifetime?'

I kept silent, not voicing my fear that if I stayed on the boat, my father might sail for longer than just a few more years. Sail until we were killed by a hurricane or shipwrecked. Sail until I was old. I didn't want to be much older than anyone else in the school. What if I was too old for regular school and they turned me away? I was sixteen and I couldn't wait, I felt my future slipping away. And perhaps Dad was right, maybe I *was* a coward, scared of sailing in cyclone season and anchoring in risky places. All I knew was that I didn't want to sail on *Vingila* any more. My father could be the captain of his ship, and I needed to be the captain of mine, whatever that was.

Dad sighed. 'Well, I can't stop you if you say your mother's already bought a ticket. At least we've still got Robert, he was never a deserter.'

Two months after I left the boat, my mother scraped together enough money for a plane ticket to South Africa to see how I was settling in. She arrived looking thin and tired, and she cried when she saw me.

Each morning I headed off in my blue dress with my hair tied back as per school regulations. Nana and Chummy remarked how much neater I had become in just a few months. I didn't tell them or my mother about the teasing I was experiencing at school, or the name calling. My chest pain eased somewhat with my mother in the house but I knew that when she left again it would only get worse. In a way getting sick was a relief because I stopped feeling so sad. I was far too ill to feel sad, and the fever blurred my thoughts into delirium and hazy dreams.

23

THE FEVER HOSPITAL

During the days before I was admitted to hospital I lay on my bed in Nana's house with my eyes closed and a jack-hammer pounding in my head. Dreams swirled in and out of my drifting consciousness and I felt my hands swell to enormous proportions, filling the room. Then my teeth grew. My jaw extended beyond the foot of the bed, gigantic – but strangely light, the cusp of each tooth rising as if it were filled with the breath of hot-air balloons. Then my body floated off the bed, enormous and weightless. My collection of dolls, those remnants of my childhood tended so carefully by Nana, rose up from the spare bed to hover alongside me. They bobbed in unseen currents, their frilled dresses and frocks – hand sewn by my grandmother – shimmering and waving as if they were underwater. It would have been peaceful if it wasn't for the anvil in my head.

'You really must try to pull yourself together,' my mother said, coming into the room and forcing me to sit up. Above the rims of her glasses I saw – from a great distance – that her habitual frown had deepened. Her cousin was visiting for tea.

'Omnia will think you're rude,' she said. 'Try to get up, please.'

When my feet touched the floor, my legs crumpled and swirly amoebae danced across my vision. I sank beside the bed and buried my face in the hanging sheets, tears sliding down my cheeks. Mom sighed and pushed her glasses back onto the bridge of her nose. The hollows of her collarbones showed above the low neckline of her blouse and her skin still bore traces of a Coral Sea suntan almost three months old.

'Okay, be like that, if you must,' she said. She was leaving soon for Australia and she thought I was putting on my illness to make her feel guilty about going.

She helped me back into bed and walked out of the room, leaving me alone. Closing my eyes I found myself at sea again, becalmed beneath a hot, tropical sun. *Vingila* plunged and wallowed on the backs of smooth-skinned waves, and the movements of my breath began melting into the motion of the water, in a ponderous, sickening roil. Then the boat, the ocean and my respiration fused into a rotating ball. I felt my skin turn black. I opened my eyes to find, with faint surprise, that I was still in a bed in Nana's house and my arms were their old putty colour and freckled, but with new lemon tones beneath the tan.

Some time later I heard the sounds of Omnia leaving. My mother's voice drifted down the passage.

'Sorry you didn't see more of Nicky, I don't know what's got into her.'

The principal of my new school, Alberton High, knew what had got into me. This was 1984 in South Africa, and for some people things were still very clear. A few days earlier I had presented myself to his office with reports of a headache, shivering and blue fingernails. I felt awful, I said, and I wanted to go home.

He shook his head sadly. I'd been in school for less than two months.

'You know what your trouble is, my girl, don't you?' he said.

I squinted at him through light which had suddenly and un-accountably grown brighter. He was bald, with a pink face and white hairs growing out of his ears. He looked as if he should be friendly, except he wasn't. As he spoke, the objects around us in the room receded and his voice reached me as if from the bottom of a jar.

'My girl,' he said, 'your trouble is that you're just not used to having walls around you for a change. That's what's wrong with you.'

But he let me go.

When I came home, my grandmother, who had great faith in doctors, suggested I visit her GP. She phoned for an appointment and the receptionist told her that the doctor was fully booked, although they could squeeze me in later with another doctor, if I was prepared to wait. I tried to remember when last I'd seen a doctor. There had been one in the Marquesas Islands when I was eleven and the skin peeled off my hands in layers, and then another time when I had infected sores on my feet and I went to the clinic in Australia. When I returned for a follow-up they had found out we were illegal and the receptionist asked us leave. Two doctors in seven years and now, possibly, a third. Dad thought doctors were a waste of time. Either they weren't around or they were too expensive, he said, and usually they didn't know what they were doing. A dentist, at least, could take out a tooth.

Mom drove me to the surgery in Nana's brown Beetle, the car my grandmother had owned ever since Robert and I were small enough to fit together in its dog-box. I folded myself through the door to collapse on the seat. When my mother started the car it hummed like an insect, the buzz penetrating my eardrums to ricochet around inside my throbbing head. Each time we took a corner it felt as if my brain shifted in my skull. I wanted to fly out the window and escape into the sky and I had started to believe it was almost possible when my mother parked the car and announced that we had arrived.

While I wobbled on unreliable legs, a receptionist wrote my name in a book and then ushered us into a waiting room filled with beige chairs and magazines with their covers torn off. Although it was summer, the place was packed with people, most of them coughing and blowing their noses into paper handkerchiefs. They glanced up as we entered and examined us with dull, expressionless faces. We settled into a pair of leatherette seats to wait. After a while my head drooped and darkness began encroaching on my vision. Conversation advanced and receded around me like surf breaking on a beach. A paralysing fatigue crept up my limbs. When the pot plant in the corner reached through the murk with a curling tendril, I asked Mom if I could lie down in the car. Tottering outside I collapsed across the back seat. My mother woke me about an hour later.

'Quick,' she said, 'come on, it's your turn now.'

The chills had vanished after my nap, along with much of the headache, but I felt exhausted. My cheeks flamed. When I closed my eyes I saw the ocean simmering beneath a burning sun. Holding my mother's arm, I walked cautiously back into the building.

The doctor was a man with big hands and thick folds of skin on the back of his neck. He had a smouldering cigarette balanced on his lower lip and the quartz ashtray on his desk overflowed with butts. He took a drag and exhaled, squinting through the smoke as I told him my story. Every second day, I said, I began shivering. It always started in the late morning. My nails turned blue. I had headaches and I had vomited several times. Pains shot through my legs. I'd been in a malaria area a few months back, and had taken prophylaxis. A small cloud of smoke hovered between us as I spoke, stinging my eyes.

'So,' he said, 'do you have a sore throat?'

'No.'

'Runny nose?'

'No.'

'Cough?'

'No.'

'Oh well,' he said sighing and taking another drag of his cigarette, 'I

352

suppose flu affects different people in different ways.'

He lifted the ashtray to reach for his script pad.

'Here,' he said, 'take these antibiotics. You can pay at the door, thanks.'

He did not get up.

The following day I said to my mother, 'My pee looks like Coca-Cola.'

'Ag,' she said, 'it must be the antibiotics.'

Her flight back to Dad and Robert and Pepe was booked and confirmed.

'Nicky,' she said, 'come back with me to Australia.'

'How can you even ask me that, Mom?'

'Please. Come back. It won't be so bad, you'll see. You can carry on with correspondence school. At least you'll be with us there. Go to high school later.'

'Mom, I miss you all so much, but you know I can't live on the yacht any more, so don't even ask me.'

Going back to Australia would be an admission of defeat. I couldn't do it. I would stay with my grandmother and go to Alberton High School where the principal believed that I needed to grow more accustomed to walls.

I overheard my mother talking to Nana. 'What if Nicky's putting this whole thing on,' she said, 'to make me feel guilty about leaving?'

I couldn't eat. My urine darkened further.

'I'm getting worried about Nicky,' Nana said the next day. 'Phone the doctor again.'

Mom called the GP who had seen me.

'Listen,' she said, 'I think my daughter might have malaria.'

'Take her for a test then, if you want,' he replied.

I pictured the mouthpiece of his telephone wreathed in smoke and imagined the smell of stale breath, greasy plastic and dead cigarettes.

The pathology service office was a subterranean cave at the end of a passage that wound beneath the local private hospital. There were no windows for light, and a fluorescent strip cast a pall on the pair of disinterested attendants.

'You do look pale,' one of them said as she placed a tourniquet languidly around my arm. I blinked to steady her wavering face. She screwed a needle into a clear plastic barrel. Slipped in a glass tube. Uncapped the needle.

Her voice and the dim contours of the cave blurred as I felt myself drifting off. The steel needle tip piercing my skin drew me back to reality, but the connection felt tenuous. Without feeling anything in particular I watched my blood spray and bubble into the glass tube.

'Malaria test, eh?' the attendant said to my mother.

Mom nodded.

'We don't see a positive malaria test often.'

The sting intensified to a burn as she withdrew the needle from my vein.

'Here,' she said, applying a puff of cotton to my inner elbow, 'push on this. Somebody will call you later with the result.'

Blood stained the cotton red. My hands were trembling so much I couldn't hold it properly.

Over the weekend my mother said she thought I looked better.

'I believe you can go back to school on Monday,' she said.

My shivering and headaches had eased and I felt too weak to argue. We hadn't heard anything from the lab.

On Monday morning at school, a group of girls in my new class looked me over with detached curiosity.

'You're so thin,' said one.

'Ja,' said another, 'and so pale. What's wrong with you?'

They regarded me for a moment as if I were somehow unclean, before turning their backs to reform a small, tight group. I sat on my bag, waiting for the bell and listening to exclusionary giggles bubble over their shoulders. The day stretched out elastically. I walked from class to class watching teachers move their lips as they chalked incomprehensible symbols on blackboards. After several years the bell rang, signalling the end of lessons, and I prepared to walk home. That morning Nana had driven me to school against my mother's wishes. She wanted to pick me up again afterwards but Mom had said no, a walk would do me good and strengthen me up. I picked up my bag which had grown incrementally heavier since the morning, and I made for the school gate. Take it slowly, I thought, you'll be okay. The air was humid with an impending thunderstorm, the grass a vivid green against patches of exposed orange earth. The distance home seemed immense. Slowly, I mumbled, slowly. You can do it.

Outside the school, I noticed my grandmother's Beetle. The driver's door burst open and she trotted over to me on stumpy legs.

'Your test results are back,' she said. 'The lab lost them, that's why it took so long. They confused your first name with your last and filed you under Martinique instead of Stilwell.'

I leaned against the car for support.

'Your test's positive. You've got malaria and the doctor wants to see you right away,' Nana said.

'The same doctor who saw me last time?'

'No, not him. My usual one. You'll like him, he's very nice.'

'Does he smoke?'

'Not as much as that other one. Now, come on, jump in. We'll pick up your mother on the way.'

At the surgery, the receptionist ushered Mom and me past the choked waiting area, directly into a consulting room where another doctor sat with his cigarette. When we entered, he stubbed it out.

'So,' he said, 'what have we got here?'

I lay on the examination couch with my school dress pulled above my waist. He stuck a thermometer under my tongue and kneaded my abdomen.

'Any headaches?' he asked.

I nodded.

'Shivering?'

'Yes.'

'Fever?'

'Yes.'

'Dark urine?'

'Not any more.'

He turned to my mother.

'I see you don't have medical aid.'

'No, we don't. We never expected anything like this.'

'She needs admission. I know an infectious disease expert in Rietfontein, he's very good. It's a government hospital but a good one. I'll give him a bell and we'll see what we can do.'

I slumped in my chair as he dialled. Malaria was bad, wasn't it? I had heard that people died from malaria. I thought about dying and wondered if I should feel afraid, or horrified. All I felt was tired. I glanced without interest at the certificates on the wall behind his desk. There weren't many. From the waiting room came the faint sound of coughing.

'Get Dr Murray at Rietfontein Fever Hospital on the line, please.'

While he waited, the GP doodled on a pad with the picture of a bloated frog holding a straw in its mouth. Through my stupor I thought the upside-down words spelled 'Spasmocanulase'. Could that be right, I wondered. Why would anyone call a medicine Spasmocanulase, and what could it possibly be used for? It sounded more mechanical than medicinal.

'Hello, is that Dr Murray? Look, I'm a GP phoning from Alberton. Yes, Alberton, on the East Rand, and I've got a little girlie here, about fourteen.'

Mom shook her head at him and mouthed sixteen.

'Sorry, sixteen. Small for her age. Anyway, her malaria smear's come back positive.'

Silence.

Then, 'From last week. Vivax.'

The voice of the infectious disease specialist buzzed in the receiver like a trapped wasp. The GP rubbed his temples with his non-doodling hand.

'Yes, I know,' he said, 'the lab lost the result. Most unfortunate. She's with me now though. Very anaemic. Splenomegaly and a bit of a liver. Low grade fever. No medical aid. Think you can you see her? Thanks very much. I'll send her over. You'll wait? Good, I'll tell them to get a move on.'

He put down the phone. 'He'll see you today.'

'Where is he?'

'At the fever hospital, Rietfontein. I'll draw a map.'

When we got home Mom talked to Nana while I lay on the couch with my face pressed against a cushion covered in pebbled fabric as rough as the underside of a sea cucumber.

'If she goes to hospital she'll need pyjamas,' my grandmother said, 'and I've noticed that she hasn't got any. Didn't you lot wear pyjamas on the yacht?'

I half opened my eyes, fighting against the couch which had grown into a giant sucker and was trying to engulf me. I closed my eyes again, and prepared to be consumed.

'Wake up, Nicky,' Mom said, giving me a shake. 'Come on, sit up. Pay attention.'

I opened my eyes with considerable effort. 'I don't own any pyjamas, Nan. I sleep in my T-shirt.'

'That old T-shirt with the holes in it? You can't wear that and a pair of pathetic panties in hospital, little girl. What are the doctors going to think? That you're some poor orphan annie, that's what. They're going to laugh at you. '

She glared at Mom.

'Doesn't Chummy have an old pair we can borrow?' my mother said. She didn't own pyjamas either; none of our family did. In hospital though, it seemed as if they were compulsory. We searched my grandfather Chummy's cupboard. Nana's wardrobe wasn't an option, she was much shorter than me, and very heavy in the thigh and bosom. Besides, she wore pink frilly nighties. After some looking we found a suitable pair of faded blue pyjamas.

'He hasn't worn these for years,' Nana said.

I tried them on, tightening the drawstring about my waist. The trouser ends flapped around my skinny ankles.

'You've lost weight,' Mom said. 'If it wasn't for the drawstring, those pants would fall off.'

'Nan's scale read 43 kilos this morning,' I said, 'five less than normal.'

'What are you going to do about slippers?' Nana said.

'Nicky doesn't have any,' Mom said. 'She'll just have to wear slops.'

Chummy got lost on the way to the fever hospital and for almost two hours we wandered through the back streets of Johannesburg. We arrived at Rietfontein Hospital as the sun was setting. The hospital, set on spacious wooded grounds, was divided into sections. We were directed to the isolation wing, a low bunker-type building. During my stay I would learn that this ward, which dealt mainly with severe viral haemorrhagic infections like Ebola and Congo Fever, was primarily for whites. Behind the isolation wing sat a small TB ward, also for whites. The bulk of the hospital, however – several sprawling wards with verandas and galvanised tin roofs – was reserved for black men with tuberculosis.

As we drove into the grounds we passed groups of emaciated men strolling under the trees, or sitting in the sun, smoking. They all wore faded blue pyjamas that flapped about their skeletal frames. Their feet were thrust into slops or shoes with trodden-down heels which they wore without socks. Most of their pants were several centimetres too short and exposed their scaly ankles.

'At least you've got the right clothes for this place, Nicky,' Mom said.

A nurse in the isolation ward told us that Dr Miller had waited until five before going home. Another doctor would handle my admission and Dr Miller would see me in the morning. She led us down a long wooden-floored passage, lined by doors which opened into small cells, each of which held a single bed, made up with starched white sheets hard as cardboard. The doors to the rooms all had spy holes; hatches which could be opened from the outside, enabling nurses to look in without opening the door. Outside my room, I had a small veranda and beyond that were dark trees and grounds which stretched into the distance. I wasn't sure if the peacocks and monkeys I saw foraging beneath their branches were real or vestiges of my delirium.

Mom helped me into Chummy's old pyjamas, unwrapped a bunch of grapes, placed it on my bedside table, kissed me and left.

'We can't stay,' she said as she walked out the door, 'because Chummy doesn't want to miss his TV programmes.'

A hard-faced nurse and a paunchy grey-haired doctor with a beard came in to see me about half an hour later. He had a stethoscope around his neck and she pushed a trolley loaded with files and tinkling thermometers in glass jars.

'So where did you catch this malaria, little girl?' he said as his hands palpated my abdomen.

'Probably the Solomon Islands.'

'Never heard of them. Where are they?'

'Near Papua New Guinea, on the equator.'

'What on earth were you doing there?'

'Sailing.'

His hand made its way toward my underarm. On route its fingers curled themselves around my bare breast.

I flinched and glared at him.

'Sorry,' he said absently and the hand moved on to my armpit.

'How long have you been sailing?'

'Seven years.'

'Seven years! And what about school?'

I turned my face to the wall. 'On and off,' I said, 'a bit in Australia.'

'I see.'

He was quiet for a moment, then he said, 'The lab test showed you have *vivax* malaria. We don't get much of that in Africa. When did you say you were in these islands?'

'Two months ago.'

'Strange, the incubation period for *vivax* is normally just a couple of weeks. Were you taking prophylaxis, by any chance?'

I nodded. 'Chloroquine.'

'That could do it. Anyway, you're lucky you didn't get sick while out there away from hospitals. You would have died.'

The doctor took the chart from the nurse and wrote a few lines then they turned and walked out the door, leaving me alone. I couldn't sleep. Light from the passage flooded through my open door. At eight o'clock the nurse came in with a handful of bitter pills for me to swallow.

'I can't sleep. Is there anything for me to do?' I asked.

'Well you can't watch television because we've just admitted a bunch of open TB cases and they're in the TV room.'

She took my pulse, wrote a note in the chart and walked out the room.

About an hour after that I began crying. Hot, salty tears slid down my cheeks to pool in my ears. The nurse stuck her head around the door.

'What's wrong with you?' she said.

'Can't sleep.'

'Oh.' She retreated again.

From the nursing office across the passage directly opposite my bed I could hear the bearded doctor who had groped my breast talking to the nurse above the sound of a kettle boiling.

'How's the one in 6B?' he said.

'Sleeping,' replied the nurse.

'Sad story. Isn't it? And 7B?'

'The girlie with malaria? She's going to give us trouble, wait and see. Not sleeping. Crying.'

There was silence for a while except for the clinking of spoons in cups and the sound of water being poured.

Then the nurse spoke. 'Strange one, isn't she. Yacht and all. I wonder what she'll do without an education.'

'I can't imagine,' said the doctor.

The nurse gave a sigh so loud I could hear it across the passage. 'Oh well, I suppose she'll find something.'

Despite feeling weepy with the dregs of the malaria and the pangs of loss and homesickness, I felt an urge to set them straight. I had plans and a clear goal. I didn't know if I would achieve what I had set out to do, but I felt that the doctor and nurse who were gossiping about me should at least know my intentions. I refused to be dismissed. Pulling myself from the bed, I made my way across the passage on shaking legs. Chummy's pyjamas flapped around my ankles.

'Excuse me,' I said, looking into the little office where they sat almost knee to knee, holding their mugs of coffee.

'Yes?' said the nurse.

My lower lip began trembling so much I wasn't sure I'd get the words out, but I did.

'I couldn't help hearing – you were wondering what I'm going to do without an education?'

They exchanged a glance. Perhaps I'd imagined their entire conversation. Maybe they'd just been sitting in silence, drinking coffee when I chanced to stumble in and begin babbling. Did they think I was crazy? I continued anyway.

'One day,' I said, my voice cracking a little, 'I plan to be a forensic pathologist.'

Then I turned and walked out of the room.

24

ALBERTON HIGH SCHOOL AND THE ISLANDS OF THE INDIAN OCEAN

After my discharge from hospital I spent a week at home recuperating. Then my mother, who had delayed her return to Australia while I was hospitalised, flew back to Robert and Dad, and I resumed classes at Alberton High. I had been in school for just a few days when Mrs de Kock, my Afrikaans teacher, sent me to see Mr Minnie, the acting vice principal of the school. From her classroom I walked down the corridor which connected the concrete blocks of classrooms to the low admin building and hall. My path took me through the Matric Garden, an 'improvement area' in which three skinny trees were struggling to reach adolescence in a patch of brown lawn. Then I crossed the tarred quadrangle where the school pupils gathered each day for morning prayers and assembly. Across a further stretch of dusty grass lay a line of asbestos prefab huts where commercial pupils took woodwork and typing classes. I tried not to think of the lavish grounds and sports fields of Brisbane State High. From the quadrangle I entered the coolness of the school foyer. As my eyes adjusted to the dim light I made out a hard bench and – in the corner – a solitary pot-plant imprisoned in a plastic tub. Mounted on the wall above the defeated-looking plant were a pair of wooden plaques bearing the names of previous sports captains and head boys and girls in gold paint. It was a short list. Next to the plaques was a framed photograph of Mr Kallman, the current principal. The walls were otherwise bare. There were no celebratory photographs of prestigious alumni. No rugby captains, no famous cricket players or professors of chemistry or molecular biology had ever graduated from Alberton High. Unlike Brisbane State High, my new school was neither old nor illustrious, nor was it known for its academic or sporting achievements. Nana and my mother had chosen the place simply because it was close enough for me to walk to and because it was cheap. Nobody ever actively recommended Alberton High. The most anyone said of the school was that it wasn't quite as bad as Hill High, in the neighbouring town of Rosettenville, where the Lebanese and Portuguese – otherwise known as the Lebs and Porras – formed gangs and fought. My mother's sister Annette, who taught at the local primary school, went so far as to advise my mother against Alberton High. Standards there were very low, she said. But my mother wasn't prepared to put my grandmother out. There would be no driving. I had to walk, and that meant Alberton High.

'Don't worry,' Mom had said to my aunt, 'Nicky's tough, she'll be fine anywhere.'

Except everything was not fine, which was why Mrs de Kock sent me to see the vice principal.

I walked through the cool foyer and knocked on Mr Minnie's door.

He didn't look up. 'Ja,' he said. 'What is it?'

The thin white line of his side parting cleaved his dark hair into a pair of unequal sections. Beneath the hair was a tight, foxy face with a severely trimmed moustache. Mr Minnie's brown suit was almost the same shade as his hair, and the knife-edged creases of his trousers terminated several centimetres above his brown socks and shiny black shoes. Like most of the staff in Alberton High he spoke Afrikaans as a first language, although he taught accountancy in English. He sometimes stood in as cricket coach, and when boys in the school needed caning and Mr Kallman the school principal was busy, they were usually sent to Mr Minnie.

'Mr Minnie,' I said, 'Mrs de Kock asked me to speak to you.'

'Ja?'

'She wants to know if I could take Immigrant Afrikaans.' I hesitated. I knew I was expected to say Sir, as the other pupils did, but I found I couldn't, it just felt too subservient.

Mr Minnie capped the pen in his hands and sighed.

'Let's get a few facts sorted out first,' he said. 'Correct me if I'm wrong, girlie, but am I to understand that you were born here in South Africa?'

'Yes.' He waited for me to say Sir and when the word didn't come, his eyes narrowed briefly in annoyance before he went on.

'So that would make you a South African citizen?'

I nodded.

'And the rules state quite clearly that the option of Immigrant Afrikaans is available only to immigrants.' He paused again. 'I think you can agree with me that you are not an immigrant.'

'Yes, Mr Minnie, but because I've been out of the country for almost eight years and haven't done any Afrikaans, Mrs de Kock thought maybe I could get an exemption.'

Afrikaans was proving to be a problem. The subject was compulsory and if I failed the end of year exam, I would not be allowed through to the next year, no matter how strong my other marks were. Furthermore, I needed to pass the subject on higher grade to get a university exemption. The other pupils had all been learning the language from grade one and even the weakest speakers were practically fluent, leaving me lost in a babble of unfamiliar gargling sounds. When presented with my first comprehension test I was not only incapable of understanding the sample passage, but had no idea what the questions were either.

Mr Minnie used the pinkie finger of his left hand to straighten an errant moustache hair.

'Martinique,' he said, 'I think there is something very important here that you have to learn.'

He paused for me to say 'Yes Sir'.

I found I couldn't do it and arranged my features instead into what I hoped was a neutrally expectant expression. This was not enough for Mr Minnie.

He coughed sharply and glared at me.

'Yes, Mr Minnie,' I said.

He blinked and said: 'I don't know where you have been running around, my girl, but in this school you will come to understand that rules are rules and they don't just get changed for people who think they are special in some way. Do you hear what I am saying, girlie?'

'Yes, Mr Minnie,' I said.

'Good. Dismissed.'

When I returned to Mrs de Kock's classroom a bristle-head boy whom the others called Storkie nudged his neighbour and said, 'Check, Mangaroo's back and she looks like Mr Minnie gave her jacks.' A trickle of sniggers spread through rows. Storkie himself got jacks regularly and one day after yet another trip to the vice principal's office had surprised the class by pulling down his pants when the teacher wasn't looking to show us the rows of welts and bruises of various ages where Mr Minnie's cane had found its mark on his buttocks.

'Hey, Mangaroo,' he sneered, 'did it hurt so much to make you cry? Tell Storkie what's wrong.'

'Oh stop it, Storkie,' one of the girls said with a giggle and a malicious smile.

I was the class joke. In Australia I had been considered an outsider, but a rather cool one. Or at least I was able to see myself as such. I dressed as a punk rocker and lived on a yacht on the river. I skipped school whenever I wanted to, I roamed the city at will and went to late night movie shows with boyfriends who were far older than me. In Alberton High I was a geek, a nerd, a dork. From the start my clothes had been wrong. In Australia it was trendy to wear long skirts and square-toed lace-ups. In Alberton baby-doll shoes were the rage and school dresses were worn very short. I arrived in my new school as a spectacularly unsuccessful cultural transplant. In the South African teen race to desirability I had backed the wrong horse. Every aspect of me was viewed with scorn – my shoes, the length of my skirt, my unshaven legs, my strange hairstyle. I realised the problem right away and took steps to change. My hemline was easy enough to fix and I begged Nana to buy me a new pair of shoes. Over time I learned to file my nails into points and shave my legs, but the damage of the first weeks at school had been done. My reputation was entrenched: I was considered clever, strange and deeply unattractive. Eventually I learned why the boys called me Mangaroo; they thought I was a kangaroo from Australia with legs as hairy as a mango pip.

One of the advantages of not having a social life was that I could concentrate on my school work. I reminded myself that I had not come to Alberton primarily to be happy (although I had hoped to find some happiness). I had left to get away from hurricanes and to achieve certain goals. I told myself that the two years of school ahead of me were like an unpleasant sea voyage which I would get through, and which would eventually lead towards the bright new future I imagined for myself. A future where I could be my own boss, have friends and wouldn't be expected to call anyone sir. For the present, however, I had no money, no social life, and very little prospect of getting a boyfriend, which was not quite how I had imagined my life would be after leaving the yacht. I had looked forward to meeting people of my own age, and now that I had, I felt lonelier than ever. Aiming for liberation, I had found something closer to exile. And I missed my brother. On *Vingila* I had been without friends for months at a stretch and I knew how to fill the gap by reading, writing in my journal and daydreaming. But I had never been without my twin. We had shared a womb and been born within fifteen minutes of each other and he had always been my defender, my playmate, my sparring partner and confidant. Nothing could fill the gap of his absence and without him I felt vulnerable and incomplete. I was glad, though, that he was not in Alberton. School work did not come as easily for him as it did for me and he would have found the place unbearably oppressive. And Nana and Chummy's fuddy-duddy ways and obsessive neatness would have driven him mad. Robert was not nearly as good as I was at pretending to be something he was not. And I could not imagine my brother lasting more than a week away from the ocean which was as much his refuge as reading was mine.

Although Nana and Chummy were friendly enough to me, our years of separation had left us interacting politely like strangers showing their best faces. For the first few months after my arrival, everyone tiptoed around one another. I tried particularly hard to be on my best behaviour. They hadn't had a teenager in the house for thirty years and I knew that my mother had promised them that I would be a good girl and not give them any trouble. Nana and Chummy, secure in the unchanged routine of a decade of retirement, did not look prepared to cope with a real teenager, and because I felt I couldn't let my mother down, I did my best to be well behaved, quiet, and disciplined. Not having friends helped. There was nothing for me to do but read and study and try to learn to speak Afrikaans. Nana arranged extra lessons with Tannie Rita, her sister, who had once been an Afrikaans teacher. Three times a week she drove me across town where Tannie Rita, a withered woman even shorter than my grandmother, pored over my homework and taught me basic grammar and beginner vocabulary. At her suggestion Nana and Chummy began speaking to me in Afrikaans and I started watching Afrikaans programmes on TV.

I found a job, working as a cashier at the OK Bazaars on Saturday mornings and Fridays after school. I sold my rarest cowrie, the *Cypraea guttata*, to a pair of collectors I found through the Pretoria Conchological Society, and together with what I earned at the OK, this gave me enough cash to buy toiletries and clothing. I also began saving a little.

On Sundays Chummy took me waterskiing on Germiston lake. At first he suggested that I might want to invite a few friends along, but after a month or so it became clear even to him that I didn't have any friends, so he stopped asking. I was a dutiful skier, but I didn't love it. The stagnant water of Germiston lake made me homesick and the sight of the little dinghies at the sailing club with their wind-filled white sails caused twinges of pain in my chest. I wanted deep, blue sea and a strong running swell. I wanted trade winds and coral atolls and what I had instead was the petrol fumes and the scream of an outboard motor on a smelly, green pond hundreds of kilometres from the ocean.

At school the days and weeks passed with a paralysing slowness. Each Monday I would tell myself that the day after the next would be Wednesday, and by then the week would be halfway gone. Friday seemed as far away as the other side of the world. School started at half past seven and it felt as if years passed before first break. At lunch I began sitting with a group of girls, although always to one side, and with the unspoken agreement that I was to be tolerated and not liked or looked up to in any way. During the afternoon lessons the second hand on my watch moved as slowly as if it were dragging its way through syrup. I was unable to identify it at the time, but I was suffering from my first exposure to chronic, intractable boredom.

Flimsy blue aerogramme letters arrived in the post box, bringing news from Australia. *Vingila* was up on the slip and my family was working hard, scraping off her barnacles and giving her a fresh coat of anti-fouling for the trip up the Great Barrier Reef to Cairns and Thursday Island. Mom wrote that Pepe had stayed on another yacht while *Vingila* was on the hard because quarantine officials forbade him to be ashore, even if he didn't leave the boat. Without Mom he had cried constantly and refused to eat and the people who looked after him were very happy to give him back when *Vingila* was launched again. My mother asked about my malaria and said she hoped I was gaining back some of the weight that I had lost. Then she mentioned a letter that they had received from Vincent in which he informed them that he was now the sole owner of *Amulet*. It seemed that when the time came to hand over occupation of the yacht, the co-owner, who wasn't a very experienced sailor, was hesitant to sail the boat alone. So Vincent kindly offered to accompany him on his first open water passage. One night, after about a week at sea, the inexperienced sailor had gone to the stern to urinate and had apparently fallen overboard. His absence wasn't noticed until several hours later, by which time, Vincent said, it was too late to begin searching. How very convenient for Vincent, I found myself thinking, he no longer has to share his boat. My family appeared to be having similar thoughts. Mom went on: your father says that guy must have been a bit of an idiot to go sailing with Vincent when he knew how much Vincent wanted the boat for himself. Now *Amulet*, with Ramone and Nadine, who was pregnant again, was on her way back to the Solomon Islands with no definite plans after that. Just before signing off her letter my mother added that Pepe, 'was almost completely better and half of the scab on his neck has fallen off'. I had not even been aware that anything was wrong with Pepe. This was just the first of several misfortunes to befall our ageing poodle.

The weeks dragged by. I went to school, came home, read library books, did my homework, walked around the block with Nana and her two miniature pinschers, and ate supper on a tray in front of the TV before putting myself to bed at nine. Summer ended and winter turned the green grass a brittle blonde. In the mornings frost lay on the ground and in the unheated classrooms of Alberton High our breaths turned to smoke when we exhaled. A daily temperature inversion pressed smoke polluted air against the earth and the atmosphere grew so dry that my nose bled daily.

Letters continued to arrive from Australia. After an extensive overhaul on the dry docks, and a thorough fumigation, *Vingila* was ready to leave Brisbane and sail to Cairns when a problem presented itself. My family's visas had expired and they received a letter informing them that they would have to leave Australia immediately and wouldn't be allowed further entry into the country. This meant sailing non-stop up the east coast and around the top of the continent to Christmas Island in the Indian Ocean. A voyage at least five times longer than anything *Vingila* had ever before attempted. Mom wrote: your father took us all to the immigration office and explained that sailing to Christmas Island would take four to five months. He said he was ready to do that if he had to, but he worried about running out of fresh food. And of course, there was also the dog. A rather frail, elderly dog. He wasn't sure the dog would make it. The immigration officer relented. You're right, he said, that's too far for any dog, and he extended their visas. So *Vingila* set off from Brisbane to sail up the Great Barrier Reef towards Thursday Island and then on to Darwin. After my family left Brisbane there was a long break in the letters and I learned later that when he got to sea Dad had decided to sail all the way north to visit Chesterfield again, that forlorn reef in the centre of the Coral Sea with its narrow sand spit and single palm tree. Hurricane Winnie, who had followed us from the Solomon Islands, had washed most of the island away and, my mother wrote, the palm is gone and at high tide there is almost nothing left to see, although the waters of the lagoon are still full of fish and coral. For a week Dad and Robert spent their days spearing fish while Mom and Pepe sat on the yacht or took short walks around the sand spit at low tide. Then a squall blew in from the south-west one night and *Vingila*, in the shallow coral-filled lagoon, snapped her anchor chain. Luckily,

Mom wrote, they were able to motor into the wind and set out both the Danforth and the new fisherman's anchor Dad had bought in Australia. It helped that there were no other yachts to get tangled up with. The next day Robert went diving and found the lost anchor and *Vingila* sailed back to Australia.

Winter wore on. To the barely concealed surprise of my grandparents who had expected me to fail, my results in the mid-year exams were good, with the exception of Afrikaans which I had failed, although not quite as badly as I had feared. Mrs de Kock was apologetic.

'I'm sorry, Nicky,' she said. 'I really wanted to pass you. You're getting better though, and if you keep trying you might just make it by the end of the year.'

When I wrote to Mom I tried to convince her that I was happy and settling in. She had been sending regular aerogrammes to both me and Nana. Dad wrote rarely and Robert almost not at all, although Mom said he checked the post office every day in the hope of finding mail from me. From Mom's letters I followed *Vingila*'s progress. I asked Nana if I could stick a map on the wall in my room tracing *Vingila*'s journey home and she replied that Chummy would never allow that because Prestik made horrible marks on the walls, so I carried a map in my head instead, and at any time knew the general whereabouts of my family. After leaving Chesterfield Reef, *Vingila* sailed back to the coast of Australia, heading north up the Great Barrier Reef to Cape Flattery, stopping at Bewick Island, Stanley and Wilkie Islands and on to Cape Weymouth and Thursday Island. From Thursday Island they set off for Darwin, anchoring in wild, remote bays where huge tidal swings left them stranded on a mudflat one night. 'The boat was heeled right over,' Mom wrote, 'and I didn't sleep all night because I kept worrying that one of the gigantic salt-water crocs that we have seen swimming around here was going to climb aboard.' When the tide rose, the crew of a passing yacht helped winch *Vingila* off the mud. In September my family left Darwin for Ashmore Reef several hundred miles westward. Ashmore had a sandy spit for an island so low it disappeared underwater at high tide. And Ashmore was hard to find, Mom had written, because the satnav stopped working and your Dad had to remember his celestial navigation again. There is even less of Ashmore than there was of Chesterfield and I don't know why your father likes these reefs, she added. Our old friends Don and Muriel on *Aries* followed *Vingila* to Ashmore Reef, and the two yachts were joined by a small, semi-open wooden skiff with a crew of three ragged Filipinos who were hunting sharks for their fins. At night Mom admitted she was afraid *Vingila* would be attacked by the Filipinos who looked a lot like pirates. Then she added that shortly before leaving Darwin they had got news that Vincent and Nadine's boat *Amulet* was back in Cairns and that Vincent had delivered a new baby brother for Ramone when Nadine had refused to go ashore to the hospital for the birth. Vincent had named the baby Elvis.

After that there was a break of about a month before I got a stack of letters from Christmas Island. There was even a letter from Dad. Christmas Island was wonderful. They wished I was there. They had made friends with some Chinese people and had sailed to anchorages all over the island where they caught trigger fish and curried them. I wouldn't believe it, but the trigger fish were just like the blackfish of Ascension, and they were delicious. Their new friend Lee had also introduced them to thousand year old eggs. I knew about thousand year old eggs from a Chinese cookbook I had read. You took duck eggs and buried them in mud or ash or wood shavings, and then you poured a bottle of rice wine over them and left them to cure for months or years, until the yolks had turned creamy and khaki-coloured and the whites turned to dark, sea-green jelly. Just reading about thousand year old eggs made me shudder. I couldn't imagine ever eating one. Dad wrote that once you got used to the idea, they tasted just fine, especially with lots of bird's eye chilli. The only thing was, they left you burping sulphur all day. I gave a sigh of relief that I was not there. I read on. Dad wrote that he had packed a few of the eggs under my bunk and was keeping them for me to taste the next time we saw each other.

From Christmas Island *Vingila* sailed further across the Indian Ocean to Cocos Keeling, where I got a letter from Mom, saying that the sharks on Cocos were very aggressive and that Robert and Dad had been caught in a feeding frenzy while spearfishing and if Don had not been passing by in his dinghy, my brother and father would probably have been eaten. The letter finished by saying that they were leaving soon for the Chagos Archipelago, a group of deserted islands in the direction of India, and I wouldn't be hearing from them for a month or two, but that Dad had said I could visit them in the Seychelles for the December holidays, if there was enough money in the bank account from the rental houses in Benoni. I phoned Nana's travel agent for a quote and checked the bank account and started looking forward to seeing my family again. I received that letter in early October and two months later, as the end of the year approached, I heard no news from *Vingila*.

The end of the year came and I passed Afrikaans with a D on higher grade. For the rest of my subjects I got As. I still had not had word from my parents and, what was worse, had no way of sharing my news because I had no address for them. It had been almost three months since I had a letter from Mom and I could only imagine they had decided to stay in Chagos. I tried not to think of other possibilities. Obviously I would not be going to the Seychelles, and when school broke up and my father's sister, Auntie Enid, invited me to spend a few weeks at their beach house in East London, I used most of my savings from my after-school job to buy a plane ticket. Then I packed my bags, kissed Nana and Chummy goodbye and left for the coast. Once in East London I tried not to worry about my family as I swam in the warm surf, read books, sunbathed and even kissed a boy who, because he had never spoken to my classmates from Alberton High, did not know that I was supposed to be unattractive.

25

MATRIC AND CHAGOS ARCHIPELAGO

In January when I returned to school I learned that our science teacher had resigned and the school board had been unable to find a replacement. Then the matric biology teacher announced that she was pregnant and would be taking maternity leave from mid-year on doctor's orders. The school board was unable to find a replacement for her either. Not having a teacher didn't bother me, I preferred learning directly from the textbook anyway. Mr Minnie informed our class that one of the ex-pupil's fathers had volunteered to give us science lessons twice a week before school as a temporary measure and our biology teacher told us that we had no choice but to cover the syllabus in double time and finish by June. Mr Minnie also informed the class that our results the previous year had not been good and that because this was to be our last year at school, and our most important one, he expected to see an improvement.

'Mr Kallman and I have decided,' he said, 'that any girl who fails a test, will get detention and every boy who fails a test, will be seeing me in my office.'

Storkie put up his hand. 'Are you talking about jacks, sir?'

Mr Minnie gave a tight smile. 'What do you think I'm talking about, boy? Furthermore, we are going to be a lot stricter on uniform inspections. We have noticed that a certain sloppiness is creeping in and we believe that this may be related to your poor academic performance. A sloppy exterior reflects a sloppy mind.'

By February I had still not heard from my family and, because I had no address, I couldn't write to them either. This was hard, because sending cheerful letters to my mother and brother, even when I wasn't happy, served to buoy me up. And although I knew they were probably okay, I was worried. At the same time I felt curiously helpless and resigned. If *Vingila* had sunk or been wrecked, there was nothing I could do about it except wait for the news to reach me. I couldn't send out a search party or rescue team. Then, in early February, about four months since I had last received mail, an envelope arrived from the Seychelles. Inside were three letters from Mom, all written from the Chagos Archipelago and dated 7 November, 1 December and 9 January. In the first letter she wrote that they had sailed from Cocos Keeling with our old friends Don and Muriel on *Aries*. The wind had been good and *Vingila* had made good time, arriving in Chagos after twelve days of easy reaching. She described Chagos as a large atoll, with several islands spread around a lagoon. The place had once been inhabited, but after an American naval base was established on Diego Garcia, 180 miles to the north, the people of Chagos had been evacuated, leaving behind a settlement which had fallen to ruin. The diving was excellent with millions of fish and Pepe was enjoying himself chasing rats ashore. She wasn't sure when they would get to the Seychelles and Dad was talking about staying in Chagos for the cyclone season which worried her because they wouldn't have enough gas, food or fuel. The second letter, which she said she was giving to *Aries* to post from the Seychelles, was dated early December, and began by saying how sad she was that they wouldn't be in the Seychelles to see me for Christmas. She hoped

I had done well in my exams.

She wrote that Chagos, like Diego Garcia, belonged to the British, and they had had a visit from a rather snooty British patrol boat. Dad attempted to buy some fruit from them and the captain replied that they had nothing to spare. A week later an American warship stopped in and, over the VHF radio, Dad tried again to buy supplies. The captain sent over an inflatable dinghy loaded with boxes of apples, tangerines, melons and fresh bread. The seaman making the delivery refused to take any payment. My mother ended the letter by writing that Pepe was getting very old. Although he still enjoyed chasing rats, his eyes were beginning to cloud and she wasn't sure if he was getting deaf or just didn't want to listen to her any more. The last letter was dated 9 January and she began by writing that they would be leaving Chagos for the Seychelles in a few days. They had found some chickens and killed a couple for lunch. There were still plenty of breadfruit and limes and Dad had seen a donkey in the old cemetery which was the creepiest place with vines growing over the old tombstones. Robert had started talking about coming home and going to school but Dad had many arguments against it, so she really wasn't sure what they would do. She would write as soon as they got to the Seychelles in a week or two.

A month passed while I waited for a letter from Mom, saying they had reached the Seychelles. A few weeks later I received a bulky envelope from Sri Lanka. Inside were two letters. One from my mother and the other from Robert. I started with Mom's first. It was dated 30 January. As you can gather, she wrote, we are still here in Chagos. Not all the news was good. Dad had been bitten on the hand by a moray eel while he washing a fish fillet in the sea. He had deep jagged wounds that had bled profusely which Mom was treating with Betadine ointment. Pepe had been in an accident which my brother would tell me more about because she still found it too upsetting. She asked me not to say anything to Nana about Pepe as it would only upset her as well. They were waiting for wind and hoped to leave Chagos soon. (At that time she didn't know that *Vingila* wouldn't leave the archipelago until early May, a full three months away.) She wrote that they were eating only fried fish and breadfruit chips because they had run out of almost all their other food. The dinghy fuel was finished and she was down to her last onion, although Dad had recently found a lemon tree near the graveyard, so she didn't think they would get scurvy. To save cooking gas they prepared meals ashore on an open fire in a fireplace they had made on the porch of the abandoned hospital. She drew a diagram of the eleven islands surrounding the lagoon and wrote that they had spent their first month at Passage Island, before moving on to Boddam Island and the old hospital. Although there were a lot of blue-bottle flies and mosquitoes, everybody, except Pepe and Dad with his bitten hand, was healthy. They were hoping that another yacht sailing from the Seychelles would be bringing them fresh supplies. Robert had started doing a bit of correspondence school at last and she was working her way through my old lessons to keep herself mentally stimulated. She finished by saying she would give the letter to some friends on a yacht called *Schieldag* who were leaving for Sri Lanka and had promised to post it for her.

My brother's letter went straight to the point. Hey sis, he wrote, you wouldn't believe it, but last Friday Pepe jumped from the boat to the dinghy and his low-slung gun hooked on the toe rail and when he landed in the dinghy there was blood everywhere and he had a bone hanging out of his bone, if you know what I'm saying. His dick was broken.

I read the sentence again. Pepe had broken his penis? I didn't know that was possible. Did a penis have bones? I read on.

'Anyway, so he had this bone hanging out and Dad tried to push it back but it wouldn't go, so the next day after the bleeding stopped we gave Pepe some Valium and I held him down while Dad cut off the bone with a pair of side cutters. The old boy screamed and fell back in a faint and now none of us can turn him on his back any more. Mom's putting Betadine on it and she says it's getting better. It looks a bit floppy but at least the old bugger can still pee all right.'

He went on to tell me about his pet barracuda Jimmy, who was about six feet long and hung around the boat all day because he couldn't catch fish for himself as he seemed to have some sort of gill injury. Robert had taken to feeding him fish heads by hand and when there weren't fish heads to spare, trolled a lure from the wind-surfer to catch food for Jimmy.

For Christmas they had caught a chicken and when my brother tried to wring its neck its head just went round and round and the eyes kept looking at him so he took it down to the sea and cut its head off with his machete instead.

'Mom doesn't want us killing any more chickens. She says there are enough fish to eat, so now we feed them coconuts instead and they are getting quite tame.'

He went on to say that in the evenings they could pick up a broadcast from the American naval base on Diego Garcia 150 miles away, and that they sometimes had a Robin Williams show which he knew I would like.

He ended the letter by saying he had to go and feed Jimmy.

In spite of Mr Minnie and Mr Kallman's measures to improve academic excellence in Alberton High, standards continued to fall. Mr Minnie called an assembly of the matrics to make a special announcement. He had received the first term results from the teachers and he was not pleased. Three quarters of the pupils taking standard grade maths had failed. Mrs van Staden's higher grade class did a little better and Mr Minnie's own accountancy class too. Physical science results were dismal. He cleared his throat and told us that apart from one pupil, not a single other student in the school – higher or standard grade – had passed. I was surprised. Learning from the textbook, as I usually did, I hadn't found the exam that difficult. Then Mr Minnie did something unexpected.

'I would like to tell you that the one pupil who passed,' he said, 'was Martinique Stilwell. Martinique put up your hand, so everybody can see you.'

I noticed that he looked tense, wound up. A muscle in his jaw was twitching.

'Martinique – the rest of you might like to know – passed with 97 per cent.'

A sound spread through the assembly hall; a low rumble which turned into something that sounded more like a hiss. Mr Minnie turned at me and nodded. He had an odd look on his face. I thought exam results were supposed to be private and I wondered what he was up to. Why had he told the whole school? It seemed unlikely that he was proud of me, and far too outlandish to imagine he hoped I'd get beaten up by my fellow students or be subjected to further social isolation. Keeping my face as expressionless as I could, I nodded back at him.

'Now the boys will see me and Mr van Wyk in my office. We are going to be very busy this morning which is why I have asked Mr van Wyk to help me. I hope you have worn your thickest underpants today, because you'll need them. Those of you boys who failed both science and maths will, of course, be getting double strokes. The girls know where to go to arrange for detention. I can see we're going to have a lot of clean, smooth desks in school, and I hope you will all learn something from this. Dismissed.'

I filed out of the hall half expecting to be lynched in the quadrangle. When a posse of students – including Storkie – approached me later that day at second break, I prepared myself for a beating. They didn't want to fight, however, they wanted to talk. Would I be prepared to give the class extra science lessons? So I began holding extra science lessons after school in Nana's dining room, leading my grandmother to believe that I had suddenly become popular. For our first lesson she even baked a cake.

In April a letter arrived from the Maldives. *Vingila* was still in Chagos. Mom wrote that the rice was finished, and also the flour. They cooked everything ashore on the fire, even morning coffee, because they were keeping the last of the cooking gas for the trip to Rodrigues. She hoped they were leaving soon but with Dad you never knew. Even the lemons on the tree were finished now, although there were still plenty of breadfruit. At night she dreamed of eating fresh bread and cheese. You wouldn't recognise your brother, she wrote, he has grown so big and muscular. There are a few other yachts here and nobody wears clothes any more except Robert, and his Speedo has so many holes in it now, I don't know why he bothers. They had had a full moon party a few months back and the couple from one yacht had brought cup cakes which made everybody feel sick and gave them nightmares. Mom wished she had an address so that I could write to her. She hadn't had news for so long except for a letter she had found in a bottle on the beach which wasn't really the same thing. She hoped that we were all healthy and that I was doing well at school and she ended by saying that she would give anything to be back home in South Africa.

My second year of school wore on. The days shortened as winter approached and the grass turned brown. I was beginning to feel the strain of being a good girl for my grandparents. I was seventeen years old and I wanted a few posters on my wall and a place I could make my own. Nana even forbade me to close the door, because 'closed bedroom doors upset your Chummy'. I was also, for the first time in my life, gaining weight, which was strange because I almost always felt hungry. Nana served small meals of chicken steaklets, and frozen fried rice from a packet. All the food we ate had either been frozen or in some way processed. Even the vegetables were frozen. She also liked cooking in bulk and freezing portions which could then be conveniently defrosted in the microwave before the evening TV programmes began. We ate early and by midway into the evening I felt hungry again and would begin snacking on biscuits and chocolate Nana kept in tins.

I had made a few friends at last, however; Julie, a girl from England who ran cross country with me and Michael, who was repeating matric and disliked Alberton High as much as I did. Michael was a plump, soft-looking boy, with the faint haze of an incipient moustache on his upper lip and wispy hair that I later learned his mother permed at home to give it more body. He had a driver's licence and rode a motorbike and sometimes, when he got the use of his older sister's car, we would skip school together and go to the movies or spend the day in the coffee shops of Hillbrow drinking Horlicks and playing backgammon. Although half a dozen students had failed their matric exams the previous year, Michael was the only one who had returned to Alberton High. He had wanted to go to a private college with his friends, but because his divorced mother could not afford private school fees he was back in Alberton High, where he was immediately identified as an outsider and subjected to the usual taunts from the rest of the class. In Michael I found a substitute for my twin brother. They weren't anything alike except for their quietness of presence, which I realised was what I was after. As the year passed, Michael and I skipped more and more classes. The teachers didn't seemed to notice, or care. In coffee shops, I helped him with his lessons and his marks began to show signs of improvement. Because he was on standard grade maths, with no option to change mid-year, a university pass was out of reach. Anyway, Michael didn't want to go to university. He didn't know what he wanted to do, just that university wasn't an option. We talked a lot about the usual teenage stuff as our friendship developed, except for the divergence our paths would take at the end of the year. Even if I didn't get in to medical school, I knew I was going to university. If I couldn't be a doctor, I would be an engineer, or a scientist of some kind. For Michael, the only certainty was at least two years in the army. About that he had no choice.

Another letter arrived from Mom. This one from the Seychelles, delivered once again via another yacht. My mother wrote that it was nearly May and *Vingila* was still in Chagos and she had had enough. She wanted to come back to South Africa, but every time she tried to say something to Dad about it, he just got angry, so she had decided it was best just to keep quiet. He had been in a very bad mood lately. Pepe at least had completely recovered from his accident. Most of the other yachts had left in April when the cyclone season ended and now there was just one other yacht left, *Sunbird* from Zimbabwe. Mom had started teaching the boy Timothy because his own mother's teaching methods were a bit erratic. At first she had thought Timothy, who was almost ten years old, had a learning disorder, until she discovered that he actually knew almost nothing, so she had started with his two times table and he was coming along.

The breadfruit were almost over and she wasn't sure what they would eat except for fish. She was keeping aside one month's worth of food for the trip to the Seychelles, although they had heard reports about how expensive it was there and Dad had started digging in his heels about going. If they didn't go to the Seychelles, she wasn't quite sure where they would go, perhaps Rodrigues or Mauritius. Either way, it was a long sail that had taken some yachts over a month because of the light, erratic winds. There was still also the threat of a late cyclone kicking about if they went south too soon. Dad and Robert were trying to ferment coconut wine because all the rum was finished and although their first attempts hadn't been successful, Robert was sure they were near a breakthrough. A few weeks previously a British patrol boat from the naval base on Diego Garcia had stopped in, wanting to know how much longer my family intended to stay. They told my mother that

Vingila had become an embarrassment to the administrators on Diego Garcia. She missed us.

As the end of the second term approached, I turned my attention to my school work. After the terrible first term results, Mr Kallman, the principal, had found a new science teacher when Mr Ashmole, who had been giving us part-time early morning lessons, had left in frustration. Those of us in his class knew why. Mr Ashmole had told us that, according to the Transvaal Education Department, the aim of teaching science was to show the splendour of the universe in such a way as to show the splendour of God. The teaching of evolution, or anything else for that matter which might throw the existence of God into doubt, was forbidden. Mrs Peters, our new teacher, agreed to come out of retirement to teach us physical science on one condition; she was a Reborn Christian and she also wanted to be responsible for our religious instruction. We were soon to discover that Mrs Peters had been reborn into the charismatic faith and what she really wanted to teach us about was the beauty of talking in tongues. Sometimes she was so enthusiastic about the miracle of talking in tongues that the time allocated to us for religious instruction wasn't quite enough and our science periods had to be used as well. Occasionally she gave demonstrations. Depending on the lesson, I read either the physics textbook or the Bible in which I had always enjoyed searching the Old Testament for the passages about masturbation, rape, and human sacrifice, and all the instances in which people who had offended God's laws should be stoned to death.

In June a letter arrived from the island of Rodrigues. I learned that at the end of May *Vingila* had finally left Chagos. Mom thought she deserved a medal of some kind for not having gone into a shop for six months, and towards the end her nightly dreams of fresh, buttered bread with cheese had become intolerable. Dad was sad to leave Chagos. He said he would have liked to stay longer and mentioned the possibility of stocking up and returning for another six months, a suggestion that found little support from Mom. Robert just said that he wanted a new Speedo because his old one had disintegrated and he didn't like spear-fishing naked.

Once at sea, Dad decided to bypass the Seychelles because he had heard the islands were very expensive and money was running low, so he changed course for Rodrigues, a small volcanic island a few hundred miles north of Mauritius. The sixth night at sea was calm, with light winds. *Vingila* was flying her working jib and an un-reefed main sail. The hatches and portholes were open and a faint breeze fanned Mom, Robert and Dad who had finished supper and were about to settle down around the table for a game of poker. Dad suddenly held up his hand for silence.

'Can anyone else hear that?' he said.

Robert thought he heard a low rumble too sustained to be thunder. The sound grew louder. Pepe whimpered and pressed himself against my mother's legs. My brother went up the hatch to look.

'I'm not sure I'd do that if I were you,' Dad said.

'Holy shit!' Robert dropped back inside, trying to close the hatch. He wasn't quick enough. A torrent of white water forced the doors apart and followed him into the saloon. *Vingila* yawed over, water cascading through every open hatch and porthole. Pepe skidded across the floor and was swept towards the engine room in a stream that had suddenly sprung up in the main saloon. In the passage his head disappeared under a wave. Mom dived after him. *Vingila* rolled over still further and the stream gurgled into the stern cabins where water was spraying onto the bunks from the open portholes.

'Freak fucking wave,' Robert said, climbing the stairs against a waterfall and trying to push the doors of the main hatch shut against the pressure of the water. 'Twenty fucking feet of white water I saw out there. Jesus Christ, a fucking huge breaker in the middle of the ocean and we're right in the middle of it.'

When *Vingila* finally righted herself and water had stopped pouring inside, Dad and Robert went on deck to check the damage. The netting on the life line was shredded and parts of the windsurfer lay in jagged pieces on the deck. The dinghy was still hanging from the stanchions, upside down as usual, which had saved it, and the mainsail and jib were intact and pulling against the light wind. Only the white, churned sea gave a hint at what had just happened.

Inside, the damage was worse. The ham radio was drenched and so was the satnav which had been giving problems anyway. Salt water had soaked the engine and the alternator. Even after Dad cleaned and bled them, the batteries wouldn't charge. Dad said he would check again in the morning and after pumping the bilges and closing the hatches they lay down on the saloon floor because all the bedding was water logged. Mom told me later that she couldn't sleep that night, or several of the nights that followed, because she kept listening out for the roar of breaking water.

Mom wrote that Dad had said I could visit them in Mauritius for a month over the June school holidays if there was enough money in the Benoni account. There was – just. After finishing my mid-year exams, I got on a plane and left the wintry highveld for the tropical island of Mauritius.

My family met me at the airport and we took a taxi to Port Louis, the harbour where *Vingila* lay anchored. In the eighteen months since I had last seen him, my twin brother had grown up; he was even more deeply suntanned than I remembered and much more muscular. His hair, bleached white by the sun, reached his shoulders in a shaggy mess. My family expressed surprised at how pale and soft I had grown, and I was shocked at how rapidly Pepe had aged. He slept most of the time, barely rousing himself for his twice daily walks ashore. His eyes were filmy and on land he tottered along stiffly, head to the ground. Sometimes he lost us and sniffed about in a panic, and when we called out to him he didn't seem to hear. Except for looking a little more thin and leathery, Mom and Dad hadn't changed much, and neither had *Vingila,* who was as rusty and battered-looking as ever. Coming down the hatch, I inhaled the familiar smell of dried fish, mould, teak and fermenting bananas and it was as if I had never been away. When mealtime came around, though, it soon became apparent that I had. On my first night my mother cooked masala potatoes, and a fish curry with coconut milk and then, out of habit, set three places at the table.

'Hey,' I said, 'what about me?'

Supper looked and smelled delicious, but when I took a mouthful a searing pain shot from my tongue, through my gums, to end somewhere in the region of my eyeballs. Beads of sweat sprang up on my forehead and the light seemed to change nature.

'My God, when did you guys start eating such hot food?' I said.

'We always eat this,' Robert said. 'You should know, you used to like chilli. What do you eat in Alberton?'

'Frozen, crumbed stuff. Packet sauces. Noodles and cheese. No spices.'

'Don't you make anything for yourself? You can cook. You're the one who started us on curry and Asian food in the first place, remember?' Mom said, calmly taking another spoonful of curry and popping it into her mouth as if it were no more incendiary than vanilla custard.

'In the beginning I asked if I could,' I said, 'but Nan wouldn't let me. She said Chummy didn't like the smell of curry in the house.'

I took another forkful of fish and had a coughing fit that was closer to choking. Salty liquid trickled from my nose.

'Just keep going,' Mom said, 'you'll get used to it.'

'Looks like you got soft there in South Africa,' Dad said, 'but we'll get you right. Then we'll feed you some thousand year eggs with bird's eye chilli. That'll get your juices going.'

We sailed *Vingila* from Port Louis, the capital, to Grand Bay on the other side of the island where there was a sheltered anchorage and a quiet yacht club in a grove of coconut palms. When we motored from the harbour and Robert raised the mainsail, it was as if a great weight lifted from my chest. The sky was blue, the sea bluer and the fresh wind blowing from shore smelled of tropical island. As the mainsail snapped taut, *Vingila* sprang to life. Mom took the helm and I hauled in the jib sheet as Robert cleated the main halyard and raised the old yellow and green drifter. Surging forward, with her low familiar hum, our 20 tonnes of steel, canvas, seashells and dried fish cleaved the water into two foamy waves at the stern, and I felt properly away from Alberton High and Germiston Lake and happier than I had been in a long time. I thought that under different circumstances, I might have been able to stay with my family and complete the circumnavigation.

Robert joined me in the cockpit where I had taken the helm from Mom who had gone below to secure a cup rolling about in the sink.

'Old boat's still got a bit of spunk in her, hasn't she?' my brother said.

I nodded and brought *Vingila* a bit closer into the wind.

'Nicky, how's Alberton? Are you happy there?'

'Sometimes,' I said, 'but I think you'd hate it. For a start there's no sea. Anyway, in six months I'm done. University will be better.'

'Is there money for university?'

'I don't know.' After paying for my flight to Mauritius the Benoni bank account was practically empty. The agent responsible for letting out the houses hadn't raised the rent in years and the tenants had sometimes gone months without paying. I had tried to tell my father that the agent was useless and he should look for another, but he hadn't believed me.

We sailed on for a while in silence. Then I said, 'Have you thought about what you'll do when you get back?'

Robert shrugged and brushed a salt-stiff strand of hair from his eyes. 'Can't say I want to do anything in particular. Guess I'll have to start school again. If we ever get back.'

'What do you mean?'

'Oh, you know Dad. Next thing he'll be turning around for Chagos again or something.'

'God,' I said, 'I can't imagine Dad in South Africa. What will he do there?'

Robert smiled. 'Well, one thing's for sure, he'll have to look for a job because from what I understand there ain't no more money left.'

'Are you still reading those cowboy books ?' I said.

I returned to Alberton High suntanned, chilli-fit, skinny again and ready for the third term. Three weeks in Mauritius had passed quickly, and with less than a thousand miles back to South Africa, my mother had assured me she would be home soon and we could be a family again. I returned to school cheerful and determined to make the best of my last five months at Alberton High. Midway through the term, the teacher trainee filling in for our absent pregnant biology teacher sent me to Mr Minnie's office for disobedience.

The substitute teacher wanted us to write out the answers to several years worth of old biology papers in full, including all the essay questions, while I preferred learning in point form; it was quicker. Besides, rushing through the biology syllabus in six months had forced me to neglect my other subjects, which I now felt needed attention. When I tried to explain this to her, she said that if I didn't obey orders she would have no choice but to send me to Mr Minnie. I lost patience. Send me to Mr Minnie then, I said, because I'm not writing out all those essays. I don't have time and my other subjects need attention if I'm going to get into medicine. Which was how I found myself at the vice principal's office where I hoped to explain myself and, given my good academic record, be given some leniency.

'Mr Minnie,' I said, 'I really need time for my other subjects. Prelims are in two weeks and I'm applying for university. I was hoping to get into medicine and I need a scholarship. It's very important for me to do as well as I can and writing out biology papers like this isn't helping.'

Mr Minnie narrowed his eyes and stroked his moustache.

'Martinique, it is not for you to decide how to study. You are the student, and it is your duty, as the student, to obey the teacher's orders. If your teacher says you must write out the essays in full, then you must write out the essays in full.'

I could have backed down then, it would have been easier.

'I'm sorry,' I said, 'I really don't have the time for that.'

'What did you say?'

'I'm not writing out biology past papers.'

'Then I have no choice, you must have detention. Five days worth, starting Monday.'

'What kind of detention?'

'The same kind of detention everybody has.'

'But prelims start soon. How am I going to study if I'm sanding desks?'

'That, my girl, is your problem, not mine. Unless, of course, you decide to change your mind and do as your teacher tells you.'

'No,' I said, 'I'm not going to do that.'

'Then I'll see you Monday, personally. And Martinique –'

'Yes?'

'One last thing.' His moustache twitched. 'You might think that you are very clever, but you still need to learn that you are part of the class. Dismissed.'

On Monday afternoon Mr Minnie, hair neatly combed and wearing a pale apricot poly-cotton shirt, maroon tie and brown slacks, was waiting for me in the detention classroom. He gestured towards a particularly defaced desk. My task was to sand the ballpoint ingrained graffiti from its surface. I took the sandpaper and its gritty texture, tugging gently against the skin of my fingertips, brought back sharp memories of the hours of sanding I had done on *Vingila*. I sat down, crossed my arms and began to cry. Mr Minnie's eyebrows shot up for a fraction of a second before knotting into a frown above the bridge of his narrow nose. He sighed and sank into a seat at the teacher's desk. My sobs intensified. My tears at first were tears of anger and frustration, although as the minutes passed, other feelings emerged, which served to make me cry harder. I cried primarily because I hated Alberton High and Mr Minnie who had power over me, but I cried also because I missed my family and I was sick of being an outcast and part of me wished I had stayed on the boat. I cried because I wished Dad could have been be different and I cried because I wished my mother had stood up to him more. I cried because I feared I might do badly in the prelims if I couldn't study and had to spend the week sanding desks, which might cost me a place in medical school. I cried because I had left the boat in search of freedom and found a different type of tyranny. While I cried, Mr Minnie sat and stared out of the window at the rugby field or doodled on a scrap of paper. Occasionally he sneaked sideways looks at me. The room was silent except for the sound of my sobs. Neither of us said a word. If I had been a boy he would have caned me and both of us knew it. He too was helpless. He knew he couldn't take my hand and force it to hold the sandpaper and move it across the desk. All he could do was watch me. My sobs grew hoarser and more choked, my eyes and face swelled and my nose blocked up, forcing me to breathe through my mouth. After a while I stopped crying and sat on the desk, swinging my legs and giving intermittent hiccups while Mr Minnie continued to stare out of the window. At the end of two hours he stood up and sighed.

'Okay,' he said, 'we're done for today.'

'What about tomorrow?' I asked, my voice thick from swelling and snot. 'Do you want me to come back?'

'No,' he said, 'don't bother.'

I wrote prelims the following week and submitted my application for medical school. Three weeks after that I received a letter informing me that I had an appointment for an interview for the degree of bachelor of medicine and surgery, which meant that of the three thousand applicants, I was among the five hundred who had made it to the next stage.

I wrote to Mom in Mauritius to tell her the news and to ask when they were coming back. Her reply described parties at Grand Baie Yacht Club, and how Robert had been going to the horse races with Mauritian friends he had made. I'm not sure when we are coming back, she wrote, when I ask your father, he gets irritable. He says he'll let me know when he's ready. She asked me to tell her how the interview went and said that Don and Muriel, who were with them, wished me luck.

Chummy drove me to medical school for my interview. I wore my school uniform, and, in spite of the heat, my blazer. I was very nervous. The building, a solid block of concrete with strange red vents in place of windows, looked intimidating. Inside the foyer, amongst the white-coated students, there were several other teenagers in school uniforms, all wearing blazers heavy with braids signifying prefect status, and with scrolls denoting scholastic and sporting performance sewn beneath the front pockets, and in some instances, down the other side of the blazer. My blazer in comparison was bare.

I took a seat and waited. After a while I was called into a room and introduced to my interviewers: a lecturer at Wits and a final-year medical student.

'Tell us, Martinique, why do you want to be a doctor?' the lecturer asked.

'I want to help people,' I said.

'Then why not be a lawyer?' the medical student said. 'They help people too, you know.'

'I don't want to help people in that way.'

'Then what makes you like medicine?'

I felt the interview wasn't going well and that, coming from Alberton High, my chances weren't good anyway, so I decided to be honest and let them make the decision as to whether I was doctor material.

'When I was very young,' I said, 'my father's parents had a farm, and we would go there every summer and my father would slaughter a cow for the table. I hated seeing it die, but once it was dead I loved watching them cut it up.'

'You did?' the medical student said.

'Yes. The inside of it – the intestines and kidneys, the liver and heart were fascinating. I found them beautiful. So mysterious, you know. Once my cousin put a cow's heart in my hands which was still beating. I won't ever forget it. I'd like to know the human body like that too.'

This was the truth. I wasn't squeamish at all. I also enjoyed gutting fish, and my brother and I would often slice open their stomachs to investigate the contents, which were often surprising.

'And if you were a doctor, what kind of doctor would you like to be?'

'A forensic pathologist.'

'Really?'

'Yes, because you get to solve mysteries and stuff. I read some books with forensic pathologists in them and it sounded fun.'

The medical student and the lecturer exchanged a glance.

'One last thing, Martinique.'

'Yes?'

'It says here on your application form that you've sailed most of the way around the world and were home schooled by your mother.'

I nodded.

'That must have been interesting.'

'Yes,' I said, 'it certainly was.'

I left the interview silently cursing myself for opening my mouth and saying such stupid things. I tried to imagine what it would be like working as a chemical engineer, which was my second choice if I didn't get a place in medicine, except I wasn't completely sure what a chemical engineer did.

I wrote to Mom saying that I had no idea how the interview had gone, we would just have to wait and see. I was, however, hoping they would be back for honours night at Alberton High. She replied that Pepe had been very sick. His kidneys had failed and he had almost died. She was praying to be there for honours night, but it all depended on Dad. She ended the rather short letter by writing that she was on her way to the vet to take Pepe for another check-up.

Before honours night, however, I had to get through the Alberton High Matric Farewell. Among the popular pupils excitement ran high for this evening of food and dancing. Many of my classmates had been planning their dresses since the previous year and considerable effort had gone into deciding on a theme, decorating the school hall and designing invitations.

'For many of you,' Mr Minnie had said in assembly, 'this will be the highlight of your school career, and for some of you even the best night of your lives.'

My mother, who loved sewing, was upset that she would not be there to make my dress and wrote letters to several of my aunts, enlisting their help in the project. I planned a black silk sheath and my hair, I decided, would be slicked sleekly back against my skull. I would look austere, serious and elegant.

'You can't wear black to your matric farewell,' my Aunt Audrey said when she took me shopping for fabric. Against my will we left the shop with three metres of shocking pink artificial silk watermarked taffeta and a pattern for a puffed sleeved dress, the only feature of which I liked was the deep V cut down its back.

My Aunt Adeline sewed the dress and Aunt Audrey took me for a fitting.

'It's stunning,' she said. 'You'll knock their socks off.'

As a concession to my desire for austerity, she had allowed me a gun-metal grey sash and a pair of matching grey high heels. In the evenings I practised walking up and down Nana's passage. I never really got the knack of heels, but I hoped it would be all right on the night. I wondered what my partner would wear. Black, I hoped. Or dark grey. With Chummy's help I had found a date at the Germiston Aquatic Club; Thys was a quiet, older Afrikaans guy I knew from the ski show. I had thought initially about asking my friend Michael, but he made it clear he wasn't going. 'I went last year and it was shit and this year will be shit as well.'

I asked Michael what he had worn.

'A pink suit,' he said. 'Actually, it wasn't quite pink, it was more of a salmon.'

Smug with a vision of myself in elegant black, because I did not yet know that I, too, would be wearing pink to my matric farewell, I teased him horribly for days. As the day of the dance approached I decided to phone my date Thys to ask what he would be wearing.

'A pink suit,' he said. Then he paused. 'Well, not quite pink actually. More of a salmon really.'

My last hope was that I would at least have sleek, slick backed hair.

Nana's hairdresser laughed when I described the hairstyle I had in mind.

'Are you crazy?' she said. 'This is your matric farewell.'

And, using the blow-dryer, and most of a can of hairspray, she transformed my fine straight hair into a mass of sticky curls that rose from my face and cascaded down my neck. As a finishing touch she added a pair of stiff wings that sprayed from my temples and kept the curls at bay.

At school that night my maths teacher didn't recognise me at first when I smiled at her.

'Nicky,' she said, 'is that you?'

Balancing precariously on my high heels I nodded, holding on to my salmon-suited date's arm for stability. Smiling was an effort, the make-up on my face felt as stiff as the curls of my gelled hair.

One of my classmates came over. Her face had been heavily plastered over too. 'You look stunning, Nicky,' she said. 'I wouldn't have believed you could be so pretty. See, all it takes is a little effort.'

My potential for prettiness was to be the theme for the rest of the evening. In fact, for weeks afterwards I was to hear the same refrain from most of the popular girls in my school. With a bit of effort, a can of hair spray and a pink dress, I too could be attractive.

By the end of the evening I had abandoned my high heels to go barefoot. Julie and I had shared a bottle of sweet sparkling wine and my gelled curls had migrated from the top of my head and were hanging somewhere in the region of my ears. Even without the heels I was staggering. When the bouncer at the after party nightclub took my arm and asked me if I'd go outside with him, I pushed a stray curl from my eye, took a last swig from the bottle and told him to forget it, I would have to be a lot drunker than I currently was to go anywhere with him. In fact, I said, from the look of him I would probably have to be unconscious. The bouncer responded by tightening his grip on my arm and dragging me through the door while simultaneously trying to kiss me. Thys, my pink-suited date, hearing my screams of protest, rushed to my rescue, receiving – in the tussle that followed – a vigorous head butt that split open his eyebrow and left blood trickling down his face and onto the pink suit.

Julie, her date, Thys and I were then asked to leave the nightclub by the manager who had come out from his office to see what the commotion was about. We drove to a koppie overlooking Alberton and there, beside Thys's yellow Beetle, we danced on the road until the first pale rim of light appeared on the horizon and I felt a thrill of joy because I knew that I was very nearly done with Alberton High.

In November when Alberton High held its annual end of year prize-giving ceremony, *Vingila,* who had left Mauritius, was in the Indian ocean several hundred miles from landfall. Only Nana and Chummy were in the hall. Nana wore nylon stockings and her best crimplene dress for the occasion and Chummy clapped so hard when I accepted the Dux Scholae Cup and the Koch Progress Trophy from Mr Minnie, that his brylcreemed side part lost its traction and came undone, sending a sweep of oily hair into his eyes. After the ceremony a photographer from the local newspaper arranged me in front of a table with my trophies and took my picture. She didn't have to ask me to smile. I hadn't stopped grinning since finding a letter in the post box earlier that afternoon informing me that I had a provisional place in medical school which would be confirmed if my final matric marks were satisfactory.

A week later *Vingila* made landfall in Richards Bay, an industrial town on the east coast of South Africa. After eight years at sea my father had completed his circumnavigation. Mom made a call from the public phone as soon as they arrived and Chummy raced off in his cream-coloured Alfa Romeo to see them. He found my parents and Robert getting drunk in the main saloon with Don and Muriel, our old friends on *Aries,* and he promptly joined the party, which by all accounts went on until quite late. I missed the celebrations because Nana forbade me to take time off school. The next day Chummy brought Mom, Robert and Pepe back to Alberton.

When my suntanned and muscular brother came into my bedroom with its candlewick bedspreads and dolls, the salty smell of him filled the place.

He plopped down on my bed.

'So this is where you sleep, sis?'

'Yup, only I'm not allowed to sit on the bed when the bedspread's on because Nana doesn't like it.'

'You're joking, right?'

Mom shared my bedroom with Pepe who was now completely blind and deaf, and had grown so stiff he could barely walk. Robert slept in the spare room. Less than a week later the three of them were gone again.

'I can't live here,' Robert said. 'Chummy keeps telling me to cut my hair and get some decent clothes. He wants me to work on the mines. He said that's what he did. I'm going back to Dad.'

'We'll see you in December when you've finished your exams,' Mom said, giving me a goodbye kiss and picking Pepe up in her arms as she ran outside to catch the lift Nana had arranged for them. And then they were gone and it was just me in my room at the desk again.

26

RICHARDS BAY

In mid-December after I had received the results of my final exams and had found a letter in the post box confirming my place in medical school, I returned to *Vingila* to visit my father. I had not seen him since his arrival in South Africa. Robert was staying with him on the boat.

Pepe was dead. In November Mom had let him out one night for a pee and, while tottering blindly around the deck, Pepe had fallen into the anchor locker, which had been accidentally left open. He had landed on the pile of chain below and had broken his back.

Mom had phoned me in Alberton.

'He was paralysed,' she sobbed. 'He couldn't move his legs, so Dad and I took him to the vet. They put him down.'

Her loyal companion, flying fish chaser and foot warmer of seventeen years was gone. After Pepe died my mother left the yacht, moved in with my grandmother and began looking for work as a substitute teacher to help pay for my impending university fees. Besides, she said, I really need a break from your father and that damn boat. Mom and I crossed paths briefly in Alberton before I packed my bags and left for the coast to stay with my father and brother for the summer holidays.

Don and Muriel met me at the yacht club gate. I hadn't seen them in almost four years. There were streaks of grey in Don's dark beard and his eyes were a little more crinkly, but other than that neither he nor Muriel had changed much.

'Nicky,' Don said, gathering me in a hug, 'we are so dang proud of you, girl. We hear you're gonna be a doctor.'

'Your dad wasn't sure when to expect you,' Muriel said. 'He and Robert had an errand to run and they said you should have a drink with us on *Aries* in the meantime.'

Don and Muriel walked me to *Aries* who was moored at the jetty for visiting yachts. *Aries*, like her owners, was ageing gracefully and looked well cared for and as sturdy and good-natured as I remembered her. Next to *Aries* lay a striking looking junk. It took me a moment to recognise her. It was the *Maria Jose*, the Chinese junk with a Swiss flag we had first met in Durban twelve years previously, before we had even launched *Vingila*. She still had sails the colour of dried blood, and white eyes painted on her black bow for her to see where she was going, but her cavernous hatches showed glimpses of a well-appointed interior now and there was outside seating with pretty cushions and an awning. Don filled me in. The Klaar siblings, Hans, Inge and Alex, were now in their twenties and all three of them were still aboard. The family had just returned from South East Asia where they had refurbished the junk using money they had made from the treasure they had found in Madagascar. While at sea on their way to Richards Bay, Ernest and his wife Ilona had fallen very ill with malaria and Hans told Don that they had no treatment aboard and his parents grew so sick he was afraid they would die. It was horrible knowing there was nothing he could do to help them. Fortunately Ernest and Ilona were still alive when *Maria Jose* made landfall. After recovering in hospital, Ernest, who had raised his sons to be sailors and navigators, told Don that he was proud that his children had sailed to South Africa by themselves.

'It's what I trained them to do,' he said. 'I feel I've done a good job.'

'Sons and daughters are useful for other things too,' Ernest went on. 'When we were last in Durban, we anchored next to a navy vessel. We put Inge on the deck in a bikini to distract the sailors, and I sent Hans and Alex to swim over and climb the stern and fetch us some strong new warps.'

Hans was twenty-two that summer and wanted to leave the junk. He had been back to Switzerland, the country of his birth, and found the only work available to him menial and intolerable. He did not see himself as either a road worker or a postman. Don told me that Hans had then applied to a university in Hawaii to study marine biology, but had been turned down because he had no educational certificates of any sort. Now he had agreed to deliver a yacht from Richards Bay to England, where he told Don he planned to buy a small catamaran with the proceeds. It was time for his own boat. Don said that, like me, Hans collected seashells and that he too knew the Latin names and current market value of almost every cowrie and cone. He could also identify many of the orchids of Madagascar, and for some time had been smuggling the plants into South Africa and selling them to collectors.

'But you, Nicky,' said Don, patting my shoulder, 'don't have to do any of that smuggling and trading stuff. You're going to be a doctor, girl.'

From the opposite bunk, Jib, the kitten I had rescued in Tahiti and given to Don as a present, narrowed her wicked eyes at me. She was fatter than ever.

'Oh look,' said Muriel, 'she's giving you kisses. That's how she shows affection, you know, when she half closes her eyes like that. How sweet.'

Later Dad and Robert found me on *Aries* and Robert rowed us out to *Vingila* who was anchored some way off shore.

'Cheapest mooring I could find,' Dad said, looking pleased.

Rust stains ran like tears down *Vingila*'s hull and I felt a surge of affection for our bulky, old boat. Patting her gold mast, I whispered, well done, old girl, you did it. She wasn't the same without Mom, though. Inside, the sink was full of dirty dishes and in Mom and Dad's cabin the bunk they had shared was unmade and the place smelled of old dog. I kept expecting to see Pepe sleeping under the main saloon table in his usual place, only to be reminded – with a jab of pain – that our poodle was dead.

Yet I was happy to be back. And I was even looking forward to a night in my bunk once I had found some clean sheets and cleared out all the sacks of warps and sails that had taken up residence on the mattress. While I made tea, Robert and I talked about the technical high school that he would attend the following year. He wasn't looking forward to it. Both he and Dad would stay on *Vingila*. It was unclear where Mom would live.

'It's just two years of school,' I said. 'They'll go quickly.'

Dad took a sip of his tea. He looked shrunken, his blue eyes watery behind his glasses and I noticed traces of grey in the stubble on his chin. I wondered what he planned to do next, now that he had finally sailed around the world. I wondered if he knew himself.

After a while my father said, 'So, Nicky, I suppose you think you're some kind of a big shot now. Going to university. Very important. Too fancy for the rest of us.'

I had not spoken to him since passing matric. I was the first member of my family to go to university and he hadn't called to congratulate me on my results, nor had he said anything about my being accepted at medical school. But Don had told me earlier that after the matric results were published, Dad had gone around the yacht club waving the paper under people's noses and telling them how his daughter had got distinctions and was going to be a doctor.

I shrugged. '*I'm* not a big deal, but going to university feels like a big deal. Scary even.'

Dad just grunted, narrowed his eyes and took another sip of tea. I knew that something had changed. My father didn't scare me any more. Nothing was explicitly stated, but I felt I had no reason to fear the Whistler now because Dad would not lift his hand to me again. Even his words had lost much of their power to hurt me, because I was the captain of another boat now, one that had already set sail for the future.

EPILOGUE

I often dream that I am back on *Vingila* and we are sailing across the lagoon of an atoll. I can see palm trees on the shore, and a line of white dwellings and the steeple of a church. As the wind fills her sails, *Vingila* surges forward and coral heads and schools of fish flash under her keel in the clear water and I feel happy and free. I awake to face the reality of a rather conventional existence. I am married and have a house and children of my own. My husband is also a doctor and we both work and our children go to school. As the years have passed and the suburban roots I planted have grown ever deeper, I am more able to appreciate the strength of character and courage that my father displayed in taking his family sailing around the world and I am grateful to him for many of the adventures of my childhood.

My father finally sold *Vingila* to Inge Klaar, Hans's sister. Inge was pregnant at the time, and had a French boyfriend. The relationship did not work out and we heard later that he had taken off with the boat, leaving her stranded. *Vingila* is now for charter in Nosi Bay, Madagascar, and Inge has another yacht, *Scallywag*. After selling *Vingila* my father began building a new steel yacht, and he is still at it.

Don and Muriel stayed on at Richards Bay too. They sold reliable old *Aries* and began building a bigger, faster boat. 'This one's going to have everything I ever wanted aboard,' said Don. On the new yacht's maiden voyage to Madagascar, the rudder broke and Don was swept overboard while trying to repair it. His body was never recovered. Less than a year later Muriel succumbed to cancer.

My mother says she is never going sailing again. She moved into a house not long after *Vingila* finished her circumnavigation, and she says she loves having a garden and not having to worry that the anchor is dragging whenever the wind blows.

My brother did not fare well at technical college. The discipline and the routine of lessons irked him, and he found that he preferred to spend his time surfing. Eventually he was conscripted into the navy where he trained to be a commercial diver. Robert now has twin girls of his own. His work on oil rigs often takes him out of the country, and although our paths have separated, we sometimes meet to surf together, and when we do it feels as if nothing at all has changed and we are twelve years old again and having fun together in the waves. Like me, he speaks of having a yacht of his own one day. For now it seems he is content with a house near the sea and a surfboard.

My two daughters have begun sailing. On weekends my husband and I take them to the stagnant waters of Zeekoeivlei, a dam which looks and smells a lot like Germiston Lake, where Chummy, my grandfather who has also since passed away, once took me waterskiing. My fair-haired children sail Optimists; stubby tubs of dinghies. I love to watch them, either from the shore or from my own sailing dinghy. They sit straight-backed, with one hand on the tiller and the other holding the main sheet. As the wind fills their sails and their boats heel over slightly, they counterbalance and the dinghies move forward, square prows pushing up little bow waves. And whenever I catch a glimpse of my daughters' faces, they are almost always smiling.

ACKNOWLEDGEMENTS

To my family: Mom, Dad and Robert, because, as they say at the Oscars, none of this would have been possible without you. I will love you always.

Kevin Patterson showed me at close range how to set about writing a book and then, after encouraging me to do the same, introduced me to Anne McDermid, my agent. Thanks for your help and advice along the way.

Justin Fox, my supervisor at the University of Cape Town MA programme, shared many lunches with me at Joe Fish where he consistently refused to eat mussels. Thank you for the effort you exerted in weeding out my semicolons, Justin, and for your diligence and thoroughness.

For thoughtful, critical reading and helpful suggestions, I am most grateful to Nic Dawes, Don Pinnock and Luke Fiske.

Alison Lowry provided excellent editorial advice, kindness and enthusiasm. For her insightful and wise attention to the manuscript, I count myself lucky indeed. Thanks also to Pam, Reneé and the people at Penguin SA.

Robert Ravensburg and David Harrison kindly provided photographs.

To Hans van Heerden, Emma Hurley and Shamima Bhorat, thanks for your friendship and support, not just with regard to this book, but for each day that we work together.

Evelyn Terreblanche, I am fortunate to be your friend. Thank you for your advice on the cover, your careful reading and for reassuring me when I needed it.

Lastly, to Bryant, who read aloud every word I put to paper, who copy-edited and just generally put up with me over the years it took to complete this book, thank you.